CONTEMPORARY AMERICAN FOREIGN AND MILITARY POLICY

Academic advisors in American government:

Joseph C. Palamountain, Jr.
Skidmore College

Martin M. Shapiro
University of California, Irvine

AMERICAN GOVERNMENT READINGS SERIES

Academic editor: Joseph C. Palamountain, Jr.

CONSTITUTIONALISM AND POLITICS: CONFLICT AND CONSENSUS
C. Peter Magrath

VOTING, INTEREST GROUPS, AND PARTIES
Bradbury Seasholes

THE AMERICAN PRESIDENCY: VITAL CENTER
Elmer E. Cornwell

CONGRESS: ANVIL OF AMERICAN DEMOCRACY
George Goodwin, Jr.

THE SUPREME COURT AND PUBLIC POLICY
Martin M. Shapiro

POLITICS, ECONOMICS, AND THE GENERAL WELFARE
Michael D. Reagan

CONTEMPORARY AMERICAN FOREIGN AND MILITARY POLICY
Burton M. Sapin

CONTEMPORARY AMERICAN FOREIGN AND MILITARY POLICY

SCOTT, FORESMAN'S AMERICAN GOVERNMENT READINGS SERIES   Joseph C. Palamountain, Jr., Academic Editor

BURTON M. SAPIN
GEORGE WASHINGTON UNIVERSITY

SCOTT, FORESMAN AND COMPANY

FOREWORD

The American Government Readings Series has been designed to meet the need of American government courses and other courses in political science for broader, more imaginative selections of supplementary readings than those found in the traditional single-volume collection. All too often, the conventional reader is sadly uneven, thoroughly unimaginative, and so inadequate that the instructor is forced to create his own syllabus to achieve satisfactory, up-to-date coverage.

The American Government Readings Series avoids these weaknesses by substituting for the chapters in the single-volume effort individual volumes edited by specialists. By providing separate readers on specific subjects, such as the presidency, Congress, and civil rights, the series offers the instructor new variety and flexibility in constructing his course. By drawing on the resources of a group of specialists rather than a single generalist, the series promises both authority and originality.

The readings in each volume are derived from a variety of sources: books and monographs, professional and popular journals, and historical documents. They introduce stimulating dialogs between advocates of conflicting points of view, thereby involving the student in significant controversy over important issues. Each collection represents a range of difficulty and includes a balance of articles chosen for general interest, research significance, and theoretical import. Chapter introductions provide essential background information, and full headnotes lead the student into the individual selections.

A unique feature of the series is the original essay with which each editor closes his volume. Analyzing current issues and research, the essays point out their relevance for the student and, in the process, heighten his awareness of what a political scientist does and how he does it.

The Publishers

CONTENTS

PREFACE

The foreign and military policies of the United States are being vigorously discussed and debated these days. The articles included in this reader should provide a solid factual and conceptual background for that discussion and for the major decisions that will be made in the coming years. I hope that students interested in American foreign policy or American government will find these commentaries thoughtful and well documented. I am confident that they will find them stimulating and extremely readable.

While the primary focus of the book is foreign policy, it attempts to illuminate the fundamental interdependence of foreign policy and military policy and to provide at least an introduction to the important problems of military decision. Some selections discuss the interest and influence of the general public on foreign and military affairs; other readings deal with the governmental machinery—legislative as well as executive—through which foreign policies are developed and carried out. Finally, there are a series of articles on specific military and foreign policy problems facing the United States today.

My concern throughout has been to select the best commentaries available on key topics and then to present them at length, in preference to a mélange of bits and pieces that would aspire to cover all possible subjects of interest.

Most of the work on this volume was done during a year as visiting professor at the U.S. Naval War College, Newport, Rhode Island. The War College provided an environment that was both supportive and stimulating. Special thanks are owed Mrs. Marion Bliss, who helped guide and supervise the enterprise.

Burton M. Sapin
The George Washington University

CHAPTER 1

THE UNITED STATES IN WORLD POLITICS

So much has been written about the sudden, massive involvement of the United States in world affairs since the beginning of the Second World War that it is difficult, in a short statement, to move beyond truisms, clichés, and basic definitions.

If this is inevitable, perhaps we do well to begin with a paragraph or two on the excitement that does, or should, inhere in the subject. It is true that the United States is a latecomer to the ranks of the principal international actors. It is also true that the leap from supporting player to superstar was made almost overnight. In the life of nations, the distance between isolationist America and what some observers have begun to call, regretfully or admiringly, imperial America is relatively short.

The term revolution is much abused these days. Nevertheless, it is quite aptly and appropriately applied to much of the international environment with which the United States has had to cope in the last 25 years — whether one is referring to military strategy and technology, the broader technological advances in transportation and communication, the political relations of nations, the disappearance of the old colonial empires, or popular attitudes and expectations around the world. World population problems are usually labeled "explosive" rather than "revolutionary."

From the point of view of the student of American government and politics, what is — or should be — utterly fascinating is the interaction of the American system with this highly complex, unfamiliar, and dangerous international environment, for which American decisions and actions represent by far the most important input made by any nation. Most of us are familiar with the salient characteristics of the American polity, but what difference do they make in the formulation and implementation of American foreign policy?

Critics bemoan the archaic and sluggish functioning of Congress, the lack of imagination and initiative in the federal bureaucracy, the widespread public ignorance and disinterest regarding foreign affairs. If they are accurate in their picture of the American governmental system as slow moving, inefficient, unrepresentative and unresponsive, what are the consequences for foreign policy performance? Has the U.S. been saved only by its great resources, providing in effect a very substantial margin for error? Or does its political system only look bad as judged by some absolute and unrealistic set of standards? Perhaps we look better when compared to other political systems and their foreign policy performances.

Whatever one's views on these questions, they are undeniably intriguing and challenging. They require looking at the relatively familiar from a somewhat different perspective: what are their consequences, what difference do they make in the way the United States of America views its international environment, conceives its interests and needs vis-à-vis that environment, and then goes about the business of pursuing and protecting those interests?

It might be noted that for those who take a strict environmental-determinist view of foreign policy, the approach just suggested is completely unnecessary, a waste of time. In other words, if one assumes that *any* Country X, confronted by Situation Y, will respond in exactly the same way, it serves no useful purpose to examine governmental structures, political processes, and socio-economic patterns in an effort to explain Country X's response. The environmental determinist's view is that the nature of the external situation determines the foreign policy response.

The pages that follow reflect the assumption that the foreign policy choices and actions of nations are a product of the interaction of domestic and international factors, both of which significantly influence and limit the options. We know much less than we should about the processes involved, particularly in terms of empirically based and verified propositions about what factors weigh most importantly under what conditions. It is assumed, however, that developing such propositions is necessary to improved understanding of the dynamics of American foreign policy behavior.

For purposes of definitional clarity, it is probably worth noting that when we refer to foreign policy, we are concerned with official, governmental actions and statements. In this connection, some observers make a distinction between international *relations* and international *politics*, reserving the latter term for the official relations of states and their governments and the former, broader term for the great variety of interactions and transactions that take place among nations which are not controlled or directed by their governments or regarded as reflecting their views. Obviously, the distinction between the two realms is by no means clear-cut, and they affect and limit one another in many ways.

It may nevertheless be useful to remember that there are, usually, designated governmental agencies and officials who represent the authoritative voice of a nation with regard to its views and policies about other nations. Obviously, they do not and cannot reflect the views of everyone in a particular nation; presumably, what they do reflect are the policy end products of the political and decision-making processes of the particular nation. Thus, in a representative democracy like the United States, one of the interesting problems to be examined is how — through what channels and processes — the wider society, the citizenry at large, exercises influence on the attitudes, views, and actions of those officially empowered to act on their behalf as a nation.

As a final introductory comment, one simple way of understanding why the United States has such great difficulties in its international relationships is to recognize that the approach we have been applying to the United States applies equally to other sovereign nations. Each nation, by sheer geographical reality if nothing else, has its own distinctive view of the world and brings to the international arena its own particular set of national interests and concerns. Basic facts of geography and history make it almost impossible to conceive of a complete overlap of interests and objectives as among two or more nations. Even U.S.-Canadian relations, on close examination, turn out to be quite complicated, sensitive and, on occasion, abrasive.

Given the central political, military, and economic role of the United States in present world affairs, most nations cannot achieve an acceptable degree of success in pursuit of their national interests without some kind of accommodation to the power and interests of the United States. At the same time, the United States, in spite of its great power, can only have a degree of success in its own larger problems and responsibilities if it is somewhat responsive to at least some of the interests of others. The resulting mélange of pressures and choices in hundreds of specific situations from day to day constitutes the workload of contemporary American foreign policy.

AMERICAN NATIONAL INTERESTS AND OBJECTIVES
Seyom Brown

The cataloguing of national interests and objectives, be they American or other, is a trying and frustrating intellectual exercise. At the very abstract level — peace, rule of law, free and expanding world trade — they are so general as to be meaningless. As one attempts to specify desired states of affairs more precisely, it is often extremely difficult to do and, from a practical policymaker's point of view, the more specific you get the more difficult it may be to get others to agree.

Even if one succeeds in spelling out detailed objectives regarding some international situation, it should not be assumed that they will provide clear and unambiguous guidance to meet all circumstances. To find illustrations of this point, one need only read some of the recent efforts, inside and outside the American government, to define the circumstances under which it might be necessary, desirable, or at least acceptable for the United States to intervene to attempt to prevent a Communist takeover in some friendly or allied nation.

Dr. Brown's analysis does not overcome all of these problems, but it represents one of the best efforts to spell out the underlying rationale for postwar American foreign policy. For some further comments on the question of national interests and objectives, see the introduction to Chapter Five of this book.

THE IRREDUCIBLE NATIONAL INTEREST AND BASIC PREMISES ABOUT WORLD CONDITIONS

National interest is more important than ideology.

John F. Kennedy

Between the lofty reiteration of outworn platitudes and the glib profession of radical alternatives are found the deepest and most persistent reasons for basic United States foreign policy. Those who fear the smallest concession to criticism will topple the whole edifice of postwar foreign policy, and those who are trying to topple it with adolescent iconoclasm, mistake the clichés for the underlying concept of the national interest. This underlying concept was indeed the source of many policy formulations — particularly the rhetoric — now regarded as Cold War clichés. But the concept antedated the Cold War and will likely outlast it. It set the boundaries to and had much to do with shaping the character of the foreign commitments and programs of

each of the Administrations described in this book. Without his profound appreciation of this same underlying concept John F. Kennedy would not have been able to accomplish as much as he did in his efforts to pry loose the barnacled formulations of the fifteen years previous to his Presidency. And only such an appreciation will allow current and future national leaders to face squarely the awful choices ahead.

The concept of an irreducible national interest is imprecise, but essential, and deeply rooted in the American political experience.

Each of the men whose constituency has been the national electorate have been intensely aware that they were bound by an historical, Constitutional, and current political obligation to service, first and foremost, at least two basic objectives of the national society: its physical survival; and the perpetuation of something called the American Way of Life — in the familiar words, "to secure the blessings of liberty to ourselves and our posterity."

Although it was fashionable in some circles during the years 1959 to 1961 to debate the proposition "Better Dead than Red" or its converse, highly placed officials were reluctant to enter into the speculative discourse, however morally instructive. The Presidential view of the matter has been constant from Truman to Johnson: the primary task is to assure that such a choice never has to be made. Foreign commitments and national security programs have been constrained by firm insistence from the White House that *both* survival and the non-totalitarian condition of the nation are to be placed ahead of all other objectives.

A third imperative with almost as much compelling force upon highest policy levels has been the injunction to promote the general welfare, or the economic well-being of the whole society. From the vantage point of the Presidency, there is a good deal of political steam in the passion of the populace to have its liberties and eat well too.

The highest officials, in their need to erect their foreign policies on the bedrock of historical consensus, often attempt to show how their actions derive from these Constitutional and constant political imperatives: we seek today, as we did in Washington's time, explains President Johnson, "to protect the life of our nation, to preserve the liberty of our citizens, and to pursue the happiness of our people. This is the touchstone of our world policy."[1] Such resounding claims are more than ritualistic bell-ringing. They are reflective of Johnson's perception that the least common denominator of political demand, from the national constituency at large, is that the President pursue *simultaneously* the nation's interest in its own survival and those conditions which allow for the perpetuation of the nation's essential sociopolitical patterns.

This perception is sustained by the dominant themes of debate between the two great political parties. The party in opposition will often accuse the party in the White House of sacrificing too much of one basic value in the service of another. But the premises of critic and defender alike are that all of the basic values—survival, liberty, and economic well-being—can and ought to be pursued at the same time; and that this irreducible triumvirate of interest must not be subordinated to other considerations.

Thus, the strongest criticisms by Democrats against the Eisenhower Administration involved the charge that the nation's defense requirements were being neglected because of a slavish pursuit of a balanced budget. The President, also fending off those in his own party who wanted to reduce defense expenditures still more, defended the existing size and structure of the armed forces with the argument that "to build less would expose the nation to aggression. To build excessively, under the influence of fear, could defeat our purposes and impair or destroy the very freedom and economic system our military defenses are designed to protect."[2]

The concept of an irreducible national interest provides no specific guidance for its implementation—therefore the debate. The point is that, in the offices of ultimate national responsibility, the concept is considerably more than a cliché. Too vague to determine programs and specific commitments, it nonetheless constrains the range of policy choices. Although the concept is dependent for its programmatic expressions upon the particular Administration's definition of the essential American liberties (how much freedom of enterprise? how much freedom of speech?), premises on what makes

the economy tick, and analyses of the capabilities and intentions of potential foreign adversaries, the basic Presidential impulse to lead the nation away from situations where ultimate choices between survival, liberty, and welfare have to be made is in large measure responsible for the central thread of continuity in foreign policy from Truman to Johnson.

No less important a reason for the continuity in foreign policy from Truman to Johnson has been the persistence of the view that the primary threats to this irreducible national interest are the spread of International Communism and another world war. The constancy as well as the changes in foreign policy which have occurred may be read as the theme and variations of the basic objective of avoiding one of these threats without bringing on the other. The two prongs of this basic objective are derived from a set of premises about world conditions, and what these conditions seem to require of the United States in order to perpetuate itself and its Way of Life. This set of critical premises—those which have persisted in top policy levels over the past twenty years and have had a pervasive impact on specific commitments and actions—can be stated as follows:

A. The Soviet Union is motivated (how strongly is a variable) to be the dominant world power, and eventually to fashion the world into a single political system based on the Soviet model. The premise that the Soviets are motivated only to secure their society against outside interference has never been bought at the highest levels of the United States government since the Second World War. However, there has been constant questioning, and occasional diplomatic probing, to determine the extent to which the actions of the Soviets to implement expansionist motives are constrained by their perception that such action may place the security of the Soviet Union in danger and/or take away from their ability to achieve domestic economic and social goals. There apparently has been increasing receptivity in White House and State Department circles, since the Cuban missile crisis, the Test Ban, and the widening of the Sino-Soviet split, toward the premise that the Soviets have seen the futility of expansionist

[1]Address by President Johnson to The Associated Press, April 21, 1965, in the *New York Times*, April 22, 1965.
[2]State of the Union Message by the President, January 5, 1956.

adventures and would now like to turn their energies to domestic development tasks.[3] But varying interpretations are made of the presumed Soviet constriction of their external power drive. It may, as some analysts suggest, be the natural result of the maturing of their sociopolitical system — a supplanting of the revolutionary leadership by a bureaucratic generation most interested in efficiency and political stability. Or, it may be primarily the result of the application of the Leninist stratagem of "two steps forward, one step backward," in the hope that a relaxation of international tension now will lead to a slackening in the West, during which time the Soviet Union will be tending to the reorientation of its economy and technology in preparation for the next phase of hostile competition. There are many versions of these theses, each suggesting a somewhat different set of United States policy responses and initiatives to the Soviet Union. Later chapters will elaborate such attempts by the United States to test the international waters to see if any of these theses should become the operating premise for U.S. foreign policy. For present purposes it is only necessary to take note of this turbulence beneath the surface constancy of the basic premise that the Soviets would be expanding if we, the United States, were not containing them. The desirability of containing the Soviets at least within their present sphere is not in question; but the appropriate role for the United States in this containment function has increasingly become a central issue of policy.

B. Another critical premise underlying the observed constancy in foreign policy from Truman to Johnson has been that in another world war the United States would quickly become a prime target for mass destruction. Early in the period the technology of warfare, plus the obvious strategies deduced from the new technology, were seen to be bringing about a situation in which the United States could not become involved in war against its largest rival without thereby placing the lives of millions of American civilians in jeopardy. By 1948 there was consensus among United States scientists and military planners that it would be only a matter of a few years before the Soviet Union developed such a capability. In the interim the Soviet Union could compensate for its strategic inferiority vis-à-vis the United States (we could already reach the Soviet Union with weapons of mass destruction from our overseas bases) by

holding "hostage" the urban populations of Western Europe. By the mid-1950s Soviet thermonuclear developments plus great improvements in their long-range strategic bomber fleet made the vulnerability of the continental United States in a world war an operating premise of military planners and top foreign policy officials. The avoidance of another world war was seen to be equal in importance to preventing the expansion of Communism. "Deterrence" became for a time the magic word, presumably eliminating the potential conflict in priority between preventing strategic attack on the United States and containing the Soviets. But the pursuit of peace could no longer be dismissed as mere rhetoric. World peace, meaning basically the avoidance of general war between the United States and the Soviet Union, had become irrevocably an *essential* policy objective — that is, a necessary means of preserving the irreducible national interest.

C. Yet prevailing premises about the distribution of international power since the Second World War would not allow the pursuit of world peace to take *precedence* over the containment of Communism. The war had left the Soviet Union surrounded by power vacuums where previously it had been hemmed in by constellations of great power. The only source of great countervailing power now was the United States. Therefore, the desire to prevent the extension of Soviet power (assuming the Soviets wanted to expand the territorial basis of their power) carried with it a responsibility for the United States to make its power available to dissuade or block the Soviets. At first, the United States tried to dissuade the Soviets from expanding by appeals to the spirit of the Grand Alliance and the decent opinions of mankind as reflected in the United Nations Charter (there was no expectation that the collective security machinery of the United Nations could be used as a coercive instrument against the Soviet Union). Under the immediate postwar assumption that the Soviets, requiring foreign capital for reconstruction, were anxious to maintain the goodwill of the West, the Truman Administration early tried by tough talk alone to induce the Soviets into a more benign posture. But as it appeared that Stalin was more anxious to take advantage of opportunities to expand his territorial base than to maintain the goodwill of the

[3]See, for example, Walt W. Rostow, "The Third Round," *Foreign Affairs* (October 1963), pp. 1 – 10.

West, the Truman Administration soon began to seek means of redressing the local imbalances of power around the Soviet periphery. At first, these efforts were concentrated in economic and social measures to reconstruct war-torn Europe and Japan. But Soviet military power plays against Iran, Turkey, Greece, and Czechoslovakia brought into prominence at the White House level premises of the critical effect of military balances, local and global, on the Soviets' propensity to expand. The Berlin blockade of 1948 apparently sealed the case for Truman, and Secretary of State Acheson was given the go-ahead to make explicit in the North Atlantic Treaty the unequivocal commitment of United States military power to counter any Soviet attempts to exploit their military superiority in Europe. In exchange for this commitment of American power the West Europeans were expected to work urgently to build up their own military power, so that the burden would not fall disproportionately on the United States. The willingness to forego even our commitment to world peace, if indeed that were necessary to prevent the Soviets from forcibly adding unto themselves the vast power potential of Western Europe, was by 1949 an explicit premise of United States foreign policy. Such explicitness was possible with respect to Western Europe because its fall to the Soviets could be defined as tantamount to "surrender." The Soviets would become the dominant world power, and could eventually overpower the United States itself.

D. Thus, the "balance of power" became the critical concept for determining the priority to be given in any specific situation to containment of Communism or the avoidance of world war, should these two objectives appear impossible to pursue at the same time. Each of the four postwar Administrations have agreed on at least this much: if a Communist success in a given conflict would critically undermine the power of the non-Communist world to dissuade the Communist world from further advances, then, presumably, the balance of power itself was at stake, and, since, by extension, this meant the survival of the United States, there was no question of where the national interest would lie. In such situations, peace would have to give way temporarily to the active containment of Communism, even if the temporary breakdown of peace would place the United States in danger of direct attack.

E. But none of these premises provided sufficient advance guidance for basic policy in situations where the overall U.S.-Soviet power balance was not thought to be immediately at stake. If the Soviets were only making a limited grab, would it be worth a world war to frustrate them? What if another Communist nation were attempting to extend its power—would we, should we, automatically equate such an attempt with an increment to the Soviet side of the global balance of power? In global balance of power terms, how should we regard the coming to power *within* nations of supposedly indigenous Communist movements? The fact that the United States, through successive Administrations, has not been able to answer such questions *in principle* in advance of unfolding situations has been in large measure responsible for some of our major policy crises over the past two decades. The decision not to bring our coercive power to bear to prevent Mao Tse-tung's victory over Chiang Kai-shek; the expenditure of blood and treasure in Korea to rectify the gross miscalculation of the Soviets that we would not be willing to intervene there to oppose aggression; the Truman-MacArthur controversy; the great debate over "massive retaliation" vs. "flexible response," and particularly its expression in NATO policy; the Quemoy and Matsu crises of the 1950s; the Bay of Pigs, the Cuban missile crisis, and the chronic problem of how to deal with Castro; the Dominican military intervention of 1965; and, of course, Vietnam—all of these have produced as much dissensus as consensus in the nation, precisely because of the existence of varied concepts of international "power."

There has been constancy at one very important level of analysis and policy. Premises of the irreducible national interest, and basic assumptions about world conditions have given persistence to the two-pronged objective of attempting to prevent the spread of International Communism and to prevent the outbreak of a Third World War. As perceived by those responsible for the conduct of United States foreign policy, this has meant primarily influencing the Soviets and the Communist Chinese not to try to expand their territorial base, and influencing other nations to pursue policies that would enhance their resistance to control by these two Communist giants.

But, the major issues have been over means,

not objectives. The problem has been essentially a problem of *power*. The difficult question has been what *kinds* of power—what capabilities—are needed to accomplish the agreed upon objectives of the nation. . . .

The objectives of containing Communism and preserving peace do not exhaust the range of objectives animating United States foreign policy since the Second World War. These have been emphasized first, however, because they have been generally accepted during the period as practically inevitable derivatives from the irreducible national interest of survival in a non-totalitarian condition.

The nation has also considered itself committed to interests of a more altruistic nature, and much of the story of the past two decades centers on attempts to reconcile the requirements of implementing these altruistic interests with the requirements of self-preservation. But again, the major arbiter of choice has proven to be the concept of the global balance of power.

LARGER INTERESTS AND THE BALANCE-OF-POWER CONSIDERATION

We have no taste for empire. We do not wish to establish a Pax Americana. Nor do we desire to act as the world's gendarme. We do not regard the dominant role of American power in so many parts of the world as a permanent—or satisfactory—state of affairs.

George Ball

The liberties and well-being of other peoples have been persistent major concerns of United States foreign policy since the Second World War. Officials of the Truman Administration regarded our sponsorship of the United Nations, the Truman Doctrine, the European Recovery Program, and Point IV as consistent with American idealism as well as self-interest. John Foster Dulles preached anti-Communism as a universal moral imperative. President Kennedy, unsentimental realist he is supposed to have been, sounded the trumpet for "a grand and global alliance" against the "common enemies of man: tyranny, poverty, disease, and war itself." His generation of Americans, said Kennedy, felt an obligation to work toward a "more fruitful life for all mankind":

To those peoples in the huts and villages of half the globe struggling to break the bonds of mass misery, we pledge our best efforts to help them

help themselves, for whatever period is required—not because the communists may be doing it, not because we seek their votes, but *because it is right.*[1]

And there can be little doubt that Lyndon Johnson believes he is giving voice to the American mainstream when he claims:

Of course security and welfare shape our policies. But much of the energy of our efforts has come from moral purpose.

It is right that the strong should help the weak defend their freedom.

It is right that the wealthy should help the poor emerge from their hunger.

It is right that help and understanding should flow from friendship and loyalty.

It is right that nations should be free from the coercion of others.

That these truths may coincide with interest does not make them less true.[2]

The difficulty, of course, has come not when such moral purposes coincide with interest, but precisely in those situations or programs where they would suggest different policies than what seem to be required by the nation's interest in its own security and welfare.

In the main, our foreign policy leadership since the Second World War has been fortunate in the large measure of coincidence between the nation's self-interest and the nation's altruistic ideals.[3] With the rival superpower propounding a monolithic global society, the traditional American commitment to *national* self-determination, now enshrined in the United Nations Charter, could be used as an ideology to firm up the will of other peoples to resist absorption in the Communist bloc. And with Communist regimes propounding and acting upon the doctrine that a highly regimented populace unquestioningly carrying out policies made at the top is necessary for modernization, the doctrine that governments derive their just powers from the consent of the governed could be one of our most powerful weapons of containment—and possibly even liberation. As Secretary of State Acheson counseled:

[1]Inaugural Address, January 20, 1961; Department of State *Bulletin*, February 6, 1961, pp. 175–76 (emphasis added).
[2]Address by President Johnson to the American Bar Association, August 12, 1964, in the Department of State *Bulletin*, August 31, 1964, pp. 298–301.
[3]For the period from McKinley to Franklin Roosevelt, see Robert E. Osgood, *Ideals and Self Interest in American Foreign Relations* (Chicago: University of Chicago Press, 1953).

Our first line of action . . . is to demonstrate that our own faith in freedom is a burning and a fighting faith. . . . And we don't restrict this belief to freedom for ourselves.

If we are clear about this, if we are full of passion about this, then we have in our hearts and minds the most revolutionary and dynamic concept in human history and one which properly strikes terror into every dictator, to every tyrant who would attempt to regiment and depress men anywhere. . . .[4]

Or as put by John Foster Dulles:

The great weakness of despotism has been, is, and always will be its disregard of the rights of man. Despotism can always be routed if free men exploit that weakness. If our example can illumine . . . the great advantages of a free society, then Soviet Communism will lose its deceptive appeal. Furthermore, it will lose its grip upon the enslaved whom it now holds. . . .

. . . I agree with . . . Walter Reuther when he said: "The quest for liberty constitutes the eventual victorious challenge to the totalitarian system."

This quest for liberty must be simultaneously pursued on three fronts—the home front, the free-world front, and the captive-world front.[5]

Characteristically, President Kennedy exhibited a more chastened view: "It is one of the ironies of our time that the techniques of a harsh and repressive system should be able to instill discipline and ardor in its servants—while the blessings of liberty have too often stood for privilege, materialism and a life of ease."[6] Still he had faith that with a national rededication to our deepest ideals, and a willingness to make the hard decisions and sacrifices that such dedication would require, the tide would eventually turn. For in the last analysis, mankind will see that "we can welcome diversity—the Communists cannot . . . we offer a world of choice— they offer a world of coercion. And the way of the past shows clearly enough that freedom, not coercion, is the wave of the future."[7]

Yet at times the magnitude of assistance required to significantly help others pursue their freedom and welfare has appeared too costly. It was 1947 when President Truman proclaimed the doctrine that "it must be the policy of the United States to support free peoples who are resisting attempted subjugation by armed minorities or outside pressures." But the universally-phrased doctrine was applied only in particular cases between 1947 and the summer of 1950. It was applied in Greece and Turkey— the crisis situations which prompted the doctrine. And the $17 billion program for European economic recovery was portrayed as its required corollary. Under cover of the same principle, Berlin was sustained by the American airlift in 1948–49, and the United States committed itself to the defense of Western Europe by the North Atlantic Treaty. But during this same postwar period the Administration did not attempt to apply the Truman Doctrine to events taking place in Eastern Europe or in China.

With respect to Eastern Europe, recalls Walt Rostow, "It was worth protesting diplomatically against Stalin's course of action and maintaining a *de jure* position of opposition to Communist takeover, but it was not worth risking American blood to prevent the outcome."[8] Similarly, a Communist regime in China was not at all desirable to those in control of U.S. foreign policy, and President Truman did all he reasonably could to prevent it. But his liberty to commit American resources to the struggle, Truman felt, was limited. As the situation deteriorated, the only remaining alternative to a Communist takeover appeared to be a large-scale intervention with American forces to bail out Chiang Kai- shek. Truman, certain that "the American people would never stand for such an undertaking,"[9] liquidated our commitment, and helped evacuate Chiang to Formosa. After these events, the Republicans blamed the Communist absorption of Eastern Europe and China on the Truman Administration, but the opposition party was notably deficient, at the time of their occurrence, in suggestions for larger United States involvements in either case.

A Republican Administration got its chance during the 1953 East German uprisings, and

[4]Quoted by McGeorge Bundy, *The Pattern of Responsibility* (Boston: Houghton-Mifflin, 1951), p. 42, from Acheson's speech to the American Society of Newspaper Editors, April 22, 1950.
[5]Address by the Secretary of State to the Congress of Industrial Organizations, November 18, 1953, in the Department of State *Bulletin*, November 30, 1953, pp. 741–44.
[6]State of the Union Message by the President, January 30, 1961.
[7]State of the Union Message by the President, January 11, 1962.
[8]Walt W. Rostow, *The United States in the World Arena* (New York: Harper, 1960), p. 178.
[9]Harry S. Truman, *Memoirs: Years of Trial and Hope* (New York: Doubleday, 1955), II, 62, 91.

then again during the Hungarian crisis of 1956, to demonstrate how high a price it would be willing to pay to support the liberty of other peoples. Again, there were certain impassable limits.

These limits are set by the irreducible national interest—the survival of the American Way of Life *here*—and premises about world conditions directly affecting this interest. Our larger interests in the liberties and well-being of other peoples has been pursued where such action is perceived as required by, or supportive of, the basic national interest. We have also expended energy and resources, in limited amounts, to support the liberties and well-being of other peoples, even though not prompted by calculations of self-interest, for the sufficient reason that "it is right." But there has been constancy over the period in Presidential refusals to service these larger interests when the action required was perceived as contrary to policies deemed necessary to secure the blessings of liberty to *ourselves* and *our* posterity.

Thus, although the objective of containment of Communist expansion was often explained to the people as motivated by our deepest desires to preserve and expand the area of freedom, the ultimate calculations underlying decisions to oppose particular Communist provocations have been in terms of the consequences of the contemplated action or inaction for the physical security of the United States, and the freedoms and economic well-being of citizens of the United States.

If the expected costs of United States intervention were very high, and the benefits problematical—as in Eastern Europe, China, and Cuba during the Bay of Pigs—valor gave way, painfully, to inaction dictated by prudence. But, where the consequences of inaction were foreseen as a disadvantageous change in the global balance of power, meaning that the United States might soon lose the wherewithal to secure its own survival in a non-totalitarian condition, decisions to counter the provocation with all that was required have been made, unflinchingly, even though the expected costs in human and material resources have been high, and, on occasion, the irreducible national interest itself has been risked.

The persisting United States commitment to defend a Western presence in Berlin (even though the balance of military force there is against us) and President Kennedy's willingness to establish a very dangerous direct confrontation with the Soviets to compel a removal of their missiles from Cuba are examples of high risks taken in "the defense of freedom" *when* the global balance of power is thought to be at stake. I am not arguing that these decisions were inevitable. I do argue that such decisions are practically inevitable when a President feels the global balance of power is at stake, because a global imbalance against us is regarded as putting our survival at the mercy of our opponents. As there is no absolute measure of power, one President may see the global balance of power at stake in a situation where another may not. Thus the premises of power held by the various Administrations is a crucial variable in explaining the changes as well as the constancy in United States foreign policy.

The more controversial decisions have involved situations where there is a highly ambiguous or tenuous relationship perceived between the liberty and well-being of others and the global balance of power, and where programs thought capable of significantly helping those in need would be very costly.

Such considerations determined the acceptance at the close of the Korean War of a stalemate based on the status quo ante rather than a pressing for "victory" to allow the United Nations to administer nationwide elections and reunify the country. The original decision to intervene to reverse the North Korean drive to take over the whole country, even though this task might be costly for us, was undertaken out of a notion that to allow the Communists to succeed in their invasion would drastically undermine the non-Communist side of the power balance. A weighty ingredient of Western power, particularly as expressed in the new North Atlantic Treaty, was thought to be the faith of our alliance partners that the United States would honor its pledges to oppose aggression. Thus, indirectly, but rather clearly to the American leadership, our own security—dependent upon Western Europe being on *our* side of the balance of power—was seen to be threatened. Consequently, it was very important to oppose the North Koreans with whatever force was necessary to throw them back at least to the line of demarcation. As it began to look as if we could defeat them in the North too, without a significantly larger operation than was already under way, our objective was temporarily expanded to include the freedom and reunification of all of Korea. But the intervention of the Communist Chinese changed the calculations of the cost of implementing this larger interest, which, after all, was not seen to be required by balance of power considerations; indeed, the maintenance of the global balance was thought to require that we husband our resources for the possibility of a greater battle with the Soviet Union over Western Europe. . . .

The lack of clarity over just which American interests were really involved did not prevent the Eisenhower Administration from assisting in the overthrow of a Guatemalan government infiltrated by pro-Soviet Communists. But in this case, the assessment of costs to the United States of the indirect assistance we rendered was made out to be very small. On the other hand, we continued to tolerate the existence of not very "free" regimes and depressed standards of living in many of our southern neighbors, since these conditions did not at the time seem to affect the balance of power, and hence United States security, one way or the other. Moreover, until the Act of Bogotá in 1960, we defended our inaction to support the political liberties and well-being of Latin Americans as consistent with the principle of "nonintervention" (self-determination) as expressed in the Inter-American treaties. The doctrine of nonintervention got fuzzy again as Castro solidified his ties with Moscow. The Kennedy Administration, inheriting the contingency plan of its predecessor, began what it thought was a low-level-of-effort counterinsurgency operation, somewhat on the Guatemalan model. But as a Communist regime in Cuba was not thought to be a crucial factor in the global balance of power, the operation was called off as soon as the costs of carrying it through were seen to have been vastly underestimated. Also, part of the uncalculated cost in the plan as originally handed to President Kennedy was the likely effect on the social reform elements in Latin America whom Kennedy was trying to court; and thus under Kennedy's premises of power, the global balance, if invoked at all as a consideration, might seem to be adversely affected even if the United States were successful in forcibly bringing down Castro.

The ambivalent United States reactions toward prospects of Communist successes in Indochina also illustrate the problems of policy when unclear global power considerations are cojoined with high costs of commitment. We assisted the French effort to keep all of Indochina out of Ho Chi Minh's hands, so long as this involved a relatively small expenditure of our material resources. Later, as the French effort collapsed, the possibility that we might decide to intervene led Eisenhower to talk for a time as if the balance of power itself was at stake—a contention hotly disputed by many of our allies and by the opposition party in Congress. After the 1954 truce, an aid program was reinstituted for South Vietnam, for the ostensible purpose of bringing about conditions that would allow for eventual nationwide self-determination. But the principle of self-determination would have to be postponed until the population could be secured against coercion by Ho's agents. During the Kennedy Administration there was reluctance to define the outcome of the continuing struggle between the Vietnamese Communists and non-Communists in stark balance of power terms. It was "their war," said Kennedy, although we would do all we reasonably could to help the non-Communist side. Furthermore, our aid was conditioned on at least a minimum respect being shown for civil liberties by the South Vietnamese regime. Later, as our help changed into direct United States involvement, carrying with it the implication of our own unlimited commitment to the maintenance of a non-Communist South Vietnam, the Johnson Administration once again defined the stakes of the conflict in global balance of power terms. Yet this definition remained under considerable dispute in the United States as the costs of implementing the commitment rose.

The foreign assistance program as a whole has been operating right in the center of this hazy area, where often the relation of any specific component of the program to basic United States security interests is not at all clear, and therefore the diversion of domestic resources to such foreign ends is disputed by interest groups within and without the government who would like comparable amounts diverted to them.

The Eisenhower Administration, with all its rhetoric about our devotion to freedom as a universal imperative, found a way, temporarily, of avoiding a systematic policy dialogue on the relationships between foreign aid, the character of recipient regimes, political liberty, and basic United States interests by making foreign assistance, for the most part, the reward of military alignment. The military balance of power was easily connected with United States security interests, and military allies were facilely portrayed as weights on our side of the balance. If economic and military assistance was necessary to assure the alignment and security of an ally, no additional rationale was necessary. It was sufficient to argue that, dollar for dollar, X amount given to the recipient allies would result in more military manpower and firepower for the non-Communist world than if that same amount were added to the United States military budget. The case within the Administration, as well as the public rationale, for assistance to regimes who preferred to remain nonaligned in the Cold War remained largely undeveloped. Although the need for such a rationale became evident to Eisenhower and Dulles by the end of their first term, the press of events and the inertia of a bureaucracy already geared to programs based on the older premises put a brake on new initiatives.

It remained for the Kennedy Administration to push with vigor a fresh set of premises on the relationship between assistance from the United States, socioeconomic reform, political democracy, and our own security. . . . Enthusiasm in the White House still had to deal with sluggishness in a Congress responsive to parochial demands, and skepticism from career administrators and diplomats more comfortable in dealings with foreign "Establishment" types than with the bristling revolutionary nationalists of the nonaligned world. The Alliance for Progress and the manifest interest by Kennedy in the new leaders of Africa produced no significant changes in the scale of our overall foreign assistance effort, nor any major reallocation of disbursements within the program. But even if the visible effects of the new orientation to foreign assistance were still primarily on the symbolic level, the realistic joining by Kennedy, MacNamara, and Rusk of our altruistic concerns for the liberties and well-being of others with a sophisticated analysis of international power relationships struck a responsive chord in the country's growing constituency of businessmen and professionals with an active interest in world affairs.

The percolation of these premises to popular levels where they could generate political steam, and therefore appropriations, was another matter. At the time of this writing the popular foreign policy issues were again regressing to "guns vs. butter" simplifications. The dollar and manpower requirements of the Great Society at home were competitive with the dollar and manpower requirements for maintaining our commitment in Vietnam, and the latter were most immediately oriented to military tasks.

The active implementation of our national belief that all men have a right to choose the leaders and the laws by which they will be governed has, at times, involved us in serious disagreement with countries whom we consider allies against Communist forms of totalitarianism. Here too, however, the litmus test for determining our predominant national interest has tended to be the balance of power consideration.

The anti-colonial revolution since the Second World War has for the most part proceeded according to its own inner dynamic, with the United States and the Soviet Union bystanders. However, the pace of adaptations by the old metropolitan nations to the assertion by their former wards of the right to self-governance *has* been subject to United States influence, the outstanding example being the Dutch acquiescence in Indonesian independence. Also, the intensification of nationalist demands for freedom from colonial overlordship was in part a function of the "moral" support given to this global movement by *both* of the superpowers. In practically all of the colonial dependencies there were Communist agents at work, but the successful leaders in most of the new nationalist parties got their revolutionary motivation from studies of the American and French revolutions and learned their socialism from Fabian professors. Lenin's theories of imperialism and capitalist exploitation were only part of the brew, which the Nehrus, the Nkrumahs, and the Sukarnos exploited with telling political effect. Political factions in their countries who were dominated by orthodox Marxist-Leninist beliefs lacked the emotional appeal of the hybrid new nationalistic ideologies. Even the Soviet Union soon recognized this and, by the late 1940s, began to court the non-Communist nationalists, often at the expense of indigenous Communist parties.

Thus, for reasons of traditional sentiment and for the hard-headed consideration of not allowing the Soviets to parade as the sole sponsors of anti-colonialism, the Truman Administration and its successors have felt it necessary to identify the United States with the aspirations of the peoples of the Third World. Each has tried, in its fashion, to give vocal support to the principle of self-determination, and some tangible evidence (in the form of technical and economic assistance) of our determination to have the new nations succeed in their experiments with democratic self-rule. But these genuine efforts to support the new nationalisms of the Third World have been circumscribed, particularly in the Truman and Eisenhower periods, by the emphasis given to the securing of the *military* components of the global balance of power. The military potential of a revived Western European technology, a girdle of military allies to prevent easy expansion by the Communist powers, and a system of far-flung bases to bring our strategic striking power within reach of the Soviet heartland were regarded as priority objectives. As these assets were, in many cases, to be provided by nations with overseas dependencies some deference to the sensibilities and the material interests of the colonial powers was thought to be a requirement of our statecraft.

Fortunately, for this purpose, the ideology of national sovereignty embodied in the United Nations Charter cut two ways: it provided a rationale for mobilizing efforts to combat Communist subversion and overt aggression; it also provided the legal excuse for refusing to take sides in disputes which fell under the "domestic jurisdiction" of another nation.

Moreover, we had a vital interest, professed and real, in reducing the resort to violence as a means of bringing about change. It was by no means clear *who* in any given anti-colonial uprising, say Algeria, was relying most on violence—those defending the existing system of public order, or those trying to overthrow it. In such circumstances our doctrinaire profession of opposition to violent methods of change was able to buttress our propensity to straddle the fence.

Early in his tenure as Secretary of State, Dulles summed up this central dilemma of U.S. foreign policy which, because of the natural course of events, was to become most intense during the late Eisenhower period:

Perhaps some of you feel that your government is not pushing political liberty as strongly as it should. I can say to you three things:

First, we are pushing for self-government more than appears on the surface.

Secondly, where we exercise restraint it is because of a reasoned conviction that precipi-

tate action would in fact not produce independence but only transition to a captivity far worse than present dependence.

Thirdly, we are alert to the possibility that the Communist threat might grow into an excuse for delay, when it is not an honest reason for delay.

There are good and sufficient reasons why the United States desires, in the United Nations and elsewhere, to show unity with its Western allies. But we have not forgotten that we were the first colony to win independence. And we have not given a blank check to any colonial power.

There is no slightest wavering in our conviction that the orderly transition from colonial to self-governing status should be carried resolutely to a completion.[10]

By the time of the Kennedy Administration most of the old colonial empires had been liquidated, so national self-determination could be professed with less qualification. Still, when it came to risking the loss of the strategic base in the Portuguese Azores, prudence prevailed, and Kennedy and Ambassador Stevenson labored to get the African nationalists to tone down demands for the United Nations to apply sanctions against the Salazar regime unless independence was granted to Angola and Mozambique.

Finally, in many of our relationships with the poorer nations our desire to act in accord with our larger altruistic interests—independent of considerations of self-interest or the power struggle vis-à-vis the Communists—produced additional dilemmas of a practical and philosophical nature. When it has come to fashioning concrete policy out of these beliefs, each of the postwar Administrations has been bedeviled by the potential contradictions between:

A. our interest in the rights of national societies to determine in their own way their own form of government (a pluralistic world society; Articles I and II of the UN Charter);

B. our interests in social justice based upon a respect for the dignity and rights of each individual human being (Part II, Universal Declaration of Human Rights);

C. our interest in the eradication of those socioeconomic conditions forcing portions of

[10]Address by the Secretary of State to the Congress of Industrial Organizations, Cleveland, Ohio, November 18, 1953, in the Department of State *Bulletin*, November 30, 1953, pp. 741–44.

the human race to live in physical misery (Point IV of 1949 Presidential Inaugural Address; Charter of Punta Del Este).

Which of these interests should we put *first*? In our rhetoric these ideals are placed side by side, with the implication that they can and ought to be pursued *simultaneously*. This is a natural extrapolation from our country's own experience, where the demand for self-government was made by men committed to the rights of individuals, and an egalitarian social ethos grew in an environment of abundance.

But many of the poorer nations of the world are run by oligarchies anxious to hold on to their social and material privileges. Economic assistance to such nations without "political strings" attached has sometimes resulted in an increase in a nation's per capita productivity and income; but often it has also perpetuated a system of social injustice. Yet is has been against our inclinations to *intervene*, by withholding or withdrawing economic assistance until major social reforms are first implemented. The Alliance for Progress made a move in this direction, but gingerly.

In other nations there is a commitment to egalitarianism with a vengeance, in which the property rights and civil liberties are trod under heel. Yet with our traditional optimism, we have been receptive to claims that such suspensions of constitutional processes are only temporary, and may—in some cases—be the necessary price for rapid socioeconomic development. We have been less willing to grant the benefit of the doubt to Communist as opposed to non-Communist reformers (such as Ayub Kahn). But even with respect to Communist regimes, as long as they seemed to be refraining from interference in the affairs of other nations, we have increasingly regarded them as fit commercial partners and possibly even aid recipients.

The hopeful "answer" to the potentiality for contradiction between our altruistic political, social, and economic interests—the insistence that all of these ought to be pursued simultaneously—has rarely worked out in practice. In attempting to apply this typically American solution to the problems of national development,

Truman, Eisenhower, Kennedy, and Johnson have run up against the hard realization that in most of the poorer nations of the world the human and material resources make for very uneven patterns of progress. In most cases an absolute insistence by us that development in political procedures, civil liberties, social reform, and economic productivity go hand-in-hand would constitute a moralistic criterion defeating progress in any of these areas. A more pragmatic attitude, variously groped for by each of the four Administrations of the period, has been difficult to sell to the Congress, however. The Legislature, acting as the broker for constituent domestic interests jealous of any diversion of resources to foreign objectives, needs either a grand moral crusade or a clear and present danger to the nation to forge a consensus in back of altruistic acts. Unable to provide the former, for the reasons just alluded to, the Executive, from Truman to Johnson, has had to fall back on the national security rationale in order to be granted the wherewithal to influence other nations in directions consistent with our larger interests.

The notion that the United States has been conducting its foreign relations as if it were a global social welfare agency and reform school is a myth derived from a reading of the rhetoric without an inspection of actual programs. As sincere as any Administration has been in professing our larger commitment to the well-being and liberties of all peoples, all have tended to decide major foreign policy questions, ultimately, in terms of the irreducible national interest: how will a given action or program affect the *power of the United States* to secure its way of life for at least its own people? What actions and programs are required in order to keep the *power of potential adversaries* below a level at which they could force the United States to choose between its survival and its way of life?

The limiting criteria for decision have remained essentially constant.

But such constancy only sets the boundary to the story. International "power" is a many-faceted thing. The successive Administrations and factions within them have varied in their premises of power—the essential ingredients and most appropriate uses.

CHAPTER 2

MILITARY FORCE AND FOREIGN POLICY

Foreign policy is concerned with American relations with foreign nations (and other political entities beyond our boundaries). Military or national defense policy is concerned with defense of the United States and, more significantly in the contemporary period, preparation and use of armed forces to otherwise protect and pursue the interests of the United States.

Even without the benefit of the classic dicta of Clausewitz and others, it should be evident that foreign policy and military policy are closely related. Both look abroad, beyond the national boundaries; both are concerned with the intentions and capabilities of other nations, aspiring to exert some influence thereon. The foreign policy perspective is broader, at least theoretically encompassing the totality of relations with other nations. The concerns and activities of the defense establishment tie it much more deeply and intimately into the domestic life of the nation.

In the past, the interdependence of foreign policy and military policy was much less widely remarked upon, studied and understood than it is today. The explanation seems rather simple. Prior to World War II, the security and very physical safety of the United States were not seen to be linked, on a continuing, urgent basis, to the general state of the international system and the particular state of American relations with other nations around the world.

Today, foreign policy as well as military policy has as its most pressing, high-priority concern the security of the nation. This is not to denigrate economic or commercial concerns or even the desire to do good internationally, but the nature of the international environment and the American role in it make national security the first-priority concern. This, of course, continues to be true for the military establishment—although the nature of some of its problems has changed markedly in the last two decades.

While the overlap in problems and responsibilities between foreign policy and military policy is substantial, each has its own special fields of activity and competence and corresponding organizational structures. The defense establishment must recruit, train, equip, and position very large military forces; this involves extensive efforts in such fields as research and development, logistics and supply, manpower management, and the choice of competing weapons systems to fill many military requirements. The problems of policy choice and control and of efficient management of this enterprise are fantastically difficult and challenging.

Managing the foreign affairs establishment (the State Department, the U.S. Information Agency, the Agency for International Development, the Peace Corps, etc.) at home and abroad represents somewhat different, if difficult, problems. But it is probably fair to say that the major problems for the foreign policy organization lie in dealing with more than a hundred sovereign nations and probably as many international organizations and agencies, somehow trying to advance or protect the interests of the United States.

Thus, there are distinctive as well as overlapping foci of interest and effort for foreign policy and military policy. In this book, major emphasis is placed on foreign policy and foreign relations, with the military establishment viewed primarily in terms of its direct involvement in and impact on U.S. foreign relations. Military establishment policy-making and management *per se* will not be given detailed consideration.

In the postwar period, the American military establishment has carried out American foreign policy in a wide variety of places and situations. Some of its activities have been traditional ones — showing the flag, show of force and, upon occasion, use of force. Others have been somewhat novel, either in concept or scale of operation — military assistance and training for the armed forces of many foreign nations, establishment of a world-wide complex of American military installations, and, perhaps most significant, stationing of substantial American military forces overseas in what is called "peacetime."

Where these military activities have been carried out on behalf of U.S. foreign policy objectives or have involved dealing with the governments and peoples of other nations, they have been subject to, and limited by, relevant foreign policy objectives and considerations. It may be argued that the foreign policy agencies and their personnel, notably the State Department and the Foreign Service, have been ineffective in enforcing these foreign policy guidelines or that the policies themselves have been mistaken in some instances. It is certainly true that these policies have on occasion been vigorously debated and resisted by the military. It would, however, be grossly inaccurate to argue that the dominance of foreign policy considerations in most of these situations, and their importance in all of them, have been rejected in principle by the military establishment.

To mention just a few examples of American military activities that require clearance or approval by the Department of State: visits of naval ships to foreign ports; signing of military assistance agreements with other nations, and the detailed assistance actually supplied; negotiation of overseas military bases, and their evacuation; and speeches by Defense Department officials, civilian or military, that have foreign policy aspects.

It may be suggested that so much military activity and use of military force on behalf of the international objectives of the United States is undesirable no matter how carefully monitored and controlled by the State Department. I would argue that the importance of the military establishment in contemporary American foreign policy is essentially a function of the violent world we live in rather than an overly aggressive or powerful professional officer corps, some conspiracy of the military-industrial complex or a fatal flaw in the American character. A brief cataloguing of the wars, insurrections, coups d'etat, and other situations involving organized violence on a large scale since the end of World War II would produce a list running into the hundreds; and the United States would more frequently be found in the role of onlooker or aspiring peacemaker rather than participant.

Foreign policy and military policy, as we have indicated, are today deeply and inextricably interrelated. For example, thermonuclear devices deliverable by intercontinental ballistic missiles represent a fundamental problem of offense and defense for the military establishment. At the same time, they add great difficulties to what would have been in any event tense, trying and dangerous relationships between the United States and the Soviet Union. These weapons have also become a major factor and problem in American relations with our NATO allies: the control of these weapons; whether or not to assist our allies in developing their own nuclear capabilities (our unwillingness to do so in the case of France certainly contributed to General de Gaulle's displeasure with the United States); and the recurring question in the minds of western Europeans as to whether and under what conditions American nuclear weapons would in fact be used in defense of Europe. Thus, major policy questions regarding these weapons concern the foreign affairs as well as military departments. Both participate in many of the decisions regarding them, and each has relevant expertise, perspective, and special concerns to contribute. In some situations, foreign policy considerations may even be overriding.

In many other areas, military policy and foreign policy considerations interact in a similar fashion. In deciding whether or not to establish (or, perhaps, to give up) an American military base overseas, a variety of foreign policy aspects (including the sensibilities and preferences of the host nation, and neighboring nations) must be weighed, but so must the military requirements for the facility and the importance of the military functions it serves.

It is precisely this intermingling of concerns and considerations that led to the development of strong politico-military staffs in both the Defense Department and the Department of State and to major personnel training and assignment programs designed to produce not only military officers with an awareness of political and economic factors that affect their military activities and responsibilities, but also foreign affairs personnel with an equivalent "feel" for military strategy, hardware, and operating problems. While the presence of Defense Department civilian and military leaders on the National Security Council and other major national decision-making bodies has been widely noted, much less attention has been given to the fact that the State Department, since the early 1960's, has been given an opportunity each year to review the draft Defense budget from a foreign policy perspective before it is actually submitted to the President.

Some would say that the last point represents more form than substance or, perhaps, that whatever the formal arrangements, the net results in terms of the overseas performance of the United States are still overweighted in the direction of military factors, military activities, and application of military force. This is certainly a point of view worth careful examination. The view taken in these brief comments is that if the consequences are indeed less than ideal, they emerge from a situation in which the United States has had to cope, in its sudden emergence as the leading world power, with an international environment characterized by a very high degree of violence and by a series of revolutions in military technology that add significantly to the difficulties of its national security and foreign relations concerns. In the process of so doing, an impressive effort has been made to develop appropriate organizational arrangements and personnel skills and attitudes. Finally, the form and much of the spirit of military activities overseas have in fact been responsive to broader foreign policy guidance and concerns.

THE PRESSURES OF MILITARY NECESSITY
Gene M. Lyons

A number of basic points about the development of postwar foreign and military policy in the United States are illuminated in Professor Lyons' extremely useful essay. His historical survey gives solid substance to the notion of the interdependence of foreign policy and military policies and problems. He also places military policy-making in its domestic political and governmental context, making clear some of the ways in which contemporary problems of military strategy, technology and posture have affected, and been affected by, American governmental institutions and processes.

The Cold War has created powerful pressures on American society, pressures which by their persistence and ubiquity could have a fundamental influence on the direction the American people move in the future. For the Cold War has strained the bonds of the democratic process, challenged the effectiveness of the American governmental system, and tested the mettle of American leadership and the American people.

The impact of the Cold War on American society can be measured in a number of ways: in terms of the size of the annual defense budget, the existence of a large standing military force, the dependence of important sectors of the national economy on military contracts, an increasing centralization of power in the executive branch of the federal government, and the psychological threat of obliteration through thermonuclear war. It can also be measured in terms of the energies it has released: advances in science and technology that have been carried ahead by defense requirements; and national programs in training, education, and anti-discrimination that have served as a catalyst for moving toward the American dream of equal opportunity for all.

Involved in the Cold War is a concept of the relationship of military force to foreign policy which is new to the American experience. This is not to suggest that the United States has never used force in seeking political objectives, or that Americans have been uncommonly pacifistic. The consolidation of the United States during the nineteenth century and subsequent American expansionism in the Pacific and the Caribbean were accompanied by a deliberate exploitation of military power. At the same time, the American Civil War was the greatest armed conflict between the Napoleonic Wars and World War I, and the first total war under modern technological conditions. Moreover, in both world wars the United States not only mobilized its full resources in support of the military efforts of the allied powers but used its considerable influence in turning allied war aims toward the military objective of unconditional surrender.

The requirements of military policy are thus not unknown in the American experience despite the tradition of anti-militarism and the relative freedom from international conflict that the United States enjoyed until the early part of the twentieth century. The Cold War is nonetheless different from earlier situations. The difference lies principally in America's new role of world leadership and in the incredibly destructive capacity of modern weapons.

The United States has come to a role of world leadership at a time of revolutionary change. The emergence of new nations from the disruption of former colonial empires, the opportunities for rapid technological development and resultant social dislocations, the development of world-wide systems of communication, and the ideological challenge of communism have combined to create an international environment of continual turmoil and tension. Within such a setting, the element of force has become a major instrument of change and military power a central factor in dealing with the problems of foreign policy. All important issues of diplomacy must be dealt with in an atmosphere highly influenced by considerations of military power.

The centrality of military policy is nevertheless complicated by the special nature of modern weapons. Nuclear weapons and long-range delivery systems offer the major powers the means of destroying their opponents in all-out war. While nations may survive a thermonuclear war to the extent that men will try to rebuild a society out of utter chaos, the destruction will be so great that it can truly be said that "total" victory is, for the first time in history, a possibility. For it would certainly be two or more generations before a nation devastated by thermonuclear war became viable once again. The use of modern weapons thus poses a moral issue of deep consequence. At the same time the issue is also one of great practical risk. Modern weapons are essentially offensive, and until a completely effective defensive system is developed, the condition in which the victor finds himself at the end of such a war may be only relatively better than the vanquished. The United States and the Soviet Union, in effect, hazard the perils of self-destruction in becoming engaged in a thermonuclear war.

The situation is also one of extreme paradox. Military power is an indispensable element of international involvement, yet the utility of military power is limited by the risks of its very use. The American response to this paradox has been a "mixed" doctrine combining the policy of deterrence and the concept of control over conflict situations. The policy of deterrence is directed against the threat of aggression and requires the maintenance of sufficient military power to threaten other major nations with unacceptable destruction if they undertake aggressive action. The concept of control involves the moderation of critical areas of tension or conflict before they reach a point where the major powers confront each other without a margin of safety and risk the danger of all-out war. The methods of achieving moderation may vary from bilateral negotiation between the two major nuclear powers to the establishment of international peace-keeping machinery under the United Nations.

One of the most important implications of the current situation, in terms of its impact on American society, is the limits which this policy places on American military power. Military power becomes a requirement but not an active instrument of policy. The usefulness of military might is measured by the extent to which it can be translated into political power. It is an umbrella under which diplomacy, economic activity, and propaganda can be employed to further American interests. Military power might have to be used, especially in response to aggression or equally serious provocation. But even when force is brought to bear, the measure of success is not the crude calculation of military victory but the more difficult dimension of political achievement.

The use of military power as a deterrent is not new in history. Deterrence was an essential function of the British navy in the era of *Pax Britannia,* and in the American experience it was a function of military outposts in protecting Western settlers from Indian attack, and of the fleet in maintaining American footholds in Central America and in the Philippines. But if the function is not new, the scope and requirements of deterrence today are broader and more complex than before, both because of the nature of modern weapons and because of the dynamics of contemporary world politics. The material requirements of developing, maintaining, and perfecting a deterrent capability, the intellectual requirements of planning and anticipating the situations in which the deterrent will have to be brought to bear, and the psychological requirements involved in the demonstrations of will and the acts of bargaining that are crucial to great power relationships — these depend on the full resources and institutions of the nation. It is the level of intensity, the degree to which the policy of deterrence involves the country as a whole, and the consequences of failure which are unique in the current context of history. . . .

In 1945 and 1946 the formulation of postwar military policy was . . . carried on amidst these conflicting motives: to proceed with the demobilization of the wartime forces; to prepare to meet commitments under the UN Charter and in settlement of the war's victory; and to provide contingencies to deal with potential Soviet expansionism. Even under the pressures for demobilization, the United States was obliged to maintain the largest peacetime military force in its history in order to meet its commitments. The question was: What system should be adopted to develop and maintain such a force?

The broad policy alternatives fell into two major categories. The first was a traditional army plan that had always been defeated by a combination of anti-militarism and indifference: to develop a system of peacetime Universal Military Training (UMT) that would provide the United States with a potentially ready force without the necessity of a large standing army.[1] The second solution was more radical and re-

lied on technological advances made during the war: to harness American air power to the atomic bomb and provide the United States with a formidable weapon of destruction with which to maintain American influence in the world.[2]

UMT was in the American tradition. It was based on the concept of a citizen army which reflected the historical distrust of military centralization and professionalism and appealed to the crusading kind of patriotism that rouses a democratic people to arms. Nonetheless, politically, UMT was unpopular. It meant foisting direct responsibilities and burdens upon hundreds of thousands of citizens soon after the end of war and the promise of relief from military obligation. It also aroused the familiar unpopularity with military life which veterans carried out of the armed services — unpopularity stemming from the waste, the chafing command system, and the meaninglessness of war aims and orders for the solitary soldier isolated from the great sweep of war. It is a great paradox that for all the adoration of military heroes and the splendid response to patriotic histrionics, military life itself remains such an unpopular existence for most Americans.

There was, on the other hand, much in favor of basing American military posture on air power and the atomic bomb. In the midst of the devastation under which both ally and enemy lay at the end of the war, these weapons were symbols of America's position as the strongest power in the world, indeed of American omnipotence. They were also the weapons that, in the popular mind at any rate, had brought victory; for the widely screened images of triumph were German cities blasted by strategic bombing and Hiroshima and Nagasaki smoldering under the first atomic bombs exploded in anger. Air-atomic power, moreover, was the instrument of "total victory" and "unconditional surrender," which were conceived to be the normal objectives of war. The cost of air-atomic power, finally, was less visible than UMT. The basic requirements were technological, and the manpower needs could be met without the imposition of an unpopular conscription. The air force had emerged from the war as the most glamorous of the services, with all the thrill and promise of advance-

[1]*Universal Military Training,* Hearings, Committee on Military Affairs, House of Representatives, 79th Cong., 1st Sess.
[2]For an excellent general review of the development of the doctrine of air power, see Bernard Brodie, *Strategy in the Missile Age* (Princeton, 1959).

ment necessary to attract young Americans. The most tangible needs were for research and development, but here there were valuable by-products as funds thus allocated would be plowed back into the economy and would assist in converting from a wartime to a peacetime economy.

American military strategy was, in fact, based on a primary reliance on air-atomic power from the end of the war until the early 1960's. Throughout these years the overriding assumption was always the need to be prepared for a world-war kind of conflict with the Soviet Union. Less compelling demands were met with ad hoc measures but no basic change in policy. The manpower requirements of keeping occupation forces in Europe and Japan in the late forties, and later of manning alliance systems in these same areas, were filled through a continuation of the wartime selective service system, renewed periodically by Congress. UMT was defeated first in 1947 and again after the Korean conflict when the unexpected need for ground forces in that war gave new impetus to exploring the possibilities for training the citizenry in arms.

The defeat of UMT after Korea was closely related to the "new look" inaugurated by the Eisenhower administration in 1953. The "new look" was not really new but rather an intensification of the priority of air-atomic power. The mottos of the new look came to be the threat of "massive retaliation" made by Secretary of State John Foster Dulles, and the promise of "more bang for a buck" made by Secretary of Defense Charles Wilson. If the new look was a shift, it was not from what had been American military policy, but from the doubts that had come to develop about that policy since about 1949.[3]

The inter-service rivalries that characterized defense organization in the late forties were more than just incidents of bureaucratic infighting; they were also disputes over strategic policy. Out of the National Security Act of 1947, the air force had emerged as an independent service, freed from subordination under the army and in possession of the main instruments of the air-atomic strategy. As the air force sought to maintain this position of preeminence, and the army turned to pick up the pieces after the first loss on UMT, the navy was likely to be caught in the middle, left with no important strategic mission. This downgrading of the navy seemed to be confirmed when, in 1949, in the

heat of the annual budget-cutting campaign that had gone on each year since the end of the war, Secretary of Defense Louis Johnson suddenly stopped allocations for the construction of the navy's prize, a supercarrier that could haul aircraft capable of carrying atomic weapons.

The navy revolted. Navy Secretary John Sullivan, who had not been previously informed of Johnson's decision, resigned. The navy-officer hierarchy organized a counter-attack group, under then Captain Arleigh Burke, which focused its attention on the air force and looked for redress from allies in Congress. The "revolt of the admirals" was on. Under the guise of what began as a congressional investigation of air force procurement methods, the navy was given the opportunity to vent its wrath, and the outburst took the form of public criticism of prevailing military doctrine. Navy spokesmen warned of the dangers of what was essentially a single-weapon strategy and were particularly critical of the adequacy of the new air force bomber, the B-36. They questioned the usefulness of the air-atomic system to deal with such ambiguous threats to the peace as Soviet pressures in Turkey and Greece and instability in the Middle East. They even raised the issue of morality and painted ugly pictures of the results of strategic bombing with atomic weapons.[4]

The immediate effects of the navy's outburst and the congressional hearings that followed were substantially nil. Neither the President nor Congress was willing to undertake a more expensive defense program. It was not a matter of substituting an aircraft carrier for an air force wing, but of *adding to* air force requirements to meet the demands of the navy, and probably the army as well. Such a move was contrary to the prevailing spirit and seemed utterly needless to those who were psychologically convinced that, if it came, the next war would be fought almost wholly from the air and would be directed against the Soviet Union itself. This spirit persisted not only against the navy attack, but also against the increasing concern in the planning echelons of the State Department that American military capability was neither large enough nor varied enough to support the full range of the nation's commitments. These doubts, expressed

[3]See the case study on the "new look" by Glenn Snyder, in Schilling, Hammond, and Snyder, *Strategy, Politics and Defence Budgets* (New York, 1962).
[4]*Unification and Strategy*, Hearings, Committee on Armed Services, House of Representatives, 81st Cong., 1st Sess.

mainly by George Kennan, then planning chief for State, led in early 1950 to a National Security Council study, NSC 68, which specifically called for larger conventional forces to fight limited wars.[5] NSC 68 had hardly appeared when the Korean conflict broke out and the United States found itself in the middle of a limited war with inadequate and poorly trained troops.

Criticism of the air-atomic strategy had also been involved in the controversy over the hydrogen bomb that began in late 1949 when the Soviets exploded their first atomic device. Work on the more powerful hydrogen bomb had been virtually halted in 1945 after the success of the A-bomb and the early decision to seek international control of atomic energy. With the collapse of disarmament talks and the announcement of the Soviet explosion, the drive to proceed with the H-bomb was again initiated. In a debate that was largely limited to the scientific community and the highest levels of government, two factions emerged. One, led by Edward Teller, urged an all-out effort on the H-bomb to insure American superiority in the arms race. The second, led by Robert Oppenheimer, cautioned against an intensification of big-weapon competition and proposed increased experimentation to develop small, low-yield atomic weapons which could be employed with discrimination and would provide multiple-weapons systems to meet a variety of conflict situations. Late in 1949 President Truman ordered work on the H-bomb to proceed. But the proposals to develop a diversified atomic arsenal were not rejected. Under Project Vista in 1951 and 1952, for example, a group of scientists at the California Institute of Technology submitted a study of the possibilities for the development and use of low-yield atomic devices; and indeed such new weapons systems actually became operational by the late 1950's.[6]

The Eisenhower administration that took office in 1953 did not wholly reject these doubts about the emphasis on air-atomic power. The administration was, however, pledged to two overriding objectives: to bring the national budget into balance in the face of soaring defense expenditures that followed the outbreak of the Korean conflict; and to get the United States out of the Korean War and avoid getting involved in similar conflicts in which no decisive solution could be pursued. These two objectives were, of course, related. Once the immediate aim of ending the Korean War was achieved in 1953, it became necessary to avoid

future "Koreas" while developing a military establishment that was kept within conservative budget limits. The way to do this, according to Secretary Dulles, was to project the strategy of air-atomic power to its full conclusion, and to lay to rest any doubts about the American will to respond to challenge. The Soviets were thus warned that the United States would respond to threats to its interests and to the peace of the world by exerting military pressures at times and places of its own choosing. No longer would the United States react to Soviet initiative or be forced to accept the battleground chosen by the communists. The ability to take the initiative away from the Soviets, and thereby to strengthen the policy of deterrence, would flow from the so-called doctrine of "massive retaliation."[7]

The Dulles doctrine was full of ambiguities. Under what conditions would massive retaliation be threatened? Could local provocation in Berlin or on the off-shore Chinese islands lead to a thermonuclear attack on Moscow with few or no intermediate steps? Even more questionable, was a thermonuclear attack a rational response to communist guerrilla activity in Southeast Asia? There is no doubt that a strategy of deterrence requires a degree of ambiguity—an element of surprise, of the unknown—to be effective. But Secretary Dulles operated under the weakness of having only one means—air-atomic power—to respond to a variety of situations. Thus, no matter how ambiguously it might be stated, the United States could support a threat only through the use of atomic power. It could well be asked whether, in an open society in which rationality is encouraged and there is a demand for political accountability, massive retaliation would, in fact, be a response to any but the most direct and provocative of communist actions. In this context, Dulles' doctrine lacked credibility.[8]

Massive retaliation was, however, only one element in the Dulles strategy. A second, and

[5]For the story of NSC 68, see the essay by Paul Y. Hammond, in Schilling, Hammond, and Snyder, op. cit.

[6]The H-bomb debate can be followed in the transcript of the Oppenheimer hearings, In the Matter of J. Robert Oppenheimer, Atomic Energy Commission (1954); see also Warner R. Schilling, "The H-Bomb Decision: How to Decide Without Actually Choosing," Political Science Quarterly, LXXVI (March 1961), 24-46.

[7]Secretary Dulles first articulated the doctrine of "massive retaliation" in a speech on January 12, 1954; see New York Times, January 13, 1954.

[8]For an early critique of the Dulles doctrine, see William W. Kaufman, ed., Military Policy and National Security (Princeton, 1956), 12 ff.

conceivably as important an element, was the insistence that threats which merited less than a nuclear response would have to be met by local forces, largely manned by nations in the area of danger. This was the implication behind General Eisenhower's pre-election evaluation of the Korean War when he said: "If there must be a war, let it be Asians against Asians, with our support on the side of freedom." It was also the basis for the drive to develop a series of defense treaties, bilateral and regional, around the world and to use American economic aid as a means of supporting local military forces needed to combat communist pressures.[9]

The Dulles strategy was thus based on a division of labor. The United States would provide the ultimate threat to communist aggression through its air-atomic power, while other nations, tied to the United States through defense treaties and military and economic assistance programs, would provide the conventional forces needed to meet local threats and pressures. The division of labor proved, however, to be unworkable. For one thing, there was no viable military capability in most of the "grey areas" in Southeast Asia and the Middle East, and no expectation that such a capability could be built. Few of the developing nations, moreover, preferred to accept this alternative to communist absorption. Except for those states under severe pressure—South Korea, the Nationalist Chinese on Formosa, and South Vietnam—they sought to play a more independent role. Indeed, some—and the most important like India and Egypt—sought a position of neutralism which would enable them to deal with the East-West conflict in terms of their own independent development rather than the strategic requirements of the great powers.

But the ultimate blow to the doctrine of massive retaliation came with the realization, in late 1957, that the Soviet Union possessed an intercontinental missile capability that made the United States itself vulnerable to direct attack. The American military advantage, critical to the Dulles doctrine, had been based on the worldwide network of the Strategic Air Command that could, from a number of positions, strike at the heart of the Soviet Union. Until the late 1950's there was no such threat to the United States itself. The margin of maneuverability in this protected position was destroyed with the launching of the first Soviet sputnik in the fall of 1957. The superiority of the United States in the arms race now began to give way to a strategic

balance between the two super-powers, as the Soviets moved to turn their potential into operational power.

The American response to the new strategic balance took several directions in the late 1950's and early 1960's. The first move was to fill in the gaps in American military strength in order to provide a broader range of capabilities, particularly for limited and internal wars. Not only were the force levels of the army increased until they reached just under one million by 1963, but military transportation facilities were expanded to provide means for airlifting large contingents of troops into danger zones. These two goals of increased power and mobility were dramatically demonstrated in the fall of 1963 when, in a trial run, troops in the strategic reserve based in the United States were flown to Europe and deployed into fighting positions during a steady three-day period of non-stop flights.[10] Under wartime conditions, circumstances of confusion, tension, and enemy action would certainly make such a transfer of forces more difficult. Nonetheless, the exercise was an impressive demonstration of the new ability of the United States to bolster the limited-war capacity of the NATO alliance in case of a Soviet threat to Europe, and to provide a viable alternative to the use of nuclear weapons.

In 1961 the Kennedy administration also took steps to develop special forces trained for guerrilla-type operations. These forces were directed against ambiguous threats to stability that arise from insurgent efforts to unseat governments supported by the United States. In the 1960's the case of South Vietnam provided an almost classic area of application for counterinsurgency operations. Threatened by rebels who were aided by the communist regime in North Vietnam, the Saigon government was a slender reed—but a reed nonetheless—on which much of the general security of Southeast Asia rested. The Eisenhower dictum of "Asians against Asians, with our support on the side of freedom" would have been disastrously ineffective in meeting the challenge. The Saigon government (in any of its forms) hardly represented "freedom"—only the best alternative in a difficult and dangerous situation. But beyond this acceptance of reality, the South Vietnamese, for good and logical reasons, lacked not

---

[9]For a study for the application of this strategy to the Korean case, see Gene M. Lyons, *Military Policy and Economic Aid* (Columbus, 1961).
[10]*New York Times*, October 23, 1963.

only the means but the will to fight unless they were sustained from outside. American assistance was thus extended beyond equipment and training to actual participation in combat operations in advisory and logistic support of South Vietnamese forces.

The development of limited-war and counter-insurgency forces broadened the range of American options and thus added credibility to the doctrine of deterrence in a way that had not been possible in Dulles' day. The major deterrent nevertheless remained the ultimate threat of strategic nuclear power, and it was this power that was now directly vulnerable to attack as a result of the Soviet ICBM capability. A first strike by the Soviets might so cripple U.S. strategic forces that effective retaliation would be prohibited. A new requirement thus had to be met—to protect the American retaliatory capability, not only the vehicles and warheads but the whole system of command and control from the President down to aircraft and missile commanders. Again, this protection was the result of intensified efforts in the late 1950's and early 1960's.

These efforts included new research and development in weapons systems, new methods of sheltering, and new tactical concepts. Advances in rocket fuels provided increased power that was also safer and quicker to ignite than earlier fuels, and thus more effective for missiles that had to be launched from concrete silos in which they were protected from all but a direct hit. Concrete "hardening" also provided protection for air installations and most importantly for the network of complex communications systems through which command and control was achieved. But beyond "hardening," the retaliatory force was protected through increased mobility—on the theory that a moving target is harder to find and hit than a stationary one. Strategic Air Command bombers were not only kept on a round-the-clock alert, but by 1962-63 a certain number were continually air-borne, ready to move toward targets should the bombers on the ground be destroyed. Finally, the navy's nuclear-powered submarine was pushed into production and, once operational, provided a weapon that could stay in motion at sea for almost a year without coming into port; which could approach enemy shores with minimum possibility of detection; and which carried sixteen Polaris missiles capable of sending nuclear warheads 2,500 miles with good accuracy.

The diversification of American military capability and the protection of retaliatory forces were, in effect, unilateral responses by the United States to the more tenuous balance of power that followed the Soviet ICBM capability. There was, however, another response which was essentially bilateral and which involved joint efforts by the Americans and the Soviets to keep the balance as stable as possible. There was, on the American side, for example, growing speculation that if the retaliatory capacity of both sides was effectively protected, the incentive for first strike would be greatly reduced since the probability of knocking out a major part of the enemy's power would be extremely low. Mutual invulnerability thus provided the kind of protection against surprise attack which it would be impossible to negotiate into a treaty. At the same time, the mutual concern for stability in the light of the consequences of miscalculation and the uncertainties of revolutionary forces in the world was an incentive for both powers to explore the feasibility of other control mechanisms. Not only was the nuclear test-ban treaty a consequence of these explorations, but perhaps more significant (though less spectacular) was the installation of a "hot line" between Washington and Moscow to permit instantaneous and continual communication in case of emergency. Such communication was essential not only to the control of conflict but to the effectiveness of deterrence. It was important to avoid precipitous action through a miscalculation of intentions; but it was also important to have a means of telling the other side when the chips were down.

Limited war, counter-insurgency, invulnerable strategic forces, arms control measures—all of these are components in a general strategy that is considerably different from the single-factor air-atomic strategy that had dominated American military doctrine since 1945.[11] It is no longer assumed that the next war will be a World War II plus nuclear weapons and missiles. Indeed, a basic objective is to avoid this kind of conflict, not only by deterring aggression through threat of unacceptable retaliation but by agreement with the Soviet Union on controlling unstable conditions that could lead to general war. At the same time, there is a preparedness—and presumably a willingness—to fight wars at lower levels of violence if American

[11]For a general review of the development of this strategy after 1961, see William Kaufman, The McNamara Strategy (New York, 1964).

political interests can be protected in no other way.

The requirements of this more complex military policy generate a stream of conflicting pressures on American society. The requirements of deterrence involve an annual budget of some $50 billion a year; armed forces stationed throughout the world; a vast network of research, development, and training facilities; a determination to use military power if necessary, and a national will to support such a decision. At the same time, the forces developed by these requirements must be controlled in order to insure rationality and to avert catastrophe. Any decision to use military power must be calculated against the political objectives to be gained or lost. Yet the size of the military establishment and the national frustration and impatience with limited achievements in reaching political goals create pressures for using military power in a less calculating way. At the same time, the dilemma of military power is related to the dual vision with which we must view the Soviet Union. We are forced to look at the Soviet Union as an enemy in order to justify the maintenance of such an enormous military establishment; but we must see the Soviets as a partner in terms of the political necessity of cooperating in order to avoid a war in which the means of destruction could virtually eliminate any chance of gaining meaningful political objectives.

The requirements of military policy and the limits of military power thus tug at American society in two often opposing directions. This is an entirely new experience for the United States, whose earlier sorties into the complexities of military policy were on an "all-or-nothing" basis. The major objective of our huge military resources is not necessarily to "win" any victories. It is to deter potential international conflict, to pursue political goals through more lasting though less decisive means than military force, and to gain the time to develop an international system, through deliberate arrangements and through political evolution, in which the present risks and dangers of war can be averted.

THE MAKING OF MILITARY POLICY

The requirements of a national security policy based on a combination of deterrence and arms control are four: (1) the development and maintenance of an effective deterrent capability; (2) decision-making procedures that are at once responsive to the complexities of contemporary world politics and to the demands of the democratic process; (3) open communications with the Soviet Union in order to avoid accidents and miscalculation of intentions; and (4) a strength of will on the part of American leaders and the people to act decisively when necessary and to resist acting too quickly when it is risky to do so.

These requirements have had important effects upon the organization of the American government. They have necessitated a centralization and amalgamation of authority in the Executive Branch of the federal government and particularly strengthened the power of the Executive Office of the President. The President, as commander-in-chief of the armed forces and chief negotiator and representative in foreign affairs, is in effect the ultimate source of authority in national security affairs. It is, for example, the President alone who can issue orders for the use of nuclear weapons. This power gives the President, together with his staff and immediate advisers, tremendous leverage in the political process through which policy and strategy are developed.[12]

In comparison, the power of Congress has steadily declined. The power of Congress to declare war, for example, has for all intents and purposes been abrogated by the changing nature of warfare. In the Korean conflict, American troops went into battle as a police action in response to a recommendation of the UN Security Council. There was no congressional declaration of war. In the Berlin Blockade of 1948-49, and in subsequent crises related to the question of access to Berlin, it has been the President, as commander-in-chief, who has made the basic decisions, decisions that had to be supported by a willingness to go to war in order to be effective.

In the Far Eastern incident of 1955, moreover, the Congress, by joint resolution, actually gave President Eisenhower prior approval to use armed force to resist efforts by the Chinese Communists to take the off-shore islands of Quemoy and Matsu; the only condition was that he first determine that such an invasion would jeopardize the security of Formosa.[13] In point of fact, the joint resolution did not give the President authority he did not already possess, both

[12]See Richard E. Neustadt, *Presidential Power* (New York, 1960).
[13]Similar congressional action was taken in support of the presidential position in the Middle East in 1957, during the Cuban missile crisis in 1962, and during the Tonkin Gulf incident in 1964. See Report No. 1329, Committee on Foreign Relations, U.S. Senate, 88th Cong., 2nd Sess., 8.

through his position as head of the armed forces and under the bilateral defense treaty with the Nationalist Chinese. But in responding to President Eisenhower's request for unequivocal support for his executive actions in the Formosan Straits—a request no doubt prompted by a desire to avoid a repetition of the method of entrance into the Korean War, in which Congress did not participate at all—Congress acknowledged the primary and dominating role of the President in issues of war and peace.

This is not to suggest that Congress plays no role whatsoever in matters of defense. No President can ignore Congress. Not only does Congress exercise powers of oversight and appropriations, but congressional support gives a sense of popular concurrence to presidential action. Congressional support is also essential to the President's domestic programs, and he is unlikely to jeopardize it by a head-on conflict on security issues if he can avoid it. At the same time, any President is certain to respect the need for preserving congressional prerogatives under the American system of government. In this respect the treaty power continues to give the Senate an important policy-making role in cases where the President feels forced or inclined to use this route to conclude international agreements. It is of course true that the President has frequently used the method of executive agreement to come to terms with other nations, a method which does not require Senate approval. But the choice of the treaty route is open to him if he wishes to emphasize the domestic support he has, or if he wishes to pay respect to the constitutional position of the Senate in foreign affairs.

Within these bounds there are obvious restrictions on the role of Congress in defense affairs because of the complexity and size of the issues, the technical nature of so many of the problems, and the numerous other demands on a legislator's time. The influence of Congress in the area of defense is, in many respects, more the result of an intervention into the executive process of policy making than an exercise of its own prerogatives. Congress has become a court of appeal for those in the Executive Branch whose positions are overruled within the executive hierarchy. This has been particularly true of the military departments who have found congressional committees a useful arena in which to battle (or re-battle) their case, either in competition with sister services or against the increasing

civilian authority that has developed in the Department of Defense. In the B-36 controversy, for example, the navy was able to bring its argument for new aircraft carriers to Congress after Secretary Johnson's decision to discontinue the program. Similarly, in the early 1960's the air force, through forceful presentation to the Armed Services Committees in both houses, was able to push the development—at least to the building of prototypes—of a manned supersonic bomber despite the opposition of the Secretary of Defense. In both cases Congress was presented with an opportunity to review not only the particular decisions with regard to the choice of weapons systems but the broad strategic implications which these choices involved.

The review of decisions that are matters of controversy within the Executive Branch is thus an important method of exerting congressional influence. It requires, however, a high level of liaison between the bureaucracy and Capitol Hill, and a kind of "open door" policy by legislators. But it is a method which is encouraged by the annual appropriations process and which directs the attention of Congressmen and Senators to those items out of the vast and complicated array of items in an annual budget of $50 billion, which are vulnerable to questioning and investigation. In contrast, the annual review of foreign and defense policy is a process in which Congress essentially learns what is going on and to which it can contribute little.[14]

Within the Executive Branch, the same problems of size and complexity which have made Congress' role so difficult have led to increasing centralization. Under the National Security Act of 1947, a national defense establishment was established as a policy making body with limited powers of coordination over the three military departments, army, navy, and air force. Amendments to the original act and general operating experience have greatly expanded this limited authority. Almost complete decision-making power now rests at the level of the Secretary of Defense and is exercised in a variety of ways: through central budgetary control and through the authority to transfer research programs in weapons systems from one service to another; through the establishment of

[14]For meaningful analyses of the role of Congress, see Samuel P. Huntington, The Common Defense (New York, 1961), 123 ff.; also Roger Hilsman, "Congressional-Executive Relations and the Foreign Policy Consensus," American Political Science Review, LII, No. 3 (September 1958), 725 ff.

such centralized functional agencies as the Defense Intelligence Agency and the Defense Supply Agency; and through the development of unified commands reporting to the Secretary and the Joint Chiefs of Staff and maintaining integrated command and training over units from all three services.

This tendency toward centralization has left the services secondary to the Defense Department in all but one major area: recruitment and promotion of personnel. This power, while residual, is not inconsequential; so long as an officer's career depends on his own service, he is most likely to follow that service's views no matter where the basis of authority in other matters is to be found. Service loyalty has thus not been substantially changed in the shift toward centralized authority. Indeed, it might have intensified as the services have sought to maintain their integrity in the face of depleting authority and to use the few independent powers they have retained.

The increase in civilian authority in the defense establishment is more than an extension of the traditional concept of civilian control of the military.[15] It is that to a certain extent, but more correctly the increased role of civilians comes from changes in the nature of warfare. The importance of weapons technology has forced the military to become increasingly dependent on civilian scientists and engineers, not only for the design and development of new weapons systems and detection devices but for their use as well. At the same time, the changing nature of weapons does not permit the military to rely wholly on previous combat experience as a guide to future wars. No one has had experience using hydrogen bombs, tactical atomic weapons, and long-range missiles. The battleground of the future is highly theoretical and the problems of troop formation, requirements, and the rest cannot be anticipated on the basis of classical military history alone; there is also much to be learned from calculated extension of the known capabilities of new weapons and the probable response of an opponent.

But the civilian role in military affairs is, above all, enhanced by the objectives of defense policy. The relationships that flow from a policy of deterrence and arms control are essentially psychological and political. The development, deployment, and use of the defense establishment must be delicately related to political objectives. The mechanisms for insuring this relationship are several. The formal method is the National Security Council, established in 1947 as an advisory board of cabinet-level officers to make recommendations to the President. As a corporate body, the Council is subject to the wishes of the President. The President has the responsibility for policy and the Council is available to him, but he is under no obligation to call the Council into session before deciding on any major policy matter. Of the Presidents since 1947, General Eisenhower used the Council more systematically than the others, developing a military staff-like system within the Council structure.

Within the Defense Department, the Secretary has his own political advisers, mainly concentrated in the office of the Assistant Secretary for International Security Affairs. In the State Department, military affairs are the concern of all bureaus, though there is special emphasis in the Policy Planning Council and in the Politico-Military Affairs Staff, the former established in 1948 and the latter in 1961. At the White House level, the President's Special Assistant for National Security Affairs not only provides the secretariat for the National Security Council but is the contact point between the President and the departments—a strategic position from which he can often match the influence of the Secretaries in the formulation of policy. Also in the White House, the Special Assistant for Science and Technology provides a second center of influence in national security affairs, as presidential adviser and as leader and coordinator for the scientific community in its role and relationship with the government.

The new demands on civilians for policy and operational involvement in military problems have precipitated a new professionalism in national security affairs, which is manifested in a number of ways.[16] There has, especially since the mid-1950's, been an increasing insistence that major political appointments in the fields of foreign affairs and defense be based on experience and special qualifications, with other criteria of political, regional, or ethnic background being subordinate. While this tendency had been followed earlier in foreign affairs, it was late coming to the defense establishment where

[15]Gene M. Lyons, "The New Civil-Military Relations," *American Political Science Review*, LV, No. 1 (March 1961), 53 ff.
[16]For a full discussion of the new professionalism, see Gene M. Lyons and Louis Morton, *Schools for Strategy* (New York, 1965).

the needed expertise was concentrated in the career military. But with the shift in specialist requirements in the Pentagon, greater care has been given to appointments. The last Eisenhower Secretary of Defense, Thomas Gates, for example, had served as Deputy Secretary, Assistant Secretary, and Secretary of the Navy immediately before his appointment, and had also had experience in the defense field during World War II and in the immediate years after the war. The Secretary of Defense in the Kennedy administration, Robert McNamara, brought special competence in the area of operations research, proven ability in large-scale management, and earlier experience in applying systematic analysis to military problems while on air force duty during and after World War II.

This insistence on competence and experience, evident at other political levels in the Defense Department, is in many respects related to the rationalization, or "intellectualization," of the policy process, for which the military was greatly responsible. This rationalization has origins in several sources. It rests, first, on the application of techniques of operations research to military operations during World War II. Both the British and the Americans found that by projecting weapons capabilities and by carefully observing response behavior, it was possible to develop more effective firing methods, evasive tactics, or other more efficient methods of operations. This consciously rational method of determining the better "use" of weapons was reinforced by expanded scientific efforts in the postwar period to produce better weapons. These two trends—better weapons and their better use—were then institutionalized in the non-profit, scientifically oriented, university-like corporations set up by the military departments (and later by the Secretary of Defense) to bring this new kind of expertise into the defense establishment. While the most successful and glamorous of these groups is the RAND Corporation set up by the air force, others, such as the army's Research Analysis Corporation, the navy's Operations Evaluation Group, and the Institute of Defense Analyses, have also made important contributions to rationalizing the policy process.

This tendency toward rationalization, based on weapons, their uses, and their costs, was joined by a second intellectual change: a more dynamic and realistic approach to the whole field of international politics and foreign policy.

In place of legalistic, goal-setting tendencies in the study of world affairs, there grew up in the postwar period a new school of realism which gave greater emphasis to the role of military power, but more importantly, to the necessity of translating military strength into political objectives. Grounded in the history of the inter-war years, the wartime experiences, and a more concentrated concern with contemporary politics, the new realism found its most articulate expression in the writings of Hans Morgenthau and George Kennan.[17] Even for those who opposed its premises, it forced a more rigorous methodology on all writers and teachers in the field, and its effects, through education, scholarship, public debate, and the changing requirements of policy makers, had, by the 1960's, given a new depth to thinking about international politics. At the same time, other advances in international studies had produced specialists in different areas of the world—Latin America, Africa, the Middle East, the Far East—in which American commitments were growing, and greater sophistication and skill in dealing with the complex interplay of political, economic, social, psychological, and military factors that are involved in national security issues.

The new expertise in defense and diplomacy poses a number of problems. There is, first of all, the real problem of bringing expertise to bear on policy in an effective way. When the issue is highly technological, there is necessarily a heavy reliance on the specialist. When the issue is less limited, more open to judgment, less susceptible to an absolute determination, a willingness to hear the expert may depend on the value that is attached to quality and depth in analysis and interpretation. However highly rationalized the policy process may become, the ultimate decisions are in the hands of the President, and his will and style dominate. While the "experts"—civilian and military—may limit the alternatives of choice, their role in making a choice depends on the President's giving them their place in the decision-making hierarchy.

This is not to say that a President—or his chief advisers—is free to ignore expert advice. He does so only at his own risk. Beyond the obvious need to take specialized knowledge into account, there is a political motive: this same advice can be made available to Congress or the press and used to demand accountability for

[17]For examples: Hans J. Morgenthau, *Politics Among Nations*, 3rd edition (New York, 1960); and George F. Kennan, *American Diplomacy, 1900-1950* (Chicago, 1961).

executive action. At the same time there is nothing "monolithic" about expert advice. Experts may differ, not only when the problems are essentially political but when they are highly technological as well. There is never only one way to attack a problem in military research and development, for example. After several stages of experimentation and testing, the factors of feasibility and efficiency may become so clear that the best solution becomes indisputable. But until that point, decisions involving time, money, and considerable effort usually must be made, and there is literally no alternative to depending upon the knowledgeable judgment of chosen experts.

The rationalization of the policy process in national security affairs thus gives tremendous power to experts in government; but it does not mean that we are moving toward government by elite. Indeed, the open nature of presidential elections, the reliance of Congressmen on parochial interests, the vital role of pressure groups in the legislative process, and the susceptibility of public opinion to mass communications, all these features of American political life serve as restrictions on complete rationalization. Even further, they may act as direct influences on policy, to restrain or provoke policy change in the face of contrary expert opinion. A basic shift in American policy toward Communist China, for example, is as much dependent on factors of domestic politics as on calculated estimates of the future of the communist bloc. Similarly, a President might easily find it necessary, because of internal pressures, to respond more openly and directly to communist adventurism than a studied analysis of the national interest dictates.

These limits on rationalization may be looked at from two points of view. They suggest that through the complex interplay of American political forces a "general will" of the people is an influence in national security policy, at least in its tone and broad dimensions. This, one might say, is a "good thing." From another perspective, however, this "democratizing" influence may be more dangerous than satisfying. In so far as the "general will" on such matters as defense and diplomacy can be determined, it is likely to be expressed in less complicated terms than the actual situation merits. At the same time, the ambiguity of dealing with the Soviet Union as both enemy and partner; the problem of determining where the objectives of international communism become subordinate to the de-

mands of Russian or Chinese national interest; the frustration of not being able to identify the "payoff" from foreign aid, military assistance, and diplomatic support; and the impatience at being forced, time and again, to explain that we are not an aggressive people—these kinds of pressures can lead to a sense of impatience to which both the President and Congress may feel obliged to respond—whether or not such a response is warranted by "external" factors.

In this kind of situation, the response of Congress is likely to be fragmented and divided, and more apt to reflect opinion than to shape it. It is the President who must balance the "feeling" of the country with the demands of his own responsibility and, if necessary, become the teacher of the people if he finds that there is resistance to what he must do. For here, as in other respects, we are left with the increasingly important role of the President as the major impact of the Cold War on the American political system. The roles of Congress and public opinion and pressure groups remain operative but highly dependent on presidential initiative. While expert advice is at a high premium, the effectiveness of the knowledgeable specialist is also tied to a responsiveness by the President. There are clearly pressures on the President to rely on expert advice: the very nature of national security issues, the importance of science and technology, the complexity of political and military factors, the need for long-range perspective, the accumulation of expertise that is available, the expectation that more and better knowledge provides a firmer basis for decisions.

But in the final analysis it is the President who must choose. He may be restrained by what he feels the country will support and how far Congress will be willing to go. His power to change the temper and direction of public opinion is not unlimited. It is nevertheless extraordinarily potent—the information he alone possesses, the monopoly he can have of communications media, the responsibility he is expected to assume, the leadership and unity only he can give. For we are living in a political system that is dominated by the presidency. This domination is not wholly the product of the Cold War. It comes from the continuing experience of dealing with crises and challenges since the Great Depression of the early 1930's. But today it is largely carried forward and expanded by the necessity of coping with problems of war and peace.

NEW APPROACHES TO DEFENSE DECISION-MAKING
Wesley W. Posvar

A great deal of attention has been directed to what many regard as a revolution in the way major defense decisions are made in the United States. A variety of terms, sometimes used rather carelessly, have been associated with this "revolution"—operations research, systems analysis, cost-effectiveness, and program budgeting among them. Credit or, in some cases, blame for these developments has tended to be given to former Secretary of Defense Robert S. McNamara and some of the brilliant economists and other analysts who served with him (the latter were referred to in the early days of his seven-year stint in office as the "Whiz Kids"). All of these approaches, however, had to some extent been applied to military decision-making before the McNamara period.

In this connection, Dr. Posvar's essay provides a useful survey and evaluation of these and other approaches to defense. Wesley W. Posvar, former professor of political science and chairman of the division of social sciences at the United States Air Force Academy, has been chancellor of the University of Pittsburgh since 1967.

The era of nuclear weapons is well understood to be a revolution in the nature of conflict. Less well understood is a similar revolution in the form of methods and concepts for the management of military force. The management revolution occurred largely as a response to the weapons revolution, induced by the need for both economy and rationality in a strategic environment of chaos and potential doom.

Albert Einstein, the dismayed founder of modern nuclear science, perceived that "our world is threatened by a crisis whose extent seems to escape those within whose power it is to make major decisions for good or evil. The unleashed power of the atom," he said, "has changed everything except our ways of thinking. Thus we are drifting toward a catastrophe beyond comparison. We shall require a substantially new manner of thinking if mankind is to survive."[1]

Although he undoubtedly had more altruistic improvements in mind, the new methods and concepts for the management of military force do constitute a "new manner of thinking," an attempt to fulfill the need Einstein expressed. The process of making decisions for national defense has been broadened in novel institutional and methodological ways. The process takes place both inside and outside government.

Legions of analysts conduct myriad studies of weapon systems and force requirements. Groups of advisers weigh the issues of war and peace and probe the meaning of those issues to a greater depth than was ever possible through the old-fashioned intuitions of battlefield commanders and political leaders. This whole development—comprised of the methods, the concepts, and the advances in strategic doctrine and theory—can be characterized as "strategy expertise." It is treated here as a development of great importance in itself, one that was jointly created and is jointly employed by military professionals and civil servants inside government and by private experts and scholars outside government. The development thus transcends the jurisdictional doubts and quarrels that often divide these elements.

There are many critics—and they would surely include Einstein if he were alive today —who deplore the fact that these intellectual energies are devoted, essentially, to the preservation of military security through the manipulation of the very military instruments that constitute the hazard. Yet there has been no other possible way to provide security. The nation-state system is a reality. Any scheme for security on a planet that contains nuclear weapons is imperfect, even inherently dangerous.

Nevertheless, it is the world's great good fortune that the United States as a mature power with unusually moderate objectives was the first to acquire the responsibility of nuclear weapons. Moreover, it is the search for restraint in the exercise of nuclear power that makes the strategic task complicated. If atomic weapons had first become available to a totalitarian state, there might have been little need for the development of strategy expertise.

ORIGINS

There are three intellectual sources of today's strategy expertise. The first is the body of military literature produced by the old professionals. Besides Clausewitz, the notables included Jomini, a contemporary of Clausewitz in the late

[1]Quoted by Hans Helmut Kirst, *The Seventh Day* (New York: Ace Books, 1959), p. 6.

eighteenth and early nineteenth centuries, and the more recent naval strategist Mahan and air strategist Douhet. These writers all made distinctive contributions to strategic theory. Both Clausewitz and Jomini undertook to analyze the phenomenon of war and its attendant practices in the context of the new era, opened by Napoleon, in which powerful European states invested all their honor and all their young manhood, mobilized by the *levée en masse,* in their contests with one another. Mahan related the employment of seapower to the strength and prestige of nations in the broad sweep of history. Douhet developed doctrines for using air weapons to attack industrial centers remote from surface armies and for committing all available forces to a strategic offensive at the outset of war.

In general, the military origin of strategy expertise was limited to such writings.[2] Beyond them, relatively little had appeared in the way of original, analytical military thought before World War II. Strategic theory was, therefore, remarkable for its sparseness. Most military writers had tended to adhere closely to the ideas of these classicists and to distill those ideas into simplified forms, such as the so-called principles of war. The field of military planning, which in the present day is so closely identified with the formulation of strategic theory, was limited mainly to problems of mobilization and to determining the initial deployments of forces in the event of war. Examples were the German Schlieffen Plan and the French Plan XVII before World War I. The interactions of military forces that would take place after their collision in the field were not an object of detailed planning. Such unforeseeable events were left, necessarily, to the initiative of the commander. In general, then, it seems not unfair to say that historically the military profession was uninterested in theory and generally unconcerned with searching for new ways to improve its efficiency as an instrument of the state.

The civilian academic community provided the next source of strategy expertise.[3] In the 1930's, the topic of war became an object of attention at several important academic centers. At the University of Chicago, Quincy Wright, professor of international relations, conducted a major research project called *A Study of War.*[4] This study undertook to survey warfare throughout history, to examine its characteristics and to identify its causes. At the Yale institute of International Studies, the nation's need for military security was examined candidly and treated as an essential element of foreign policy—an uncommon approach for those times. A number of important books were produced there by a group of scholars, of whom Nicholas J. Spykman and Arnold Wolfers were the most prominent.[5] In New York City, the New School for Social Research, a center for prominent refugee scholars from Europe, organized a faculty seminar that treated war as a contemporary social phenomenon.[6] At the Institute for Advanced Study in Princeton, Edward Mead Earle established a faculty seminar in military affairs.[7]

All these scholarly ventures had a common source in the study and teaching of international relations at the university level. Thus, these efforts represented a major development in the academic discipline of international relations, an initial departure from the traditional emphasis on international law, international organization, and diplomacy as the generally accepted bases of international order. The significance of that departure may be difficult to appreciate now that three decades have intervened, but it cannot be overstressed. Disenchantment with the failure of the League of Nations and the dismal failure of utopian schemes such as the Kellogg-Briand Peace Pact outlawing war had begun to chill the hopes and disturb the basic assumptions of professors specializing in international relations. The problem of war, it appeared, was not to be solved solely by legal devices; more realistic and penetrating insights into the very nature of war were required.

[2]See Edward Mead Earle, *Makers of Modern Strategy* (Princeton: Princeton University Press, 1943), Chaps. 4, 5, 17, and 20; Bernard W. Brodie, *Strategy in the Missile Age* (Princeton: Princeton University Press, 1959), Chap. 3.
[3]The general content of the next paragraphs follows Gene M. Lyons and Louis Morton, *Schools of Strategy* (New York: Frederick A. Praeger, 1965), Chap. 2.
[4]The result was a published work of impressive scholarship, a major influence on the students who participated in its preparation and upon numerous others who have used it since. Quincy Wright, *A Study of War* (Chicago: University of Chicago Press, 1942). Harold Lasswell produced his important *World Politics and Personal Insecurity* (New York: McGraw-Hill, 1935), as a consequence of studies begun in connection with Wright's project at Chicago.
[5]For example, see Nicholas J. Spykman, *America's Strategy in World Politics* (New York: Harcourt, Brace, 1942), and Arnold Wolfers, *Britain and France Between Two Wars* (New York: Harcourt, Brace, 1940).
[6]The product was a volume titled *War in Our Times,* eds., Hans Speier and Alfred Kähler (New York: W. W. Norton, 1939).
[7]This led to the brilliant collection of historical essays, *Makers of Modern Strategy* (important military thinkers from Machiavelli to Hitler). This volume, appearing as it did during World War II, served as a historical capstone, a definitive evaluation of three centuries of strategic development, just at the time when warfare was making its most radical break with the past and entering the nuclear era.

Nevertheless, scholarly interest in war remained at a fairly abstract level during the 1930's. Not until World War II did scholars plunge themselves into an active strategic role, accepting the cruel character of the international environment as something to be accommodated to if it could not be changed. Only after 1945 did many scholars become willing to concentrate on the problem of improving the efficiency of military force as an instrument of the state.

The third intellectual origin of current strategy expertise is less easy to trace. It may be described loosely as "scientific," for it grew out of the technological enterprises of World War II. An aspect of that war quite without historic precedent was the mobilization of a large part of the scientific establishments of belligerent nations, including tens of thousands of their best technical minds. The amazing collection of talent assembled in the Manhattan Project for the development of the atomic bomb is the best example of such activity, but only an example.

Among the welter of scientific activities in World War II, there appeared one specialty particularly relevant to the appearance of strategy expertise. This specialty eventually developed and merged with the military and academic antecedents already described. It began with the *ad hoc* efforts of scientists to improve the operational efficiency of military forces in combat. These efforts acquired the label "operational research," later called "operations research" or "operations analysis."[8]

Individuals or teams of scientifically trained analysts observed combat operations, gathered statistics, and, through mathematical analysis, endeavored to develop more efficient procedures and doctrines for the employment of forces. For instance, using data about the interceptions of enemy submarines and shipping losses to those submarines, they were able to recommend a more productive search pattern for antisubmarine vessels. In air operations, they treated such questions as the preferred size and shape of bomber formations and the best routes for penetration of enemy territory. In general, they developed a methodology and set of skills that were remarkably useful in their applications to military problems.

DEVELOPMENTS IN ANALYSIS

In the postwar period, other methods and techniques were soon added to the repertoire of the military analysts. Some of them were derived from major theoretical advances. Highspeed computers came into prominent use, and the science of linear and dynamic programming was advanced. Not only war-game playing, but also game theory, soon came to be prominent objects of attention of the strategy experts, under the impulse provided by the theoretical formulations of John von Neumann and Oskar Morgenstern.[9] In game playing, two branches of effort, both experimental, appeared. One employs "rigid" games, which have fixed rules and procedures, and very often are based upon complicated mathematical models of war. Thus, a series of wars can be "fought" in a computer to test the effectiveness of a given weapon under varying assumptions about enemy attack plans. "Non-rigid" games involve role-playing by individuals, who simulate decision-makers in conflict situations. These games can provide experience to the players for dealing with several kinds of abstract problems: Judging relationships between different instruments of their own action; judging the effects of counteraction by an antagonist; and sensing the nature of uncertainties and unknowns in a conflict environment. Such games are therefore valuable for teaching students of foreign policy. They are also useful for preparing real decision-makers to cope with anticipated international crises with scenarios set in trouble-spots like Viet-Nam and the Congo. The utility of games, however, does not extend to discovering answers to policy problems or revealing desirable courses of action, as wishful proponents are sometimes tempted to claim. For decision-makers, there can be no substitute for reality.

The economic mode of decision-making

Bernard Brodie anticipated the future shape of strategic analysis in 1949, when he pointed out that the methods of economics had great promise for application to a new science of strategy. Both fields, he asserted, are basically

---

[8]Having begun in Great Britain, operations research was quickly taken up in the United States and applied throughout the combat arms in all theaters. A thorough technical account of the early development of operations analysis by the U.S. is provided by Philip M. Morse and G. E. Kimball, *Methods of Operations Research* (New York: Technology Press and John Wiley, 1958).

[9]John von Neumann and Oskar Morgenstern, *Theory of Games and Economic Behavior* (Princeton: Princeton University Press, 1947). For a historical survey, see Clayton J. Thomas, "Military Gaming," in Russell L. Ackoff (ed.), *Progress in Operational Research*, Vol. I (New York: John Wiley & Sons, 1961), Chap. 10.

concerned with the problems of allocating scarce resources in order to achieve stated aims.[10] Since that time, economists have taken the lead, not only in theory, but also in applications.

For example, at The RAND Corporation, procedures were developed for thorough measuring of the costs of new weapon systems.[11] These procedures took account not only of the obvious costs of procurement, but also of indirect costs like installations and supply, as well as future costs like fuel and personnel pay. Simple as it seems, The RAND costing technique was a breakthrough in determining price tags for multibillion dollar programs that had previously been undertaken without any reasonable conception of what their ultimate costs might be.

From the efforts of the early strategic economists, there followed directly a complete overhaul of budgeting and weapons selection procedures in the Department of Defense. When he moved from The RAND Corporation to become Comptroller of the Department of Defense in 1961, Charles J. Hitch exercised a historic opportunity to translate theory into practice.[12] Under Hitch's leadership, the whole defense budget-formulation procedure was pulled together, costing methods were streamlined, and the planning and programming cycle extended five years into the future. While the budget submission to Congress is required to be organized in functional funding categories, such as personnel pay, construction, and aircraft procurement, these categories did not lend themselves to evaluating program decisions. So a system was introduced for identifying the costs of individual programs and program "packages," grouping together the costs of forces according to mission, like strategic war forces and transport forces. All these improvements enabled decisions about major weapon systems to be made more rationally, better matched to their mission. They clarified the strategic choices that had been implicit in earlier budget decisions — for example, the fact that to withhold funds from an air base hardening program is to reduce the "strike-second" capacity for nuclear retaliation, and, therefore, to reduce the stability of the deterrent posture.

Nevertheless, the costing of defense programs remains a complex procedure. There are many imponderables, such as the safety of crews, the morale of civilians, and the good will of allies, that are true values, even though they do not carry dollar signs. The decision-maker must assign them some weight when he makes his choices. There are also many technical problems in costing. For example, if an attack carrier with its air group is compared with a land-based air group, what portion of the land base costs are chargeable to that group when the base may have many other tenants? The answer may determine which of the air groups looks cheaper. Another difficult area is that of "residual" costs. Suppose there are two weapons with the same basic mission, a cheaper one with a five-year life expectancy, and a more expensive one that will not require replacement for ten years. How should they be reflected in a five-year budget? Should the cost of the latter weapon be discounted to show its residual value after five years? Or will it be obsolete then, in any case? This, and countless similar questions, are matters of opinion for the decision-maker.

Systems analysis

The cardinal development in the new methodology for defense decision-making is really elementary in concept—an amalgamation of all these analytical methods in the procedure called "systems analysis." In a technical sense, systems analysis means the investigation and comparison of the effectiveness and costs of alternative means (systems) of accomplishing a stated objective. More broadly, it deals with the whole process of allocating defense resources. From another standpoint, systems analysis can be regarded as the product that emerges when experts from various disciplines are brought close together under favorable circumstances of organization and communication—experts who share attention to common tasks. It is a process whereby the whole is made to exceed the sum of its parts. In the words of one of its pioneers, systems analysis "permits the judgments of experts in many fields to be combined to yield

[10]Bernard Brodie, "Strategy as a Science," *World Politics,* I (1948 – 49), 467 – 88.
[11]Charles J. Hitch, David Novick, and associated economists at RAND developed and refined these techniques and proposals, which were later implemented under Hitch's leadership as Assistant Secretary of Defense, Comptroller. Key RAND publications were David Novick, *Efficiency and Economy in Government Through New Budgeting and Accounting Procedures,* The RAND Corporation, Report R-254, Santa Monica, Feb. 1, 1954; and Charles J. Hitch and Roland N. McKean, *The Economics of Defense in the Nuclear Age,* R-346, The RAND Corporation (Cambridge, Mass.: Harvard University Press, 1960).
[12]Charles J. Hitch, *Decision-Making for Defense* (Berkeley: University of California Press. 1965).

results that transcend any individual's judgment."[13]

Systems analysis has been made a central element of the defense decision-making apparatus, along with the streamlined costing and budgeting procedures that were introduced in 1962 by the Defense Comptroller. In 1965, systems analysis was institutionalized in the office of the new Assistant Secretary of Defense (Systems Analysis), where studies are made of the cost and effectiveness of major prospective programs, such as the B-70, the Polaris submarine, the multipurpose F-111, and the nuclear-powered aircraft carrier. The first incumbent, Alain C. Enthoven, also devotes a major share of his efforts to fostering the use of better analytical techniques throughout subordinate staffs of the armed services.

To the uninitiated, systems analysis still conjures up an atmosphere of the occult. By mysterious mathematical processes, it is supposed that the practitioners of systems analysis produce solutions of remarkable advantage to their client, but quite beyond his capacity for comprehension. Granted that many of the computations involved are complex and require advanced training, it is still important to realize that systems analysis rests on simple logic and on the scientific method of diligently collecting, testing, and comparing data. It is, in this sense, operations research expanded to solve larger-scale problems.

Some of the best results of this kind of analysis can be shown to derive from nothing more mysterious than common sense. The classic example cited is that of the new operations researcher reporting to duty in the field, and at once encountering a long delay in the mess line waiting for soldiers to wash and rinse their mess kits. There were two tubs for washing and two for rinsing. He quickly observed that it took the average soldier three times as long to wash as to rinse. Applying his analytical powers to this problem, he produced the recommendation that, instead of two tubs for washing and two for rinsing, there should be three for washing and one for rinsing. Lo and behold, the delay in the mess line was eliminated. An equally simple analysis resulted in a World War II decision to increase the size of shipping convoys. Observations showed that the number of ships lost per convoy remained fairly constant, whether the convoy was large or small. By increasing the size of convoys, then, total losses were reduced.[14]

Moreover, even the most complicated analy-

ses are built on an elementary concept, that of marginal comparison. This means that alternative weapon systems are compared on the basis of the marginal increases, or the increments, in effectiveness that can be obtained by adding a given amount of resources to each. A very large program, in which a huge investment has already been made, may show only a modest increase in effectiveness when added funds are funneled into it. In this case, the program is well along in the stage of "diminishing returns."

The marginal concept may be illustrated in a simple numerical example. Suppose there is a force of 300 missiles, each with a 30 per cent probability of target destruction, aimed at 100 different targets. Using a simple binomial equation, it can be calculated that such a force, on the average, would destroy 67 of these targets. If the force were increased to 600 missiles, the same calculation would show 88 targets destroyed. This is an increase, or marginal effectiveness, of only 21, due to diminishing returns. Similarly, a force of 645 missiles can be calculated to destroy an average of 90 targets. At this level, an additional 45 missiles (marginal cost) would eliminate only two additional targets (marginal effectiveness).

These figures do not constitute an argument against adding missiles to the force. The extra targets destroyed may well be worth the extra cost, high as it is. But the figures do prompt the analyst to search for alternatives and to examine their marginal effectiveness, too. Perhaps, for the same investment, it will be found more productive to purchase manned bombers, electronic aids for the existing missile force itself, or something else.

At the national level, then, the kind of problem treated by systems analysts often consists of comparing major program alternatives, in what is called the "cost-effectiveness study." The computations may require banks of computers, miles of digits, and formidable mathematical models. The important judgments, however (as well as the big mistakes), are not esoteric perceptions, but applications of basic economics. Systems analysis means, simply, that, for a giv-

[13]F. R. Collbohm, "Project RAND," an address before the Scientific Advisory Board (Santa Monica: The RAND Corporation, March, 1955), P-707, p. 5. An excellent introduction to the techniques is provided by Herman Kahn and Irwin Mann, "Techniques of Systems Analysis," RM-1829-1, The RAND Corporation, Santa Monica, June, 1957; and "Ten Common Pitfalls," RM-1937, The RAND Corporation, Santa Monica, July 17, 1957.
[14]Morse and Kimball, op. cit., pp. 3–6.

en expenditure of resources, the performances of alternative systems are carefully compared, whether in combat, in the laboratory, or on paper. The systems in competition may be alternative small arms for Viet-Nam or alternative Intercontinental Ballistic Missiles. Conversely, the military task may be assumed as a constant—such as the destruction of a target system—and the cheaper way to carry out the task is selected between such alternatives as B-52 bombers or Minuteman missiles. (It would be erroneous, of course, to seek "least cost" and "most effectiveness" simultaneously. One or the other quality must be held constant for the sake of comparison.) Systems analysis also means searching for new alternatives in the broadest possible context. Before funds are committed to one mission, it is desirable to look at all other possible missions. Perhaps the over-all defense posture can be improved more by leaving the offensive forces unimproved and adding instead to air defense forces or to limited war forces.

A notable example of the broad kind of investigation is The RAND Report R-266, *The Selection and Use of Strategic Air Bases*, completed in 1954. After lengthy study, that report recommended reliance on lightly-manned and pre-stocked bases overseas, to be used for rapid forward staging of bombers in the event of war. The resultant saving in construction costs of the previously planned, more elaborate bases was $1 billion. More significant, however, was the fact that the study inevitably dealt with general strategic issues—the extent and dependability of U.S. alliances, assumptions about the political circumstances in which war might begin, and the nature of the strategy of deterrence. It also led to collateral studies of programs for airborne alert, base hardening, early warning, bomb-detonation alarm, and others.[15] R-266, therefore, became far more than a technical project. It employed extensive logistic analysis, but it also required the best judgment of economists and political scientists.

Systems analysis at the national level is, therefore, more dependent on good reasoning and reliable data—always fortified by common sense—than on obscure mathematical formulations. The outcomes are usually forthright and easily comprehensible: The B-70 is a more costly method of delivering nuclear weapons in retaliation than other available aircraft and missiles; a civilian shelter program, at initial levels of expenditure, is a better investment for saving lives in the event of nuclear attack than an Anti-Ballistic Missile; a more productive way to apply resources to aircraft carrier forces is to buy more carriers and fewer aircraft than originally programed. This latter finding relies on more rapid shifting of aircraft, as they are needed, back and forth between previously deployed carriers.

The incisive reasoning that is required in systems analysis is most usefully applied to the definition and demarcation of the problem under study itself. The study may be too narrow, and thus exclude useful considerations, or it may be too broad, and thus be inconclusive. It may pertain to the wrong period; it may suffer from an orthodox bias or an excess of zeal for change. One analyst recounts his own experience in the early postwar design of strategic bombers to be used in the middle 1950's. He expended much effort in investigating the problem of tail turret design for effective aiming of machine guns at attacking fighters. He then suddenly realized that by the time these bombers were in service, air-to-air missiles would have made his guns obsolete. He had been studying the wrong problem.[16] (The bombers, by the way, were built with tail turrets.)

One of the most beneficial results of the introduction of systems analysis at the national policy level, therefore, has been to draw widespread attention to the importance of judgment in defining a study. Underlying assumptions, previously taken for granted, are now thought through and made more explicit. If they are not, the result can be embarrassing. The systems analysts in the Office of the Secretary of Defense spend much of their time probing for errors in the definition and scope of studies made by lower agencies. Does an Air Force justification for air-to-surface weapons take account of the availability of artillery? Does an Army study of intra-theater airlift requirements assume such short legs of resupply and such limited airstrip availability that it erroneously slants the findings against larger Air Force transport aircraft? Conversely, the service staffs probe for loopholes in Defense analyses. Does a Defense study of, say, the numerical need for

[15]*The RAND Corporation, the First Fifteen Years* (Santa Monica: The RAND Corporation, 1963), p. 16; and E. S. Quade (ed.), *Analysis for Military Decisions* (Santa Monica: The RAND Corporation, November, 1964), Chap. 3.
[16]Quade, *op. cit.*, p. 301. For an extensive discussion of technical errors, see Chap. 16. See also Kahn and Mann, "Ten Common Pitfalls," *op. cit.*, and Hitch and McKean, *op. cit.*, Chaps. 9–11.

ICBM's, base its results on a too benign intelligence estimate of enemy forces? In this manner, the whole nature of the defense policy dialogue in the Pentagon is changing. The new goal of partisanship is to produce red faces on those whose errors of judgment are uncovered. This seems to be a somewhat more productive way to channel strategic debates than in former times, when assumptions were too often implicit, data were inaccessible or concealed, and budgetary disputes were won or lost in back-room compromises or in bombastic confrontations.

Some critics, nevertheless, point out the deleterious effects of all these methodological changes on the corporate well-being of the defense establishment. They complain of over-centralization of decisions and warn against undermining of military professionalism. Whether the critics are right or wrong in their general accusations, most of those who can remember how the system of defense decision-making worked earlier take a temperate, if not an enthusiastic, view of the changes in methodology. Those earlier years were characterized by an exaltation of "pure" military requirements, the hidden rollback of expenditures, and the "cost-squeeze" and consequent cancellation of programs that had been initiated without knowledge of whether there might be room for them in subsequent defense budgets.

Estimates of the savings effected by the new procedures run into many billions of dollars. One high official affirms that the United States has been able, so far, to fight a major war in Southeast Asia while maintaining its strategic posture and also avoiding general mobilization only because of the economies obtained by the new defense budgeting and analytical procedures. Whether or not his claim is extravagant, it should be acknowledged that management efficiency and good military professionalism ought to be natural companions. Ultimately, there is reason to expect that most of the present frictions in defense administration will dissipate of their own accord, when wider acceptance and use of the new management tools improve the quality of the output and, consequently, strengthen the position of the military staffs.

DEVELOPMENT OF CONCEPTS AND THEORY

Looking beyond the methodological successes and the dollar savings provided by strategy expertise, one finds another kind of contribution of immeasurable but probably even greater val-

ue to the nation. This is in the abstract realm of theory, concept, and doctrine.

From 1956 to 1959, for example, The RAND Corporation conducted, on its own initiative, a study of civil defense in the United States. Although there was no conclusive result in the form of a national program for civil defense, it increased national leaders' awareness of the possible effects of nuclear war, and it undoubtedly improved the climate for acceptance of realistic security programs in general.

Albert Wohlstetter's article, "The Delicate Balance of Terror,"[17] which had considerable public impact, was the unclassified outcropping of a series of vitally important studies that revealed the technical problems of maintaining an effective posture of deterrence. As a consequence of these and other efforts, concepts of deterrence have become more sophisticated, able to distinguish between the forces required for first- and second-strike, and able to treat deterrence by strategic forces or threats other than all-out war. These phrases may not presently stimulate much excitement, but it is useful to recall the comparative lack of understanding of such matters a few years ago. (Wohlstetter, for example, earlier encountered resistance in official circles to the notion that to suffer a surprise attack might make a decisive difference in the ability of United States strategic forces to strike back.)

Some of the major new landmarks in the development of military thought have appeared as published books. William Kaufmann's *Military Policy and National Security*[18] raised vital questions about the efficacy of deterrence as conceived in the mid-1950's; Samuel P. Huntington's *The Soldier and the State*[19] provoked a thoughtful public discussion about the proper role of the military profession in this country's government; Thomas C. Schelling's *The Strategy of Conflict*[20] opened a new vista for studying relations and communications between military antagonists. Any bibliography in this area contains many other examples of great merit.

[17]Albert Wohlstetter, "The Delicate Balance of Terror," *Foreign Affairs*, Vol. XXXVII, No. 2 (January, 1959), and "Scientists, Seers, and Strategists," *Foreign Affairs*, Vol. XLI, No. 3 (April, 1963).
[18]William W. Kaufmann, *Military Policy and National Security* (Princeton: Princeton University Press, 1956).
[19]Samuel P. Huntington, *The Soldier and the State: The Theory and Politics of Civil-Military Relations* (Cambridge, Mass.: The Belknap Press, 1957).
[20]Thomas C. Schelling, *The Strategy of Conflict* (Cambridge, Mass.: Harvard University Press, 1960).

In considering all of these contributions together, it appears that a new body of strategic theory is beginning to take shape. It draws upon game theory, theories of bargaining and communication, and certain propositions of economics, such as the duopolistic competition of firms.[21] The new theory illuminates the nature of modern conflict. It contributes to refinement of the policy of deterrence of nuclear war. It fosters better understanding of the nature of nuclear stability. And it opens the way for arms control, explained as a "shared interest" between adversaries in such goals as accident prevention and, if war should occur, damage limitation.[22] (They are goals that may require, paradoxically, increased defense expenditures.) The jargon of the new body of theory has grown to include such terms as escalation, intra-war communication, city hostages, crisis management, and limited strategic war—some of them simplistic notions, all of them representative of earnest efforts somehow to improve national security in a setting of unprecedented international insecurity.

In the domain of strategic theory, then, there occurs the full blending of the sources of strategy expertise. The earliest source, the ideas of military writers like Clausewitz and Mahan, has direct relevance as a preface to the newer concepts of strategy. The same is true of the academic source, the prewar studies of international politics that now acquire special urgency in the environment of nuclear weaponry. And the scientific source—operations research expanded into systems analysis—provides a methodological framework upon which new theory can be built.

LIMITATIONS

The new approaches to defense decision-making were described as productive of greater efficiency and actual monetary savings. There can be no question that the policy of the United States is deeply affected when many prominent officials in the Joint Staff, in the Office of the Secretary of Defense, in the Department of State, and even in the White House spend hours absorbing the ideas of strategic thinkers by reading their reports and books—and without the distractions of office politics and personalities that usually accompany officials' involvement in such subjects. The policy revolution, then, is proving to be a potent response to the nuclear weapons revolution.

One is left feeling some uneasiness, nonetheless, regarding the new approaches to defense decision-making. One cause for concern is the fact that strategy analysts are subject to the impulse to "optimize" their sphere of investigation—reaching to the ultimate scope, the whole of national policy and international security. They enter the obscure realm where the ends and means of high policy are weighed and mingled through political judgment, where objectives and criteria for strategic programs shape as well as reflect the strategic environment of the future. Their impulse toward generalization is not undesirable in itself; it stems from a natural striving for the broadest possible studies, encompassing as many relevant assumptions as possible.

The concern, then, lies in whether the governmental system and its leaders have the capacity fully to understand and to incorporate this expertise into the decision-making process in a politically responsible manner. To be more specific, systems analysis has been successively expanded to incorporate more uncertainties, incommensurables, and unknowns. When it is necessary for analysts to make assumptions about who might deliberately launch a general war, which countries might acquire (or even which should acquire) independent atomic forces, or which economic and political factors will decide the future alignment of underdeveloped countries, they have arrived at the highest level of policy. Expert advisers may also be impelled to consider the whole scope of policy, because they often feel better equipped to do so than the government officials whom they advise. The danger is that the top government official may be limited in his ability to comprehend an analytical study that is implanted with policy assumptions; he is certainly limited in the time he has available for reasoned contemplation of the complex issues involved in such a study.

Another difficulty of defense decision-making is even more profound. Strategy expertise has developed better ways to handle the unknown.

[21]The pioneering work was Schelling, *The Strategy of Conflict.* See also Kenneth Boulding, *Conflict and Defense* (New York: Harper and Brothers, 1962); Anatol Rapoport, *Fights, Games and Debates* (Ann Arbor: University of Michigan Press, 1960); Klaus Knorr and Thornton Read, *Limited Strategic War* (New York: Frederick A. Praeger, 1962).
[22]Representative of the arms control literature are Donald G. Brennan (ed.), *Arms Control, Disarmament, and National Security* (New York: George Braziller, 1961); and Thomas C. Schelling and Morton H. Halperin, *Strategy and Arms Control* (New York: The Twentieth Century Fund, 1961).

Through statistical techniques and decision-making methods, the government is now aided in dealing with the uncertainties of the present and future in research, development, and long-range planning activities. The arena of international conflict, however, is an amorphous sphere of unpredictable, unaccountable, and incomprehensibly complex human initiatives. Despite successes in coping with uncertainties, therefore, strategy expertise is destined to remain "suboptimal"—inadequate—in relation to the broad creative challenges of strategy. For there is obviously a difference between anticipation and creativity, between exercising prudent choice in respect to the future and employing imagination. The great initiatives of international politics arise from the womb of change. The economic mode of selecting courses of action among definable alternatives, however, represents a commitment to the kind of alternative that can be defined.

Bernard Brodie pointed out that systems analysis pertains not so much to the fine determination of the highest point of a curve, as to ascertaining whether it is acceptable to be on that particular curve at all.[23] Creativity is the discovery of altogether new curves. Strategy analysts may assist in discovering them, but they are not able to furnish marvelous techniques for doing so. The decision to send a manned expedition to the moon was a creative decision, right or wrong, and one which would not meet the test of any normal economic criteria.

In a deeper philosophical sense, the future is not only unknown but unknowable. This fact presents a particular hazard for creativity in national policy—the temptation to pursue utopian solutions. To be able to visualize a resolution of the problems raised by the existence of nuclear weapons is to be deceived by one's own desire. Hegel, who made the highest claims for historical inevitability, nevertheless denied the possibility of insight coming to the aid of those who attempt to set the course of history: "Philosophy always arrives too late for that. . . . The owl of Minerva begins its flight when dusk is falling."[24]

The breadth of judgment, then, that is needed to transcend the limits of analysis and methodology must reside in the decision-maker himself. Otherwise, he would be no more than the efficient manipulator of power. He would be limited to mechanical perceptions of international conflict, bound by techniques and procedures, and constrained from the creative search for new solutions. He would lack the understanding of the real stakes of conflict, the values inherent in the political system that he serves. The wisdom that is required to strike a balance between resolution and restraint in the use of nuclear power would be wanting.

[23]Bernard Brodie, "The Scientific Strategists," in *Administration of National Security* (Selected Papers by the Subcommittee on National Security Staffing and Operations of the Committee on Government Operations, U.S. Congress, Senate [Washington, D.C.: Government Printing Office, 1962]), p. 198.

[24]Quoted in Carl J. Friedrich, *The Philosophy of Hegel* (New York: Random House, 1954), p. 227.

POST-VIETNAM ROLE OF THE MILITARY IN FOREIGN POLICY
Maxwell D. Taylor

General Taylor personifies in his career the greatly increased role of the military establishment and the professional military man in the making and carrying out of national policy. General Taylor served as Chief of Staff of the United States Army and, after a period of retirement, returned to active duty to serve, first, as military adviser to President Kennedy, then as chairman of the Joint Chiefs of Staff, and, finally, as United States Ambassador to South Vietnam.

It is also worth noting that General Taylor is usually categorized as a "military intellectual," thoughtful and self-conscious about his role as a professional officer, deeply interested in military strategy and broader national policy as well as military tactics and operations, and also, in his case, in the improved organizational effectiveness of the U.S. government in the national security field.

It is therefore particularly interesting to get his reflections on the contemporary role, limitations, and problems of the military regarding foreign and defense policy and on some of the longer-term consequences for the military establishment of the war in Vietnam.

Reprinted from *Air University Review*, July-August 1968, Vol. XIX. No. 5.

In keeping with our intense concern about Asia in general and Southeast Asia in particular, it has occurred to me that it might be of interest to reflect on the condition of the armed forces after termination of the Vietnam conflict and the effect of that conflict on the role of the armed forces in foreign policy. A unique requirement is placed upon the military profession to anticipate change in time and to adapt thereto the conduct of its primary business, national security. The importance of quick perception and adaptation derives from the vital nature of national security and the disasters which may ensue from gross error in adjusting to its evolving needs. Unhappily, the timely anticipation of change is not easy because of the many variables which enter into the national security equation. National security is both a state of mind and a power relationship based upon the international distribution of resources of all kinds, upon attitudes and policies of governments, upon personalities of leaders, upon economic cycles, and upon the ebb and flow of ideologies. National security is affected by human emotions and motives arising from greed, fear, and fervor. Finally, in its narrowly military connotations, it is affected by changes in strategy, tactics, and weaponry.

It is with these thoughts in mind that I have undertaken to identify some of the changes which appear to be taking place in these broad fields bearing upon foreign policy and national security and then draw some conclusions with regard to the probable or possible effects on the role of the armed forces.

To start from fundamentals, let us first remind ourselves that the role of the armed forces as presently stated in official literature is to support and defend the Constitution of the United States against all enemies, foreign and domestic; to insure by timely and effective military action the security of the United States, its possessions, and areas vital to its interest; to uphold and enhance the national policies and interests of the United States; and, finally, to safeguard the internal security of the United States. In short, the armed forces exist to defend our form of government and the constitutional principles upon which it stands, to guarantee our physical security and the safety of our material possessions, and, in general, to advance our national interests wherever found.

I would call your attention to at least two characteristics of this mission. The first is that the mission is not solely the responsibility of the armed forces. In its overseas aspects, the mission that I have described is a reasonably complete statement of the goals of our entire foreign policy, supported by the totality of our national power, of which the armed forces are merely the military component. As such, they must work in combination with other components — political, diplomatic, economic, moral, and psychological — in order to carry out the foreign policy objectives of our government.

The second characteristic I would mention is the round-the-clock aspect of the military mission in foreign policy. There was a time when most people considered the armed forces an institution of importance only in time of war. There is an old English saying that the soldier in time of peace is like a chimney in summer. I can recall when, shortly after World War I, I returned as a second lieutenant to visit my old grandfather, a Civil War veteran, that I had great difficulty in explaining to the old gentleman really how I was earning my pay. He could not understand what an army did when there was no shooting war in progress. And I must say his questioning attitude was justified by the conditions faced by the armed forces between World Wars I and II.

In that period we had solemnly outlawed war as an instrument of policy; we were branding our munitions makers as "merchants of death," and it was taking ambitious second lieutenants nearly twenty years to become a captain. Today, this isolation of the armed forces from the realities of life in time of peace is a thing of the past. It is a hard fact of the present that the armed forces are on duty around the clock, and in a sense they never enjoy holidays or Sundays. But if most of our citizens recognize a continuing peacetime role for the armed forces, I think that many would still make a sharp distinction between their role as discharged in peace and in war. In spite of the teachings of Clausewitz as to the kindred nature of war and policy, many of us still feel that the transition to war in some way abrogates the peacetime roles, alters the relations of a citizen to his government, and surrenders the conduct of war and large parts of the related foreign policy into the hands of the military.

In World War I, the French political leaders liked to quote Talleyrand to the effect that war is too serious a business to be left to the military — a fact which indicated that, in the view of these French leaders, most people considered that the soldiers were, or perhaps should be, in charge in time of war. I would say that most of the officers of my generation would have been inclined to agree with this concept and to have labeled as political interference the intervention of civilian authority in time of war—in any field other than the broadest aspects of foreign policy. Also, all the officers in this same era were taught in the military schools that the mission of the armed forces in time of war was the destruction of the armed forces of the enemy. That destruction equated to the military victory for which General MacArthur proclaimed there is no substitute.

I have mentioned these past concepts because I feel that significant changes are occurring which bear importantly upon them and upon the future role of the armed forces.

In pursuing this subject, for completeness I would like to review the means and methods available to the armed forces in performing their role in foreign policy. Then I shall discuss the new factors arising which bear upon the choice of means and methods and, hence, upon the role of the armed forces in the support of foreign policy.

The armed forces exert their influence through various forms of military force, either potential or actual, derived from the men, weapons, organization, and discipline which are their primary sources of strength. This military force in its various configurations provides a means by which the leaders of government may bend the will and influence the conduct of adversaries in conformity with the requirements of the national interest as interpreted at a given time and place. To these leaders falls the choice of methods in using this military force. Even without an exercise of choice, the mere existence of the armed forces contributes to the support of foreign policy, serving as a mute Big Stick that adds persuasiveness either to quiet talk or to noisy threats. But if mere force in-being does not suffice, the civilian leaders may then call the armed forces into action at varying levels of controlled violence.

In limited war, the armed forces may be used to impose limited damage and limited loss on the enemy, to obtain concessions that are likely to be something less than vital to either party. In total war, they may undertake to render the enemy helpless and defenseless by the destruction of his armed forces, of his leaders, of his government, of his economy, and even of his entire people. Following victory, they may then be called upon to occupy conquered territory and to join in repairing the damages of war to which they have contributed. All such actions take place within and as a part of foreign policy in its broadest meaning, not as a substitute or replacement for that policy. Clausewitz made this point long ago, and I think it is still valid.

In addition to the military means and methods available to the armed forces, there are also nonmilitary ways for them to support foreign policy. They do so by participating in peace-keeping operations, generally under international control, as in the Congo or in the Western Hemisphere as the agent of the Organization of American States. Through the administration of military aid programs, they exert an important influence in the field of foreign relations. I have often thought that our military school system, in accepting thousands of foreign officers and soldiers for instruction, is perhaps the most effective single instrument of foreign policy for broadly influencing foreign attitudes toward the United States.

The performance of the armed forces in civic action is well known. That term, I believe, was coined at the end of the Korean War, when in a relatively short time the armed forces of the United States, later assisted by those of Korea, quickly brought aid to the devastated countryside and performed miracles of quick restoration, doing things impossible in the short run for the long-term programs of economic aid.

So much, then, for the means and methods of the armed forces in support of foreign policy. Now let me move to the subject which I think is the most pertinent to the theme of this presentation. What new factors are arising which bear upon the choice of means and methods in the future?

I would single out three factors which have arisen or are arising and which unquestionably will affect the future role of the armed forces in foreign policy. The first is the fear of World War III, which is a primary preoccupation of the political leaders of all nations. The second is the multipolar distribution of power which has followed the disruption of the Sino-Soviet bloc. The third is the aftermath of the experience of the Vietnam war, with its many lessons which, if understood and heeded, are sure to affect our future use of military power.

First, there are the effects of the general fear of World War III. This fear dates back to the use of nuclear weapons in World War II and expresses itself today in many ways. One is the emphasis on the deterrent role of the armed forces as the primary justification for their existence. The fear of World War III has made all responsible leaders cautious and inclined to examine their every move in relation to the possibility of World War III.

It is a curious thing, however, in considering the deterrent effect of the armed forces, that, in a sense, we can undermine this effectiveness by talking too much about it. The more one stresses the purely deterrent role of the armed forces, the less convincing that deterrent tends to become. This paradox arises from the nature of the elements which make for effective deterrence. Deterrence requires strong armed forces in-being, directed by resolute leaders clearly ready to use them and served by a command and control system which will assure getting their orders to the right place at the right time. Thus, the unquestioned will and the clear capability to use force become the strongest guarantee of not having to use it at all. Any suggestion that it is only for deterrence and somehow only for show and never for use works in a contrary way on the effectiveness of deterrence. Thus, it is not enough to talk a good game of deterrence; it is quiet, unruffled readiness to perform that really counts.

So, then, my first point regarding this fear of World War III is to note the increasing emphasis on the deterrent role of the armed forces. Growing out of this same concern is a tendency toward greater and more detailed civilian control of the armed forces. This tendency feeds on the fear that World War III will happen through mistake, through the error of a field commander, or through some other form of military miscalculation and is encouraged by the efficiency of our telecommunications which allows authorities in Washington to communicate almost instantaneously with commanders in any quarter of the globe.

Historical examples of the past prompt our civilian leaders to feel that they should assume a greater responsibility for intervening in military affairs. The example of General MacArthur as a field commander who changed the objective of an entire war in midstream is a case in point often cited in justification of the need of greater civilian control.

President Kennedy was greatly impressed by Barbara Tuchman's book, *The Guns of August,* which, as he interpreted it, exposed the pre-1914 generals to the charge of having made mobilization plans so rigid that political leaders in the critical days of 1914 were deprived of all options in making decisions affecting the destinies of their nations. The President was inclined to attribute to the generals the fault for this—a criticism which led me to fight back as best I could, maintaining that it was the politicians at fault, because they never should have let the generals plan without political guidance. At any rate, this feeling of the need for options is very much on the minds of our civilian leaders today, who do not want to find themselves boxed into a corner by military imperatives in a time of crisis. We can expect them to insist on maintaining options and alternatives, and to demand greater flexibility in military planning.

Next, there is the trend toward gradualism in the use of military force, which also arises from the fear of World War III. This trend has been encouraged by our experience in the Cuban missile crisis, which is often cited as a successful example of the use of restrained, graduated force. Although our government did not get all that it might have wanted in this confrontation with the U.S.S.R., it got all that was essential—and without World War III. That success, as interpreted by many observers, resulted from the fact that we remained in constant communication with Moscow, that we moved carefully, slowly, explaining what we were doing and why we were doing it, at the same time preserving a posture of unquestionable determination to see the thing through. This experience encouraged the gradualism which has characterized our strategy in Vietnam and which has often been disparaged by military critics. I shall return to this point later.

The second new factor which bears upon the future role of the armed forces in foreign policy is the fragmentation of the Sino-Soviet bloc. We should remind ourselves from time to time how the world looked to us ten years ago during the eyeball-to-eyeball confrontation of the Western and the Sino-Soviet blocs, when the great and overriding fear was of general nuclear war. Since then, the growing split between the Soviet Union and Red China, beginning with the withdrawal of the Soviet technicians from China in 1960, has drastically changed the political balance of power throughout the world. That split may well be recorded by historians as the most significant political event of the postwar period.

One result of it has been the growing possibility of a Soviet-U.S. détente, a prospect which some of us may regard as premature and perhaps illusory. It has also resulted in replacement of the former bipolarity of the power confrontation by a multipolar distribution of power and the creation of new foci of power in many quarters of the world. Consequently, we now have to concern ourselves with parts of the world which in the past were considered neuter in a strategic sense. Our experiences in Cuba, the Dominican Republic, the Middle East, Laos, and now in Vietnam remind us that multipolarity—while reducing the danger of a great nuclear war—carries with it challenges which are new and in some ways more difficult to cope with than the grim simplicity of the former confrontation with the Sino-Soviet bloc.

Let us now consider the third factor which has arisen since World War II which bears upon the role of the armed forces in foreign policy. It is the Vietnam experience, which is a case study of the consequences of the multipolarity to which I have alluded. It is hard at this point in time to draw all the lessons of Vietnam; even to attempt to do so is to invite debate, since anyone who seeks to identify lessons undertakes to interpret and to assess praise or blame for motives and actions. But at least we can say without fear of contradiction that our experience with the so-called "war of liberation" technique in Vietnam will have a bearing on the future participation of the armed forces in support of foreign policy. It is a challenge which I personally believe to be serious, in spite of efforts in some quarters to depreciate the sincerity of Lin Piao in describing how the "war of liberation" technique would, in the future, be the favorite device for the expansion of militant Communism. He emphasized in his famous speech on the subject that after the successful application of this technique in South Vietnam it would be applied not only in Asia but in Latin America and Africa as well. Further, he went on to explain why the Communist leaders had concluded that the "war of liberation" should be the preferred technique. He pointed out that general nuclear war was universal suicide and that, since even limited nonnuclear war could so easily expand to general nuclear war, limited war also is too dangerous. Hence, the "war of liberation," which tunnels under the conventional defenses of a country, was to be the preferred way for expanding Communism.

This feeling by the Communists that limited war is too dangerous for indulgence in is very

interesting, since it parallels up to a point our own thought on this matter. We also believe that general nuclear war must be deterred at all costs. But, at least prior to Vietnam, we had not been inclined to reject limited war as a form of military force which might be used in the national interest under certain circumstances. However, current events in Vietnam are causing us to reexamine our views on this subject. President James Perkins of Cornell, in a recent article, has posed the problem very clearly. He points out the great difficulty in rallying this country behind a foreign issue involving the use of armed force which does not provide an identified enemy posing a clear threat to our homeland or to the vital interests of long-time friends. As many of our citizens view the situation, Vietnam does not meet these criteria—hence their dissatisfaction with our growing involvement. For the future, Dr. Perkins concluded that

We now have to give more attention to the public understanding, to the importance of international support and cooperation, and to the need for increased development assistance as a more effective way of forestalling the circumstances that invite aggression. In the end we may feel as restrained in invocation of limited deterrence as we earlier did in the application of massive retaliation.

One finds much in the Vietnam experience to justify these views of Dr. Perkins.

Because of the tendency to move cautiously to avoid the risk of World War III, as a matter of deliberate policy we have exercised extreme prudence in applying military pressures in Vietnam. But however praiseworthy this restraint may be from some aspects, this slow application of military force is antithetical to the American disposition. It requires too much time and patience to obtain results. And we are finding in Vietnam, as in former episodes of our history, that these are national virtues in short supply.

A perceptive British critic, *The Economist*, observes that what the Americans may run out of is not material resources to continue to prosecute the war but patient public support for the whole idea of limited war. As long as the Vietnam experience is fresh in our minds, it is safe to say that the United States for a long time will be slow to engage in new military adventures far from home where the national interest is not more easily discerned than in the present Southeast Asian involvement.

That leaves us, of course, with the question of how to cope with a "war of liberation." Can we make no military response between a Lebanon-scale demonstration and a massive intervention in force to resist this threat? It is true that we can hope to anticipate situations where "wars of liberation" may occur and by nonmilitary civil means attempt to change the local conditions and eliminate the causes of political disintegration. But anticipation, of course, does not answer the entire question. We cannot afford to lose the deterrent effect of our forces in discouraging small aggressions. This is a point to which I will refer later.

Another point which is arising from the Vietnam experience is our growing resistance as a people to the role of world policeman which seems to be thrust upon us. We did not seek it, we do not want it, we do not like it. But, at the same time, our conscience reminds us of our responsibility to contribute in accordance with our means to the maintenance of worldwide peace and stability. But not wishing this task, we are inclined to look about in the hope of finding some way out of our predicament. Can't someone else take over?

At the same time that we are looking for outside help, we are experiencing a growing disillusionment with the capabilities of international organizations. We have tried to get the United Nations to help us in Vietnam, and we have been rejected. We have seen the great difficulty of peace-keeping efforts on the part of international bodies in Africa and the Middle East. So as we look at the problems of the emerging nations, we are at a loss to decide how to cope with the many focal points of unrest. We do not want to be the world policeman, but there seems to be no one else to do the job.

The dilemma urges us to greater wisdom and selectivity in deciding where our true interests lie in the worldwide scene. We find ourselves asking whether we have interpreted correctly our national interests in Vietnam and whether we are prepared to do better in choosing our course when similar situations arise in the future. The means taken to assure better selectivity are likely to react on the role of the armed forces in their support of the ultimate decision.

Another derivative of our Vietnam experience is the realization of the tremendous importance of the home front in support of foreign policy. We are learning how different it is, as Dr. Perkins has mentioned, to rally our people behind a distant cause which has no clear relationship with our immediate interests. We are seeing the effects of the misgivings of our people with regard to our growing involvement in Vietnam and to our apparent assumption of the role of gendarme of the universe. These misgivings among our people provide us with a forceful reminder of the essentiality of the support of the home front if we are to continue to use our military strength effectively in support of foreign policy—particularly if the scene of action is far from home. It is not an exaggeration to say that the outcome in Vietnam will be influenced as much by the attitude of the home front as by the conduct of our men who are fighting the battles.

Apart from other factors, our difficulties in closing ranks in support of this undeclared war are compounded by the competition for resources between the requirements of Vietnam and our domestic programs—by racial issues purporting to find some linkage between the Vietnam war and racial discrimination, by conflicts between liberals and conservatives, by contention between the executive and legislative branches of government, and then by just plain politicking with the Vietnam issue. This division at home has been furthered by the behavior of the publicity media. Free from any form of censorship in Vietnam which would be normal under conditions of war, they have reported the situation in such volume and profusion as to create much of the confusion that exists in the minds of those of us who depend upon press, television, and radio for our information. In the aftermath, we are going to have to think very hard about the proper role of these media as an influence upon the outcome of foreign policy.

I come now to the end of the discussion of the new factors bearing upon the role of the armed forces in their participation in foreign policy. I would now like to speculate a bit—though speculation is always dangerous—as to possible changes in the role of the armed forces which these factors may produce.

I would not expect any significant change in the formal statement of the roles and missions of the armed forces which I cited at the start. That mission is stated in broad terms which seem adequate to continue to guide the armed forces in their support of foreign policy. But without any change in the stated role of the armed forces, I would certainly expect the trend towards increased civilian control over military operations to be a phenomenon which is here to stay. I think it is here to stay because the reasons for it which I enumerated are likely to remain valid for a long time to come.

If in making this statement I may have distressed some of my military friends, I now bring them compensating good tidings. In my judgment, the armed forces in the future will have the opportunity to participate to a much greater degree than ever before in the formulation of foreign policy. Just as Talleyrand said that war is too serious a thing to be left to the military, I would say that the deterrence of war and the maintenance of peace are matters too serious to be left either to the military or to the civilians, but must be the result of an integrated effort of all parties. I see signs which encourage me to believe that our civilian leaders accept this fact and can be expected to act in consonance with it.

To illustrate this point, I should like to mention something that may or may not be generally known. President Kennedy, following the disastrous Bay of Pigs affair, took a significant step in recognizing the need for greater military participation in foreign policy formulation. On 27 May 1961 he called in person upon the Joint Chiefs of Staff at the Pentagon and discussed their relation to him. He reminded them of their duties as the advisers to the Commander in Chief and expressed the hope that their advice would always come to him directly and unfiltered. He also stated explicitly his view that this advice of the Chiefs could not and should not be purely military, since most of the problems with which he was concerned were shot through with political, economic, and psychological factors as well as military, and that he as President must take all factors into account. While he expected the Chiefs to present the military factor without fear or hesitation, he wanted them to know that he regarded them as more than military specialists and looked to them to help him in fitting military requirements into the overall context of any situation because he recognized that the most difficult problem in government is to combine all assets in an integrated, effective pattern. This verbal statement to the Chiefs was recorded in National Security Action Memorandum 55 of June 1961. To anyone not familiar with it, I suggest it would make interesting reading.

President Johnson has also acknowledged the growing importance of the military contribution to foreign policy. He did so in the decisions contained in National Security Action Memorandum 341 of March 1966. This is the document which charged the Secretary of State, as the agent of the President, with the overall direction of all interdepartmental activities overseas and directed him to set up a series of interdepartmental committees to help him carry out this new mandate. The most important of these committees is called the Senior Interdepartmental Group, chaired by the Under Secretary of State and including as a member the Chairman of the Joint Chiefs of Staff. At the level of the Assistant Secretary of State, National Security Action Memorandum 341 directed the establishment of Interdepartmental Regional Groups, chaired by an Assistant Secretary of State and including a representative of the Joint Chiefs of Staff.

Thus, for the first time, the Joint Chiefs organization has been fitted by executive authority into the planning and implementation process of foreign affairs, and the military voice has been given a forum in which it can be heard and its influence exercised in an environment conducive to effective integrated action.

This new place at the national council table offers a great opportunity to the armed forces and should end the myth that the military voice is not being heard at the top level of government. I often have occasion to chuckle as I read some of the Washington columnists. It seems to me that one morning one of them produces a column which proves conclusively that President Johnson has sold out to the military; the next day I read a column that is just as convincing in proving that the Joint Chiefs of Staff are being ignored and the civilians are making all the military decisions. It seems to me that the number of articles on both sides of the issue are so nearly equal that it suggests we are striking not a bad balance in Washington in accommodating the role of the military in the formulation of policy.

Now let us give some thought to the future size of the armed forces and the effect of that size on their role in foreign policy. It is possible to make a good case for the need for larger armed forces after Vietnam and an equally good case that they should be smaller. In favor of bigger forces, one can point to the increased needs of deterrence in a world of multipolar power where there will be many calls to many parts of the world requiring strong, highly mobile, ready forces. Furthermore, the reluctance to call up reserve forces to meet the needs of Vietnam has made us uncertain of their availability in future emergencies. Thus, there is the question in our contingency planning whether we can safely count on the reserves in the future. The question is heightened by the civil unrest at home which may require the retention of the National Guard in its state role and its exclusion from overseas missions. Such considerations as these argue for larger regular forces in-being in the post-Vietnam period.

But if it is possible to make the case for an increased establishment, I can also make a strong case for the opposite view. At least I can point to tendencies which will have the effect of reducing the armed forces.

The first obvious one is that after every war there is an immediate move to reduce military spending; and, because of the high cost and unpopularity of Vietnam, I would expect this urge to be even stronger than in the past. Furthermore, the needs of our domestic programs which have been delayed or set aside by the requirements of Vietnam will demand attention and provide added arguments for a reduction in military spending.

Monetary policy may also contribute to a cutback of military spending and of all overseas activities and thus work at odds with our foreign policy objectives. Some economists are convinced that the continuation of a fixed exchange rate will eventually make it impossible for the U.S. to finance overseas activities at past levels without serious domestic consequences. They argue that as we run out of gold we must bring our balance of payments into equilibrium or pay our overseas accounts with dollars saved by deflationary austerities at home. The alternatives to this unattractive prospect would be to raise the dollar price of gold, to supplement gold by some form of international currency such as the special drawing rights which are now being considered, or to adopt a flexible exchange rate independent of gold. All these measures raise objections of varying degrees of seriousness which make unlikely the early adoption of any one of them.

In the meantime, we may run the risk of having the present monetary policy impose restrictions on foreign policy which will work against our genuine national interests. Thus, in the final analysis, we will have fiscal, economic, and domestic reasons for limiting our overseas commitments after Vietnam. In combination, these factors are likely to exert a depressive effect on the size of the forces which the Congress will be willing to support.

There is considerable uncertainty as to the combined effect of these various factors with regard to the composition and strength of the post-Vietnam armed forces. But if I were asked to guess, I would expect that we will have smaller forces, at least in the immediate post-Vietnam period, characterized by greater emphasis on quality, mobility, and professionalism. There is likely to be every effort to do away with the draft and to depend entirely upon volunteers to maintain the armed forces, but with greater expenditures in pay of personnel. This reduction in size may be offset by a reduction in overseas responsibilities, because one consequence of our Vietnam experience is certainly going to be a review of all worldwide commitments with military implications.

Let me mention one last aspect of the role of the armed forces in support of foreign policy which we seldom think about but which is of tremendous importance. It is the need for the armed forces to do their part in assuring the support of the home front for the foreign policy of our government. I revert to our experience in Vietnam and the great difficulty we are having in aligning our people solidly behind that policy. But having said that the armed forces should do something about the home front, I recognize the very real difficulty of suggesting practical measures. I do think that we can help by word and deed in setting forth to our fellow citizens the legitimacy of the military role in a democratic society and the indispensability of military power as a part of national power in support of our foreign policy.

In so doing, we must show that we of the military have a sincere respect for the responsibilities of our civilian leaders and understand the supporting role of the military to that leadership. We must demonstrate in our behavior that we do not think exclusively in terms of force in solving the world's problems, that we can and do act not just from the military interest but from the national interest. Such a posture, faithfully sustained, will go far, I believe, in convincing our citizens that the military voice speaks with a competence and a responsibility which deserve close attention in the councils of government. Respect for the character and competence of the armed forces is one part—and a most important part—of respect for the competence of government and for the soundness of its policies.

POLITICO-MILITARY PROBLEMS AND RESOURCES

John C. Ausland

In the spring of 1961, the Department of State established a Politico-Military Affairs staff and attached it to the office of the Deputy Under Secretary of State for Political Affairs. The latter is the State Department official short of the Secretary of State himself responsible for working closely with both the Department of Defense and the Central Intelligence Agency.

The establishment of the Politico-Military Affairs staff was an attempt to strengthen the personnel resources and expertise available to the top officials of the State Department for dealing with those problems which significantly involve both military and foreign policy considerations. This staff, for example, was made responsible for coordinating the State Department review of the military budget referred to in the introduction to this chapter. It was also an obvious central point of contact and coordination for Defense Department officials having business to conduct with the State Department.

Mr. Ausland is a career Foreign Service Officer specializing in politico-military affairs. At the time this article was written, he was serving as director of one of the major units within the Politico-Military Affairs staff. It is from this vantage point that he viewed the national security problems that would face the Nixon Administration as it took office in January 1969.

Whatever the new administration does about the management of our national security, one thing is certain—it is not going to convert the Pentagon into a rest home for soldiers and diplomats. Even if Congress manages to slash the cost of our defenses, it will eat up a large share of the national budget. Thus, one of the new administration's main tasks will be the management of sizable armed forces, which will continue to play a significant—if, hopefully, diminishing—role in our diplomacy.

Because it is difficult, if not impossible, to separate the management of our armed forces from our strategy, I propose first to examine the main politico-military problems which will confront the next President. I will then examine some of the needs and resources for more effective management of these problems.

NETTLES FOR THE NEW PRESIDENT

While a number of issues could be tackled under this heading, I will deal briefly with only four of the more prickly: strategic forces and disarmament; Vietnam and United States forces abroad; strategic mobility and United States bases; and military assistance.

Strategic forces and disarmament

Since the missiles and bombers of the Soviet Union are the main threat to our existence, the decisions of the next administration regarding our strategic forces could be critical. Given the pace of the technological revolution, the President will have to make literally dozens of important decisions regarding weapons systems. However, in contrast with the past, foreign policy considerations will play a much more important role. The President will be concerned not only with the defense of the United States, but also, more than heretofore, with the impact which his decisions will have on our relations with the Soviets, the Chinese, and our allies.

There are several reasons for this. The primary one is the possibility of Soviet-American agreement to limit the strategic arms race. Another cloud on the horizon—but this time dark—is the growing nuclear power of Communist China. (Thus far, we have tended to assume that the Chinese nuclear problem will be a carbon copy of the Soviet, but this is not necessarily the case.) The other factor complicating discussion of our strategic forces will be the continuing possibility of an increase in the size of the nuclear club, the Nonproliferation Treaty notwithstanding. The new administration will have to deal with both the specter of proliferation and the demand for greater assurances from prospective members of the club.

How will these crucial problems be managed? The President will be compelled to take a close interest in them, since he will have to make many of the decisions. As did previous Presidents, he will look primarily to the Secretary of Defense and the Joint Chiefs of Staff for advice on our strategic-force structure. He should, however, find himself looking more than did his predecessors to the Secretary of State for advice on political considerations bearing on strategy and force structure. If for no other reason, this will probably be insured by the talks with the Soviets, which have already brought the State Department and the Arms Control and Disarmament Agency (ACDA) from the wings into center stage on strategic arms questions.

From *The Annals* of the American Academy of Political and Social Science, Vol. 380 (November 1968). Reprinted by permission of the American Academy of Political and Social Science and the author.

All of this raises the question whether our government is properly organized and staffed to deal adequately with these problems. In addition to the White House, a number of departments and agencies are involved, including the State Department, the Pentagon, the Arms Control and Disarmament Agency, the Atomic Energy Commission, and the Central Intelligence Agency.

Under the Johnson administration, problems related to strategic forces and disarmament were dealt with in several forums. Decisions regarding American strategic forces were dealt with in one of Secretary McNamara's draft Presidential Memoranda, as a part of his Five-Year Force Structure and Financial Program. While the Department of State has played a role in this process, it can only be described as modest. Disarmament problems have been the primary responsibility of the Arms Control and Disarmament Agency. While the Departments of State and Defense have been deeply involved in disarmament, the State Department staff has been very small and—though extremely able—probably inadequate.

This tendency to deal with force-structure and disarmament questions separately may have been satisfactory for the limited test ban, outer space, and nonproliferation treaties. The current talks with the Soviets, however, go to the heart of the nation's strategic forces, and it is essential that the President have advice, on both force structure and disarmament, based on well-coordinated staff work of both the diplomatic and defense agencies. Before dealing with this problem, however, I would like to sketch the other major defense issues which will confront the President.

Vietnam and United States forces abroad

If the problems related to strategic forces loom large, those concerning our general-purpose forces (army and marine divisions, carrier task forces, tactical air forces, and the like) are no less portentous. The largest question mark concerns the outcome of the Vietnam war. The lack of an answer to this makes it devilishly difficult to project the future size and deployment of our general-purpose forces. It is, however, possible to make one prediction with a reasonable amount of confidence. While the impact of events such as the Soviet occupation of Czechoslovakia will play a role, the next administration will almost certainly want to re-

consider the number of American forces abroad. The specific issues will concern what forces should be left overseas and the pace of any withdrawals. But the broader foreign policy issues will relate to how the process is managed so that any withdrawal of forces is not seen by either allies or potential aggressors as a fundamental change in United States commitments, which would encourage aggression or create political instability.

Obviously, the State Department and our diplomatic missions abroad should play a leading role in these decisions with regard to the size and pace of any reductions and the manner in which other countries are dealt with. Unfortunately, in the past, our diplomatic establishment has not always taken the lead but has tended to react to pressures from Congress and the Pentagon. It is essential, however, that the next administration determine in advance where it wants to go and how it wants to get there.

Strategic mobility and United States bases

At the same time that the reduction of United States forces abroad is being weighed, there will be several related problems to be dealt with. These are the implications of the new lift capability our forces are acquiring and possible adjustments in our base structure abroad. After years of talk about it, the C-5 aircraft will soon be flying trucks and tanks around the world. Supplemented by the C-141 for personnel, the Military Airlift Command will acquire in the 1970's a much greater ability to move whole army divisions from one continent to another quickly. If Congress approves the Fast Deployment Logistics Ship, the Navy's ability to move combat forces will take a similar leap.

While digesting the significance of these strides in mobility, the next administration will also be confronted with considerable turbulence in our base arrangements abroad. The simple fact is that many other countries are getting tired of having American bases on their soil and want either to curtail their use or to get rid of them.

The new administration will have at its disposal a study by a joint State Department–Defense Department study group on our bases. This will, however, be only an introduction to the problem, and our diplomatic and defense establishments will have to work very closely together in dealing with the interrelationship between our growing strategic mobility and shrinking base structure.

Military assistance—a dwindling asset

Not unrelated to these problems is the question of the future of the military assistance program. After two decades, this bold experiment is in serious trouble. There are a number of reasons for this, not the least of which is the general feeling that many of America's allies are not doing enough for themselves. Furthermore, the shock of seeing some of our friends using or threatening to use United States arms against each other has not helped.

For some years now, Congress has been placing considerable pressure on the administration to reduce the military assistance program. Whereas at its peak in 1952, it was $5.74 billion, in 1967 it was $790 million.[1] The new administration may very well want to consider whether it should continue to give military assistance at all—and particularly new equipment—to other than a few key countries.

If ever there was an aspect of the military world on which the new Secretary of State should be the President's primary adviser, this is it. Congressional legislation places this responsibility on him, as follows:

Under the direction of the President, the Secretary of State shall be responsible for the continuous supervision and general direction of the assistance programs authorized by this Act, including but not limited to determining whether there shall be a military assistance program for a country and the value thereof, to the end that such programs are effectively integrated both at home and abroad and the foreign policy of the United States is best served thereby.[2]

It is important that he exercise this authority, working closely with the Secretary of Defense, as well as with other parts of the government.

THE MANAGEMENT ALTERNATIVES

Having sketched the key politico-military issues which will confront the next administration, I would now like to turn to their management. . . . I will limit myself to commenting on the major alternatives from a politico-military point of view.

No matter how the White House staff is organized, its primary role should continue to be to get the key problems before the President in a timely manner and in a form which makes the issues and alternatives clear. It seems to me evident that many of the questions discussed above cannot properly be settled at any lower level. I think it would be unfortunate, however, if the White House staff attempted to take on the job of co-ordinating the day-to-day work of the Departments of State and Defense.

If, however, the White House is to resist this temptation, the Departments of State and Defense will have to provide evidence that it is unnecessary. While co-ordination between Foggy Bottom and the Pentagon has improved considerably in recent years, it is still far from perfect. Too many officials in the State Department are still disinclined to exert the leadership which is required of them, and too many officials in the Pentagon are still inclined to proceed on their own on courses of action with foreign policy implications without consulting the State Department in a timely fashion.

One key to this problem will be the relations of the President, the Secretary of State, and the Secretary of Defense. If they do not work effectively together, we will be in trouble, for they will set the tone for the work of the staffs: Presidents and Cabinet officials surely do not get better staff work than they demand.

Good working relations at the top are, however, not enough. If the senior officials are to be spared, it is essential that there be some arrangement for co-ordinated staff work. While there is no easy answer to this need, I believe that President Johnson was on the right track when he issued National Security Action Memorandum 341 in 1966. This gave the Secretary of State responsibility "for the over-all direction, co-ordination and supervision of interdepartmental activities of the United States overseas." It also established the Senior Interdepartmental Group, chaired by the Under Secretary of State, and the Interdepartmental Regional Groups, chaired by the appropriate assistant secretaries. Unfortunately, these groups got off to a slow start and did not really get rolling until late in 1967. It is, therefore, still too early to tell exactly what they will do and how well they can do it.

The possible functions of these groups include planning and policy, operations, and crisis-management. Because this is a large subject, I shall limit myself here to saying that experience, to date, indicates that their main effort should be in the planning and policy area. For

---

[1] U.S., Office of the Assistant Secretary of Defense (OASD), for International Security Affairs (ISA), *Military Assistance Facts* (Washington, D.C.: U.S. Government Printing Office, 1968). (The 1967 figure does not include military assistance to South Vietnam.)

[2] Section 622 (c) of the U.S. Foreign Assistance Act of 1961.

example, the SIG-IRG mechanism might be a good one through which to do the staff work regarding a significant adjustment in the United States forces or bases abroad so as to get the issues to the Secretaries of State and Defense and the President. It would not lend itself to carrying out the decision.

If, however, the country directors, the IRG's, and the SIG are to do their job adequately, they will have to develop better techniques to deal with some of our more complicated problems. Take, for example, a country in which the United States has a large number of forces and bases, as well as economic and military aid programs. What is the proper mix of these expensive programs? No one department or agency can answer this question. It is essential, therefore, that some co-ordinated interagency analytical technique be employed.

While a certain amount of progress has been made in this direction, particularly in the Latin-American Bureau, much remains to be done.

Now, just a word about task forces. While many officials considered these somewhat of a joke early in the Kennedy administration, there is now a broad consensus that many problems simply cannot be dealt with in a routine manner. It is generally accepted that task forces are particularly useful in dealing with crises. They could also be used more to deal with significant politico-military problems, particularly those which require interagency analysis of the possible "trade-offs" between alternate United States resources (such as economic aid, military assistance, and United States forces).

PROBLEMS IN THE DIPLOMATIC ESTABLISHMENT

If the State Department is going to play its proper leadership role in politico-military problems, the Secretary of State must set the pace. In the first instance, he should assume "the over-all direction, coordination, and supervision" of the other foreign affairs agencies—the Agency for International Development (AID), United States Information Agency (USIA), and ACDA. In order both to do this and control the work of the State Department, he should make some drastic changes on the floor on which he will have his office. The most important change that should be made is to carry out the recommendations of the Herter Committee to appoint an Executive Under Secretary to act as general manager of the State Department. This official should, among other things, supervise the SIG

staff on behalf of the Under Secretary. He should also be responsible for management of interagency planning and programming.

Within the regional bureaus, the senior deputy assistant secretary should be responsible for management of the IRG, as well as interagency regional and country planning. He will need a staff to help him do this. Since the role of mathematics in this work is an important—if limited—one, at least some of the officers should be trained in quantitative analytic techniques.

Abroad, the institution of political advisers to major military commands is now pretty well established. The new Secretary of State should, however, insist that his department resist the temptation to use these positions to take care of deserving but less effective senior officers.

There are a number of things which could be said about politico-military problems in embassies, but I shall limit myself to one. The next President should re-examine a significant gap in the authority of the ambassador. This was contained in the following paragraphs of President Kennedy's letter of May 29, 1961:

Now one word about your relations to the military. As you know, the United States Diplomatic Mission includes Service Attachés, Military Assistance Advisory Groups and other Military components attached to the Mission. It does not, however include United States military forces operating in the field where such forces are under the command of a United States area military commander. The line of authority to these forces runs from me, to the Secretary of Defense, to the Joint Chiefs of Staff in Washington and to the area commander in the field.

Although this means that the Chief of the American Diplomatic Mission is not in the line of military command, nevertheless, as Chief of Mission, you should work closely with the appropriate area military commander to assure the full exchange of information. If it is your opinion that activities by the United States military forces may adversely affect our over-all relations with the people or government of _____, you should promptly discuss the matter with the military commander and, if necessary, request a decision by higher authority.[3]

[3]U.S., Senate, Foreign Relations Committee, *Additional Material on Administration of the Department of State*, July 31, 1962.

These instructions are all right in a case like Germany, where the ambassador and the general have plenty of time to work out their relations. But, what about a case like that of the Dominican Republic, where an ambassador and a joint task force commander suddenly found themselves thrown together in a confusing situation. If they can co-operate, the confusion is at least reduced. But suppose they do not?

I believe that, in the case of contingency operations, the ambassador should be in charge. Now, I realize that the military do not like the idea of having troops "under" a civilian. I should like to remind them, however, that both the President and the Secretary of Defense are civilians. There is one point on which I sympathize with them. Not all of our ambassadors would be qualified—or even willing—to perform such a role. There is, however, a solution to this problem: appoint able ambassadors. And I assume that no competent ambassador in such a situation would normally attempt to direct the tactical employment of troops. I use the word "normally" advisedly. Sometimes tactical orders can be significant, as the decision in the Dominican Republic to establish a logistic line from the airport to United States forces at the Hotel Ambassador. This became, in effect, the line between the opposing Dominican forces.[4]

EDUCATING THE FOREIGN SERVICE ON MILITARY MATTERS

This brings us directly to the heart of the matter, the education of Foreign Service officers on military matters. The record on this score since World War II has been rather good. Many Foreign Service officers have had at least some form of military service, although I have the impression that the percentage has decreased as compared with the years immediately after World War II. A great number of the senior officers have attended one of the senior war colleges. Furthermore, an increasing number of officers are working with and for the military, either in the Pentagon, at one of the service schools, or at a military command headquarters. (A recent meeting in Washington of those officers currently on such duty collected over fifty.) Those State Department officials thrown in contact with the military officers assigned to the State Department learn a great deal from them.

Having said this, I should add that I would consider it a mistake for the next administration to assume that no improvements can be made. I stress this because even the best organization cannot soar above the level of the people who comprise it. Allow me to suggest a few areas for examination.

The State Department could make greater use of the outside research organizations with respect to politico-military problems. If it cannot get its own budget increased, it should make a greater effort to influence the ways in which the Department of Defense and the Arms Control and Disarmament Agency spend their research funds.

The State Department should start a regular officer-exchange program with some of these research organizations.

The State Department should employ, for at least one-year tours of duty, more academicians who specialize in military matters.

The Foreign Service Institute should strengthen its politico-military program, which is now minimal, and should have military officers on its staff. This program should be directed primarily at junior- and middle-grade officers. It should also include correspondence courses on politico-military subjects.

The State Department should be vigilant against the assignment of mediocre officers or time-servers to work with the military. The best way to do this is to insure that officers assigned to these jobs are rewarded and that the skills which they gain are employed in future assignments.

The State Department should train more officers in quantitative analytic techniques. In this regard, it should assign several officers to the Office of Systems Analysis in the Pentagon. Both agencies should profit from it.

Military officers should be assigned to the SIG and IRG staffs.

In brief, if the next administration is to meet its challenge abroad, it will need all the help that it can get. While I hope that military force will play a smaller role in our foreign affairs in the future, it would be utopian fantasy to pretend that it will play none—or that by ignoring the military factor, it will go away.

Since World War II, steady—if uneven—progress has been made in improving the management of our national security problems. The next administration should build on the achievements of its predecessors, and not try to start all over again.

[4]John B. Martin, *Overtaken by Events* (Garden City, N.Y.: Doubleday, 1966), p. 680.

CHAPTER 3

POLITICS, PUBLICS, THE MEDIA, AND THE NATIONAL CHARACTER

Politics, publics, the media, and the American character represent a shorthand reference to those politically relevant factors outside the formal governmental machinery. The fundamental questions that concern us are how they do, and how they should, affect foreign policy.

While there has been a great deal of research on some of the individual elements—the press, political parties, voting—and their impact on foreign policy, we are not in a position to weigh or compare their influence on foreign policy outputs in any quantitative or even systematic way. For example, there is a considerable literature that deals with the role of the press and, to a lesser extent, the other mass media, the nature of the treatment they accord various types of public policy issues, how reporters do their work in Washington and elsewhere, and so forth, but if you ask what difference all of this makes in terms of foreign policy consequences, it would be difficult if not impossible to get a reasonably precise answer.

Since there are identifiable people and agencies responsible for the making and carrying out of foreign policy, they do provide a well-defined focus for studying the impact of these nongovernmental factors. Rather than viewing the latter as free-floating forces that somehow make a difference, it is at least worth inquiring how those in the foreign policy business are affected by them. This will not give us all the answers we need, but it represents a step in the right direction. For example, public opinion polls provide periodic reports on what the public thinks, supposedly, about various policy issues or political personalities. As students of foreign policy, the additional question we should ask is how these polls are being interpreted by the people responsible for making foreign policy. This kind of data on what the public thinks about something is often not very reliable. However good or bad the polls are, they nevertheless do not become significant in terms of policy consequences until the President or the Secretary of State or the Secretary of Defense has looked at them and made some policy change or adjustment in response to them. Admittedly, the chain of influence may be more complicated: e.g., executive response to Congressional pressure which is in turn a response to the polls.

It has been argued that the combination of his rapidly falling public support as reflected in the opinion polls and then the strong showing of Senator Eugene McCarthy in the New Hampshire primary were regarded by President Johnson as significant and provide at least part of the explanation for his decision not to run for the Presidency, and for some of the changes made in our Vietnam policy in March 1968. The point is that an assessment of consequences is essential in analyzing the role of such factors.

Decision makers can be influenced by other elements in the domestic political setting. These may take the form of conscious efforts to exert influence: letter writing to legislators and executive officials; resolutions voted at meetings of large organizations; or running a full-page advertisement in the *New York Times*. On the other hand, foreign policy makers may act on the basis of their own perceptions of the domestic political climate, as reflected not only in public opinion polls but in political campaigns, election results, and newspaper editorials.

Another influence of the society is a little more subtle. It is the values and attitudes that the decision makers have "internalized" as members of the society. Here, one encounters another slippery concept, something called "the American character" or, closely related, "the American style." To state the matter in overly simple terms, are there any common characteristics or values shared by most Americans because we have lived together in a certain kind of society, in a certain part of the world, with a certain set of institutions, over a certain period of time? And if so, what difference do they make in terms of American foreign policy choices and performance?

Let us assume, for example, that most Americans tend to be pragmatic types, concerned not with deep philosophical or ideological questions but rather with the solving of practical problems. There is certainly a strong element of the pragmatic in the American way of life, and it can be very attractive, appealing, and productive. On the other hand, as applied to a difficult and unfamiliar foreign situation and milieu, this short-range, problem-solving, let's-get-the-job-done attitude may get us into trouble. Some critics argue that this is exactly what happened to the United States in Vietnam. In all fairness, however it should be pointed out that the pragmatic approach has sometimes proved quite effective, even overseas.

If these brief comments about American pragmatism are at all close to the mark, they suggest that analysis of the American character may provide useful insights into American foreign policy decisions and problems. The great difficulty with such an approach as a reliable tool for foreign policy analysis is that it involves, first, developing some agreement on this elusive phenomenon called the American character and then assessing in a systematic fashion the ways in which it seems to influence foreign policy.

Public opinion is a term often abused in the discussion and study of public policy. A few clarifying comments may help. First of all, there are many publics. Secondly, there is a very broad range of opinions among those publics. The range runs from people with no opinions or little empirical basis for the few views they may have, to people whose opinions have a strong underpinning of information and considered thought.

On many matters, there are large groups in the country who have little information, no opinion, and couldn't care less. Different groups of people are stimulated or activated by different subjects. Some people have strongly-held and well-grounded views in one particular field, for example, civil rights or urban problems. The concern of many more is triggered by so-called "pocketbook" issues.

It is also fair to say that short of major crises and, particularly, of military involvements like Korea and Vietnam, most people in this country pay relatively little continuing attention to foreign affairs. Typically, the public begins to follow foreign policy issues with the same intensity and interest as domestic issues in the case of a large-scale military involvement like Korea or Vietnam. The latter affect the citizenry at large in terms of higher taxes, large numbers of men drafted for military service, and other dislocations to the personal lives of individuals; in terms of clear, direct, and substantial impact on the lives of many, they are very much like major domestic policy issues. Most other foreign policy matters simply do not have such direct and obvious effects on the mass of the public.

If one assumes the necessity or desirability in a democracy of a certain level of public understanding and public involvement in the making of major policy choices, this analysis of public opinion and foreign policy may be rather depressing. Clearly, we do not have and cannot have a kind of town-meeting democracy in our national affairs. Even if it were possible, it would not be desirable in foreign affairs in the sense that the vast majority of citizens have neither the knowledge, the training, nor the developed judgment to make day-to-day foreign policy decisions of the sort now required.

What is both impressive and reassuring is that our political leaders and our opinion leaders

—businessmen, churchmen, educators, labor leaders, the press, radio and television—all the people we pay attention to, act as if the public were alert, concerned, and listening to what these leaders have to say about public policy, including foreign policy, issues. Therefore, they discuss and debate the issues actively, continuously, and at times with great intensity. Since they seem to assume that these public debates and discussions are important, they become so.

Sometimes the nature of the debate is not as lucid and rational as the scholar would like. Nevertheless, looking back over the history of the American involvement in world affairs since the end of the Second World War, one finds a series of great debates about foreign policy—the Truman Doctrine of aid to Greece and Turkey, the Marshall Plan, troops to Europe in connection with the organization of NATO, the relief of General MacArthur in 1951 and the larger issues of Far Eastern policy involved in the Korean War, and, finally, Vietnam. Often, there has been a great deal of excitement and emotion generated; at the same time, some good discussion, analysis, and commentary on what was happening usually emerged and helped focus for the public the different views of the problem and what should be done about it.

Finally, in this area of public opinion, there is some recent evidence which suggests the possibility that "the attentive public," those with a deeper and more sophisticated interest in public affairs, is beginning to expand in size, to become a larger proportion of the American public. Certainly the civil rights movement, beginning in the late 1950's, stimulated an interest in public policy among many not previously involved. This interest was sustained by deep concern about the war in Vietnam. These and other critical problems of the 1960's have undoubtedly stimulated the interest and involvement of many not previously concerned with public policy. Assuming that this is a desirable development, an important question over the next few years will be to see how many of these people sustain their interest beyond the one or two current problems that now concern them. (For a more detailed discussion of this point, see the selection by Professor Rosenau.)

What can be said about the foreign policy consequences of parties, politics, interest groups, and elections? Often, the most effective political pressure on the executive will not be direct but, rather, indirect, through the Congress. In other words, if you are a member of an interest group and want to have some impact on a foreign or domestic policy issue, as a matter of tactics your best gambit may be to convince some congressmen to support your views. They can then bring these views to bear on the executive much more effectively than the pressure groups themselves.

It does, however, seem generally agreed that organized interest or pressure groups are not an important factor in foreign policy. (The picture is quite different for domestic policy issues.) They are least important on the big issues; they are most likely to have some impact on a narrow matter which clearly affects the interests of particular American groups. On major foreign policy problems like NATO, East-West relations, or foreign aid, the issues involved are usually so complicated and there are so many interested groups trying to press their views, that there is probably a tendency for them to cancel one another out, leaving considerable freedom to the policy makers (who may well have major differences among themselves).

When the United States was negotiating a peace treaty with Japan in the early 1950's, there was little broad public attention to or concern with it. On the other hand, Japan's return to complete independence was likely to affect specific American economic interests. In this particular case, intense concern was expressed by the American fishing industry on the West Coast, which was in fact able to exert sufficient pressure to protect its interests. Thus, the narrower the foreign policy issue and the more directly it affects identifiable American domestic interests (often these are economic), the more effective the pressure of interested groups is likely to be. The larger the foreign policy issue, the less effective it will be.

In the case of elections and voting behavior, a crude proposition would be that specific foreign policy issues do not seem significantly related to the choice of candidates. In other words, a candidate's position on a particular foreign policy question does not usually seem to be a significant factor in voters' decisions. (United States policy regarding Israel in those districts with heavy Jewish populations would seem to be one notable exception, although a serious candidate would be most unlikely to make himself vulnerable on this score.)

While the specific foreign policy views of candidates usually do not affect elections, general orientation toward international affairs and an indicated competence in foreign affairs seem to make a difference, particularly at the Presidential level. Certainly one element of Senator Goldwater's difficulties in 1964 was that he did not project to the public either a deep understanding of foreign affairs or the assurance that he would deal with foreign policy problems with balance and judgment. This may also help explain Governor George Romney's inability to establish himself as a leading Republican contender in 1968.

It is clear that American foreign policy is thoroughly enmeshed in the larger American political milieu. However, as I have indicated, we are simply not in a position to indicate clearly and authoritatively the net impact of these nongovernmental factors on foreign policy. We are left with partial views and impressions offered tentatively and modestly. The American political system does seem to get its critical foreign policy issues aired and debated though the timing is not always propitious and the manner far from elegant. Further, there seems little doubt that the American public has greatly increased its knowledge and matured in its responses to international problems over the past two decades. Both these characteristics, in my view, were manifested in the continuing and heated debate and discussion of Vietnam policies in 1967 and 1968. However one may view the merits and demerits of the policies themselves, I think that Americans can take some pride in the response of their political system to this most complex and painful foreign policy problem.

THE ATTENTIVE PUBLIC AND FOREIGN POLICY
James N. Rosenau

Without a doubt, one of the most important books published by an American political scientist in the postwar period is Gabriel Almond's *The American People and Foreign Policy*, which first appeared in 1950. In a formulation which has continued to be quite influential, Almond divided the American public into three major groupings: the mass public; the attentive public; and the elite. In brief, the mass public, representing the overwhelming majority of the nation, was neither well-informed nor greatly interested in foreign affairs; the elite provided the leadership in developing the opinions of the nation. The attentive public, roughly estimated at ten to fifteen per cent of the population, was viewed as relatively well-informed, concerned about problems and issues, but not in a position directly to affect policy outcomes (though perhaps serving as a critical audience for views presented by elite opinion leaders and makers).

In two earlier studies, Professor Rosenau has contributed to the development and clarification of these concepts and the empirical basis for them. (See *Public Opinion and Foreign Policy*, 1961; and *National Leadership and Foreign Policy*, 1963.) For those who still treasure a town-meeting view of democracy or a Jeffersonian view of the virtues of the average citizen, the work of scholars like Almond and Rosenau on American public opinion has had a depressing effect. In the selection that follows, Rosenau provides a modestly encouraging theory: namely, that the attentive public has been expanding in size in the course of the 1960's.

In the section of his monograph that has been omitted, Rosenau goes on to provide some evidence for his theory, using trends in the receipt of letters from the public by the White House, Senator Philip A. Hart (D., Mich.), and the *New York Times* and the *New York Post*. The data from all these sources do in fact indicate the same clear trend—significantly more letters received from the public. Rosenau views this as preliminary supporting evidence for a hypothesis which obviously needs considerable further exploration.

Almost everywhere people are bored by foreign policy.

> *The Economist,*
> October 10, 1964,
> p. 117.

[Norman R. Morrison,] a Quaker official described by friends as upset over Administration policy in Vietnam, burned himself to death in front of the river entrance to the Pentagon late this afternoon.

> *New York Times*
> November 3, 1965,
> p. 1.

Reprinted from a monograph sponsored by the Center of International Studies of the Woodrow Wilson School of Public and International Affairs, Princeton University, copyright, March 1968.
Ed. note: Some of the footnotes have been omitted.

These two accounts of behavior on the part of citizens were published thirteen months apart, and the discrepancy between the indifference described in the one and the tragic action described in the other vividly poses the problem examined in the ensuing pages. What, we shall be asking, is happening to citizenship between elections? In this era when ideology is said to be ending and alienation mounting, is attentiveness to foreign policy growing or is apathy deepening? Are more people more mobilizable or has affluence overwhelmed commitment? If the very technological developments that render issues complex and confound the citizen also place him closer to the course of events and facilitate his comprehension of them, will the latter consequence tend to offset the former?

These questions are easier to raise than to answer. The little systematic evidence that is available points to one set of conclusions, while one's impressions of recent events lead in a contrary direction. On the one hand, there are extensive studies and data that depict a scarcity of persons in the United States who consistently keep abreast of public affairs and who can thus be considered to compose the Attentive Public. On the other hand, the extremity of the act of self-immolation over the situation in Vietnam seems symbolic of a growing involvement in the course of events between elections.

To unravel these contradictory tendencies, our analysis will proceed in four steps. First, we shall look at some of the findings bearing upon the size of the Attentive Public. Next, we shall note the impressions that lead us to conclude that these findings convey a misleading picture of present and future trends. Third, we shall develop an empirical theory of the dynamics of attentiveness which will provide a basis for predicting slow and continuous growth in the relative size of the Attentive Public. Finally, we shall present new data designed to serve as a preliminary test of the growth pattern predicted by our theory. [Ed. note: This last section has been omitted.]

AN ACTIVE MINORITY

Notwithstanding the importance of the roles played by the Attentive Public, by almost any quantitative standard its ranks are not large. The varied and intensive activities of attentive citizens tend to give an exaggerated picture of the number of persons involved. The very intensity of one group's behavior will often capture headlines that, in turn, provoke equally

intense activity on the part of opposing groups. As this spiraling process continues, the extent to which concern is widely shared tends to be exaggerated. The vigorous demands and angry protests of the Attentive Public may command the respect of officials and attract the attention of news media, but in proportion to the population as a whole its members constitute a distinct minority.

It is difficult, of course, to describe the size of the Attentive Public in the United States with a precise figure or percentage. Much depends on the criteria used to classify persons in its ranks. Since different observers use different definitions and measures of attentiveness, the resulting estimates often vary considerably. Whatever criteria are used, however, they never yield figures that portray the Attentive Public as a majority of the citizenry. The varying estimates always fall within a range that does not exceed 50 percent of the adult population at its upper limit.

That virtually any criteria lead to a conception of the Attentive Public as an active minority can be readily illustrated. Contrast, for example, the circulation figures of newspapers and magazines that report and analyze public affairs in a serious and extended fashion with those of printed media that treat such matters in a cursory and simplified manner. Perhaps the most striking comparison is provided by the often-cited difference between the readerships that the *News* and the *New York Times* enjoy in the world's largest cosmopolitan area: in 1965 the daily circulation of the *News*, a tabloid that reports on scandal and sex far more vividly than on issues of public policy, was 2,170,373, whereas the corresponding figure for the *Times*, with its thorough treatment of public affairs, was 652,135.[1] Or consider—to lift the contrast to a national and weekly or monthly level—the difference between the number of subscribers to such politically oriented publications as the *Atlantic, Harper's,* the *National Review*, and the *Reporter*, on the one hand, and the circulation of such essentially unpolitical magazines as *Cosmopolitan, Holiday, Redbook,* and *Sports Illustrated* on the other: none of the first four reported a 1965 circulation of more than 278,957, while none of the last four circulated fewer than 825,863 copies.[2]

Nor is the picture altered by comparisons of the audience for entertainment and for public

[1] N.W. Ayer and Son's Directory Newspapers and Periodicals 1965 (Philadelphia: N.W. Ayer and Son, Inc., 1965), p. 1263.
[2] Ibid., pp. 1428–36.

affairs programs presented by the electronic media. One elaborate analysis of the television viewing habits of 2,427 adults, for example, found that only 4 percent cited "regular news" first as their "favorite program," that only a slightly higher proportion (7 percent) specified "other information and public affairs" programs first, that the average viewer prefers programs "that provide pleasant relaxation rather than serious stimulation," and that "aside from the day's news and weather—which he watches regularly—he rarely uses the set as a deliberate source of information, and he is extremely unlikely to turn on serious and informative public affairs presentations."[3] Indeed, myriad anecdotes could be cited to show that most citizens resent the intrusion of public affairs into their viewing hours. Just as criticism from soap-opera viewers is invariably aroused by coverage of emergency daytime meetings of the United Nations Security Council, so was the ire of sports fans raised to unprecedented peaks when the orbital flight of Gemini 5 was unexpectedly hampered by electrical power problems and the networks canceled coverage of two exhibition football games until the problem was solved and the safety of the astronauts assured.[4] Similarly, when President Johnson scheduled a 9:00 p.m. appearance before a joint session of Congress to appeal for a law guaranteeing Negroes the right to vote, the event was covered in New York by the three television networks and, as a result, the independent stations in the city enjoyed "substantial increases" in the size of their audiences, winning viewers who usually watched network entertainment shows that had been canceled.[5]

The minority status of the Attentive Public is even more clear-cut in studies of political behavior itself. While this status can only be inferred from the data on mass media consumption, it is directly evident in the findings of researchers who have probed the practices of citizenship. Summarizing a number of studies pertaining to questions of foreign policy, for example, Hero observes that "possibly as many as 15 percent of American adults display a significant degree of interest in world affairs" and that "many of these interested citizens possess only rather trivial or peripheral information on international relations."[6] A dramatic illustration of this general point was provided by a finding that, in 1964, 28 percent of a representative sample of 1,501 adult Americans were "not aware that most of China is now ruled by a Communist government."[7]

The findings for attentiveness to domestic affairs reveal perhaps a slightly greater degree of activity and involvement, but again none of the figures even approach a majority of the citizenry. A national cross-section sample of 8,000 respondents, for example, was found to include 21 percent who reported discussing public issues with others "frequently" and 13 percent who said they had conveyed their opinions on a public issue to congressmen or other public officials "one or more times in the past year."[8] Likewise, a nationwide sample used to study the 1964 presidential election yielded the finding that "only about 15 percent of the adult population reports ever having written a letter to a public official, and of the total stream of such letters from the grass roots, two-thirds are composed by about 3 percent of the population."[9] Similarly, while many Americans are "joiners" and belong to a vast array of formal organizations, it has been estimated that only 31 percent belong to organizations that "sometimes" take a stand on public issues.[10] Still another dimension of activity was probed in a nationwide sample of 970 American adults, only 27 percent of whom reported that they "regularly" followed "the accounts of political and governmental affairs," while 53 percent responded "from time to time" and 19 percent answered "never."[11]

With respect to local affairs, too, the percentages fall short of the halfway mark. In a sample of 525 registered voters in New Haven, for ex-

---

[3]Gary A. Steiner, *The People Look at Television: A Study of Audience Attitudes* (New York: Alfred A. Knopf, 1963), pp. 126, 127, 228–29.
[4]One network received 1,625 telephoned objections to the cancellation in New York, 1,800 in Los Angeles, 1,200 in Chicago, 1,400 in Washington, 300 in St. Louis, and 100 in San Francisco. *New York Times*, August 22, 1965, p. 73.
[5]*New York Times*, March 17, 1965, p. 91.
[6]Alfred O. Hero, *Americans in World Affairs* (Boston: The World Peace Foundation, 1959), p. 6.
[7]Martin Patchen, *The American Public's View of U.S. Policy Toward China* (New York: Council on Foreign Relations, 1964), p. 5.
[8]Julian L. Woodward and Elmo Roper, "Political Activity of American Citizens," *American Political Science Review*, Vol. XLIV (December 1950), pp. 874–76.
[9]Philip E. Converse, Aage R. Clausen, and Warren E. Miller, "Electoral Myth and Reality: The 1964 Election," *American Political Science Review*, Vol. LIX (June 1965), p. 333.
[10]Robert E. Lane, *Political Life: Why People Get Involved in Politics* (Glencoe, Ill.: The Free Press, 1959), p. 75.
[11]Gabriel A. Almond and Sidney Verba, *The Civic Culture: Political Attitudes and Democracy in Five Nations* (Princeton: Princeton University Press, 1963), p. 89.

ample, Dahl found that 47 percent discussed local affairs with friends, that 27 percent communicated their views to local officials, that 16 percent had had contact with New Haven officials, and that only 13 percent had "done anything actively in connection with some local issue or local problem—political or nonpolitical." Only 3 percent of Dahl's sample cited all four of these activities, and 40 percent did not cite any of them.[12] Even smaller rates of participation are reported by Presthus: using samples of 479 and 655, he found, in two small communities of upstate New York, that no more than 1 percent discussed any of ten different issues with a friend, that not more than 5 percent attended any public meeting connected with the processing of nine of the issues, and that not more than 3 percent "contributed work or money" in connection with nine of the issues. (The tenth issue, raising funds for a hospital, elicited some activity from 38 percent of the sample.)[13]

But there is no need to pile finding upon finding. The general pattern remains consistent throughout all the studies that touch upon citizenship between elections. Indeed, it is even evident in the activity that occurs *during* elections. Of the nearly 1,800 citizens who made up a representative sample used to study the 1956 presidential election, 28 percent were found to have tried to convince others to vote in a particular way, 10 percent reported contributing financially to the campaign of a party or candidate, 7 percent said they attended "political meetings, rallies, dinners, or things like that," and 3 percent cited "other" types of work during the campaign.[14] In short, it is difficult to quarrel with the overall conclusion that "a really intense commitment to politics probably is limited in American society to a small fraction of political activists"[15] and that, viewing the electorate as a whole, "about one-third . . . can be characterized as politically apathetic or passive; in most cases, they are unaware, literally, of the political part of the world around them. Another 60 percent play largely spectator roles in the political process; they watch, they cheer, they vote, but they do not do battle. In the purest sense of the word, probably only 1 or 2 percent could be called gladiators."[16]

A GROWING MINORITY?

Yet absolute data are not trend data. To conclude that attentiveness is not a pervasive phenomenon between elections is not to say anything about emerging patterns. There is no reason to presume that the size of the Attentive Public is constant in proportion to the population. On the contrary, there are reasons to speculate that in the long run its ranks will swell at a faster rate than those of the citizenry as a whole.

Our speculations along these lines are, it should be noted, contrary to many prevailing notions about the impact of affluence and industrialization upon the individual in modern America. Satiated by luxury, stultified by television, atomized by large organizations, deprived of complaints by the welfare state, isolated from the centers of political decision by the sheer magnitude and complexity of society, the individual is said to be turning away from public affairs rather than toward them. The old blueprints of order and life in community, society, and world no longer seem appropriate to the intricacies of life in the space age. Science defies Marxism, guerrilla warfare confounds democratic liberalism, urban life overwhelms traditional conservatism. At the same time, the outmoded values have not been replaced by new ones that provide a means of comprehending and evaluating the new issues of our time and that thus give direction to political energies. Accordingly, it is alleged, people are either retreating to anomic forms of satisfaction or they are returning to the comforting folds of family and church. Whether the behavior is deviant or conventional, moreover, the result is said to be the same: the citizen seeking anomic pleasures and his church-going counterpart searching for fundamentals are both being moved by intensely personal drives. They share an inward orientation and selfishness that, the argument concludes, preclude the concern for other people and the commitment to larger goals on which involvement in politics is presumed to rest. The arena of public affairs offers little pleasure or excitement in comparison to the three-week tour of European capitals, the television spectacular, the family outing, or the narcotic dose.

There is, of course, much to be said for this

[12]Robert A. Dahl, Who Governs? Democracy and Power in an American City (New Haven: Yale University Press, 1961), pp. 277–79.
[13]Robert Presthus, Men at the Top: A Study in Community Power (New York: Oxford University Press, 1964), pp. 259–62.
[14]Angus Campbell, Philip E. Converse, Warren E. Miller, and Donald E. Stokes, The American Voter (New York: John Wiley and Sons, 1960), p. 91.
[15]Ibid., p. 104.
[16]Milbrath, Political Participation, p. 21.

line of reasoning. Wealth is widespread and unprecedented luxury is now enjoyed by a great many people. Crime, drug addiction, juvenile delinquency, and other forms of anomie are national problems, and they do seem to be linked to larger social trends. It is also true that statistics on family life and religious practice reflect the patterns described. And certainly the television screen commands the energies and dampens the imaginations of millions of citizens. Nor can it be denied that one need look no further back than the 1950s for a convergence of these tendencies and a resulting torpor pervading the national community.[17]

Notwithstanding these tendencies—and, in a curious way, partly because of them—there remain compelling reasons to speculate that contrary tendencies are also operative and that, on balance, these will foster a growth in the ranks of the Attentive Public. Before we consider these reasons, however, it must be emphasized that we are not positing a rapid and widespread increase in citizenship between elections. Sudden spurts of such activity seem highly unlikely in view of all the incentives to apathy that have for so long kept down the ranks of the Attentive Public. Indeed, if a sudden and sharp rise in the attentiveness of the citizenry were to occur, it would be more likely to reflect a temporary, impetuous, or moody expression of increasing malcontent than a structured and sustained concern about the course of events. From the perspective of political stability, it is quite appropriate that travel, television, and family occupy the time of people. Any quick and pervasive turn away from such pursuits to public affairs could only signify an era of disruptive politics, and it is not such an era that we foresee when we predict the growth of the Attentive Public. Rather, our speculation concerns a small, but nonetheless steady, expansion in the number of citizens who develop and maintain a continuing interest in public affairs. Stated in crude quantitative terms, the tendencies we shall be discussing are not likely to accelerate the rate of growth of the Attentive Public by more than, say, one-tenth of one percent a year. In the long run, such a rate can have profound consequences for the conduct of public affairs, but for the moment we are asserting only that its inception has occurred, and nothing in the ensuing analysis is intended to imply a larger scale of change.

The origin of such an assertion is, admittedly, a highly impressionistic interpretation of recent history. The 1960s appear vastly different from the 1950s. Torpor seems to have given way to the protest march, the teach-in, and the petition. The Satisfied American appears to have been replaced by the Mobilizable American. Where the debilitating influences of material abundance once seemed to dominate the concern of elites, the limits of civil disobedience now appear to be the focus of their attention. Where everyone once seemed preoccupied with his pocketbook, increasing numbers now appear even more concerned with their consciences. Where letters-to-the-editor columns once seemed short and filled with trivia, they now seem long and full of agitated reactions to public affairs. Where students once seemed lethargic and involved in conventional study, they now appear to include the rally and the picket line among the places where learning can be obtained. Where the heroes of mass culture once adhered to an unwritten rule prohibiting political commitment, now "the mounting tensions of the cold war seem to be inducing more and more Hollywood stars to take a stand on political issues."[18] Where the national scene once seemed to be dominated by modes of consumption, it now conveys the impression of being pervaded by acts of expression. Indeed, it is from the perspective of a surge toward expression that the instances of self-immolation become especially meaningful. Whatever else they may represent, such actions are an extreme form of expression, and it is symbolic of the changes in the 1960s that individuals have seen fit to resort to expressions of this kind.

Appearances, of course, can be deceptive. Conceivably these signs of a growing involvement in public affairs are only a temporary, impetuous, and anomic spurt of activity fostered by discontent over the conflict in Vietnam. Or possibly the appearance of growing involvement is nothing more than greater activity on the part of the same minority that has always constituted the Attentive Public. Possibly we have mistaken qualitative innovations in the form of activity for quantitative changes in the

[17]For provocative analyses that posit the 1950s as an era of national torpor, see Robert L. Heilbroner, *The Future as History* (New York: Harper and Brothers, 1960); Emmet John Hughes, *America the Vincible* (Garden City: Doubleday and Co., 1959); Karl E. Meyer, *The New America: Politics and Society in the Age of the Smooth Deal* (New York: Basic Books, 1961); W. W. Rostow, *The United States in the World Arena: An Essay in Recent History* (New York: Harper and Brothers, 1960); and Meg Greenfield, "The Great American Morality Play," *The Reporter*, June 8, 1961, pp. 13–18.
[18]*New York Times*, August 5, 1965, p. 15.

amount of it. Teach-ins reflect attentiveness and protest marches reflect mobilizability, but do they also reflect a more widespread practice of citizenship between elections? Is the Attentive Public growing or merely becoming more visible? The foregoing impressions of the 1960s provide no clear-cut answer, and unfortunately the available findings cannot be transformed into trend data that are appropriate to test the validity of these impressions.

Without denying that the intensity of citizenship in the 1960s may convey a misleading picture of its extent, we are nonetheless inclined to reemphasize our original impressions and to interpret the recent trends as signs of growth in structured and sustained attentiveness rather than as an impulsive and transitory surge of activity. We do so not because such an interpretation is more pleasing, but because a number of reasons can be adduced that make it seem more appropriate as an explanation of recent trends in citizenship activity than any of the existing theories of anomic behavior in an affluent and industrial civilization. Theories of anomie and alienation may be applicable to certain societies, but they leave too much unexplained about modern American society. Thus we have had to develop what might be called a "theory of issue-area attentiveness." To anticipate the ensuing analysis, it is our reasoning that the 1960s have marked the convergence of a number of historic patterns conducive to active citizenship between elections, that the very forces which have given rise to an era of affluence have also fostered attentiveness, and that small but discernible accretions to the Attentive Public will therefore be revealed if appropriate trend data can be accumulated.

The conjunction of two long-term historical patterns, one immediate historical circumstance, and an hypothesis about the habitual character of attentiveness forms the basis for our conviction that the 1960s reflect a trend toward a more active citizenry. Perhaps the most important of these factors is the long-term trend toward greater educational opportunity. Required by technology, facilitated by affluence, and demanded by the enlarged aspirations of an upwardly mobile people, the commitment to education and to the acquisition of training have steadily expanded and, in the last decade, have reached the point where more than half of each year's high school graduates go on to college. In 1966, for example, 4,673,026 students were enrolled in college, a figure that represents a 5.8 percent increase over the previous year, a 52 percent increase since 1961, and a 113 percent increase since 1956.[19]

Nor is the educational trend confined to formal institutions of learning. A growing number of adult education programs relevant to public affairs are being conducted by many types of organizations and associations, by the mass media, and even by government officials. Where college reunions once consisted of wild parties, now they are also—or even wholly— the scene of serious discussions led by the faculty. Where trade unions once supplied members with newspapers containing social news and information on the bread-and-butter issues of labor-management relations, now they also offer summer school courses on world affairs and educational materials on specific issues of foreign policy. Where businessmen once equated their responsibilities with production and profit, now a "social responsibility theme seems suddenly to have gathered a streamroller momentum" and "in speech after speech in recent months executives have urged their colleagues to take a more active role in politics and civic affairs, to join the war against poverty, to improve relations with government, academic circles and students."[20] Where newspapers once stressed their entertainment features, now they also give prominent space to their public affairs columnists and advertise them in a "spectacular and expensive way."[21] Where local radio and television stations once left public affairs programming to the networks, now some 20 percent of such radio stations and some 30 percent of such television stations "have reached the point where they do more than give routine attention to news and show real responsibility and quality in their news services."[22] Where the television networks once confined public affairs programs to the least desirable viewing hours, now they are capable of devoting three and a half hours of prime evening time to a panoramic survey of U.S. foreign policy. Where government officials once conducted their activities at their own convenience, they are now more inclined, for a variety of reasons, to adjust the form and

[19]Garland G. Parker, "Statistics of Attendance in American Universities and Colleges, 1966–67," School and Society, Vol. XCV (January 7, 1967), p. 22.
[20]Robert A. Wright, "Beyond the Profits: Business Reaches for a Social Role," New York Times, July 3, 1966, Section 3, p. 1.
[21]Ben H. Bagdikian, "A Golden Age of Oracles," Columbia Journalism Review, Vol. IV (Winter 1966), p. 11.
[22]William A. Wood, "The Sound of Maturity," Columbia Journalism Review, Vol. IV (Winter 1966), p. 7.

timing of their deliberations to the habits of the Attentive Public: more than 400 members of Congress, for example, conduct regular interview programs for local radio and television stations[23] and, even more significant, in 1965 the President delivered his State of the Union address to Congress at 9:00 p.m. for the first time, thereby exposing a nationwide television audience to proceedings that previously had started at noon.

Just as these trends in formal and adult education are bound to have enormous consequences for the expansion of the economy and the continuing pace of technological change, so are their political repercussions likely to be extensive. With more and more citizens receiving formal education, with increasing emphasis upon adult education, and with the means of communicating information and ideas becoming ever more efficient, it seems highly improbable that increases will not occur in the degree of attentiveness to public affairs. There is nothing magical about education, to be sure. Possession of a college degree or exposure to the State of the Union address is no guarantee that an individual will acquire sensitivity to politics. For most individuals, however, formal training does seem to make a difference. One of the most consistent findings of social science is that, in general, the more education a person has, the more likely he is to follow the course of events and engage in attentive citizenship. For example, earlier it was noted that only 7 percent of the citizenry regard information and public affairs programs as their favorite television fare, but this is an overall figure and it changes considerably when broken down in terms of seven different levels of educational accomplishment: 4 percent at the lowest level (six years of grade school or less) and 23 percent at the highest level (post-college) cited such programs, and the figures for the intervening levels increased progressively with the amount of education.[24] While this is not to say that the membership of the Attentive Public will grow in proportion to the increase in educational attainments of the citizenry, it does seem plausible that the increase will provide both the incentive and the capacities for an expanding membership.

The second long-term pattern is hardly less significant and also derives from the pace of technological change. It might be called the "shrinkage" factor, since it reflects all the ways in which the rapid and dynamic developments in communications and transportation have shrunk social and political distances within and between nations. Comsat and the jet are symbolic of changes that culminated in the 1960s and that have heightened the interdependence of communities. Today an event in one part of the world can have repercussions in every other part. An assassination in Dallas is, within minutes, a searing experience in Buffalo and a painful one in Buenos Aires. An astronaut's blast-off into outer space is a moment of tension in millions of living rooms. A power failure in Toronto is a night of darkness in New York City. One man's admission to the University of Mississippi is an eventual education for thousands. A war in Vietnam is, for the Village Board of Irvington-on-Hudson, N.Y., the occasion for a resolution supporting the foreign policy of the federal government.[25] The international or national event, in short, *is* personal experience and daily life, with the result that it is increasingly difficult not to be aware of public affairs.

The culmination and success of the civil rights movement in the early 1960s constitute the immediate historical circumstance that leads us to believe that events have conjoined to initiate a trend toward more active citizenship between elections. Education provided an increased capacity for attentiveness and the shrinkage factor fostered a greater motivation to be attentive, but there still was lacking an expanded basis for confidence that utilization of the new talents and expression of the new motives would justify the time and energy required. This the civil rights episode supplied in a vivid way. The relationship between citizenship activity and the new civil rights legislation in 1964 and 1965 was unmistakable to anyone who followed the course of public affairs. As a result, we would argue that what has aptly been called "subjective political competence"[26] — the belief that through active citizenship one can evoke a response from government and thereby affect the course of events — was given an enormous nationwide lift. Not only did the prolonged and widespread resort to nonviolent techniques of protest produce a visible readiness on the part of federal officials to press for the adoption of remedial civil rights legislation, but it also legitimized the conviction that the individual citizen could contribute to the out-

[23]*New York Times*, August 1, 1965, p. 63.
[24]Steiner, *The People Look at Television*, p. 126.
[25]*New York Times*, December 3, 1965, p. 3.
[26]Almond and Verba, *The Civic Culture*, Chap. 8.

come of the policy-making process. At what other time in modern American history has active citizenship seemed so efficacious as it did when demonstrations in Birmingham served as the immediate impetus for President Kennedy's submission of a greatly broadened civil rights bill to Congress in June 1963; when the House Judiciary Committee approved the bill within two months after the "March on Washington" in August 1963; when a vast letter-writing campaign was followed by the defeat of a Senate filibuster and passage of the bill in May-June 1964; and when demonstrations in Selma preceded President Johnson's request for and Congress's acceptance of new voting rights legislation in the spring of 1965? These developments, moreover, were accompanied by a less spectacular but no less successful effort on the part of the peace movement to provide support for the nuclear test-ban treaty, which was ratified by more than two-thirds of the Senate in September 1963.

Officials, events seemed to be saying, are more accessible than ever. Communications do reach them and do produce reactions. Indeed, President Kennedy even spoke explicitly of his accessibility when asked at a news conference whether a "Women Strike for Peace" demonstration in front of the White House was useful: "I saw the ladies myself [through the window]. I recognized why they were here. There were a great number of them. It was in the rain. I understood what they were trying to say, and, therefore, I considered that their message was received."[27] To be sure, the civil rights movement still has many goals to realize and the peace movement has found success more elusive in the Vietnam crisis, but, nevertheless, the fact that officialdom can be responsive has been established for the present generation.

One type of evidence that leads us to cite the civil rights movement as a source of increased attentiveness to public affairs is the intensity of subsequent controversies and the techniques used to wage them. Many of the issues that have arisen since the 1964–1965 successes of the civil rights movement appear to be marked by the same intense involvement and the use of the same forms of protest as were characteristic of the public's participation in the civil rights debate. We would contend, for example, that it is no mere coincidence that the debate on the Vietnam situation from 1965 to the present has involved numbers of people and reached peaks

of intensity through picketing, rallying, letter-writing, and other methods of communicating support or dissent that have no parallel in the foreign policy area. The ambiguous nature of that war and its escalation are no doubt especially conducive to controversy, but this is hardly a sufficient explanation for the breadth and depth of the debate. The Korean War, which was also undeclared and conducted in a distant Asian land for limited purposes and with modern weapons and pinpoint bombing, was certainly not marked by domestic controversy as heated and pervasive as that which has accompanied every stage of the Vietnam conflict. Since the methods of protest and counterprotest in regard to Vietnam are so similar to those introduced in the civil rights episode, it seems reasonable to explain at least a part of the controversy over Vietnam in terms of an expansion of subjective political competence among the citizenry.[28]

Nor, it must be stressed, has the contagion of the civil rights episode been confined to the issue of Vietnam. In the New York area alone, for example, the months immediately following the enactment of civil rights legislation witnessed a march by 4,000 postal workers demanding pay increases,[29] a protest by 35 elderly women who demonstrated against the extension of Interstate Highway 287 through historic sites by ensconcing themselves in the bulldozer's shovel,[30] a threatened boycott of classes by City College students opposing a proposal to introduce tuition fees,[31] and a sit-in by 400 residents of Mount Vernon who objected to the rebuild-

[27]New York Times, January 16, 1962, p. 18 (brackets in the original).
[28]A good case in point is the large extent to which the American clergy have protested U.S. policy in Vietnam. Quite apart from the traditional pacifism that has marked a small segment of the clergy for decades, reaction to the conflict in Vietnam has been manifest among thousands of clergymen throughout the country. Indeed, the National Emergency Committee of Clergy Concerned About Vietnam had 145 local chapters within a month after it was organized. That this activation of the clergy arose out of an expanded subjective political competence acquired earlier in the decade is readily apparent in the following explanation of the changed behavior: "The most important immediate cause of the current wave of protests has been the civil rights movement. In the period following the Freedom Rides of 1961 large numbers of churchmen got their first taste of leadership in a major social movement. Their success, which surprised many, prompted radical rethinking of their role as clergymen and led to the present mood of 'stand up and be counted.'" Edward B. Fiske, "War and the Clergy," New York Times, February 15, 1966, p. 2.
[29]New York Times, July 24, 1965, p. 19.
[30]Ibid., May 25, 1965, p. 43.
[31]Ibid., November 14, 1965, p. 58.

ing of the outmoded Cross County Parkway into a superhighway.[32]

One meaning of all these diverse activities seems clear: whatever guidance ideologies may have provided in the past, the present is marked by attentiveness to specific issues and sensitivity to their boundaries. Technological change, the very factor that rendered ideological frameworks obsolete, has also equipped some citizens with the capacity to discriminate and the motivation to follow events in the nuclear age. Thus overriding precepts have given way to issue boundaries as bases for approaching public affairs. Unable to fall back on grandiose value systems that provide the judgments to be made about any situation, but at the same time better able and more inclined to assess situations, members of the Attentive Public are readier to seek comprehension and evaluation of issues in their own terms. Where an all-encompassing system of thought may have once served to guide them through the maze of never-ending problems that mark local, national, and international life, now they rely on several belief systems, each of which is internally consistent and independent of any other. Rather than adhering to a "conservative" or "liberal" philosophy, the attentive citizen has, among others, a civil rights philosophy, a war-peace philosophy, and a resource utilization philosophy. What a member of the literary fraternity has said about his colleagues can also readily be used to describe active persons in a variety of professions: "Not many writers are today really more interested in a worked-out political ideology or large-scale political involvement than they were, say, in 1960, yet on a series of specific political-moral issues, they do respond with vigor and sometimes passion."[33]

The present-day member of the Attentive Public, in other words, does not move erratically from issue to issue, searching for meaning in a complex world, but rather he makes his peace with complexity by accepting it and fragmenting it into manageable issue-areas. The quick shifts in attention that some view as disoriented and anomic are thus, for members of the Attentive Public, no more than pragmatic adjustment to the fast-moving pace of events. In the words of one member, "I am quite crisis- and issue-oriented."[34]

This is not to deny, of course, that some members of the Attentive Public possess such crude ideas about public affairs that they are unable to sustain their membership after an issue that engaged their simplistic value structure wanes. Indeed, elsewhere we have noted that the Attentive Public consists, at any moment in time, of a permanent core of multi-issue members and a number of single-issue persons whose identity is continuously changing as the rise of new issues and the attenuation of old ones activate and dissolve corresponding attention groups.[35] Obviously our theory of issue-area attentiveness does not account for the temporary and fluctuating presence of the latter among the Attentive Public. The evidence that the less a person participates in public affairs the more his attitudes toward them are likely to be simplistic and unstable is too persuasive for us to identify them as more than momentary members of the Attentive Public. What we have been discussing, however, are the multi-issue citizens who have a broad-gauged and consistent concern about public affairs. It is they whom we envision as equipped with complex belief systems and as emerging in greater numbers from the educational upsurge, the shrinkage factor, and the experiences of the early 1960s.

Our theory has one other main component —namely, an hypothesis about the process by which the increased capacity for attentiveness acquired through education interacts with the greater subjective competence acquired through experience. Thus far the analysis has tended to presume that the former precedes and facilitates the latter. Now we need to make explicit our hypothesis that the reverse process is also operative and that the interaction between education and experience is mutually reinforcing. That is, it seems reasonable to expect that for some persons the experience of developing a philosophy to cope with events in one issue-area heightens subjective political competence and thereby encourages the further development and articulation of philosophies that are appropriate to other areas. Attentiveness thus tends to sustain itself. It becomes, as it were, a habit—at least it becomes habitual for those whose objective and subjective competence has reached a point at which they are able to discriminate is-

[32]*Ibid.*, May 19, 1965, p. 1.
[33]Irving Howe, "The Writer Can't Keep to His Attic," *New York Times Magazine*, December 5, 1965, p. 44.
[34]Sally Cook, an activist student at the University of Chicago, quoted in the *New York Times*, September 5, 1965, p. 45.
[35]Rosenau, *Citizenship Between Elections* (mimeographed, 1967), Chap. 1.

sue boundaries and to overcome the paralyzing temptations of simplistic generalizations.

The habit-forming nature of attentiveness is a central feature of our theory because it suggests that not every person who enters the Attentive Public on a single-issue and temporary basis will necessarily return to a condition of apathy as the problem that engaged his attention passes from the scene. Such a return may well mark the behavior of the vast majority of any attention group, but for a few citizens—those whose educational attainments and tolerance for complexity are sufficient to sustain a multi-issue concern about the course of events—the experience of a single issue may serve as the basis for new citizenship habits. In attentiveness, as in everything else, one has to begin somewhere, and for some individuals the initial impetus toward permanent membership in the Attentive Public may be provided by a "big" issue that momen-

tarily breaks down the habits underlying apathy. Each major crisis of public affairs, in other words, may leave in its wake a residue of new multi-issue recruits to the Attentive Public. If dynamic national leaders can bring about the politicization of citizens, so can momentous national issues. More specifically, just as the appeal and style of a Woodrow Wilson, a Franklin Roosevelt, an Adlai Stevenson, or a John Kennedy appear to have enlarged the Attentive Public by heightening the salience of public affairs, so may the Cuban missile crisis and the Vietnam conflict have served to solidify the habit of attentiveness for many citizens. Indeed, as we have already suggested, the civil rights episode probably accomplished more in this regard than the combined efforts of all the national leaders and organizations who have sought to generate active citizenship between elections in the last fifty years.

THE PRESS, THE PUBLIC, AND FOREIGN POLICY
Bernard C. Cohen

The relationships among public opinions and attitudes on foreign policy questions, the nature and extent of coverage of these in the mass media, and the decisions actually taken regarding them by responsible government officials are not only complex; they are not even well understood.

In the selection that follows, Professor Cohen explores some of the relationships between treatment of foreign policy issues by the press and public opinion in this field. As in the case of the preceding selection by Professor Rosenau, his point of departure is the differentiation between the mass public, the attentive public, and the elite, as originally suggested by Gabriel Almond. It is interesting that both men focus their attention on the attentive public.

It is perhaps worth noting in passing that while considerable research has been devoted to the various ways in which the press affects foreign policy, relatively little attention has so far been given to the impact of television. The possible significance and uniqueness of the latter medium have been underscored by the war in Vietnam, literally brought into the households of millions of Americans via the evening news.

At a number of points in the preceding chapters we have referred to aspects of the problem

of foreign policy judgment and decision-making by public audiences in the light of low-volume, discontinuous, *post hoc* coverage of foreign affairs in the American press. Here we shall confront more directly the significance of foreign policy coverage for the non-governmental side of the foreign policy-making process, beginning with the notions of the relationship of press to public and to foreign policy that prevail among practicing journalists.

The belief among newspapermen that the citizen's requirement for more and more information about public affairs must be met by wider and wider distribution of news and opinion has its source as much in the historical development of the American newspaper as in the independent elaboration of a democratic political ideology. In the first half of the nineteenth century, the conditions of newspaper publishing favored journals of limited circulation, which were aimed at small and specialized communities of interest. It was only in the latter half of the century that a developing technology and an in-

From The Press, The Public and Foreign Policy, in *The Press and Foreign Policy* by Bernard C. Cohen (Copyright © 1963 by Princeton University Press; Princeton Paperback, 1965). Reprinted by permission of Princeton University Press.
Ed. note: Some footnotes have been omitted.

creasing urbanization made possible the larger journal that "synthesized the newspaper-reading audience by appealing in a single paper to a wide range of interests."[1] Once the process was under way, competitive pressures sustained it; the increasing investment that newspapers represented in plant and in news-gathering facilities necessitated increased advertising revenues, which in turn meant that newspapers had to appeal to larger and larger publics by including in one inexpensive paper all the subjects and features that separate audiences had hitherto found in specialized publications. The big city newspaper had acquired much of its present form by the last quarter of the nineteenth century, and set the model for the papers in the rest of the country.[2]

One result of this homogenization of the newspaper was the homogenization of the concept of the newspaper reader; the special interests of special readers were substantially lost in the adaptation of the newspaper to the interests, standards, and pastimes of a mass public that was lightly educated and in the market for diversion and amusement. Foreign affairs, a special subject that would have been easy to handle in the era of special-audience newspapers, came to public attention just at the time when the newspaper had successfully absorbed all areas and all subjects. The means of giving it wide public distribution were thus at hand when the movement for more democratic control of foreign policy spread in the early twentieth century. The juncture of these two phenomena further strengthened the image held by journalists (and others) of an undifferentiated mass audience for foreign affairs who should be and could be reached by foreign affairs coverage in the newspapers and, once reached, would be an unparalleled force, by virtue of its informed opinions, for wisdom and peace in the conduct of foreign policy.

In its capacity to withstand the direct and indirect assaults that have been made on this image in the years since it took clear shape, the American press has demonstrated not only its resilience but also its insensitivity to insight and knowledge. One of the earliest and most enduring attacks came from a young journalist; Walter Lippmann brilliantly dissected the theoretical premises underlying the role of the press in the public life of the American democracy, arguing that "It is not possible to assume that a world carried on by division of labor and distribution of authority, can be governed by univer-

sal opinions in the whole population. . . . Acting upon everybody for thirty minutes in twenty-four hours, the press is asked to create a mystical force called Public Opinion that will take up the slack in public institutions."[3] The burden of Lippmann's criticism has been supported in recent years by the main lines of social science research in the field of mass communications, and also in the specific area of public opinion and foreign policy. This research has pointed to the differentiation in exposure and receptivity of individuals to communications on various subjects, and has stressed the connections between this communications behavior and political, social, and psychological variables. This line of inquiry in the communications field, focusing also on the different political and social roles of various audiences, has invaded modern schools of journalism and their affiliated research institutions as well as their professional journals; yet it has not made much of a dent in the public philosophy of practicing journalists in the foreign affairs field, who seem to possess only the vaguest and most fragmentary notions of whom they are writing for, and the uses that this audience makes of their work But what are the essential facts of the situation, and what do they suggest by way of alternative possibilities on the part of the press? How much is read, and by whom?

We noted in an earlier chapter that the volume of international news was a small proportion of total news space in most newspapers, and that it was small in absolute terms as well. And we indicated then that if little foreign affairs news was published, even less was read, on the average (a most important qualification). The extent of such readership is suggested in the American Institute of Public Opinion's readership survey of 51 newspapers, conducted for the International Press Institute; of the daily average of 106 column inches of international news from home and abroad that was published, the average number of column inches actually read by adult readers came to 12, or about a half a column. It was further estimated that only two and one-third minutes were devoted to reading this material.[4] Other studies suggest the same

[1]Bernard A. Weisberger, The American Newspaperman, p. 89.
[2]Ibid., esp. chaps. 3 and 4.
[3]Walter Lippmann, Public Opinion, p. 274.
[4]The Flow of the News, pp. 62–63.

general pattern of over-all readership of foreign affairs news.[5]

These figures are likely to dismay anyone who is intensely interested in international affairs and who shares a philosophic concern for extensive public participation in foreign policy-making. They are also confusing to newspaper people, who often overlook the fact that these data represent an *average* of very different levels of interest in and exposure to foreign affairs news. The reactions of the press, in the face of this kind of evidence, are manifested in a continuing "debate" over who is to blame for the situation: the public, the newspapers, or both. One point of view claims that the reader sets the pace, that popular demand will not support greater coverage or more analytical content, and that the comparatively low volume of foreign affairs news in American newspapers represents the editor's normal response to lack of reader interest. A United Nations reporter, for example, said, ". . . I don't absolve reporters, editors and publishers and networks entirely of blame in this matter, but they cannot go beyond what the public demands."[6] And a columnist explained why foreign correspondents write material that does not get into the papers: "It goes back to exactly the same thing we've been talking about—the American people are too distracted, too busy, too indifferent. They don't want it."[7] This side of the debate has been able to introduce, as evidence to support its claim, the results of public opinion polls showing that the public is substantially satisfied with the existing amount of foreign affairs coverage in its newspapers, and is unwilling to see local or national news reduced in order to give more space to foreign news.[8]

In view of the strength of their conviction that the reader determines the character and amount of foreign affairs news that is published, it is interesting that so few newspaper people acknowledge the inconsistencies that it gives rise to: in particular, the common situation wherein the newspaper gives the reader only a minimal dose of foreign affairs news, on the ground that he is not interested in the subject and will not take any more of it, and then puts that small dose on the front page and in lead positions (in line with the recommendations of the wire service budgets), where it presumably responds to what editors refer to as "the public's news values." This circumstance points to the role of the press in forcing foreign policy material to the forefront of policy attention even though the large majority of the population would be as happy to see it sink into oblivion—and indeed immediately consigns it there. It is in this sense that the press should be seen as a significant part of the public audience for foreign policy, a creator of a structure of policy attention that has a very limited additional public audience and may never even be recorded in the mind of the *average* newspaper reader.

The contrary position in this argument is that the state of foreign affairs coverage, and therefore of readership, reflects editorial choices, and hence that editors and publishers rather than readers are responsible for the current conditions of coverage. News from Latin America provides a current case study of a situation in which the blame for the lack of material in the press is assigned, explicitly or implicitly, to the editors. Barrett and Kimball quote a UPI general news manager, Earl J. Johnson, who said: "After more than 20 years of pushing Latin American news on the wires, I've concluded that very few editors are really interested. Much is said at inter-American press meetings about the importance of printing more news from Latin American countries. But not much is done about it when the North American delegates return to their desks."[9] An Associated Press house organ recently raised the question, "Is there a gap between what managing editors tell us they want and what their papers actually print? . . . Recently Max Harrelson spent two weeks in Canada, then wrote a five-part series on Canada-U.S. relations. William L. Ryan put in two months on a Latin American tour. . . . Harrelson's series was used in 11 of 40 AMs [morning papers] checked. Two articles by

[5]Cf. Alfred O. Hero's canvass of the literature, *Mass Media and World Affairs*, Boston, World Peace Foundation, 1959, pp. 80–81.
[6]Pauline Frederick, NBC reporter, in UMBS series: "The United Nations Reporter."
[7]Marquis Childs, in *ibid.*: "The Foreign Correspondent."
[8]See, e.g., results of AIPO polls conducted for the International Press Institute between February 16 and May 18, 1953, as reported in *The Flow of the News*, p. 58: "Would you like to have your newspaper reduce the amount of local or national news in order to give you more foreign news?" Would—8 per cent; would not—78 per cent; no opinion—14 per cent. Thomas A. Bailey, in *The Man in the Street*, New York, Macmillan Co., 1948, p. 306, reports comparable results (but no figures) in a 1946 poll.
[9]Edward W. Barrett and Penn T. Kimball, "The Role of the Press and Communications" in American Assembly, *The United States and Latin America*, Columbia University, 1959, p. 96; Johnson's AP counterpart said much the same thing.

Ryan from Brazil showed in 14 of 50 AMs. . . ."[10] Leo Rosten candidly put the responsibility on the editors, with the argument that "giving the public what it wants" is another way of saying "what we [i.e., the editors] *say* the public wants."[11] Another important and familiar claim on this side of the debate is that the average reader is actually a lot more interested in foreign affairs than he is given credit for, and that his disinclination to read foreign affairs material in the press is due to the complexity of the material that is presented to him. The burden of altering this situation is thus transferred to reporters and editors, who are challenged, in Lester Markel's words, to present foreign news "in terms that are correct, concise and, above all, clear."[12]

Finally, there are others who are frankly puzzled over the location of responsibility, or who regard it as a "vicious circle," with both parties equally at fault. Thus, "Newspapers do not emphasize foreign affairs because the people are not interested, and the people are not interested because they do not find much foreign news in their papers."[13] This position is no doubt closest to the truth in the sense that the pattern of coverage is a response to perceived interests and priorities at both ends of the line. When the editor fails to draw attention to a subject because the prevailing news judgments give priority to other topics, then the majority of readers who are only marginally interested are not persuaded that it is important enough to read; and the editor in turn looks at the readership figures and draws justifiable conclusions about what people are reading. But the vulnerable part of this chain of reasoning, and of the whole argument, is the failure of the vast majority of reporters and editors to differentiate among their readers[14] — to understand that some of the public *will* read more foreign affairs news if it is offered to them, even though there may be no new recruits to the over-all readership ranks of foreign affairs news. What patterns of readership are involved here?

Readership of foreign affairs news is a poorly understood subject despite the attention that has been paid to the problem of audience analysis in communications research. One reason for this is that efforts to delineate the audience structure of the media of mass communication have rarely focused explicitly on foreign affairs news as a classification of newspaper content. Another reason for the uncertainties is that the

available data are apparently misleading, in the sense that they appear to overstate both the extent and the depth of newspaper reading in the foreign affairs field. To ask a sample of respondents where they get their information about foreign news events,[15] and to learn that between 44 and 50 per cent of the respondents get most of their foreign affairs information from newspapers and a similar proportion from the electronic media, implies a level of exposure and information-seeking that exaggerates the true state of affairs.[16] Similarly, to learn that "For their news on foreign affairs, more than 90 per cent of the population depends principally on . . . the radio and the daily newspaper,"[17] or even that about 90 per cent of the population reads a daily newspaper, is also suggestive of a much higher state of exposure to the news in it than is actually the case. Studies of communities deprived of newspapers in the course of strikes make the point that newspapers fulfill social and psychological functions more often than intellectual or intelligence functions, even when readers express their loss in terms of missing "what is going on in the world."[18] A more accurate impression of the extent of readership of

[10]Associated Press, "AP Log," March 2–8, 1961.
[11]Leo Rosten, The Washington Correspondents, p. 268.
[12]Lester Markel, "The Flow of the News to Marilyn Monroe," Problems of Journalism, 1960, p. 77.
[13]Martin Kriesberg, "Dark Areas of Ignorance," in Lester Markel, ed., Public Opinion and Foreign Policy, New York, Harper and Bros., 1949, p. 62. Barrett and Kimball cite Herbert Matthews of the New York Times on "the vicious circle of Latin American coverage. . . . The failure to provide the news perpetuates the ignorance of the reader, and this ignorance leads to the lack of interest." (Op. cit., p. 87.)
[14]In Chapter IV we noted that some correspondents expressed an awareness that they were writing for a less-than-mass market, but that on the whole, apart from a handful of newspapers and correspondents, this had little impact on foreign affairs reporting.
[15]Cf. surveys by NORC and AIPO, the former quoted in Paul Lazarsfeld and Patricia Kendall, Radio Listening in America, New York, Prentice-Hall, 1948, p. 34, the latter in The Flow of the News, p. 58, both of which are cited in Theodore Kruglak, The Foreign Correspondents, p. 41n.
[16]Cf., e.g., the data of this kind on p. 58 of The Flow of the News, and the data showing the low levels of information actually held by readers, on the pages immediately following.
[17]Cf. Martin Kriesberg, "Dark Areas of Ignorance," in Markel, ed., Public Opinion and Foreign Policy, p. 60.
[18]Bernard Berelson, "What 'Missing the Newspaper' Means," reprinted from Paul Lazarsfeld and Frank N. Stanton, eds., Communications Research, 1948–1949, in Wilbur Schramm, ed., The Process and Effects of Mass Communications; Charles F. Cannell and Harry Sharp, "The Impact of the 1955–56 Detroit Newspaper Strike," Journalism Quarterly, XXXV, No. 1, Winter 1958, pp. 26–35; Penn T. Kimball, "People Without Papers," Public Opinion Quarterly, XXIII, No. 2, Fall 1959, pp. 389–98.

international news is suggested by data from a survey in Albany, New York, in 1949.[19] Forty-seven per cent of the respondents read "just the headlines" of the national and international news, 4 per cent did not read even that much, and another 4 per cent read "not much more than headlines." At the other end of the spectrum, 6 per cent claimed to read both kinds of news "very carefully," and another 1 per cent read international news carefully, but not national news. In the middle, 33 per cent picked and chose among items, and "sometimes read carefully, sometimes not." V. O. Key's interpretation of these data is that "Day in and day out the odds are that less than 10 per cent of the adult population could be regarded as careful readers of the political news,"[20] and one would have to knock a few percentage points off even that figure for news of foreign affairs.

Who are these few careful readers? They seem to be the same few people who show up as well-informed on repeated surveys of information on international affairs, the people whom Gabriel Almond called the "elites" and the "attentive public."[21] Readership of foreign affairs news increases with age, education, and economic status; with an increase in these variables, the newspaper is used increasingly for information and decreasingly for entertainment; more men than women read such news; the larger the community (counting suburbs as part of metropolitan areas), the higher the interest in and readership of international events. Basically, however, it is educational level and socio-economic status that seem to be the best predictors of newspaper readership of foreign affairs.[22]

The significance of all this is generally missed by newpapermen, many of whom tend to think that the market for foreign affairs news can be — and should be — enlarged by techniques of simplifying the news and making it more attractive, or even by providing more of it. But an individual's exposure to foreign policy communication and his interest in international affairs that directs that exposure are concomitants of attitudes that have deep roots in his psychological orientations and his social setting. And so long as this is the case, the important variables in determining interest and participation in foreign affairs and exposure to information on the subject will be found chiefly in the life patterns of individuals, in the things that are relevant to their perceptions of and orientations to the political universe, and only marginally in such ephemeral things as the way foreign affairs stories are written for the newspapers, the amount of pictorial or human-interest content in them, and so forth. These relevant variables change slowly, and they are not readily amenable to modification by the stream of information the very exposure to which they in fact regulate. Consequently, the hope that the audience can be expanded significantly by a greatly simplified discussion of foreign affairs is illusory. It is no doubt true that most newspaper readers find foreign affairs news rather complicated and difficult to understand, but it does not necessarily follow that their interest would be stimulated if the material were presented in more simplified ways or more abundantly. It is equally likely that their basic disinterest in the material contributes to their impression of its difficulty. Furthermore, even if the hope were not illusory, even if one could succeed in attracting substantially larger numbers of readers to a discussion of foreign affairs that has been simplified by the use of pictures and one-syllable words, leavened with human interest, and related to everyday life on Main Street, the degree of simplification involved would be so great as to cause some doubt whether there would be any net increase in the capacity of the American people to understand and think through the undeniably complex issues of international relations. In other words, simplification might succeed in drawing a new audience, but to material that is so far from reflecting difficult international political realities as they confront responsible statesmen that it has no politically relevant public opinion uses.

[19]Survey Research Center, *Interest, Information, and Attitudes in the Field of World Affairs*, Ann Arbor, Mich., 1949; these data are reproduced in V. O. Key, Jr., *Public Opinion and American Democracy*, as Table 14.5, p. 352.

[20]Key, op. cit., p. 353. He also suggests the importance that should be attached to headlines over national and international news stories, when that is all that half the people read; the suggestion is made via a reference to Percy H. Tannenbaum, "The Effect of Headlines on the Interpretation of News Stories," *Journalism Quarterly*, XXX, No. 2, Spring 1953, pp. 189-97.

[21]Gabriel Almond, *The American People and Foreign Policy*, New York, Frederick Praeger, 1960.

[22]Cf. Wilbur Schramm and David M. White, "Age, Education, and Economic Status as Factors in Newspaper Reading," reprinted from *Journalism Quarterly*, XXVI, No. 2, June 1949, in Schramm, ed., *Mass Communications*, pp. 438-50; and Hero, op.cit., esp. chap. 4, "Newspapers and World-Affairs Communications," which summarizes much of the literature on this subject. See also Key, op.cit., and Kenneth P. Adler and Davis Bobrow, "Interest and Influence in Foreign Affairs," *Public Opinion Quarterly*, XX, No. 1, Spring 1956, pp. 89-101.

Since the available evidence suggests that the chief market for foreign affairs coverage in the American press is a small policy and opinion elite, and a somewhat larger attentive public whose personal characteristics and interests are much the same as those of the policy and opinion elite, though their roles are not so specialized, it is important to think about foreign affairs coverage in terms of its relevance and usefulness for the professional and personal interests and needs of this audience. This argues for a quantitative and qualitative improvement, an up-grading, of foreign policy news and comment, rather than the down-grading that is implicit in the attempt to attract new people into the audience. What this up-grading would mean for reporters and editors we shall explore further in the next chapter. But two problems immediately arise in connection with such a suggestion, and should be disposed of first: the philosophical problem wrapped up in "the people's right to know," and the practical problem of ensuring the survival of newspapers and even cultivating their prosperity through mass circulation.

Let us consider the latter first. The present endeavors of reporters and editors represent a compromise between the foreign policy interests of a few and the news values or tastes of a mass audience that "ought" to be interested in foreign affairs but presumably has to be seduced into reading about them. The practical effect is that the specialists and the attentive few are thus drawing and depending heavily on material written for a mass market that is relatively indifferent to the effort made on its behalf. This compromise is clearly not to the taste of any of the parties involved. Those who are steady consumers of foreign affairs news are dissatisfied with the daily fare they get in almost all American newspapers, to judge from the comments of foreign policy officials and of Congressmen, from the running criticism of the press in intellectual circles, and from the 8 per cent of the population who would like to see newspapers reduce the amount of local or national news in order to make more space for foreign news.[23] The large majority that rarely or never looks at foreign affairs news is most likely neutral towards its presence, in the sense that it is merely something these people walk around; but their non-readership is itself a good measure of their preference for other kinds of newspaper content.

It is possible to conceive of ways to satisfy the needs or preferences of a small audience for a higher order of foreign policy intelligence without raising the costs of publication, and without changing the character of a newspaper in ways that might alienate the larger numbers of non-readers — granting, however, that we do not even know what kind or proportions of material would give offense to people who do not read it.[24] The important obstacle, it would seem, has been thinking about this problem in the context of the customary shape and format of the daily newspaper. But there is no reason why larger amounts and different kinds of foreign affairs content, whatever its sources, need take up more front-page space than at present, or be reflected more often in the dominant headlines. Since it would be meant to serve a specialized audience, it could be handled like other materials that have few customers, like financial news or shipping news (or even materials like comics and sports that have many customers!): whatever was not deemed important by conventional standards could be put in an unobtrusive place without much regard for format, headlines, and the other trappings of "news." It is possible in this way to think of substantially increasing the amount of foreign affairs information in the average newspaper without changing the overall identity of the newspaper and with only a very marginal increase in the costs of production.

Since such an endeavor would take nothing away from the present exposure of the general public to foreign affairs news, there could be no complaint about it on philosophical grounds that cannot already be leveled at the mass media. Despite the low level of attentiveness to problems of foreign policy and the low priority given them by the public at large, one can justify the general order of importance that the press attaches to a few foreign policy questions on the ground that it is important to pretend that everybody is listening — that acting *as if* foreign affairs were of widespread public interest has important consequences in the realm of public confidence in the basic actions of government. This particular function, however, can no doubt continue to be served by the present (comparatively small) allocation of front-page foreign affairs news, thus permitting us to think about addi-

[23]See fn. 8, *supra*.
[24]As we pointed out earlier, there is no satisfactory evidence on what makes a paper succeed or fail, so far as the amount of space it devotes to international affairs is concerned. For the argument that "a publisher with the necessary resources and talents who wishes to run a paper with serious international content may make a go of it even in relatively 'unfavorable' communities," see Hero, *op.cit.*, p. 101.

tional coverage more in terms of the particular needs of particular audiences. In any case, since there is considerable evidence that much of the information on world affairs currently at the disposal of the general public comes to it not directly from the media but at one remove or more, via people who have a greater interest in the subject and expose themselves to mass media discussions of it,[25] any alternative that increases the flow of information and analysis to these primary consumers should result in a subsequent larger flow to *their* secondary audience. Thus the broad political-philosophical purposes of press coverage of foreign affairs can be served by additional news that is directed primarily towards its few direct and heavy readers than to its many marginal scanners.

Further support for this argument stems from the point, made earlier, that the press is itself one of the most important components in the public audience for foreign affairs. From this point of view, greater press responsiveness to foreign policy developments and problems of foreign affairs, even in the form of specialized inside-page coverage of them, would inherently enlarge the scope of interaction between the government and its foreign policy public. Hence, increased coverage and more substantial analysis of more specialized problems as well as of issues already "in the news" would be an

important contribution to democratic foreign policy-making even if this material were read only by foreign policy officials and a small group of attentive citizens. At its best, it might narrow the range within which major miscalculations in policy might be made as a consequence of insufficient exploration of alternatives and their implications within the confines of a bureaucratic structure, and as a consequence of insufficient interchange of value premises and preferences among policy officials and articulate people on the outside. The history of America's China policy after the Second World War should stand as a vivid reminder of the things that can happen when the political interests of outside publics have not been engaged in policy discussion and formulation.

But a problem still confronts us. There are also many historical examples of rigidities introduced into foreign policy when the political interests of outside publics *have* been engaged—for instance, America's China policy after the Korean War. This reminds us that wide public participation is not the only criterion of a good foreign policy, or the automatic guarantee of one.

[25]See Key's summary of the literature on these propositions, *op.cit.*, pp. 359–66; in addition, see Elihu Katz, "The Two-Step Flow of Communication," *Public Opinion Quarterly*, XXI, No. 1, Spring 1957, pp. 61–78.

FOREIGN AID AND AMERICAN POLITICAL CULTURE
Michael Kent O'Leary

One of the more mystifying phenomena of American foreign policy has been the apparent ambivalence of the American public, and the American Congress as well, regarding American foreign aid programs. Supporters of foreign aid cite a continuing series of public opinion polls that indicate broad public support for foreign aid. At the same time, senators and representatives presumably well tuned to the grass roots seem to get the message of increasing public resistance to foreign aid expenditures. Indeed, the ambivalence is reflected in increasingly large cuts in economic and military aid budgets while at the same time a considerable variety of American aid efforts continue to go on from year to year.

Professor O'Leary provides an interesting analysis of the American political attitudes that seem to have these contradictory policy implications and consequences. He also suggests how general notions about the American character can be translated into more specific, politically relevant terms.

We can best begin to appreciate American thinking about foreign aid by considering the general cultural and ideological environment in which public judgments and evaluations are made. Foreign policy is physically and psychologically remote from most people. Events are so complex and obscure that detailed understanding is beyond the capabilities of all but the expert. As a substitute for sufficient knowledge most people, occasionally even experts, will interpret events in terms analogous to their own experiences, their own traditions, and their own previously established judgments of right and wrong in matters of public policy. We laugh at the sign, "My mind is made up, don't confuse me with facts." Yet this is a slogan we all follow to some degree in making comprehensible an otherwise intolerably complex and uncertain world. We fashion judgments, especially about new policies, on the basis of what we already know and believe.

Our concern with the cultural underpinnings of opinion leads us to expect opinions and attitudes to be formed not so much through deliberate thought and analysis as through reactions to "images" or generalizations about foreign aid. We will investigate, in other words, the affective rather than the effective bases for judgments about foreign aid.[1]

Americans rely on three principal sets of criteria in evaluating foreign aid: whether foreign aid policies are consistent with traditional American responses to the international environment; the role of foreign aid in current diplomatic strategy; and the place of foreign aid in the area of government economic policy.

INTERNATIONALISM

It has been argued that the sentiment of the American people has historically followed well-defined alternating "moods" in the degree to which internationalist activity is favored.[2] The present is clearly a period of extroversion characterized by an initial presumption in favor of international activity. The frequently described postwar "revolution" in American foreign policy consists in part of public endorsement of increased economic, political, and military activity overseas. In opinion surveys, the public has repeatedly placed questions of war and peace and other international matters at or near the top of the list of the major problems facing this country.[3] Since the last years of World War II, approximately three-fourths of those polled have acknowledged the need for America to take an active role in world affairs.[4]

Approval has also been high for policies of economic assistance abroad. The Marshall Plan enjoyed high levels of support,[5] and even aid for economic development, the more controversial aspect of aid policy, has received more than 60 per cent approval as a *general* proposition.[6] In the press and elsewhere, most public comment presumes the need for some sort of aid, although, as we shall see, there is little consensus as to the details of an optimum foreign aid program.

The exact reasons for this internationalist outlook are not easy to determine, but perhaps a chief factor is the venerable ideal of an American "mission" throughout the rest of the world.

This attitude was born in the American Revolution and nurtured in the geographical and economic expansion of the nineteenth century. It reached an aggressive adolescence at the turn of the century and, having attained a somewhat subdued maturity since 1900, it still operates to give strength to the feeling that America can effect an uplifting of the quality of life in foreign nations. Such an attitude does not necessarily imply support for any one type of foreign policy. In some cases the notion of American uniqueness may even lead to a kind of national parochialism calling for exclusion from contacts with the benighted foreigners. But for the most part it helps create support for an activist, even aggressive, style of foreign policy.

The concept of mission has included a strong dose of humanitarianism, a component which lends support to certain forms of foreign aid. The strength of this idealism and humanitarianism can be surprising. On two occasions in 1943 over 80 per cent of survey respondents indicated a willingness to remain on the despised rationing system for another five years, ". . . to help feed the starving people in other countries."[7] In 1959, 73 per cent of poll respondents approved an idea to create a "Great White Fleet" of unused Navy vessels fitted out "as hospital ships, food supply ships, training schools and the like" for the benefit of poorer nations.[8] In March 1966, 61 per cent of a survey named building hospitals, training nurses and doctors, and providing medicine as the kinds of foreign aid which they favored most.[9]

Coupled with humanitarianism as a motivating force in the American missionary ideal is the belief that the "American way of life" —however variously that may be defined—can

[1]For a historian's well-balanced critique of generalizations about national opinions, see David M. Potter, *People of Plenty* (Chicago: University of Chicago Press, 1954), especially pp. 41–42. Also see V. O. Key, *Public Opinion* (New York: Knopf, 1961), pp. 49–50.
[2]Frank R. Klingberg, "The Historical Alternation of Moods in American Foreign Policy," *World Politics*, IV (January 1952), 239–273.
[3]American Institute of Public Opinion [hereinafter cited as AIPO], *Public Opinion News Service* (September 15, 1957); AIPO poll #610 (February 1959); AIPO poll #612 (March 1959); AIPO poll #616 (July 1959); AIPO poll #618 (September 1959); AIPO poll #635 (September 1960).
[4]See, for example, Key, op. cit., pp. 106–107.
[5]National Opinion Research Center, *American Programs of Foreign Aid* (February 1957), processed, pp. 2, 4 [hereinafter cited as NORC].
[6]Ibid., pp. 16, 21.
[7]Ibid., p. 2. Italics added.
[8]AIPO poll #617 (August 1959).
[9]Ibid., (March 1966).

be exported to the advantage of other nations. This feeling, based on America's self image as "a unique combination of economic power, intellectual and practical genius, and moral rigor,"[10] has contributed important, if selective, support for aid programs. It has helped lead to the high popularity of those aspects of foreign aid which involve Americans in face-to-face relations with foreigners for purposes of teaching, training, and instructing. Such a feeling helps explain the results of the 1966 poll cited earlier, in which between 61 and 65 per cent of the survey favored aid programs in the fields of education and agriculture assistance.[11] This feeling has meant continuing public support for the Point Four technical assistance component of foreign aid which was more popular, in the view of at least one government official, than even the Marshall Plan.[12]

More recently, the American dedication to spreading Americanism has led to enthusiastic support for the Peace Corps.[13] Popular approval is due in large measure to the Peace Corps' image as a means of sending abroad a host of selfless Americans to work with backward peoples and thereby, in the phrase of Sargent Shriver, the Peace Corps' first director, to "energize" activity in the host country.[14] The Peace Corps also profits from the attraction of citizen diplomacy, which has always been at least a minor theme of the patriotic missionary ideal. Indeed, the two-year limit on the tour of Peace Corps volunteers (with a slightly longer limit for the staff) is an echo from the diplomatic style of a much earlier day, when the tenets of Jacksonian democracy called for tenure of about two years in all diplomatic posts.[15]

As we look closely at the characteristics of the American missionary spirit we can see that it contains the seeds of its own negation. If most Americans, as Geoffrey Gorer has argued, consider that taking part in an international undertaking means simply "extending American activities outside the boundaries of the United States,"[16] it follows that foreigners are often expected to reciprocate with appropriately compliant behavior.

Most Americans can scarcely be said to apply close analysis to the detailed consequences of aid policy. But there is evidence that many Americans nevertheless share a general expectation that foreign aid will help "sell" or transmit Americanism abroad. In 1949 the National Opinion Research Center asked a sample of the population whether they thought foreign aid helped the United States. Those who considered aid helpful (55 per cent of the sample) were then asked to give the reasons for their opinions. Of this group, just under half gave answers classifiable as "helps us politically," which seemed to mean either that aid would make others like the United States more, or that it would make them more like the United States: "builds good will, promotes friendly feelings toward us"; "they'll be on our side in case of war"; "it's good propaganda for democracy, capitalism."[17]

Hans Morgenthau has noted the similarity between Wilsonianism and present-day thinking about foreign aid:

Wilson wanted to bring the peace and order of America to the rest of the world by exporting America's democratic institutions. His contemporary heirs want to bring the wealth and prosperity of America to the rest of the world through the export of American capital and technology.[18]

We might amend this to say that many of his contemporary heirs want to outdo Wilson by exporting political *and* economic institutions through foreign aid.

It should be easy to see how undependable is the support for foreign aid which flows from the missionary spirit. Only frustration and disappointment can result from expectations that aid recipients will mesh their foreign policy with America's, will come to resemble America in their political, economic, and social systems, or even will feel more favorably disposed to America as their benefactor.

Indications of public sensitivity to inadequate foreign responses are not difficult to find. As far

[10]William Appleman Williams, The Tragedy of American Diplomacy (Cleveland: The World Publishing Co., 1959), p. 24.
[11]AIPO poll (March 1966). The same types of aid received 85 per cent approval in an earlier survey (NORC, p. 16).
[12]Willard L. Thorp in Grayson Kirk, et al., The Changing Environment of International Relations (Washington, D.C.: The Brookings Institution, 1956), p. 118.
[13]See, for example, AIPO poll #640 (January 1961).
[14]Meet the Press, 5 (December 24, 1961), 10.
[15]Warren Frederick Ilchman, Professional Diplomacy in the United States 1779–1939 (Chicago: University of Chicago Press, 1961), p. 35.
[16]Geoffrey Gorer, The American People (New York: Norton, 1948), p. 224.
[17]NORC, pp. 7–8.
[18]Hans J. Morgenthau, The Purpose of American Politics (New York: Knopf, 1960), p. 190.

back as the late 1940s, when public support for the Marshall Plan was running between 56 per cent and 73 per cent of those interviewed, the NORC uncovered a strong undercurrent of something less than enthusiasm over Europe's own part in the recovery program. On two occasions (December 1947 and April 1949) respondents were asked whether they thought Europeans were working as hard as they could, or whether they were depending too much on the United States for help. It was felt by 64 per cent and 58 per cent of those answering, respectively, that the Europeans were overdependent on the United States.[19] Even earlier soundings of opinion had discovered the same sort of feeling. In October 1945, respondents were asked a two-part question: Should loans for recovery be made to our three wartime allies—England, Russia, and China? If loans were made, would the countries repay them? The replies demonstrated two things about public feeling: the chances for repayment were thought to be rather slim; and the sentiment in favor of such a loan to each country varied with the expectation that the country would repay, with China receiving the most favored public judgment (see Table II-1).

TABLE II-1   PUBLIC OPINION CONCERNING LOANS TO ENGLAND, RUSSIA, AND CHINA

	Expectation that a loan would be repaid		Agreement that such a loan should be made
	IN FULL	IN PART	
England	9%	36%	33%
Russia	24	34	40
China	33	34	63

SOURCE: NORC, p. 3.

The negative side of America's response to international aid was illustrated in 1949 by a poll in which those who opposed aid to underdeveloped countries were asked to give their reasons. Over 50 per cent indicated a fear that the psychological rewards of aid would be insufficient—that the recipients would not be grateful, or that aid was in itself inconsistent with American traditions of self-help and minding one's own business.[20]

A more recent example shows how this belief in a unique American mission works both for and against foreign aid. In 1961 there was a brief period of public discussion concerning the desirability of assisting the Ghanian government to build a hydroelectric dam on the Volta River. Most of this discussion, both favorable and unfavorable, was concerned scarcely at all with the economic or technical feasibility of the project. Instead, concern was expressed about the degree of democracy or dictatorship existing at the time in Ghana, and about the extent to which President Nkrumah was favorably disposed toward the Communist Bloc. Those who favored the project argued that American aid would make Ghana's politics more free and stable. Many were opposed because they wondered, with the *Philadelphia Inquirer*, if nations anywhere would see an advantage "in practicing the principles of democracy and freedom, and supporting the fight against communism," since we would be giving money to a government which did neither of these things.[21]

There is a final point about the twofold impact which the American missionary attitude has upon the support of foreign aid. Negative feelings represent much more than simply a diminution of the base for positive reactions. As an aid program departs from those characteristics which make it appear to be essentially American life transplanted abroad, the idealism becomes dampened and the missionary feeling may turn inward, rejecting foreign aid. The workings of this anti-aid syndrome can be easily summarized: Americans tend to assume that other nations want the essence of our political and economic institutions, and that they have the means to obtain them. When this anticipated "universal aspiration toward Americanism"[22] is not manifested in the nations that we help, American fears of being rejected and exploited can lead to an abandonment of international cooperation. Every deviation from American policy goals, every unfriendly gesture by Latin Americans, Africans, or Asians, becomes new justification for cutting down or eliminating aid. As Gorer has summed up this attitude, "People so perverse as to choose to remain foreign deserve no help."[23]

[19]NORC, p. 7.
[20]Ibid., p. 18.
[21]For a survey of such public discussion see Department of State, American Opinion Report (January 16, 1962).
[22]Gorer, op. cit., p. 225.
[23]Gorer, op. cit., pp. 230–231. See also Potter, op. cit., pp. 111–112; Key, op. cit., pp. 213–214; Almond, op. cit., pp. 54–68.

A second major aspect of opinion revolves around consideration of foreign aid's role in American diplomatic strategy, especially in cold-war competition with China and the Soviet Union.

Foreign aid gains support insofar as it is seen as a potent anti-Communist weapon, improving the living standards of others to make them less susceptible to communism, and as an inducement or reward for nations allying themselves with the United States against immediate or potential Communist aggression. Support for the Marshall Plan can be traced in large measure to the widespread feeling not only that American aid to Europe would help prevent the spread of communism by external aggression in Europe but also that in the absence of aid some of the domestic politics of countries would probably become dominated by Communists.[24]

The image of aid as a direct anti-Communist tool has also led to support for military assistance. A series of polls since June 1950 has shown that 60 per cent or more of the population has supported the general notion of military assistance to European and Asian allies.[25] As we shall see later, however, Americans have their doubts about military aid, too.

The view of aid as a diplomatic tool likewise fails to evoke unmixed support. The widespread simplifications involved in opinion-formation are nowhere more apparent than in the case of diplomatic strategy. If aid is to be supported as a tool against international communism, it therefore must not be used ambiguously. Thus, assistance to Communist countries, or even neutrals is highly inconsistent with the general attitudes favoring aid.

This uncertainty or even antipathy toward aid to non-allies was clearly shown in a series of 1956 polls which asked whether we should continue to aid "some countries like India, which have *not* joined us as allies against the Communists." The expressed sentiment was as much as 43–50 per cent against continuing such aid.[26]

The American approach to foreign policy commonly distrusts any sharp and basic disagreement with America's conception of world affairs, and includes an active sensitivity to being rejected or exploited by others. This is part of the reason for the extreme bitterness of newspaper and other public reaction to India's military seizure of the Portuguese territory of Goa in 1961. This action was interpreted as an anti-Western and anti-American move just a short time after Prime Minister Nehru, who had received much aid from the United States, had visited this country and had received considerable editorial sympathy.

Another reason for the difficulty of reconciling the concept of aid as a means of advancing the national interest with the policy of aid to nations which do not share American purposes is the unwillingness of the American public to accept the uncertainty of diplomacy—the persistence of its problems and the tentativeness of its opportunities. In arguing as to who should receive aid, public judgments tend toward polar extremes: if a Sukarno or an Nkrumah initiate anti-American actions, they are impossible to deal with and wholly undeserving of aid. If they make the slightest friendly gesture or, better yet, if they are overthrown, then things look much rosier in that region of the world, and the foreign aid gamble is held to be justified. The basic problem remains much the same now as when de Tocqueville, in his study of America, noted that democracy appeared "better adapted for the conduct of society in times of peace, or for a sudden effort of remarkable vigor, than for the prolonged endurance of the great [international] storms that beset the political existence of nations."[27]

For whatever reasons, the American has typically reacted in extremes to foreign policy challenges. He tends to wish to solve international problems by either unentangling precept or short-term massive intervention. This approach is applied to foreign aid as well as other foreign policies. In 1949, when sentiment was 70 per cent or more in favor of aid to underdeveloped countries, a sample of those who approved was asked if the United States should "put up some of the money for this purpose" or "just help in other ways." The division was even (46–46 per cent) between those who were willing to expend money for this purpose and those who selected the unspecified "other ways," which probably seemed less costly and less entangling.[28]

[24]NORC, pp. 5–6.
[25]*Ibid.*, pp. 12–13. But see below for some complications in the support of military assistance.
[26]NORC, p. 19; and *Minnesota Poll on Foreign Aid* (no place of publication: November 17, 1961, processed).
[27]Alexis de Tocqueville, *Democracy in America* (New York: Vintage Books, 1958), vol. I, p. 237.
[28]NORC, p. 16.

When the choice has been between economic and military aid the pattern has been similar, though more complex. Between June 1948 and December 1952, the NORC conducted seventeen polls which included questions regarding economic aid. Favorable opinion averaged 62 per cent.[29] During approximately the same period (April 1948 through June 1950) a series of questions was asked regarding military aid. Support was about ten points lower, averaging 53 per cent.[30] Similarly, on seven occasions in the 1950s, respondents were asked direct questions as to which they would prefer sending, military or economic aid. In every case economic aid was preferred over military, by margins averaging 36 per cent.[31] On the other hand, after the outbreak of the Korean War support for military aid was much higher. From July 1950 to November 1956 support for military assistance averaged 70 per cent in a series of twelve questions.[32]

In early 1966 a survey showed that the more entangling forms of aid—military assistance, road building, and assistance for capital projects such as factories—were the least popular forms of aid. These forms were chosen by an average of 24 per cent, as opposed to the most popular item, educational assistance, which was chosen by 64 per cent.[33] We are a task-oriented society, and will favor even hazardous and expensive actions if they are measurably achieving some goal. But in the absence of clear-cut goals and achievements, we are likely to limit our risks as much as possible. As V. O. Key concluded, we show a strange mixture of verbal toughness and "of the trustfulness of a delighted puppy when treated in a friendly manner."[34]

The increase in support for military assistance after the outbreak of the Korean War was not simply a shift from pacifism to blind militarism, but rather a change in the interpretation of the international situation. Previously, secondary means were thought sufficient to meet the demands of the international situation; later, both the wealth and the armed force of the United States were seen as necessary to eliminate a state of affairs intolerable because of its threat and ambiguity. It must be remembered that this proposed military assistance which received increased support was not for Asia, where fighting was taking place, but for Europe, where the need for the military was only potential.

The tendency to react in extremes can also be seen in the continuing public debate concerning aid to Communist countries such as Poland and Yugoslavia. Opponents of such aid base their case on the assertion that Poland and Yugoslavia still remain anti-American and pro-Russian in so many respects as to make them unqualified to receive our aid. Those favoring aid do so on the grounds that in the absence of our aid all is lost and that Yugoslav and Polish leaders will be forced to "go all the way back to Moscow."[35]

We can, in other words, speak of a widespread failure to appreciate that both the gains and the losses of diplomacy often are limited and temporary. Americans overestimate both the impact that aid can have on a given international situation and also the degree of change that can be expected during any short period. . . .

FOREIGN AID AS AN ECONOMIC QUESTION

Foreign aid, being to a large extent an economic policy, is also judged in terms of economic assumptions and doctrines. As already noted, some of the support which aid has received comes from the belief in the efficacy of a kind of international "full belly" policy as a barrier to the growth of communism within nations. The polls indicate that Americans associate high living standards in both Europe and Asia with low levels of communism.[36]

Economic development has been favored not only as an anti-Communist device, but also as one way in which America could export the economic aspects of Americanism—a healthy, affluent, and, most especially, free enterprise economic system. The passage of time has shown how radically this goal differs from what is, in fact, achievable. Anticipation of widespread imitation of American economic practices no longer serves to back up support for foreign aid.

Polls in the 1940s show support for aid on the basis of more narrowly conceived economic considerations. In the last year of World War II, 78 per cent of respondents agreed with the proposition that "we'll have the best chance of having prosperity in this country by helping other countries in the world get back on their feet . . ."; and 57 per cent agreed that "if our government keeps on sending lend-lease mate-

[29]Ibid., p. 9.
[30]Ibid., p. 12.
[31]Ibid., p. 15.
[32]Ibid., p. 12.
[33]AIPO poll (March 1966).
[34]Key, op. cit., pp. 213–214.
[35]Department of State, American Opinion Report (July 3, 1962).
[36]NORC, pp. 5–6, 17.

rials, which we may not get paid for, to friendly countries for about three years after the war . . . this will mean more jobs . . . for most Americans. . . ."[37] In response to open-end questions on reasons for liking the Marshall Plan after it was under way, 44 per cent of respondents who favored the Plan volunteered their expectation that it would help the United States economically.[38]

Although . . . arguments are still made in behalf of foreign aid on the basis of its favorable impact on the American economy, such arguments are now sharply challenged. It may very well be that one of the most potent arguments against foreign aid is now the economic one, in particular that aid is too expensive.

It must be pointed out that opposition to aid on the basis of cost, while important, is a secondary phenomenon. The American citizen will support the spending of his tax dollars for many different reasons — altruism, national emergency, or narrow and immediate self-interest. In the philosophical limbo in which foreign aid finds itself, no consistent clear-cut rationale has been advanced to convince any large numbers of people of the wisdom of spending several billions of dollars a year for aid.

The relative saliency of anti-foreign-aid opinions within the context of cost was demonstrated in a 1959 Gallup Poll which asked whether it was preferable to cut back on government spending or to increase taxes. To this vague proposition an unsurprising 72 per cent chose cutting back on spending. This group was then asked what things they would like to see cut back. Of a long list of activities considered expendable, foreign aid was mentioned most frequently — in 30 per cent of the cases, twice as much as the second-place item.[39] A 1949 NORC poll found that the single most frequently mentioned objection to foreign aid was the cost — especially the problems of "sending money overseas" when things needed to be done at home.[40] A 1965 survey found that three times as many people feel we are giving too much aid as feel we are not giving enough.[41]

The anti-spending component of negative attitudes about foreign aid has continued to be rather consistent over time, and is apparently independent of the changing currents of political debate. In 1959, for example, the question of whether to raise or lower the defense budget was being hotly debated in Washington. The Gallup Poll, in order to find out what the public was thinking about this issue, asked respon-

dents to note the budget items for which they thought the government should spend more or less money. In the list of things for which the government should decrease spending, defense was in third place, named by 9 per cent of respondents; leading this last was foreign aid, named by 17 per cent.[42]

On the other hand, when respondents are asked open-end questions about governmental problems *not* in the context of spending, foreign aid does not invoke the same high degree of negative response. In December 1959 the Gallup Poll asked respondents what topics they would like to discuss in letters to their congressmen. Cutting taxes (named by 14 per cent) and labor legislation (named by 10 per cent) headed this list — after the 18 per cent who knew of nothing to write. Opposition to foreign aid was far down the list, mentioned by only 2 per cent.[43]

INTERRELATIONSHIPS OF OPINION

We can now inquire about the impact on public opinion of the many contrasting images of foreign aid which might activate conflicting attitudes of the man in the street: exporting the American way of life vs. dangerous and uncertain international involvement; worthy assistance to people in need vs. undesirable governmental spending; building bulwarks against communism vs. helping nations which may seem all too friendly to communism.

Some notion of current judgments of aid may be gained from a Gallup Poll of early 1966: "In general, how do you feel about foreign aid, are you for it or against it?" A bare majority, 53 per cent, were in favor of foreign aid, 35 per cent were against it, and 12 per cent had no or uncertain opinions.[44] Earlier polls show about the same distribution of opinion, indicating the persistence of general opinion patterns.[45] This consistency of the general response, coupled with the wide swings in responses to variously worded questions, takes us back to the primary point

[37]Ibid., p. 3.
[38]*Ibid.*, p. 8.
[39]AIPO poll #609 (January 1959).
[40]NORC, p. 18.
[41]"America's Mood," *Look* (June 29, 1965).
[42]Cited in Key, *op. cit.*, p. 430. For more recent public expressions of opposition to the financial aspect of aid see *ibid.*, pp. 35, 161.
[43]AIPO poll #622 (December 1959).
[44]AIPO poll (March 1966).
[45]See AIPO poll #596 (March 1958); *ibid.*, #667 (February 1963); and *Newsweek* (August 26, 1963), p. 27. Gallup has asked about general approval of foreign aid four times since 1958, with an average favorable response of 55 per cent.

of this chapter. Foreign aid means many things, some favored and some feared. To appreciate public judgments more fully, we need to ask not only what factors influence opinion about aid, but also what their relative strengths are.

To begin with, aid benefits simply from being an internationalist policy. Some additional characteristics of aid which increase its public approval are: programs which seem to export elements of American society and values (ideological aid); programs which contain elements of humanitarianism; programs which support international allies; programs which involve few foreign entanglements; and programs which are low in cost. Conversely, other qualities of aid programs increase the likelihood of opposition: programs which aid nations that do not share the United States' view of the cold war; programs which involve relatively deep entanglement in international problems; and programs which are costly.

Predictably, positive characteristics appearing together in an aid program intensify support, while combinations of negative characteristics intensify opposition. The Marshall Plan was directed toward a group of familiar countries which increasingly came to be thought of as allies vis-à-vis the Communist world; Marshall aid also had a more or less definite price tag and fairly well-defined goals and time limit. Aid to underdeveloped nations, on the other hand, is directed toward a host of unfamiliar peoples and societies whose international loyalties are uncertain at best, and is of open-ended cost, uncertain ends, and indefinite duration.

Specific poll questions bear this out. In 1955 and 1956 the NORC asked a series of questions concerning economic aid. These questions sought opinion on the economic, and therefore relatively unentangling, form of aid and also aid to "countries that have agreed to stand with us against Communist aggression," thereby stressing two of the positive factors mentioned above. The average rate of approval for this type of aid was 83 per cent. At the same time the respondents were asked about giving economic aid to "countries like India, which have *not* joined us as allies against the Communists." The average approval of this proposition—a desirable type of aid to non-allies—was only 49 per cent.[46]

Similar evidence of the interaction of positive and negative factors can be found in public comment on policies of giving food to people in Communist countries. Opinion seems to be divided about evenly. Some, even among those who generally oppose aid to Communist countries, say we should not use starvation as a weapon. Others reply that sending food to starving peoples in Communist countries is doing them no favor if it helps strengthen their oppressive governments.[47]

It appears that the elements affecting evaluations of foreign aid may be tightly compartmentalized in the public mind. It will be recalled that in one previously cited poll only 33 per cent of respondents approved of a loan to England when they were asked about it within the context of the cost, through a preliminary inquiry into whether or not the loan would be repaid. In the same poll 82 per cent agreed that "the United States should continue to give relief to the people in European countries that were occupied by the enemy—such as France and Greece."[48] It is possible, of course, that the sharp difference in answers to these two questions is a result of strong anti-British and pro-French and Greek feeling by the sample interviewed. But it seems more reasonable to account for these differences by the wording of the questions, one stressing the strong negative factors of cost and possible non-repayment; the other stressing a positive factor—humanitarian assistance.

This compartmentalized thought also occurs in relation to other aspects of opinion about foreign aid. In an investigation of the relationship between opinions on cutting taxes and on supporting foreign aid, V. O. Key found that only one-fifth of those he studied "maintained a consistent position on both issues. . . . It may be that only about one-fifth of the population can be relied upon to give a consistently sensible and firm support to interrelated policies of the kinds described."[49]

WEIGHING POSITIVE AND NEGATIVE FACTORS

What are the relative weights of these positive and negative factors, or their ability to influence opinion in one direction or another?

Some of the polling on foreign aid is helpful in this process. Many poll questions are worded in such a way as to elicit opinion about different kinds of aid. By comparing responses to poll questions on different aspects of the aid program we can make inferences about the relative

[46]NORC, p. 19.
[47]Department of State, *American Opinion Report* (January 16, 1962).
[48]NORC, pp. 2–3.
[49]Key, *op. cit.,* p. 166.

popularity or unpopularity of various kinds of aid. We can make such comparisons most effectively when two conditions prevail: (1) A given question pertains to two factors on which opinion seems to be based; (2) A set of two or more such questions has one factor in common. We compare, for example, the responses to a question regarding ideological-type aid to neutrals with responses to a question regarding humanitarian aid to neutrals in order to determine the ranking of the missionary and humanitarian factors. . . .

Through this method we have obtained the rankings of four of the positive factors and three of the negative. In the order of their ability to provoke a favorable response, the positive factors are: ideological aid, humanitarianism and low involvement (of equal weight), and aiding allies. The negative factors, in order of their importance in influencing a negative response, are: aid to neutrals or non-allies, high cost, and deep involvement.

The importance ascribed to ideological missionary feelings is to some extent borne out empirically since this style of aid tends to rank not only as the strongest positive factor but also as more influential than any of the three negative factors listed. Also, the factors which can logically be paired—aid to allies and aid to non-allies, low involvement and great involvement—do not have equal weight. The positive influence exerted by aid to allies is less strong than the negative influence of aid to non-allies. And low involvement is stronger than its negative equivalent.

Thus, an aid program which gave assistance to allies and non-allies would tend to lack public support. Key's research has given indirect support to this point. Opinions opposing aid to neutrals (non-allies) are held with an intensity more than two and one-half times greater than opinions favoring such aid.[50]

Similarly, if one segment of the population saw an aid program as requiring deep involvement while an equal segment saw it as requiring little involvement, the program would benefit in terms of popular support.

The reasons for these uneven rankings are not always clear. In the case of aid to allies vs. non-allies, asymmetry may result from the general association of allies with the negative concepts of deep involvement and possible high cost. In the same way the negative strength of deep involvement may be weakened by its tendency to be associated with either missionary or humanitarian activities.

The analysis also shows, however, that these factors cannot be given even ordinal rankings which hold in every case. A "humanitarian, aid to allies" question and a "humanitarian, high cost" question, for example, have the same level of public approval. This presents a paradox in formal logic but not necessarily in social psychology. It seems reasonable for a strongly held factor such as humanitarianism either to cancel out negative factors with which it is associated or to make accompanying positive factors irrelevant.

. . . .

There is an important reason why foreign aid receives especially ambiguous treatment in the partisan political process. Foreign aid offers no opportunity for candidates to tap a consistent set of opinions. As pointed out [above] . . . , the opinions and attitudes necessary for support of foreign aid are internationalism, including long-term involvements with foreign nations, a belief in the exportability of the "American way of life," a tolerance of "deviant" international behavior on the part of aid recipients, and a certain amount of sanguineness about governmental spending.

We have already seen how these beliefs may work against one another in some cases. Support for aid on the basis of exporting "Americanism" will tend to decrease tolerance for neutralist and socialist foreign governments. Acceptance in principle of unpopular and unfamiliar behavior patterns may often be accompanied by a decreased willingness to become extensively involved with other nations.

Furthermore, these values are diffused throughout American society, not concentrated in a politically effective fashion. Foreign aid thus falls into a pattern consistent with what we know about the interplay of values relative to foreign affairs. Internationalism (whether the expansionist or cooperative version) and isolationism, on the one hand, and various domestic beliefs on the other, have existed historically in a series of changing associations which defy analysis or generalization.[51]

The past is rich in examples. Consider the following statement of a Republican official serving a Democratic President, concerning his administration of aid to war-torn Europe:

[50]*Ibid.*, pp. 212–214.
[51]Some of those associations are concisely related in Max Lerner, *America As a Civilization* (New York: Simon and Schuster, 1957), pp. 889–891.

My job was to nurture the frail plants of democracy in Europe against . . . anarchy or communism. And communism was the pit into which all governments were in danger of falling when frantic peoples were driven by the Horsemen of Famine and Pestilence.

While the words could very well be those of Paul Hoffman, the first administrator of the Marshall Plan, the speaker in this case was Herbert Hoover, Woodrow Wilson's Relief Administrator at the end of World War I. The last stage of Hoover's career saw him cast in the role of defender of the faith of economic conservatism behind the wall of a fortress America. But in earlier years he was an active prophet of Wilsonian internationalism, casting out the devils of deprivation and preaching salvation through a belief in democracy and sound business principles.[52] Both positions have been, and still are, representative of large elements of American thinking. Hoover's early reputation was sufficiently persistent to induce President Truman to ask him to serve again as a "Relief Ambassador" after World War II.[53]

Present-day American society contains intricate combinations of pro- and anti-aid attitudes. Individuals at the upper scale of income and status are among the most internationally inclined. They travel the most, read the most public-affairs magazines and newspapers, and discuss international issues. This helps create a favorable attitude toward foreign aid. On the other hand, these groups are also the most conservative economically. Their antipathy to government spending counteracts, at least in part, enthusiasm for foreign aid.

Lower socioeconomic groups operate from a reverse set of motivations. Their feelings run strongly toward the nationalist, hard-line style of foreign policy. The risks involved in aid to underdeveloped, neutralist nations seem scarcely worth the effort. They are, however, much less concerned about government spending. Government programs, domestically at least, benefit them more than other groups.[54]

Comparing two of the attitudes favorable to foreign aid, internationalism and economic liberalism, Key has shown that high levels of both occur together in only about 9 per cent of the population. The conjunction of internationalism and conservatism occurs in 5 per cent, isolationism and liberalism are espoused by 14 per cent, and the most anti-aid combination, isolationism and conservatism, occurs in 12 per cent of the

sampled population. (Excluded from these figures are those who wish to keep the economic status quo and those with no opinion.)[55]

Patterns of conflicting opinions can also be uncovered by comparing the poll eliciting opinion on the Peace Corps, which offered a good index of opinions on cooperative internationalism, with the results of a question on government spending and the level of taxation, which provided an indicator of domestic conservatism.[56] By dividing the population according to occupation and cross-tabulating the rankings on the two questions we get results somewhat different from Key's, but still showing the majority of the population (55 per cent) in the two ambiguous positions, internationalist-conservative and isolationist-liberal. The remainder is divided equally between the strong pro- and anti-foreign-aid combinations.

We can further assess the political implications of opinion by examining the taxes vs. spending question. As we said, when respondents who favored reduced spending were asked to name those policies they considered most eligible for government economies, they frequently mentioned foreign aid. However, those same respondents are *more* favorable than the other groups to the kind of foreign aid represented by the Peace Corps. The high levels of Peace Corps support come about largely because this particular program is strongly supported by some groups which have low levels of approval of foreign aid in general.[57] A reason for this was suggested by former Peace Corps Director Sargent Shriver:

We appeal to the spirit of personal initiative, to the spirit of volunteering to do something for your country, to be patriotic. These are some of the qualities that right wing people look for in the American personality and character.[58]

[52]This story is recounted in Richard Hofstadter, *The American Political Tradition* (New York: Vintage Books, 1960), pp. 283–314. The quotation is found on p. 289.
[53]Harry S. Truman, *Year of Decisions* (New York: Doubleday, 1955), p. 472.
[54]See Key, *op. cit.;* and Seymour Martin Lipset, *Political Man* (New York: Doubleday, 1960).
[55]Key, *op. cit.,* p. 157.
[56]AIPO polls #609 (January 1959) and #640 (January 1961).
[57]The three occupational groups which alone gave over 60 per cent support to foreign aid on the general question supported the Peace Corps by an average of 73 per cent. The remainder of the population, averaging 47 per cent on foreign aid in general, supported the Peace Corps by an average of 69 per cent.
[58]*Meet the Press,* 5 (December 24, 1961), 3–4.

ONE THING WE LEARNED
Bill D. Moyers

Earlier, we referred to the work of Gabriel Almond and others on American public opinion and foreign policy. Their picture of a relatively uninformed and uninterested mass public has led many to ask how this state of affairs can be made consonant with a representative democracy and, in any event, whether it leaves the mass of the citizenry completely helpless and without recourse in the face of governmental foreign policy decisions, some of them literally matters of life and death.

The war in Vietnam seems to have demonstrated that, with regard to the broad directions of national policy, the President needs a solid basis of support for the courses of action he is pursuing. If it is notably lacking, this may become at a certain point so unsettling and so fraught with political burdens and costs that it does have an impact on policy. This is not to say that in 1967 and 1968 a broad national consensus developed regarding what should be done in Vietnam. What did seem to develop, however, was a strong sense of unease and of dissatisfaction from a number of different quarters with the what and the how of American policy in Vietnam. Finally, this made a difference, in terms of the political fortunes of President Johnson and the Democratic Party and of the U.S. policies being pursued in Vietnam. A roughly similar case history can be sketched in the case of the American involvement in Korea fifteen years earlier.

Mr. Moyers' essay suggests some of the problems and ambiguities in the assessment of public opinion from a Presidential perspective. Some of his interpretations of American opinion can be debated; for example, his view that public resistance to the idea of withdrawal from Vietnam reflects primarily a rigid, simplistic anti-communism. However, his effort to suggest the essential, limiting role of the public in a situation like Vietnam, and the complex relationships of public attitudes and Presidential performance, is stimulating reading, particularly in view of his own experience as a key Presidential staff assistant.

Whatever else we may say of the dissent to the war in Viet Nam, it has effectively reminded us that we are still a democracy. Some may demur that we did not need to be reminded so noisily, but the fact remains: so many Americans turned from indifference or passive skepticism to outright opposition that the policy had to be changed. There comes a time, in foreign affairs as in domestic policies, when "the people" will be heard.

The tradition of dissent, of course, has been upheld by those who were its targets as well as by those who, not always with the best of manners, exercised their right to be heard. Even when they would not publicly admit it, or admitted it grudgingly, most of the top officials I knew in Washington agreed with Woodrow Wilson's assertion: "We do not need less criticism in time of war, but more. It is to be hoped that the critics will be constructive, but better unfair criticism than autocratic suppression."

The preoccupation with the tradition of dissent, however, obscured another basic tradition of U.S. foreign policy, whose neglect has done more to turn public opinion against the war than any other factor. I mean the tradition of *consent*. Our system assumes a sense of participation by the people in the making of critical national decisions. When that sense of involvement is absent, when the public feels excluded from the judgments that are made in its name, a policy is doomed from inception, no matter how theoretically valid it may be.

There is a continuing tension in American democracy between the "will of the people" and the judgment of their chosen representatives. It was brought home to me during the week of crisis surrounding the march on Selma, Alabama, in 1965, as the President and his advisers met in the Cabinet Room to discuss alternative courses of Federal action. At a particularly exasperating moment, when no option appeared likely to succeed, one man exclaimed wearily: "If we only knew what the people of this country really wanted us to do about civil rights. . . ." The President studied his adviser for thirty seconds, then answered: "If we knew what they wanted us to do, how could you be sure that we should do it?"

Presidents feel this tension acutely, for they are not only politicians responsive *to* the people, but chief executives and commanders-in-chief responsible *for* the people. They know, often too well for their own peace of mind, that the people may not know best, that democracy can become, in Oscar Wilde's words, "the bludgeoning of the people by the people for the people."

Reprinted by special permission from FOREIGN AFFAIRS, July 1968. Copyright by Council on Foreign Relations, Inc., New York.

Presidents also know first-hand the frustrations of trying to divine public opinion toward foreign policy. For one thing, they realize that many people have more opinions than facts, and that the less some men know, the louder they shout. Americans are capable of a very high noise factor, especially when they take passionate feelings for pertinent information.

It is fashionable today to claim that we are better informed about foreign policy than ever before. No doubt that is true, but we ought not to assume that because we are better informed we are also well informed. Alas, we are not. At the White House, for example, we were impressed and discouraged by reliable studies which indicated how poorly informed many Americans really are.

One study by the Survey Research Center of the University of Michigan, made for the Council on Foreign Relations,[1] revealed that one-fourth of the respondents were not aware that Mainland China was ruled by a communist government. A Gallup poll in 1964 revealed that two-thirds of the American people had paid little or no attention to developments in South Viet Nam, although the United States had been involved there for ten years. It is small wonder, then, that it took almost two years for a majority of people to know and react demonstrably to what was happening there.

These surveys are not isolated studies. They are substantiated in other examinations of public opinion by such serious students of American attitudes as Lloyd Free and Hadley Cantril. Their recent study[2] is a thorough and illuminating analysis of the fundamental assumptions underlying the way Americans react to specific issues. I do not recommend it for those who believe that anyone can grow up to be Secretary of State. In one survey, for example, one in four respondents had never heard or read of the North Atlantic Treaty Organization, and only 58 percent knew that Russia was not a member. These and other findings led Free and Cantril to conclude that two-fifths of the American people appear to have too little information about international matters to play an intelligent role as citizens of a nation fully engaged as the major power in the world.

Public ignorance is not the only handicap a President must overcome in trying to determine what people will accept or support in foreign policy. Public opinion, as every President has learned, is a highly variable quantity.

President Truman discovered this during the Korean War. Two months after the commitment of American troops, 65 percent of the people interviewed in a Gallup poll said the United States had not made a mistake. Six months later, only 38 percent said we had not erred. By July 1951, not quite a year later, a majority of Americans wanted a truce under any circumstances. The undulating nature of public opinion was not lost on Lyndon Johnson. In December 1965, when Lou Harris reported that the "overwhelming majority of the American people — 71 percent — are prepared to continue the fighting in Viet Nam until the United States can negotiate a settlement on its own terms," the President remarked to his associates: "An overwhelming majority . . . for an underwhelming period of time . . . wait and see." The wait was relatively brief. In March 1968, 49 percent of the people interviewed in a Gallup poll would say the United States had made a mistake in sending troops to fight in Viet Nam — a percentage that had steadily risen from 25 percent in March 1966. Seven in ten doves thought we were wrong to have become involved in Viet Nam, a Gallup poll reported, but, perhaps more surprisingly, four in ten hawks did so as well.

We were also aware that public opinion, in addition to being highly variable, is replete with incongruities. The example I most vividly recall concerned the attitudes of young people toward the war in Viet Nam. Samuel Lubell reported in 1965 that our policy there was supported by three out of four college students in New York State. Free and Cantril discovered in the same year that it was the young who most favored stepping up the war. Yet, as we have all seen, the core of the Viet Nam protest movement has been on college compuses. The age-group which provided the original escalation with its strongest support has also provided the most articulate and belligerent opponents to the war.

The phenomenon President Johnson has faced, of course, is that most Americans are both hawk *and* dove, a situation which has made the incongruities of public opinion all the more deceiving. Various profiles of public opinion, the most notable by Seymour Lipset,[3] have emphasized this aspect of American attitudes.

[1]A. T. Steele, "American People and China." New York: McGraw-Hill, 1966.
[2]Lloyd A. Free and Hadley Cantril, "The Political Beliefs of Americans." New Brunswick: Rutgers University Press, 1967.
[3]Seymour Martin Lipset, "Doves, Hawks and Polls," *Encounter*, October 1966, p. 39.

Sixty percent of the people in one poll expressed opposition to bombing large cities in North Viet Nam, but 61 percent said they were for bombing industrial plants and factories. Three out of five, in other words, were for bombing but they were not for bombing cities. At first blush this seems to be inconsistent, but what it meant, as Lipset concluded, was that Americans wanted the war to end as soon as possible, even if escalation was the way to do it. This explains why the President's standing in the polls increased sharply after he ordered a bombing pause in late 1965 *and* after he ordered the resumption of bombing when the pause did not produce negotiations.

In a survey conducted by the National Opinion Research Center of the University of Chicago, 84 percent of the respondents favored American negotiations with the Viet Cong if they were willing to negotiate, and a majority of 52 percent were willing to approve forming a new government in which the Viet Cong took part. But the same sample of respondents who were for compromise turned hawkish when asked: "If President Johnson were to withdraw from Viet Nam and let the communists take over, would you approve or disapprove?" There were 81 percent who disapproved, and 56 percent would not even agree to withdrawing our troops gradually and letting the South Vietnamese work out their own problems.

There is an explanation for this seeming contradiction, a hangover, no doubt, from the harsher ideological clashes of the 1950s. It is that "communism" as a word still triggers an almost visceral response in a majority of people. The better-informed public is aware of the growing divisions and dissimilarities within the communist world, but, as we saw earlier, most Americans are not *well* informed. For many, "communism" is an intelligible abstraction that subsumes much complexity. I remember one poll in which people were asked if they thought communists were deeply involved in civil-rights demonstrations. Of the people with college education 37 percent said yes, against 48 percent of the high school graduates and 54 percent of the grade school graduates.

What is the practical implication at the moment of this residual animosity to and concern about communism? It is what a scientific study of public opinion reveals in depth—that most Americans want peace in Viet Nam, are prepared to accept some degree of compromise with the enemy, but will not accept an end result which is a conclusive victory for communism. Their objective is peace without the expansion of communism, a goal that scarcely lessens the difficulty of the talks in Paris. Every President learns to live with this ambivalence in public opinion. He knows that in his constituency are numberless legions of people who share the attitude of one respondent to a poll: "My hope is for peace in the world—and if not that, the complete destruction of both Russia and China."

II

So much for the tension between public opinion and public officials. It should be obvious that a President faces no quest more difficult than the search for an accurate reading of how far and how fast he can lead the people. As difficult as the task is, he must try. He must try because there are questions on which governments dare not act without evidence of genuine support. When policies and laws outdistance public opinion, or take public opinion for granted, or fail to command respect in the conscience of the people, they lose their "natural" legitimacy.

As with any rootless condition, the democratic experience then becomes infected with malaise. People feel estranged from their government, seemingly powerless to alter the way things are. They may challenge policy, usually in demonstrations, but their chances of changing policy are slim. Their impotence leads either to numbed apathy or, more dangerously, to outright hostility.

This is what happened over the last twenty-four months in this country as opposition to the war in Viet Nam swelled to an overpowering crescendo. It did not happen, in my opinion, primarily because some people thought the war immoral, and some thought it illegal and some thought it simply unwinnable at an acceptable cost. I think it happened because a majority of people believed the war undemocratic—waged in violation of the tradition of consent which is fundamental to the effective conduct of foreign policy in a free society. The war was begun, enlarged and is still being waged without a clear declaration of support by a majority of the American people. I do not suggest that a war can be justified merely because it enjoys majority support, but I am sure that in this day of mass and immediate communications it is impossible to sustain successfully even a justified war to which people have not given their consent. Viet

Nam has proven that good intentions on the part of a nation's leaders will not substitute for the conscious involvement of the people in the decision to go to war.

What happened to permit this war to grow to such consuming proportions without involving the people in an act of support? For one thing, what Arthur Schlesinger, Sr., called "the humane presuppositions of democracy" were at work in the beginning of this war just as they were in similar undeclared wars in the past. These humane presuppositions "tend to make both political leaders and people blink away the possibility of armed strife in the abiding hope that reason and mutual concession will prevail."[4]

American officials did expect reason and mutual concessions to prevail in 1964 and 1965, and they did not believe it would be wise to ask the public for a declaration of support for a war that did not at the moment seem inevitable. They believed that Hanoi would listen to reason, or be frightened off by the flexing of our muscles, or be tempted to share in the lucrative rewards of economic coöperation if war were averted. None of these hopes materialized, of course, but by that time we had edged into a major war on the mainland of Asia without fully alerting the American people to its potential dimensions and without seeking their direct consent.

War is clearly one of those questions on which a government—a democratic government—dare not act without evidence of genuine support. In this case, that support was not deliberately withheld—it simply was not sought. And it was not sought because few if any officials anticipated the war would ever reach the proportions that would require a declaration.

Closely related to this judgment is the other condition that permitted so wide a gap to separate public opinion from public policy—the persistent failure of American officials, in most of the wars we have fought, to prepare the public mind for the ordeal or to clarify in advance the issues of principle. One reason for this is the natural official penchant for secrecy. People are willing to go along with the withholding of information when national security is involved. But the moment secrecy is perceived as secretiveness there is likely to be an emotional reaction of intolerance.

There is also a natural tendency for people in positions of high administrative responsibility to develop great confidence in their own judgments. They feel more competent than others to survey situations and make the right judgments. This, of course, is their job. But when the public is involved, officials fail to realize that this confidence must be communicated with more than an announced decision. A chief executive cannot expect people to have confidence in his judgment simply because it is his. He must indicate what are some of the major considerations he has taken into account so that people will know that what he has decided is both the right and effective policy to pursue. The people will allow a President significantly more latitude with respect to means than to ends, but he must make them feel a part of his decision and a partner in the policy.

Winston Churchill, who had in 1909 defined democracy as "the occasional necessity of deferring to the opinions of other people," understood this as few wartime leaders have. He believed that people should be involved. When events turned, he went to the people to explain what had occurred and why. He was careful and patient to explain rather than simply to announce his policies, insisting that people not only pass upon the decisions through their elected representatives but that they take their share of the responsibility.

American leaders, on the other hand, are not in the habit of explaining themselves. As Walter Lippmann has said, "They announce, they proclaim, they declare, they exhort, they appeal, and they argue. But they do not unbend and tell the story, and say what they did, and what they think about it, and how they feel about it. Thus the general atmosphere is secretive and standoffish, which certainly does not warm the heart in time of trouble."

I think these words describe the inhibitions on dialogue and participation—the twin elements of consent—that caused some earlier wars to be as unpopular and as divisive as Viet Nam. The War of 1812 barely won the support of Congress—the resolution passed by a majority of but three to two of the entire membership —and even then was denounced by the Massachusetts Senate as "founded in falsehood" and "declared without necessity." In 1844 James K. Polk precipitated war by marching troops into territory claimed by both sides

[4]Arthur M. Schlesinger, Paths to the Present, New York: Macmillan, 1949.

and announcing arbitrarily that the Mexicans had started the conflict. "War exists," he informed Congress, "and, notwithstanding all our efforts to avoid it, exists by the act of Mexico itself." The opposition was bitter, and after two years the House resolved by a vote of 85 to 81 that the war had been "unnecessarily and unconstitutionally begun by the President of the United States."

It may appear from our Viet Nam dilemma that we learned little from those earlier experiences about the necessity of consent. I am more hopeful. The reaction to the war has been so fierce and sustained that I cannot see future decisions involving similar consequences being made without asking the people to share more fully in the responsibility. The day has passed, I believe, when the "functional equivalent of a declaration of war" will be tolerated after the fact. The foreign policies of our government must be squared with the long tradition written by John Adams into the Proclamation adopted by the Council of Massachusetts Bay in 1774: "As the happiness of the people is the sole end of government, so the consent of the people is the only foundation of it, in reason, morality, and the natural fitness of things."

CHAPTER 4

FORMULATING AND IMPLEMENTING NATIONAL POLICY

Since the making of foreign policy and national defense policy are thoroughly enmeshed in the American political and governmental system, they are bound to reflect larger patterns and problems in it. Thus, it can be assumed that the separation of powers (significantly modified by checks and balances), primacy of the executive, relatively weak and decentralized political parties, and a highly pluralistic political milieu have consequences for externally, as well as domestically, oriented policies. The nature of these consequences, and how they may differ for foreign policy, is of course of great interest to the student of foreign policy.

The same student is also inevitably caught up in some of the continuing debates about how the U.S. government can be made to function more effectively—what personal qualities and political skills are necessary or highly desirable for an effective President, how can staff support for the President be better organized and of higher intellectual quality, what is the ideal role for Congress in public policy-making, how can the related activities of a variety of government agencies be better coördinated for the sake of increased policy consistency and improved program operation?

It is interesting to note in this connection how perspectives on various governmental institutions change in the light of changing policy problems and the way they are handled by particular incumbents. For example, most students of the Presidency (most notably and recently Professor Richard Neustadt) have viewed the President as the main dynamic motive force in the American government. Neustadt's major concern in his study of *Presidential Power*[1] is that the President be an effective politician, in other words, that he be able to get the job done. The underlying assumption is that what he and his colleagues in the executive want to do, particularly in foreign affairs, is usually closer to the right thing than any Congressional or public preferences. The executive knows more and has more expertise and seasoned judgment available to it than, for example, the Congress. The latter has tended to be viewed as a nuisance, a handicap, sometimes indeed a major burden and roadblock to a more effective American foreign policy.

Periodically, though, Congress regains some favor in the eyes of its critics. Those who felt that the Eisenhower Administration was doing too little in both defense and foreign policy suddenly rediscovered the Congress. Key committees and key legislators were urged to push the executive into action.

[1] Richard E. Neustadt, *Presidential Power: The Politics of Leadership* (New York: John Wiley, 1960).

More recently, the fierce policy disagreements on Vietnam have triggered some second thoughts on Presidential dominance in foreign affairs and the delights of having a high-energy, deeply committed, seasoned politician in the White House. Apparently, this is viewed as highly desirable as long as the incumbent is making the right policy choices by the lights of his critics. When he is not, the picture suddenly looks rather frightening.

Once again, there has been renewed interest in what the Congress can do. Senator Fulbright (D., Ark.), chairman of the Foreign Relations Committee, responded with a series of public hearings on major foreign policy problems, revolving around but not limited to Vietnam. Congressional focusing on more fundamental policy issues instead of programmatic details (the latter seems to be the preference of many Congressmen) has long been urged by many students of Congress. The Vietnam debate seems to have stimulated just such an effort. (See the selection by Fulbright below.)

In the process of taking a hard look at the Presidency and Congress in the light of Vietnam, some foolish and exaggerated things have been said. Lyndon B. Johnson was a very long way from Caesar. Some useful results, however, may have emerged. A fresh, critical look at the foreign policy powers of the President, and at the implications of Presidential style and behavior, particularly in situations of major international crisis, was certainly in order. While there are no easy answers, certainly no formal or constitutional solutions, to the dilemmas of literally worldshaking decisions that one man may have to make, it is essential that the problem be reflected upon deeply and critically from time to time.

It is similarly useful to take an occasional, critical look at the accepted clichés about the Congress. In *The Arrogance of Power*, Fulbright argues that Congress has abdicated more of its powers than it needed to in the foreign affairs field and, furthermore, that it has not been allocating wisely those energies devoted to foreign policy. As suggested, Fulbright himself has taken some steps designed to right the balance as he sees it.

Indeed, a reasonable defense can be made of the practice of annual Congressional cuts in foreign aid authorizations and appropriations, if not of some of the specific, very substantial amounts of recent years. Feeling strongly that these programs have often been oversold and poorly managed but in no position to pinpoint detailed shortcomings, an understandable and even reasonable response is to reduce the monies voted and let the executive do the pruning and economizing.

Another classic problem in American government and public administration involves the coordination at home and overseas of the many agencies whose responsibilities and activities impinge to greater or lesser degree on American foreign policy and foreign relations. In the ultimate sense, this is the President's job; practically speaking, he needs all the help he can get, in terms both of effective subordinates and facilitating organizational machinery.

Overseas, the choice of U.S. foreign policy leader and coordinator is a reasonably clear one—the U.S. ambassadors heading the U.S. missions in various countries. The problems here revolve around finding the appropriately talented and motivated men to fill these positions and providing them with the powers, the staff, and the organizational procedures necessary to make their work effective.

At home, in Washington, the scale of the problem is so immense in terms of the number of agencies, subagency units, and people involved that the solution cannot be so simple. Debate has often centered on the alternatives of State Department leadership or substantially strengthened Presidential staffs. So much depends on the individuals filling the key positions that one is inclined to be skeptical about the solution that appears ideal in the abstract. In practice, efforts have been made, particularly in the last ten years, to strengthen the foreign policy leadership mandate as well as the organizational and personnel capabilities of the Department of State while at the same time Presidents continue to provide themselves with whatever immediate staff assistance they regard as necessary to meet their own overriding national security responsibilities.

A simple guide to the labyrinth that is the foreign policy organization is to recognize that it reflects quite clearly the *extensive* and *intensive* character of the American involvement abroad. The many instruments, some new, some old, available to the United States for the carrying out of its foreign policy purposes are reflected in the many agencies that have a share of the foreign policy "action." The depth and intensity of American involvement are indicated by those agencies whose work brings them to the very heart of other societies—the Agency for International Development, the Peace Corps, the Information Agency. The global range of American interests is reflected in the country desks and regional offices that are to be found not only in the State Department but in every other major foreign affairs agency in Washington. Just how comprehensive American overseas activities and concerns have become is reflected in the fact that the Treasury and Agriculture Department representatives and the commercial attachés in many American missions abroad have been joined by science attachés and, more recently, Atomic Energy Commission representatives. Can the Space Administration be far behind?

NATIONAL LEGISLATURES AND CHIEF EXECUTIVES
Kenneth N. Waltz

In a postscript essay on the study of foreign policy at the end of this volume, the editor argues that one major direction for improvement would be to make research and teaching in this field much more *comparative* in nature. For a long time, we in the United States have been too parochial in our study of international politics, focusing too much attention on American policies and concerns and looking at world problems from a predominantly American perspective.

Such an approach is understandable but not desirable, and this is not simply a question of being broadminded or sophisticated in our approach to foreign affairs. For one thing, studies of the foreign policies and policy-making processes of other nations should help put our own system and its problems in better perspective. For another, it is sometimes quite refreshing, even shocking, to look at another nation's policy from its own perspective. It often turns out to make much more sense than it did as viewed from Washington or Des Moines. If one makes a serious effort to separate French policies from the special style, manner, and world-view of General de Gaulle, there is much in them that makes sense, given France's situation in and view of the world. Interestingly, the early months in office of DeGaulle's successor, M. Pompidou, brought no major changes in French foreign policy.

In his book *Foreign Policy and Democratic Politics*, Professor Waltz has made a bold and ambitious effort to compare the American and British political systems in terms of their consequences for the foreign policy performance of the two nations. In the process, he provides just the sort of perspective on the American system suggested above. He also raises serious questions about the clear superiority of British institutions assumed by many Americans. The selection that follows suggests the thrust of his stimulating analysis.

We can now trace some implications of the propositions made in Chapter 3. There, more emphasis was placed on Prime Minister and Parliament than on President and Congress. In considering the daily performance of governmental tasks, this emphasis will be reversed. Congress, more troublesome than Parliament, is also politically more important; and outwardly at least the political life of the President is more difficult than the Prime Minister's.

CONGRESS AND FOREIGN POLICY

In the history of the United States, fewer than ten treaties have been defeated because of the rule requiring approval by two thirds of the Senators present. Other treaties that were lost were unaffected by the rule, for they received less than a simple majority anyway.[1] Since the narrow rejection of the Versailles Treaty that contained the League Covenant as an integral part, no major treaty has been lost in the Senate. But then, between the two wars, none came

From *Foreign Policy and Democratic Politics* by Kenneth Waltz, pp. 96–119. Copyright © 1967, by Little, Brown and Company (Inc.). Reprinted by permission of the author and publisher.
Ed. note: Some of the footnotes have been omitted.
[1] Dexter Perkins says that a total of four treaties have been lost because of the rule. *The American Approach to Foreign Policy* (Stockholm: Almqvist & Wiksells, 1951), pp. 155–56. Royden J. Dangerfield finds seven treaties defeated in this way up to 1928, to which must be added the defeat in 1935 of the Protocol by which the United States would have become a member of the Permanent Court of International Justice, which was defeated by 52 votes for and 36 against. *In Defense of the Senate: A Study in Treaty Making* (Norman: University of Oklahoma Press, 1933), pp. 311–12. For the period since World War II, see David Nelson Farnsworth, *The Senate Committee on Foreign Relations* (Urbana: University of Illinois Press, 1961), chap. 4.

before it. The importance of the two-thirds rule as a barrier to international actions a President may wish to take cannot be measured simply by the number of treaties that have failed. Some failures were spectacular and have been thought to be highly damaging to the United States and to the world. Because of the two-thirds rule, the President may refrain from negotiating treaties he would otherwise try to conclude, or he may attempt to tailor to the Senatorial temper those that he does submit for approval. At the turn of the century, Secretary of State John Hay, his difficulties over Senatorial passage of a peace treaty with Spain in mind, once exclaimed:

A treaty of peace, in any normal state of things ought to be ratified with unanimity in twenty-four hours. They wasted six weeks in wrangling over this one, and ratified it with one vote to spare. We have five or six matters now demanding settlement. I can settle them all, honorably and advantageously to our own side; and I am assured by leading men in the Senate that not one of these treaties, if negotiated, will pass the Senate. I should have a majority in every case, but a malcontent third would certainly dish every one of them. To such monstrous shape has the original mistake of the Constitution grown in the evolution of our politics. You must understand, it is not merely *my* solution the Senate will reject. They will reject, for instance, any treaty, whatever, on any subject, with England. I doubt if they would accept any treaty of consequence with Russia or Germany. The recalcitrant third would be differently composed, but it would be on hand.[2]

Do such experiences, or the more memorable rejection of the League of Nations Covenant, demonstrate that the two-thirds rule is a bad one? Treaties become the supreme law of the land and, because they do so, require more than a simple majority of a single chamber. Yet treaties are made with other sovereign states and thus do not easily lend themselves to the devices appropriate to domestic legislation. Hamilton described the treaty provision as "one of the best digested and most unexceptionable parts" of the entire Constitution.[3] Nonetheless, it has from time to time been suggested that an ordinary majority of both Houses would be preferable to requiring two-thirds approval by the Senate. To change the rule by amending the Constitution would, however, be of little conse-

quence; for by using executive agreements or concurrent resolutions and simple legislation, if Congress is willing, the President can accomplish most of his foreign-policy desires.

The treaty rule is relevant then in two cases. The first of them causes no domestic trouble at all. It is the regulation of the routine relations between the United States and others, as is done by the many friendship, commerce, and navigation treaties, according to which international business is daily conducted. The other is the exceptional act of policy, which may be new, expensive, dangerous, or large in importance and which may have implications that extend over a number of years. In such matters, the President and State Department must consider the temper of the Senate and the mood of the country, prepare the way by exhortation and education, seek to change opinion if possible, and amend or add provisions to the clauses of treaties if necessary. It is sometimes said that only a few still worry about the restriction upon the power to conclude treaties, and that among those few are the President, officials of the State Department, and other executive officers concerned with foreign affairs. The habit of American government is first to exaggerate the obstacles to movement and then to work furiously to surmount them. This is known colloquially as "running scared," which is a healthfully invigorating exercise. It may well be that such measures as the Atlantic Defense Treaty and the Test Ban were won by such handsome margins (82 to 13 and 80 to 19) in part because Presidents Truman and Kennedy acted as though they might possibly not be approved at all. The wide margins by which they passed helped to establish the solidity of the American commitment.

The Atlantic Defense Treaty, for example, was made in accordance with the Vandenberg Resolution, which had been worked out in conferences among Marshall and Lovett of the State Department and Vandenberg and Connally of the Senate, with the occasional participation of John Foster Dulles. It was submitted to the Senate on April 12, 1949, debated on the floor on July 5, and finally passed on July 21. The delay was inconvenient; many of the statements

[2]Quoted in Henry Adams, *The Education of Henry Adams* (New York: Random House, 1931), p. 374.
[3]Alexander Hamilton, John Jay, and James Madison, "The Federalist No. 75," *The Federalist: A Commentary on the Constitution of the United States* (New York: Random House, 1937), p. 485.

made in the debate and during committee hearings were an embarrassment to American diplomacy. As one of many examples, consider the following discourse:

MR. CONNALLY. Regarding the inquiry propounded by the Senator from California [Knowland], of course we are interested in the peace of the world. But that does not mean that we shall blindfold ourselves and make a commitment now to enter every war that may occur in the next 10 years, and send our boys and resources to Europe to fight.

MR. DONNELL. I am glad to hear the Senator say that.

MR. CONNALLY. That is the view some people seem to take of the whole situation. The nations in Europe are not fighting now. All the outrages which have been committed seem to be tolerated by the people of the countries involved. I do not approve of them, of course. But I do not believe in giving carte blanche assurance to these people, "Do everything you want to do, you need not worry, as soon as anything happens, we will come over and fight your quarrel for you. In the meantime you may have a good time, and bask in the sunshine of leadership which you do not deserve."[4]

Such statements must awaken some doubts abroad, even among those who know that they should be discounted. The words in themselves are harsh, and Connally was at the time the Chairman of the Senate Foreign Relations Committee. Because of the opposition of some Senators and the doubts entertained by Robert A. Taft, who in the end voted against the Treaty anyway, the language of the Treaty was weakened. An attack against one member was still defined as "an attack against them all," but now it was added: to be met by such action as each state "deems necessary."[5] The Treaty finally gained acceptance by a vote of 82 to 13. If the long process of examination and approval was a spectacle, it was at least an edifying one. Anyone who cared could learn much about the Treaty, the arguments for and against it, and the condition of the world that in the majority view made it desirable. The process was costly; it was also beneficial. Delay, embarrassment, and some obscuring of every state's commitment were the price paid; gaining wide support in the Senate and among the public was ample compensation. Some may cavil at the conclusion

because it treats cavalierly a cardinal rule of the old diplomacy: that the language of all treaties be entirely precise. The rule is surely important in drawing a boundary, regulating trade, or setting the procedures of diplomatic intercourse. It is less so in such matters as we are discussing. The purpose of the Treaty was to get the states party to it to cooperate militarily, and possibly in other ways, over a period of at least twenty years. The accomplishment of such a purpose cannot be assured by the language of a treaty. The obligation to rally around at a moment of peril, because it may require the greatest of national sacrifices, will depend more on what happens after a treaty is made than on the words recorded in it. For these reasons, a hard-won but real national commitment is preferable to the gaining of an easy but nominal assent. If the treaty provision is not, as Hamilton thought, near to being the best part of the Constitution, it is far from being the terrible mistake that Secretary Hay understandably thought it to be. The requirement of a two-thirds vote remains, but it is no longer a major impediment to a foreign policy of action and involvement.

In a period when international involvements have been accepted as necessities even when they have been painful, the two-thirds rule has not kept the President or the State Department from fashioning suitable international arrangements. One must then wonder if the rule ever was a basic cause of American difficulties. It is not likely that the United States, even if she had joined the League of Nations, would have assumed greater international responsibilities in the years between the wars. If Woodrow Wilson had behaved more like a peacetime Prime Minister than like a President, by testing the ground carefully, avoiding a fight in the Senate, and foregoing a campaign in the country, the occasion for condemning the treaty rule would have been avoided entirely. But the United States would also have been less well educated and prepared for the international role that since 1941 has been hers to play.

Other types of Congressional obstruction have been more worrisome lately: among them, the constant disposition of Congress to pry into administrative details and to investigate officials and superintend their work. It is often feared that Congressmen acting as critics and investi-

[4]*Congressional Record*, XCV, Pt. 1 (81st Cong., 1st sess., 1949), 1165.
[5]The North Atlantic Treaty, Art. 5.

gators may harry the officials and the diplomats who need time to think, may frighten them into timidity where boldness is required, and may block their attempts to move with subtlety to meet complex and shifting situations whose implications most Congressmen are not equipped to comprehend.

Harold Nicolson, giving an Englishman's impression of American diplomats, wrote in the 1930's: "They enter a conference as Daniel entered the den of lions conscious that it is only their bright faith and innocence which will preserve them from the claws of the wild beasts by whom they are surrounded." He went on to describe the brash confidence of American businessmen negotiating with foreigners and marveled at the contrast between them and timid American ambassadors. Charles W. Thayer, himself a Foreign Service Officer for more than two decades, took notice of Nicolson's remark in order to point out that the cause of the diplomats' quavering was not, as Nicolson suggested, fear and suspicion of Continental diplomatists but rather their dread of the combined isolationist convictions and punitive powers of Congress.[6]

While the inclination to isolationism has waned, Congress has retained the power to tamper with policy and interfere with its conduct. Because the approval of appropriate Congressional committees is essential to the legislative success of a program, governmental officials are effectively constrained to submit themselves to Congressional scrutiny. John Foster Dulles estimated in November of 1955 that since becoming Secretary of State he had met "more than 100 times with bipartisan congressional groups."[7] Dean Acheson, reconstructing the period of his service in that office, complained that one-sixth of his working days in Washington were spent in preparing for and meeting with Congressional committees or less formal groups of Senators and Representatives; and he was able to point to the months of May and June of 1951 as a period when fully one half of his time was spent in these ways.[8] The Secretary, of course, is not the Congressman's sole source of information. Deputies, Assistant Secretaries, and assorted experts or interested parties inside and outside the government are also invited or required to appear before committees. They cannot be made to reveal all the executive branch may know or do, but they cannot avoid divulging a great deal. Congress, though it sometimes complains that it is kept in the dark, is clearly the best informed legislative body in the world.

Is the result worth the price paid to achieve it? Acheson and others have wondered if spending so much time informing and attempting to placate Congress represents the best use of the Secretary's talent and energy. Congress can be asked to exercise restraint and to remember that executive officers have other things to do, but major changes in practice are not likely to occur. Congressmen have the privilege of asking in committee; the Members of the Commons have the privilege of asking on the floor of the House. In the absence of effective ways of gaining information and pressing questions home, the House of Commons experiences increasingly the malaise that comes with performing an important task weakly. The American Congress often appears tedious and presumptuous, willful and capricious, in the exercise of the powers of investigation and criticism with which it is plentifully endowed. But if an effective, partly independent critic is desired, it is difficult to say, and secure by appropriate institutional arrangements, "Thus far and no farther." With pleasing brevity, Max Beloff has set forth a standard account of America's internal difficulties in foreign policy, some of them generated by the separation of powers. At the Berlin Conference of 1954 he found that Dulles was to some extent in the position of Molotov and somewhat in the position of Bidault and that Eden was differently placed from either of them. Like Molotov, Dulles was guided in his policy by ideological commitment. The question of America's recognizing Red China was conditioned partly by belief and thus became less a matter to be determined by international political calculation. Such decisions were also susceptible to the pressures of Congress and public opinion, however, and this fact established a similarity to Bidault. Both he and Dulles were without reliable majorities in their legislative assemblies. Congress could and did demand the right to control Dulles "in every detail," and in the power to ratify treaties and to appropriate money it possessed adequate means for the purpose. The President or the Secretary

[6]Thayer, *Diplomat* (New York: Harper, 1959), p. 72.
[7]Dulles, "News Conference Statement," *Department of State Bulletin*, XXXIII, No. 859 (December 12, 1955), 965–66.
[8]Acheson, *A Citizen Looks at Congress* (New York: Harper, 1957), pp. 65–66.

of State can, as Beloff put it, try "to muster a majority in the country which will bring pressure to bear upon a recalcitrant Congress. All the history of the last forty years goes to show how extremely difficult this is." The difficulty, he concluded, lies not merely in ideology but also in national institutions and long-standing habits: distrust of the executive, suspicion of the expert, great confidence in the right and the ability of the people to pronounce on complicated matters of policy.[9]

To take a final example of this viewpoint, George F. Kennan remarked, in an early expression of the theme he continues to hum, that history "does not forgive us our national mistakes [in foreign policy merely] because they are explicable in terms of our domestic politics. If you say that mistakes of the past were unavoidable because of our domestic predilections and habits of thought, you are saying that what stopped us from being more effective than we were was democracy, as practiced in this country. And, if that is true, let us recognize it and measure the full seriousness of it—and find something to do about it." The crucial words are "as practiced in this country." He is not saying that all democracies must be disadvantaged, but simply that the American democracy is. He doubts that the problem of making and conducting an adequate foreign policy "is soluble without constitutional reform—reform which would give us a parliamentary system more nearly like that which exists in England and most other parliamentary countries, a system in which a government falls if it loses the confidence of its parliament."[10] A Parliamentary government, Kennan believes, is able to frame and conduct its program without debilitating and disruptive interventions from the politicians. Either the government is able to carry out the policy that its wisdom dictates or, having lost support, it gives way to another that will in turn be able to act in accordance with its best judgment. His experience as Ambassador to Yugoslavia caused him to urge more strongly than ever that Congress should leave the executors of policy unmolested so that they may consistently apply their expert knowledge in ways they have learned to know are wise.[11] Arguing that Congress and the two great political parties must support what the international well-being of the country requires, he summons the ghost of Meinecke to assert the "priority of foreign policy"—that is, "the external problems of the country should be given

precedence over the internal ones, and . . . foreign policy should not be permitted to become a function of domestic-political convenience." Few will quarrel with the need to put convenience aside. But the larger question raised by Kennan is whether or not the old institutions and ordinary procedures of American government serve sufficiently well, even with all the adaptations that have resulted from the three great centralizing experiences of this century—world wars, extended depression, and protracted Cold War. Must we, as he urges, further "centralize and strengthen the conduct of foreign policy," which would require, among other things, a more forbearing Congress? Kennan has sharply pointed out that his activities as Ambassador were unfortunately circumscribed by the State Department and still more seriously limited whenever any question he raised had to be considered by two or more departments or agencies. The "main impediments" to his work, however, lay in "legislative action" restrictive of the Ambassador's activity and derived from "Congressional policy," which rigidly regulated American aid to Yugoslavia. He concludes his comments on Congress by remarking that had he known how little value Congress would assign to his judgment, "in the light of an experience of nearly thirty years in the affairs of the Eastern European area," he would not have accepted the appointment.

George Kennan is an exceptional person, who deserves well of the country he has served. In general, however, one must be skeptical in the face of the bureaucrat's claim to superiority in imagination, initiative, intelligence, or wisdom. Congress is not known for its readiness to defer to authority, which is both a source and a sign of

[9]From a paper given by Professor Beloff at the Conference on Teaching and Research in Comparative Government, held by the Italian Political Science Association in April, 1954. The paper is reproduced, in part, in Gunnar Heckscher, *The Study of Comparative Government and Politics* (London: Allen & Unwin, 1957), pp. 136—42. Beloff is obviously referring to the 1954 Berlin Conference, though 1947 is printed in the book. See also his National Summer School Lecture, "The American Role," in *World Perspectives* (London: Conservative Political Centre, 1955), pp. 52—61; and his book, *Foreign Policy and the Democratic Process* (Baltimore: Johns Hopkins Press, 1955).
[10]Kennan, *American Diplomacy, 1900–1950* (Chicago: University of Chicago Press, 1951), pp. 73, 94.
[11]Kennan, *On Dealing With the Communist World* (New York: Harper & Row for the Council on Foreign Relations, 1964), pp. 3—6, 20; J. Robert Moskin, "Our Foreign Policy Is Paralyzed," *Look*, XXVII (November 19, 1963), 25—27; "Impressions of a Recent Ambassadorial Experience," press release from the office of Senator Henry M. Jackson, November 3, 1963. The attributions that follow are from the latter source.

its strength; and one cannot know how different, and possibly how much better, the bureaucracy itself is because of Congressional interference and meddling. Bureaucracies, unmolested, are not famed for their creativity. If they display the virtues of integrity and competence, little more can be asked. Congress, as a restraint upon the executive, displays a different set of virtues. Harshly critical attitudes and harassment that pries information loose are outstanding among them. Questioning by the Senate Foreign Relations Committee once revealed that the Ambassador designate to Ceylon did not know the name of the country's Prime Minister. Reflecting upon the ignorance and incompetence that Congressmen sometimes uncover, a veteran British civil servant in an erratically brilliant book found occasion to remark that some British envoys would display a similarly "abysmal ignorance" if only they were publicly examined.[12] Knowledge without imagination and competence within narrow limits would perhaps more often be discovered, but the important point remains: in Britain one has to guess; in the United States one can more easily know. It is well to have officials interrogated and their performance surveyed by a body whose approval or disapproval makes a difference. The harmful effects of the process are offset if the difficult and important task of checking and prodding a bureaucracy of immense size is accomplished.

THE SEPARATION OF POWERS AND THE PROBLEMS OF DEADLOCK

The Report of the Plowden Committee on the *Control of Public Expenditure* states, with apparently no thought that the judgment is controversial, that "The Government could hardly make its own surveys fully available [to Parliament], since limits are quickly reached in the practicable disclosure of the Government's judgments of future uncertainties and intentions in detail for several years ahead in defence, major economic policy, and of course in social policy and in legislation."[13] In the United States, executive privilege is a matter of recurrent controversy. Not all things are revealed by the President and other officials, nor can they be, but clearly Congress would not tolerate a situation remotely approaching the British condition, where general statements by Ministers replace detailed descriptions of programs and a

careful account of how money requested will be spent. The fusion of executive and legislature, as in Britain, means that one must control the other. The separation of legislative and executive branches, as in America, places each in a position of strength.

Congress as an organization may be energetic, enterprising, and fearless, which does not in itself mean that Congress functions admirably as part of a political system. When strong powers contend, the outcome of the struggle must often be in doubt. Half a century ago, Max Weber argued that:

It is impossible for either the internal or the foreign policy of great states to be strongly and consistently carried out on a collegial basis. . . . Collegiality unavoidably obstructs the promptness of decision, the consistency of policy, the clear responsibility of the individual, and ruthlessness to outsiders in combination with the maintenance of discipline within the group. Hence for these and certain other economic and technical reasons in all large states which are involved in world politics, where collegiality has been retained at all, it has been weakened in favour of the prominent position of the political leader, such as the Prime Minister.[14]

Inertia in American foreign and domestic policy has disturbed many students of politics. Out of the wealth of his knowledge of American politics, V. O. Key, Jr., concluded that American political procedures notoriously encourage delay.[15] Stanley Hoffmann has drawn attention to the massive immobility of American policy.[16] Alastair Buchan has attributed the frustrations felt by Europeans in dealing with the United States in part to "a cumbrous process of internal debate," which makes American policy "extremely hard to alter."[17] The critics are legion, and many of them carry great weight. Much of

[12]George K. Young, *Masters of Indecision: An Inquiry into the Political Process* (London: Methuen, 1962), p. 160.
[13]Lord Plowden, *et al.*, *Control of Public Expenditure*, Cmnd. 1432 (London: HMSO, 1961), par. 74.
[14]*Max Weber: The Theory of Social and Economic Organization*, A. M. Henderson and Talcott Parsons, trans. (New York: Oxford University Press, 1947), pp. 399, 402.
[15]Key, *Public Opinion and American Democracy* (New York: Knopf, 1961), p. 45.
[16]Hoffmann, "Restraints and Choices in American Foreign Policy," *Daedalus*, XCI (Fall, 1962), 689–90.
[17]Buchan, "Partners and Allies," *Foreign Affairs*, XLI (July, 1963), 627.

the criticism singles out Congress for special abuse. President John F. Kennedy, for example, in a press conference held shortly before his death, remarked with some feeling that while he remained responsible for protecting "the national interest," Congress threatened to deny him the means of doing so.[18] Some have seen a too massive continuity and, when alacrity of response is required, a tendency to react cumbrously to crises. Others have argued that the American democracy can act only in crises and that the separation of governmental powers divides political responsibility, renders policy discontinuous and incoherent, and makes the United States difficult for other nations to deal with.[19] These different judgments are not necessarily in contradiction. One vice may lead to another, and the American democracy may act the more impetuously in crises because it is unable to alter its courses of action in between them. Its policy may occasionally veer wildly from one line to another because every line is taken too late and clung to though the conditions that would once have made it appropriate have long since disappeared.

Max Weber's argument that collegiality "obstructs the promptness of decision" finds substantiation, it seems, in American institutions. Since the capacity to act with dispatch is essential to the proper conduct of foreign policy, it is well to consider his judgment carefully. The American government has been described as habitually deadlocked. The undisciplined parties permit the famous Midwestern Republican and Southern Democratic coalition to block the many programs of which its members disapprove and leave the President unable to move the recalcitrant Congress. James MacGregor Burns has argued the case at length. Despite the weight of opinion in their favor, Burns tells us, key domestic measures that were also of indirect importance to our foreign policy were blocked by the Congress in both the Eisenhower and Kennedy Administrations. "It is notable," he says, "that Kennedy's major foreign-policy proposal of 1961—long-term financing of foreign aid—failed at the very time that the nation was aroused over crises in Berlin and Southeast Asia. Perhaps the American people have become so benumbed by constant emergency that a crisis no longer serves the old function of providing broad support for government action."[20] The effects of economic aid can be felt only over a period of years, which is presumably why Burns is so concerned about its long-

term financing. It is difficult then to see what the crises he mentions may have to do with accepting a proposal affecting the process by which funds are allocated. It is easy to argue that long-term financing would be preferable but difficult to demonstrate what is usually assumed: that, given the continuity of the American aid program on the present bases, long-term financing would make truly important differences.

Like many others, Burns wants the American government to break out of its immobility in foreign and military policy. He suggests not only that the disorder of parties and the chaos of Congress impede prompt and effective action but also that there are bold programs promising success, which a more sensible political system would put into effect.

Vastly stepped up educational and cultural exchange, broadening of the powers of the United Nations, more sophisticated and longer range programs of economic aid to the new nations, the establishment of international universities and cultural centers, increased international collaboration in social and natural science and in space technology, follow-up action to the President's "declaration of interdependence" of the Western nations—the possibilities are almost limitless.[21]

The possibilities may be limitless, though from Burns's list this would never be guessed. The list is a mixture of items of controversial merit and of peripheral international political importance. The generally uninspiring quality of the items listed makes one wonder if there really has been such a discrepancy between what has been done and what might have been accomplished by a system of government in which the chief executive and other officials concerned with foreign policy were able to move more freely.

One who describes a nation's political system and practices as notoriously slow and frequently immobile may mean to say that other political systems are better suited to their tasks, or he may have in mind a vaguely imagined ideal system that would provide a better balance be-

[18]Kennedy, "News Conference on Foreign and Domestic Matters," New York Times, November 15, 1963, p. 18.
[19]Walt W. Rostow, The United States in the World Arena (New York: Harper, 1960), p. 509; and the letter from Earl Attlee, Daily Telegraph (London), August 9, 1960, p. 10.
[20]Burns, The Deadlock of Democracy (New York: Prentice-Hall, 1963), p. 4.
[21]Ibid., p. 5.

tween leisured contemplation and the resolution of issues. Burns comments upon America's hesitation to adopt anti-depression measures in the 1930's but understandably fails to argue that other countries did any better. He regrets that the United States waited too long before beginning to aid the underdeveloped countries but fails to remark that, belatedly or not, the United States did lead the way. Comparison with the performance of other political systems makes clear that over any period of, say, five or ten years much is done by the American government. Mere measures of quantity, however, will not suffice. One wants to know especially whether or not action is taken with the promptness required by international events and if the meshing of the many elements of foreign policy is decently accomplished.

One would expect that the United States, like any country that effectively lays claim to the allegiance of its citizens, would be able to act quickly and easily at moments of crisis, when patriotic impulses push the people together and time for the raising of dissentient voices is lacking. One would then like to know if political leaders are sensitive and courageous in the identification of crises or are instead inclined to explain that all is well until everything goes wrong. The government's reaction defines as a crisis the situation that the actions of others have created. It is then almost a truism to say that new and costly policies are created only in reaction to crises. The American government since the war has been impressively ready to say that difficult situations abroad should be treated as though they were crises, which the United States should seek to meet or to mitigate. In no strict sense was it necessary to describe the plight of West European countries after the war as constituting a crisis for the United States. A similar statement can be made about the attack on South Korea, about Communist China's pressure upon the islands of the Formosa Strait, and about other cases.

In responding to crises, the United States has acted to retrieve immediate situations, but the actions have also occasioned broad innovations in policy and efforts on a grander scale. The boldness, coherence, and innovative skill of President Truman's foreign policy, built piecemeal in response to the appearance of dangers abroad, is surely impressive. The years since his Presidency have not been years of immobility in foreign policy but have instead been a time of calm persistence in the application and elaboration of a policy soundly conceived. Errors and occasional uncertainty are inevitable in any policy. Whether or not specific actions are to be applauded, however, America's policies in the Far East and elsewhere cannot be called irresponsible, unrestrained, or impetuous.

The President proposes; Congress disposes. But the President proposes many things, and Congress often disposes of them summarily. Because it frequently rejects proposed legislation, Congress has suffered a reputation for doing nothing. From the open manner in which agreement is sought and the periodic difficulty of securing it, the existence of stalemate is sometimes deduced. The process by which stalemate is avoided is taken as proof of its presence. In England, the political system discourages the open making of efforts to forge agreement on policies, lest dissension within parties be revealed. Under such circumstances, what Ministers ask for is nearly identical with what the legislature gives them, which is mistakenly taken as indication that leadership is strong, action is easy, and policies are properly coordinated.

But if the struggle over policy between the President and Congress is conducted as a competition in power, can one assume that the legislative product will often meet the needs of the day? Just as struggle is wrongly identified with stalemate, so competition is mistakenly associated with unpredictability. Of Fords and Plymouths one can say with near certainty that they will be very much like Chevrolets, and in most years the new models of all three manufacturers will look much like the old ones. So it has ordinarily been from one year to the next with foreign-aid bills, military budgets, and American policy toward particular countries and areas. Why this is so is made clear in part by identifying the aspects of policy that are argued about. Who "lost" China? Why was "victory" in Korea not gained or even sought? Will the foreign-aid program be adequate after Congress has gone over it? In such arguments over policy, the questions essentially at issue are not about whether in principle to accept a program costly in dollars and sometimes in lives. Rather, the participants ask how well a program has been carried out, just how far the country should commit itself, and whether or not the rewards will be proportionate to the costs. Majority opinion about America's role in the world is firmly established, which frustrates the excluded minority and leads them to noisy dissent. The range of opinion that has effectively set the terms of political competition is quite narrow, which helps to make policy stable. The continuity of policy is also promoted by the institutional relation of President to Congress and by the fluidity of the Congressional parties.

EXECUTIVE LEADERSHIP

One of the errors commonly made in assessing the merit of American government is to assume that because a series of pitched battles are fought within Congress and between Congress and the President the policy that emerges must be as messy as the process by which it is made. Professor Herman Finer, for example, has rightly remarked that the American government at times speaks with many voices. As an instance, he cited Henry Wallace's effort, in 1946, to undercut the State Department's foreign policy and turn America toward conciliation of Russia. Finer failed, however, to notice that the incident provoked a quick clarification of America's direction and purpose. American policy toward Palestine, Finer added, was hopelessly muddled, "for so incoherent had the process of policy making been that the administration had never counted and accepted the cost" of its own recommendation. Palestine was thereby condemned to bloodshed.[22] The British politician L. S. Amery had already attributed that unhappy result to "the weak compromises, postponements, and fluctuations" of British policy, which is a sounder conclusion since Britain's responsibility had been paramount. Amery, indeed, offered Britain's policy on Palestine as a typical instance, one in which "the Foreign Office, anxious to avoid immediate trouble with the Arab States, has generally for many years now been at variance with such constructive policy as the Colonial Office has wished to carry out."[23] Turning back to Finer, we find that he offers finally, as an "incident full of instruction to the student of American government," the $1.5 billion reduction of funds for the European Recovery Program that Representative Taber led the Appropriations Committee and the House to make in June of 1948.[24] Finer told only a part of the story; much of the amount cut by the House was restored in the final appropriation. And he failed to see, in 1949, that ERP, generously supported despite Congressional trimming, was well on the way to its outstanding success. Finer has fallen into confusion by concentrating on

process without paying attention to outcome. He also constantly implies and occasionally argues that a different process, one more like Britain's, would be much superior. If a policy made smoothly will surely be integrated, then the acceptance by Parliament of the Prime Minister's policies can be identified with the realization of coherence in the government's program.

It is at this point instructive to look at Amery's analysis more carefully. Having served in the Commons for thirty-four years (about half of them in office in a number of departments), he chose to repeat in the lectures he published in 1947 words that he had written in the mid-1930's. They are worth repeating once more. There is, he asserted from his own experience,

very little Cabinet policy, as such, on any subject. No one has time to think it out, to discuss it, to co-ordinate its various elements, or to see to its prompt and consistent enforcement. There are only departmental policies. The "normal" Cabinet is really little more than a standing conference of departmental chiefs where departmental policies come up, from time to time, to be submitted to a cursory criticism as a result of which they may be accepted, blocked, or in some measure adjusted to the competing policies of other departments. But to a very large extent each department goes its own way, following its own bent and its own tradition, fighting the "Whitehall War" to the best of its ability. . . .

The whole system is one of mutual friction and delay with, at best, some partial measure of mutual adjustment between unrelated policies. It is quite incompatible with any coherent planning of policy as a whole, or with the effective execution of such a policy. It breaks down hopelessly in a serious crisis where clear thinking over difficult and complex situations, definite decisions (not formulae of agreement) and swift and resolute action are required.[25]

The fiction of Cabinet responsibility dissuades Parliament from trying to find out what has actually gone on and leads some political

[22]Finer, *Theory and Practice of Modern Government* (rev. ed.; New York: Holt, Rinehart & Winston, 1949), p. 678.
[23]Amery, *Thoughts on the Constitution* (London: Oxford University Press, 1947), p. 94.
[24]Finer, *Theory and Practice of Modern Government*, pp. 678–79.
[25]Amery, *Thoughts on the Constitution*, p. 87.

scientists to assume that the Cabinet's imprimatur on a policy is certification of its coherence. What has actually gone on for the most part is that the Prime Minister has presided, as a good chairman should, while each department has pursued its own policy. What Amery observed and deplored, Ivor Jennings made into a maxim of proper British governance. A Prime Minister in peacetime, he asserted, "ought not to have a policy. If he has able ministers, he ought to rely on them, and policies should come from Departmental ministers, assisted as they are by all the knowledge and experience that their Departments can offer." In Jennings's view, the good Prime Minister will offer his Ministers political advice, and in Cabinet he will conciliate and encourage them.[26]

In Britain, the government's program is normally a patchwork of the policies of different departments. In the United States, the government's program has come to be the President's, actually as well as formally hammered into shape by him and his immediate assistants. In commenting upon the reaction of Congress to the legislative initiatives of Alexander Hamilton, Professor Lawrence H. Chamberlain remarked that despite "its growing reluctance, Congress could not resist the potent combination of information and concrete proposal which has ever been the special advantage of the executive."[27] Least well can Congress do so, it should be added, when the movement of events requires that response be rapidly made. With the growing importance of foreign affairs, the President's legislative star has further ascended. Until quite recently, the President's commanding presence has only sporadically been felt. The policies of the government have, through most of American history, depended on Congressmen's interests, public pressures, the force of events, and the fancies of Presidents. Radical changes in practice have recently been made. As Richard E. Neustadt points out, "In 1937, Mr. Roosevelt was bitterly attacked for sending prepared bills to Congress. In 1953, Mr. Eisenhower was attacked by his own partisans for failing to do so. In 1961, Mr. Kennedy not only recommended a complete roster of legislation but sent accompanying draft bills, over his own signature, to the two Houses of Congress."[28] Traditionally the strong President was the one who pressed his policies upon Congress. All Presidents now do so, including Eisenhower after his first year in office. The personal initiatives "of this century's

'strong' Presidents," guiding the economy, acting to prevent strikes or bring them to a conclusion, integrating foreign and military policies, "have now been set by statutes as requirements of office."[29] Thus Neustadt refers to the "routinized responsibility to take the policy lead" and to the "regular routines of office," which make Presidential leadership in legislation as commonplace as the veto power in Herbert Hoover's day.[30] Still, in leading the country, heading the administration, and shaping the legislative program, may it be, as Neustadt suggests, that the President's mode of action is "less creativity than crystallization"? While he "needs to be an actor" may he instead be "pre-eminently a reactor"? Does he typically "choose" rather than "originate"?[31]

To originate is scarcely an everyday task; most work must be less demanding than creation if the office of the President is to be endured by any man. Neustadt's evaluations are wholly perceptive, though he takes for granted a degree of initiative and an amount of originality in fashioning programs that, in order to draw a just comparison with England, should be more heavily emphasized. Whether or not it is adequate for Presidents to crystallize rather than to create depends on the quality of the original ideas and how easily they gain the President's attention. Whether or not reaction is a satisfactory substitute for action depends on how quickly issues are defined and problems thrown up to the highest levels of government. Whether or not a Presidency whose incumbents choose rather than originate can be safely sustained by the country depends on how soon the President is inclined to get into the line of departmental decisions and how varied are the perspectives, commitments, and talents of officials subordinate to him. The analysis in Chapter 3 and considerations that are presented in Chapter 6 sup-

[26]Jennings, *The British Constitution* (3d ed.; Cambridge: Cambridge University Press, 1950), pp. 164–65.
[27]Chamberlain, *The President, Congress, and Legislation* (New York: Columbia University Press, 1946), p. 11.
[28]Neustadt, "Staffing the Presidency: The Role of White House Agencies," in Senate Subcommittee of the Committee on Government Operations, *Administration of National Security, Selected Papers* (87th Cong., 2d sess., 1962), p. 130.
[29]Neustadt, "The Presidency at Mid-Century," *Law and Contemporary Problems*, XXI (Autumn, 1956), 611.
[30]*Ibid.*, p. 623; Neustadt, "Presidency and Legislation: Planning the President's Program," *American Political Science Review*, XLIX (December, 1955), 1014.
[31]Neustadt, "Presidency and Legislation," p. 1015; "The Presidency at Mid-Century," p. 622; "Staffing the Presidency," p. 131.

port the conclusion that on all of these counts one can expect more sparkling performances from Presidents than from Prime Ministers.

Prejudice against a separation of political powers rests in important part on the notion that from the executive offices of government will emerge programs whose merit and coherence are assured if only the legislature refrains from tampering with them. Purely hierarchical arrangement, in which each office is subordinate to another until one reaches the head of government at the apex, is, however, a simple impossibility. Rule without what Weber called collegiality is inconceivable. The relevant question would then seem to be, which of the different types of collegial arrangement will encourage coherence of policy, persistence of action, the spirit of sacrifice where desirable, and ruthlessness to outsiders if that should be required.

The President, though he does not get all of his program approved and gets little in exactly the form he has asked for, chooses the terrain on which legislative controversy occurs. Congressional legislation of major public importance is rare. The position of the President as leader of the nation and chief artificer of its policy has been ground so deeply into the American system that even President Eisenhower could not consistently maintain his disinclination to play the foremost role. Crucial problems will be treated by the Congress largely in terms posed by the President. At the height of the Indochinese crisis in May of 1954, Representative Rayburn remarked that the Democrats were "ready to cooperate in a sound foreign policy" provided they knew "what that policy is."[32] That Rayburn, better than anyone else in the last fifty years, could have persuaded the House to follow his lead, makes his comment all the more significant. He was seeking a chance to back a policy, not to make one, well appreciating that Congressional government is inappropriate to conditions of complexity and crisis, which are the two outstanding characteristics of the day. Even those who wish to obstruct a particular program look to the President for a lead and bitterly complain if his requests are not fully and clearly set before the Congress. Just listen to the complaint that Senator Wayne Morse lodged against President Johnson: "He doesn't want to tell the country the form in which he, as Commander in Chief and President of the United States, thinks foreign aid legislation ought to be passed, which might I say is just elementary in

this system of representative government. The country has the right to look to the President for recommendations as to the form it ought to take instead of passing the buck to the Congress."[33] The crucial problems will be treated in the President's terms, and the problems that Congress takes to be crucial will be the ones that the President describes as being so.

Still, losing legislation is a Presidential way of life. Why should anyone expect that the policies that clear the Congressional hurdle will represent just about all the legislation that the interests of the nation can be said to require? Losing is serious if the legislation is urgently needed. But if it is, the success of the President is likely. Presidents concentrate on gaining Congressional support for the policies they believe to be most important. No President will get *every-thing* he may wish for. Most Presidents, however, can get *any one thing*, if only they "wish" for it hard enough. This conclusion rests firmly on a tripod whose three legs are the institutionalized leadership of the Presidency, the nature of foreign-policy problems, and the fluidity of the parties in Congress. The first two have been discussed; the third we now turn to.

THE INTERRELATION OF LEGISLATURES AND EXECUTIVES

In England, compromises are made within the parties, which try hard to maintain a publicly united front. Whether or not the distance between parties is wide, the choices of the voter are clearly distinguished. A majority gained in a national election is a majority for a party that will be able to carry out its advertised program. Majorities gained by American parties have, in contrast, been termed "Make-Believe Majorities."[34] It cannot be assumed that a victorious party will hold together sufficiently in Congress to put into effect any of the platform on which the party stood before the people. Those who highly value clarity of choice will prefer the system that forces firm compromises to be made within parties prior to the holding of elections. At what price, one may wonder, since benefits seldom come free, has clarity of choice been

[32]*New York Times*, May 14, 1954, p. 1.
[33]Senate Hearings before the Committee on Foreign Relations, *Foreign Assistance, 1965* (89th Cong., 1st sess., 1965), p. 202.
[34]James MacGregor Burns, *Congress on Trial* (New York: Harper, 1949), p. 39.

purchased? The British parties supposedly "give the national welfare right of way over minority interests." Although concessions are made to interests it is said that "those concessions are never so fundamental as to endanger seriously the party's loyalty to its national program."[35] But how was that program made up? The belief that the balance between sectional and national interests will always be justly struck is a baffling one. When parties are in close contention for office, the votes of small groups may be needed for victory. Leaders may then require their disciplined parties to accede to the demands of pressure groups in order to secure the votes of their members.[36] Some policies will be adopted in order to heighten the parties' appeal. Others will be forgone in order to avoid the disruption of parties. The better a party is disciplined, the more easily it obeys the electoral imperatives. Because both the perpetuation of a governmental party in power and the reputation of its opposition depend upon party unity, the temptation to avoid major issues while accommodating minor interests is great.

It is sometimes thought that majority governments are able to move easily, for with disciplined parties the government can act according to the will of what may be half of approximately one half of the nation. One should say instead that British majoritarian governments cannot often enough act boldly on matters that are at once important and controversial, for the half of the nation that the government happens to represent must be substantially agreed, in the person of its representatives, before policy will ordinarily be essayed. A Prime Minister refrains, if he can, from asking for policies that will split his party or spread discontent within it. The relation between the management of groups and the content of policy is more clearly seen within the Labour Party than among the Conservatives. Hugh Gaitskell, having lost to the unilateral disarmers at the party's Scarborough Conference in October of 1960, continued to fight for his policy within the party. A year later, at Blackpool, he was vindicated. In his campaign to amend the public-ownership clause of the party's constitution, however, he had to give way. By a combination of victories and defeats, the party's policy was rendered less firm and less coherent, less appropriate to the country's needs and less attractive to the people than Gaitskell and one group of the party's leaders had thought it could be. The leader of the Labour Party has been comfortable in his office only when he has been able to maintain an effective alliance with a group of powerful trade unionists. In order to be able to do so his preference among policies must not be widely different from theirs.[37]

Leaders of parties in power have an easier time controlling their followers than do leaders of the opposition. Labour's leaders appear to have more trouble than their opposite numbers in the Conservative Party. This is partly because Labour is less often in power, partly because Labour settles its differences in public more often than do the Conservatives, and partly because Labour is a movement as well as a political party, and ideological commitment makes compromises difficult to fashion. The Conservative Party has been described as "a collection of evanescent pressure-groups"; Labour, as "a coalition of parties." The Conservative Party, more homogeneous than Labour, has no permanently alienated factions to deal with. The Conservative Party is made up of individuals whose views vary with issues; the Labour Party to a larger extent is composed of groups of some permanence, each with convictions about policy.[38]

If the government is to act, the party that has formed it must move nearly in unison. Whether the tendencies within parties are rooted more deeply in ideology or material interest, it is seldom easy for them to remain united in the face of great and new public issues. Important disagreements within the party are reason for postponing action until accommodations can be reached. The leader, whether of the government or of the opposition, becomes the target of contending individuals or groups and may preserve himself and strengthen his rule by long withholding his blessing from any of them. Reluctance to press for policies that are controversial characterizes British government on both

[35]Ibid., pp. 38–39.
[36]The argument is beautifully developed by J. Roland Pennock, "'Responsible Government,' Separated Powers, and Special Interests: Agricultural Subsidies in Britain and America," American Political Science Review, LVI (September, 1962), 621–33.
[37]The six largest unions command a majority of all the votes at Labour Party Conferences. On the processes of union decision, see Alan Fox, "The Unions and Defence," Socialist Commentary (February, 1961), pp. 4–9. On the wider subject, see Martin Harrison, Trade Unions and the Labour Party (London: Allen & Unwin, 1960).
[38]S. E. Finer, H. B. Berrington, and D. J. Bartholomew, Backbench Opinion in the House of Commons, 1955–59 (Oxford: Pergamon Press, 1961), pp. 112, 122–24.

foreign and domestic fronts. In international situations that do not immediately and directly threaten the position of Britain, party unity may long be maintained, while decisions on policy are held in abeyance. More often than is the case with domestic problems, however, international events force the hands of Prime Ministers and deny them the luxury of time to work their political wiles on the party. At least since World War II, discipline has most often broken on questions of defense and foreign policy.[39]

The difficult processes of grouping and defining, of compromising and amending, must somewhere take place. The American system, unlike the British, throws questions unresolved by the parties or by the electoral process into the Congressional arena. Congress, openly wrestling with problems that have no solution and publicly pondering the imponderable, is in ill repute for the way it does its job. It is not incompetence and obstructionism that gain Congress its bad reputation but rather its visibility together with the difficulty of the tasks it undertakes. In the United States we know comparatively little, and in Britain nothing at all, of ignorant and silly suggestions that executive officials may have made and fought for within the bureaucracy. A Congressman of little knowledge and no influence may have his nostrum emblazoned in headlines. He may thereby do more to stimulate the wise to resist him than to endanger the country's policy. The Congressional visage is nevertheless disfigured.

Congress investigates the administration and superintends the bureaucracy. In Congress, legislative ideas and governmental programs germinate, the President's proposals are criticized, bills are amended in order to improve them and altered to bring them into accord with the national temper and sectional habits, some measures are hastened and others delayed, interests are mediated and the needs of the country debated. Congress legislatively imposes its views, or seeks to, upon programs and policies that are still controversial. It becomes involved in the processes of policy at the stage where final decisions have not yet been made, doubts still exist, and difficulties are unresolved. Parliament is informed of decisions only after they have been made and cannot know of the pressures and arguments that formed them. Congress acts and is criticized; the House of Commons does little and is assumed to be competent if only someone would give it a job to do. Meanwhile committees and commissions are asked to do what representative assemblies ought to.[40]

Where government operates through a series of *ad hoc* majorities, the hand of the chief executive is strengthened. Since the late 1800's, the discipline of British parties has become increasingly firm. This means, as noted above, that decisions tend to be avoided or postponed for the sake of party unity. It is therefore odd that England has continued to be thought of as a country of strong executive leadership. The absence of party discipline in the United States means that the President seldom gets the support of all the members of his own party in Congress, but it also means that the opposition party will aid the President on all of the many occasions when its unity lapses. A system of casual majorities enhances the role of the person who can put them together. If there is to be persistently strong leadership, the President must supply it. The organization of Congress and the composition of the political parties give him numerous opportunities to do so. Groups are fluid, their members crisscross, interests and ideas conflict and overlap. Congeries of shifting interests and the comparatively even distribution of wealth permit one to say that the country, at least aside from the South, is homogeneous.[41] In a homogeneous country, groups can easily be shuffled. Though the point is not merely geographic, a look at electoral maps does confirm the proposition. In 1896, 1916, 1932, and 1948, the Democratic candidates were weak in the Northeast and strong in North Central and Western States. In 1904, 1920, and 1940, the pattern was reversed. Presidential candidates are better able than their opposite numbers in Britain to vary the image of their parties by putting together different electoral coalitions. It is at this point that the future President begins to emerge as a national leader. If his bid for office is successful, he then becomes the one who devises the legislative strategy by which Congressional groups

[39]W. L. Guttsman, for example, counts twelve important cases of opposition from within the party to Labour's policy from 1945 to 1954. Nine were foreign-policy or military matters. "Changes in British Labour Leadership," in Dwaine Marvick, ed., *Political Decision-Makers* (Glencoe, Ill.: Free Press, 1961), p. 127.

[40]See the list of Committees of Inquiry into Social and Economic Matters appointed from 1958 to 1962, with an indication of subjects considered, in Bernard Crick, *The Reform of Parliament* (London: Weidenfeld & Nicolson, 1964), Appendix F.

[41]The many statements that England is a remarkably homogeneous island should be read as meaning that the crevice between classes runs throughout the land.

are combined and recombined according to issue. Thus is his power in devising and securing a program completed. And if parts of his program are not passed, it is Congress, not the President, who is most often blamed. Thus is his power preserved.

The existence of broad national agreement on matters of foreign policy, the fluidity of parties, and the strong position of the President enable one to say that any crucial problem of foreign policy will be acted upon in terms that the President himself sets. The American variety of collegiality has not destroyed the coherence of foreign policy. In Lord Bryce's view, the reproach of democracy was its incompetence in foreign policy born of executive weakness. The virility of Congress has permitted the development of great strength in the Presidency without the risk of Presidential dictatorship.

THE SENATE AND THE SENATOR
J. William Fulbright

For many years students and critics of the American Congress have urged that Senators and Representatives, and the committees through which most of their legislative work is done, review and redefine their priorities and their allocations of time and effort. Congress, it has been argued, can better contribute to the development of wise national policies and programs by focusing its attention on major lines and directions of policy rather than the detailed nitpicking and kibitzing of policy execution by executive agencies.

In the past seven or eight years, stimulated in part, but not wholly, by his concerns about the war in Vietnam, Senator Fulbright has attempted to play such a role. While many have questioned his views and some his motives, there can be no doubt that he has helped stimulate and lead public discussions of major foreign policy issues through his speeches, lectures and three important books (*Prospects for the West*, 1963; *Old Myths and New Realities*, 1964; *The Arrogance of Power*, 1966).

A representative assembly, wrote John Stuart Mill, has the responsibility "to be at once the nation's Committee of Grievances and its Congress of Opinions; an arena in which not only the general opinion of the nation, but that of every section of it, and, as far as possible, of every eminent individual whom it contains, can produce itself in full light and challenge discussion; where every person in the country may count upon finding somebody who speaks his mind as well or better than he could speak it himself . . . ; where those whose opinion is overruled feel satisfied that it is heard, and set aside not by a mere act of will, but for what are thought superior reasons, . . ."[1]

The American Constitution entrusts these functions to the Congress and particularly, in matters of foreign relations, to the Senate, which has the responsibility to review the conduct of foreign policy by the President and his advisers, to render advice whether it is solicited or not, and to grant or withhold its consent to major acts of foreign policy. In addition the Congress has a traditional responsibility, in keeping with the spirit if not the precise words of the Constitution, to serve as a forum of diverse opinions and as a channel of communication between the American people and their government. The discharge of these functions is not merely a prerogative of the Congress; it is a constitutional obligation, for the neglect of which the Congress can and should be called to public account.

In recent years the Congress has not been fully discharging these responsibilities in the field of foreign relations. The reduced role of the Congress and the enhanced role of the President in the making of foreign policy are not the result merely of President Johnson's ideas of consensus; they are the culmination of a trend in the constitutional relationship between President and Congress that began in 1940, which is to say, at the beginning of this age of crisis.

The cause of the change is crisis. The President has the authority and resources to make decisions and take actions in an emergency; the Congress does not. Nor, in my opinion, should it; the proper responsibilities of the Congress are those spelled out by Mill—to reflect and review, to advise and criticize, to grant or with-

[1]John Stuart Mill, *Considerations on Representative Government* (New York: Harper and Brothers, 1867), p. 116.

hold consent. In the last twenty-five years American foreign policy has encountered a shattering series of crises and inevitably, or almost inevitably, the effort to cope with these has been Executive effort, while the Congress, inspired by patriotism, importuned by Presidents, and deterred by lack of information, has tended to fall in line behind the Executive. The result has been an unhinging of traditional constitutional relationships; the Senate's constitutional powers of advice and consent have atrophied into what is widely regarded as, though never asserted to be, a duty to give prompt consent with a minimum of advice.

This situation is not fundamentally the fault of individuals. It is primarily the result of events, and the problem is not one of apportioning blame but of finding a way to restore the constitutional balance, of finding ways by which the Senate can discharge its *duty* of advice and consent in an era of permanent crisis.

Presidents must act in emergencies, especially when the country is at war, and of the last five Presidents only one has not had to wage a sizable war for at least a part of his period in office. Beset with the anxieties of a foreign crisis, no President can relish the idea of inviting opinionated and tendentious Senators into his high-policy councils. His reluctance is human but it is not in keeping with the intent of the Constitution. As representatives of the people Senators have the duty, not merely the right, to render advice, not on the day-to-day conduct of foreign policy, but on its direction and philosophy as these are shaped by major decisions. I conclude that when the President, for reasons with which we can all sympathize, does not invite us into his high-policy councils, it is our duty to infiltrate them as best we can.

A distinction, to be sure, must be made between the making and the conduct of foreign policy. In a number of speeches in recent years, I have deplored the tendency of Senators and Representatives to interfere excessively in the *conduct* of policy, by advising on and complaining about the routine activities of American diplomats, especially those below the top level, and by such practices as the use of the annual foreign-aid debate as an occasion to air extraneous grievances—extraneous, that is, to foreign aid—ranging from Ecuadoran incursions on the rights of California fishermen to proposals for the withdrawal of most-favored-nation trade treatment from Yugoslavia.

The philosophy and direction of foreign policy are a different matter altogether. It is ironic that the Congress, while steadily if erratically expanding its incursions on the day-to-day *conduct* of policy, where its influence is inappropriate and often mischievous, has just as steadily been resigning from its responsibilities in the *making* of policy. It is the latter trend which poses the more serious problems for the nation, and it is my hope, as I shall explain further, that through its extensive public hearings on Vietnam, China, and other issues, the Senate Foreign Relations Committee is contributing to a revival of the Senate's traditional authority in foreign affairs and thereby to the restoration of a proper constitutional balance between the Executive and the legislature. It is too soon, however, to judge whether the revival of debate in the Senate signals the beginning of a trend toward constitutional readjustment or is only a manifestation of widespread anxiety about the war in Vietnam.

DECLINE OF THE SENATE

I have had some personal experiences which illustrate the extent to which the trend toward Executive predominance has gone and the extraordinary difficulty a Senator has in trying to discharge his responsibility to render useful advice and to grant or withhold his consent with adequate knowledge and sound judgment.

The Bay of Pigs

In the spring of 1961 I was invited to participate with President Kennedy's advisers in the deliberations preceding the Bay of Pigs expedition. The President's deference to the Chairman of the Senate Foreign Relations Committee was inspired not by constitutional considerations but by a coincidence. A few days previously, at the time of Congress's Easter recess, the President had let me hitch a ride to Florida on his plane. During the flight I heard his advisers discussing a plan for the invasion of Cuba. I was less than completely astonished because rumors of an invasion were widespread at the time and, in fact, I had already prepared a short memorandum advising against the project. I discussed the matter with President Kennedy on the plane, giving him a copy of my memorandum; upon my return to Washington he invited me to a meeting with himself and his senior advisers at which my reasons for opposing the invasion of Cuba were given a full and fair hearing.

It was a mark of President Kennedy's magnanimity that I was not subsequently banished from the Presidential plane, but neither did any subsequent trip have such interesting results. Nor, indeed, can this episode be regarded as a manifestation of the advice-and-consent function of the Senate; I was the only Senator involved in the fateful deliberations preceding the Bay of Pigs and my involvement was an accident.

The Cuban missile crisis

The Cuban missile crisis of 1962 more typically illustrated the respective roles of President and Congress in the making of a critical decision. Many of us at that time were in our home states campaigning for re-election. When the President called some of us back—the Congressional leadership, appropriate committee chairmen, and ranking minority members—we were not told the nature of the emergency about which we were to be consulted or informed, but of course we were able to guess the approximate situation. None of us aboard the Presidential plane which had been sent to pick us up on October′ 22, 1962, however, had any official knowledge of the crisis which in the following hours was to bring the world to the brink of nuclear war.

We convened at the White House at five P.M. and were briefed by the President and his advisers on the crisis and on the decisions *which had already been taken* on how to deal with it. When the President asked for comments, Senator Richard Russell of Georgia and I advocated the invasion of Cuba by American forces, I on the grounds that a blockade, involving as it might a direct, forcible confrontation with Russian ships, would be more likely to provoke a nuclear war than an invasion which would pit American soldiers against Cuban soldiers and allow the Russians to stand aside. Had I been able to formulate my views on the basis of facts since made public rather than on a guess as to the nature of the situation, I might have made a different recommendation. In any case, the recommendation which I made represented my best judgment at the time and I thought it my duty to offer it.

The decision to blockade Cuba had already been made. We had been summoned to the White House, as it turned out, not for a consultation but for a last-minute briefing. The meeting at the White House broke up after six P.M.,

and President Kennedy went on television at seven P.M. to announce his decision to the American people. In his book on President Kennedy, Theodore Sorensen refers to the temerity of those of us from the Congress who expressed opinions at the White House meeting as "the only sour note" in all of the decision-making related to the Cuban missile crisis.[2]

The Dominican intervention

On the afternoon of April 28, 1965, the leaders of Congress were called once again to an emergency meeting at the White House. We were told that the revolution that had broken out four days before in the Dominican Republic was completely out of hand, that Americans and other foreigners on the scene were in great danger, and that United States Marines would be landed in Santo Domingo that night for the sole purpose of protecting the lives of Americans and other foreigners. . . . None of the Congressional leaders expressed disapproval of the action planned by the President.

Four months later, after an exhaustive review of the Dominican crisis by the Senate Foreign Relations Committee meeting in closed sessions, it was clear beyond reasonable doubt that although saving American lives may have been a factor in the decision to intervene on April 28, the major reason was a determination on the part of the United States government to defeat the rebel, or constitutionalist, forces whose victory at that time was imminent. Had I known in April what I knew in August, I most certainly would have objected to the American intervention in the Dominican Republic. I would have objected for a number of excellent reasons, not the least of which was the violation by the United States of the Charter of the Organization of American States, a treaty which had been solemnly ratified with the consent of the Senate.

The Gulf of Tonkin resolution

Almost nine months before the Dominican intervention, on August 5, 1964, the Congress received an urgent request from President Johnson for the immediate adoption of a joint resolution regarding Southeast Asia. On August 2 the United States destroyer *Maddox* had reportedly been attacked without provocation by North Vietnamese torpedo boats in the Gulf of Tonkin,

[2]Theodore Sorensen, *Kennedy* (New York: Harper & Row, 1965), p. 702.

and on August 4 the *Maddox* and another destroyer, the *C. Turner Joy*, had reportedly been attacked again by North Vietnamese torpedo boats in international waters. In addition to endorsing the President's action in ordering the Seventh Fleet and its air units to take action against the North Vietnamese attacks, the resolution authorized the President "to take all necessary steps, including the use of armed force," against aggression in Southeast Asia.

Once again Congress was asked to show its support for the President in a crisis; once again, without questions or hesitation, it did so. The Senate Foreign Relations and Armed Services Committees endorsed the resolution after perfunctory hearings and with only one dissenting vote on the morning of August 6. After brief floor debate the resolution was adopted by the Senate on August 7 by a vote of 88 to 2 and by the House of Representatives on the same day by a vote of 416 to 0.

The joint resolution of August 7, 1964, was a blank check—so it has been interpreted—signed by the Congress in an atmosphere of urgency that seemed at the time to preclude debate. Since its adoption the Administration has converted the Vietnamese conflict from a civil war in which some American advisers were involved to a major international war in which the principal fighting unit is an American army of hundreds of thousands of men. Each time Senators have raised questions about successive escalations of the war, we have had the blank check of August 7, 1964, waved in our faces as supposed evidence of the overwhelming support of the Congress for a policy in Southeast Asia which in fact has been radically changed since the summer of 1964. We have also been told that we can exercise the option to withdraw the support expressed in the resolution at any time by concurrent resolution—an option so distasteful to most members of Congress, because it would surely be interpreted abroad as a repudiation of the President's leadership, as to be no option at all. Still, when the Senate on March 1, 1966, tabled Senator Morse's motion to rescind the resolution, the Administration chose to interpret this vote as an endorsement of its policy in Vietnam.

All this is very frustrating to some of us in the Senate but we have only ourselves to blame. Had we met our responsibility of careful examination of a Presidential request, had the Senate Foreign Relations Committee held hearings on the resolution before recommending its adoption, had the Senate debated the resolution and considered its implications before giving its overwhelming approval, and specifically had we investigated carefully and thoroughly the alleged unprovoked attacks on our ships, we might have put limits and qualifications on our endorsement of future uses of force in Southeast Asia, if not in the resolution itself then in the legislative history preceding its adoption. As it was, only Senators Morse of Oregon and Gruening of Alaska opposed the resolution.

As Chairman of the Foreign Relations Committee, I served as floor manager of the Southeast Asia resolution and did all I could to bring about its prompt and overwhelming adoption. I did so because I was confident that President Johnson would use our endorsement with wisdom and restraint. I was also influenced by partisanship: an election campaign was in progress and I had no wish to make any difficulties for the President in his race against a Republican candidate whose election I thought would be a disaster for the country. My role in the adoption of the resolution of August 7, 1964, is a source of neither pleasure nor pride to me today.

Many Senators who accepted the Gulf of Tonkin resolution without question might well not have done so had they foreseen that it would subsequently be interpreted as a sweeping Congressional endorsement for the conduct of a large-scale war in Asia. Literally, it can be so interpreted, but it must be remembered that the resolution was adopted during an election campaign in which the President was telling the American people that it would be a mistake for the United States to become involved in a major war in Asia while criticizing his opponent for proposing just that. This may explain the perfunctory debate of August 1964 but hardly excuses the Congress for granting such sweeping authority with so little deliberation. It was a mistake which I trust will not soon be repeated.

The Asian Doctrine

With such experiences in mind as those which I have described, I think it extremely important that the Senate consider the implications of the Johnson Administration's evolving "Asian Doctrine" before it becomes an irrevocable national commitment undertaken by the Executive without the consent or even the knowledge of the Senate.

Under the emerging "Asian Doctrine" the

United States is taking on the role of policeman and provider for all of noncommunist Asia. Defining Asia as "the crucial arena of man's striving for independence and order," the President, without reference to the United Nations or the obligation of other countries, declared in a speech in July 1966 "the determination of the United States to meet our obligations in Asia as a Pacific power," denounced those—whoever they may be—who hold to the view that "east is east and west is west and never the twain shall meet," and laid down certain "essentials" for peace in Asia, all requiring a predominantly American effort for the shaping of a "Pacific era."[3]

In a television interview on April 19, 1966, Vice-President Humphrey defined the Honolulu Declaration resulting from the President's meeting with Premier Nguyen Cao Ky of South Vietnam in February 1966 as a "Johnson Doctrine" for Asia, "a pledge to ourselves and to posterity to defeat aggression, to defeat social misery, to build viable, free political institutions, and to achieve peace. . . ." Acknowledging these to be "great commitments," the Vice-President went on to say: ". . . I think there is a tremendous new opening here for realizing the dream of the Great Society in the great area of Asia, not just here at home."

All this must come as a big surprise to Senators who have not even been informed of these sweeping commitments, much less asked for their advice and consent, but the President's close friend and biographer, Mr. William White, reported in one of his columns that the "Asian Doctrine" has been in the President's mind for five years, and Mr. White should know.[4] To the best of my knowledge, however, it has not been in the mind of the Senate, whose consent is required for treaties, or of the Congress as a whole, which is empowered by the Constitution not only to "declare war" and to "raise and support armies" but "to pay the debts and provide for the common defense and general welfare of the United States."

THE SENATE AS A FORUM OF DEBATE

How then can the Senate discharge its constitutional responsibilities of advice and consent in an age when the direction and philosophy of foreign policy are largely shaped by urgent decisions made at moments of crisis? I have no definitive formula to offer but I do have some ideas as to how both the Senate as an institution and an individual Senator can meet their constitutional responsibilities.

The Senate as a whole, I think, should undertake to revive and strengthen the deliberative function which it has permitted to atrophy in the course of twenty-five years of crisis. Acting on the premise that dissent is not disloyalty, that a true consensus is shaped by airing differences rather than suppressing them, the Senate should again become, as it used to be, an institution in which the great issues of American politics are contested with thoroughness, energy, and candor. Nor should the Senate allow itself to be too easily swayed by Executive pleas for urgency and unanimity, or by allegations of "aid and comfort" to the enemies of the United States made by officials whose concern with such matters may have something to do with a distaste for criticism directed at themselves.

It is sometimes useful and occasionally necessary for Congress to express prompt and emphatic support for the President on some matter of foreign relations. It seems to me, however, that we have gone too far in this respect, to the point of confusing Presidential convenience with the national interest. It is perfectly natural for the President, pressed as he is to make decisions and take action in foreign relations, to overemphasize the desirability of promptness and unanimity. But the Senate has its own responsibilities, and however strongly feelings of patriotism may incline it to comply with the President's wishes, the higher patriotism deriving from its constitutional trust requires it to reply to the President in effect: "Mr. President, we will take your urgent request under immediate advisement; we will set aside our other legislative business and will proceed as rapidly as orderly procedure permits to hear testimony and to debate and act upon your request. We will not, however, except under conditions of national emergency, set aside the normal procedures of committee hearings and deliberation and debate on the Senate floor. We regret any inconvenience which this may cause you, but just as we are cognizant of your obligation to act, we know that you are cognizant of our obligation to inform ourselves and deliberate in order to be able to give you our best possible

[3]Speech to American Alumni Council at West Sulphur Springs, West Virginia, July 12, 1966.
[4]William S. White, "Asian Doctrine," The Washington Post, July 19, 1966.

advice. We know you are aware that we render this advice not only in the hope that it will be a service to your Administration but also as an obligation to our constituents—an obligation, Mr. President, which we feel bound to meet even if, for one reason or another, our doing so subjects you to certain inconveniences."

It must be admitted that vigorous debate in the Senate can be misunderstood abroad. It seems reasonable to suppose that the debate on Vietnam has given the Viet Cong, the North Vietnamese, and the Chinese a distorted impression of internal divisions within the United States. I regret this effect very much, but I cannot accept the conclusion that it is necessary or proper to suspend the normal procedures of the Congress in order to give our adversaries an impression—an inaccurate impression—of American unanimity. I, as one Senator, am unwilling to acquiesce, actively or tacitly, to a policy that I judge to be unwise as the price of putting the best possible face on that policy. To do so would be to surrender the limited ability I have to bring influence to bear for what I would judge to be a wiser policy and would constitute a default on my constitutional responsibilities and on my responsibilities to the people of my state.

The major part of the burden of criticism in the Senate naturally falls to the opposition party. Under normal conditions, the duty is one which the opposition is only too glad to perform. Only occasionally does it happen that the party out of power is so feeble or so much in agreement with the President's policies or both that it fails to provide responsible and intelligent opposition. Under such unusual circumstances, when the proper opposition defaults, it seems to me that it is better to have the function performed by members of the President's party than not to have it performed at all.

THE COMMITTEE ON FOREIGN RELATIONS

In the winter and spring of 1966 the Senate Committee on Foreign Relations engaged in an experiment in public education. The Committee made itself available as a forum for the meeting of politicians and professors and, more broadly, as a forum through which recognized experts and scholars could contribute to Congressional and public understanding of a number of aspects of the foreign relations of the United States, some short-term and specific, others long-term and general. During the second session of the 89th Congress the Commit-

tee, meeting in open session, heard testimony by specialists on Vietnam and the Vietnamese war, on China and her relations with the United States, on NATO and American relations with Western Europe; and finally, in an experiment that I believe to be unprecedented, the Committee heard testimony by distinguished psychiatrists and psychologists on some of the psychological aspects of international relations. It is my hope that these experiments have contributed to public education and also that they have made a beginning toward restoring the Senate to its proper role as adviser to the President on the great issues of foreign policy.

I believe that the public hearings on Vietnam, by bringing before the American people a variety of opinions and disagreements pertaining to the war and perhaps by helping to restore a degree of balance between the Executive and the Congress, strengthened the country rather than weakened it. The hearings were criticized on the ground that they conveyed an "image" of the United States as divided over the war. Since the country obviously *is* divided, what was conveyed was a fact rather than an image. I see no merit in the view that at the cost of suppressing the normal procedures of democracy, we should maintain an image of unity even though it is a false image.

The hearings on Vietnam were undertaken by the Senate Foreign Relations Committee in the hope of helping to shape a true consensus in the long run, even at the cost of dispelling the image of a false one in the short run. They were undertaken in the belief that the American people and their government would profit from an airing of views by forceful advocates from within and outside the government. They were undertaken in the belief that the best way to assure the prevalence of truth over falsehood is by exposing all tendencies of opinion to free competition in the market place of ideas. They were undertaken in something of the spirit of Thomas Jefferson's words:

I know no safe depository of the ultimate powers of the society but the people themselves; and if we think them not enlightened enough to exercise their control with a wholesome discretion, the remedy is not to take it from them, but to inform their discretion.[5]

[5]Thomas Jefferson, Letter to William Charles Jarvis, September 28, 1820.

Many times in the past the Senate Foreign Relations Committee has served as the forum for a national debate and in some instances its proceedings have had the effect of translating a consensus of values into a consensus of policy as well. One notable instance was the debate on the nuclear test ban treaty in the summer of 1963. For three weeks the Foreign Relations Committee, with members of the Armed Services and Atomic Energy Committees also attending, met in open session to hear vigorous arguments for and against the treaty by witnesses from the government, from the universities, and from other areas of private life. Each day's discussion was transmitted to the American people through the press. The result was that the Foreign Relations Committee was able to serve simultaneously as both an organ of Senate deliberation and a forum of public education. In the course of those three weeks and the Senate floor debate that followed, support for the treaty steadily grew and the treaty was finally ratified by a vote of 81 to 19. Through the medium of open discussion and debate an existing consensus for peace as an objective was translated into a policy consensus for the test ban treaty as a means of advancing it.

The Foreign Relations Committee contemplates additional proceedings pertaining to major questions of American foreign policy. It is our expectation that these proceedings may generate controversy. If they do, it will not be because we value controversy for its own sake but rather because we accept it as a condition of intelligent decision-making, as, indeed, the crucible in which a national consensus as to objectives may be translated into a consensus of policy as well.

THE INDIVIDUAL SENATOR

A Senator who wishes to influence foreign policy must consider the probable results of communicating privately with the Executive or, alternatively, of speaking out publicly. I do not see any great principle involved here: it is a matter of how one can better achieve what one hopes to achieve. For my own part, I have used both methods, with results varying according to circumstances. Other things being equal—which they seldom are—I find it more agreeable to communicate privately with Democratic Presidents and publicly with Republican Presidents. Since 1961, when the Democrats came back

to power, I have made recommendations to the President on a number of occasions through confidential memoranda. I have already referred to the memorandum I gave to President Kennedy regarding the Bay of Pigs.

In June 1961 I sent the President a memorandum protesting public statements on controversial political issues made by members of the armed forces under the sponsorship of right-wing organizations; it resulted in the issuance of an order by Secretary of Defense Robert McNamara restricting such activities and it also produced a lively Senate debate in which I was accused of wishing to "muzzle the military."

In April 1965 I sent President Johnson a memorandum containing certain recommendations on the war in Vietnam, recommendations which I reiterated thereafter in private conversations with high Administration officials. When it became very clear that the Administration did not find my ideas persuasive, I began to make my views known publicly in the hope, if not of bringing about a change in Administration policy, then at least of opening up a debate on that policy.

On the afternoon of September 15, 1965, I made a speech in the Senate criticizing the United States intervention in the Dominican Republic. That morning I had sent a copy of the speech to President Johnson, accompanied by a letter which read as follows:

Dear Mr. President:

Enclosed is a copy of a speech that I plan to make in the Senate regarding the crisis in the Dominican Republic. As you know, my Committee has held extensive hearings on the Dominican matter; this speech contains my personal comments and conclusions on the information which was brought forth in the hearings.

As you will note, I believe that important mistakes were made. I further believe that a public discussion of recent events in the Dominican Republic, even though it brings forth viewpoints which are critical of actions taken by your Administration, will be of long term benefit in correcting past errors, helping to prevent their repetition in the future, and thereby advancing the broader purposes of your policy in Latin America. It is in the hope of assisting you toward these ends, and for this reason only, that I have prepared my remarks.

On the basis of the testimony given in the Foreign Relations Committee, I have concluded that the primary cause of our mistakes in the Dominican Republic was faulty advice that was given to you in the critical last days of April 1965. I believe that it would have been extremely difficult for you to have made any decisions other than the ones that you made on the basis of the information that was given to you; this point is made in two different places in my speech. Nor is the purpose of this statement recrimination against those who seem to have committed errors of judgment; the officials involved are men of competence and integrity, who appear, however, in this instance, to have offered faulty recommendations. I am interested solely, as I know you are, in helping to lay the basis for more successful policies in the future.

Another purpose of my statement is to provide a measure of reassurance for those liberals and reformers in Latin America who were distressed by our Dominican actions, just as you did in your outstanding statement to the Latin American ambassadors on August 17. I believe that the people in Latin America whose efforts are essential to the success of the Alliance for Progress are in need of reassurance that the United States remains committed to the goals of social reform. I know that you are doing a great deal to provide such reassurance and one of my purposes in this speech will be to supplement your own efforts in this field.

Public—and, I trust, constructive—criticism is one of the services that a Senator is uniquely able to perform. There are many things that members of your Administration, for quite proper reasons of consistency and organization, cannot say, even though it is in the long term interests of the Administration that they be said. A Senator, as you well know, is under no such restriction. It is in the sincere hope of assisting your Administration in this way, and of advancing the objective of your policy in Latin America, that I offer the enclosed remarks.

My speech generated a controversy. A number of my colleagues in the Senate expressed support for my position; others disagreed. Much of the criticism, to my surprise and disappointment, was directed not at what I had said about the Dominican Republic and Latin America but at the propriety of my speaking out at all. Taken aback by the consternation caused by my breach of the prevailing consensus, I made the following remarks in the Senate on October 22, 1965:

There has been a good deal of discussion as to whether it is proper for the Chairman of the Senate Foreign Relations Committee to make a speech critical of an Administration of his own party which he generally supports. There is something to be said on both sides of this question and it is certainly one which I considered with care before deciding to make my speech on the Dominican Republic. I concluded, after hearing the testimony of Administration witnesses in the Committee on Foreign Relations, that I could do more to encourage carefully considered policies in the future by initiating a public discussion than by acquiescing silently in a policy I believed to be mistaken. It seemed to me, therefore, that, despite any controversy and annoyance to individuals, I was performing a service to the Administration by stating my views publicly.

I do not like taking a public position criticizing a Democratic Administration which in most respects I strongly support; I do not like it at all. Neither do I like being told, as I have been told, that my statement was "irresponsible" or that it has given "aid and comfort" to the enemies of the United States. I am quite prepared to examine evidence suggesting that my statement contained errors of fact or judgment; I am not prepared to accept the charge that a statement following upon many hours of listening to testimony in the Foreign Relations Committee and many more hours of examining and evaluating relevant documents was "irresponsible." Nor do I take kindly to the charge that I gave "aid and comfort" to the enemies of the United States. If that accusation is to be pressed—and I should hope it would not be—an interesting discussion could be developed as to whether it is my criticisms of United States policy in the Dominican Republic or the policy itself which has given "aid and comfort" to our enemies.

A Senator has a duty to support his President and his party, but he also has a duty to express his views on major issues. In the case of the Dominican crisis I felt that, however reluctant I might be to criticize the Administration—and I was very reluctant—, it was nonetheless my responsibility to do so, for two principal reasons.

First, I believe that the Chairman of the Committee on Foreign Relations has a special obligation to offer the best advice he can on matters of foreign policy; it is an obligation, I believe, which is inherent in the chairmanship, which takes precedence over party loyalty, and which has nothing to do with whether the Chairman's views are solicited or desired by people in the executive branch.

Second, I thought it my responsibility to comment on United States policy in the Dominican Republic because the political opposition, whose function it is to criticize, was simply not doing so. It did not because it obviously approved of United States intervention in the Dominican Republic and presumably, had it been in office, would have done the same thing. The result of this peculiar situation was that a highly controversial policy was being carried out without controversy—without debate, without review, without that necessary calling to account which is a vital part of the democratic process. Again and again, in the weeks following the Committee hearing I noted the absence of any challenge to statements appearing in the press and elsewhere which clearly contradicted evidence available to the Committee on Foreign Relations.

Under these circumstances, I am not impressed with suggestions that I had no right to speak as I did on Santo Domingo. The real question, it seems to me, is whether I had the right not to speak.[6]

It is difficult to measure the effectiveness of a Senator's speech, because its effect may be something *not* done rather than some specific action or change of policy on the part of the Executive. Generally speaking, it seems to me that a Senator's criticism is less likely to affect the case in point than it is to affect some similar case in the future. I am inclined to believe, for example, that my criticism of the State Department in the summer of 1965 for its failure to give public support to the Firestone Tire and Rubber Company when that company was brought under right-wing attack for agreeing to engineer a synthetic-rubber plant in Rumania, while it did not revive that transaction, may have encouraged the State Department to give vigorous and timely support to a number of tobacco companies who were subsequently criticized by extremist groups for their purchases of tobacco from certain Eastern European communist countries. As to the effect of my Dominican speech, it may have been a factor in the Administration's subsequent support of democratic government in the Dominican Republic, repairing thereby some of the damage wrought by the intervention of April 1965 in support of the

Dominican military. Its more significant results will be shown in the reaction of the United States government if it is again confronted with a violent revolution in Latin America.

As to my criticisms and those of my colleagues regarding the Vietnamese war, their effect remains to be seen. Thus far they have clearly failed to persuade the Johnson Administration to reconsider its policy of military escalation. It may be, for the time being, that those of us who deplore American involvement in the Vietnamese civil war will have to be content —in the manner of the British Labour Party at the time of Suez and of the French intellectuals who opposed the colonial wars of the Fourth Republic—with demonstrating to the world that America is not monolithic in its support of present policies, that there are other tendencies of opinion in the American democracy, tendencies which, though temporarily muted, are likely to reassert themselves and to influence American foreign policy in the future as they have in the past. This function alone gives meaning and purpose to the dissent on Vietnam.

Before considering how he will try to influence events, a politician must decide which events he proposes to influence and which he will leave largely to the determination of others. The Senate consists of a hundred individuals with fifty separate constituencies and widely varying fields of individual knowledge and interest. There is little that a Senator can accomplish by his own efforts; if he is to have an effect on public policy, he must influence his colleagues. Sometimes, but not often, a colleague's support can be won by charm; it can certainly be lost by rudeness. Occasionally it can be won by persuasive rhetoric; more often it is gotten by trading your support on one issue for his on another, or simply by a general practice of limiting your own initiatives to matters of unusual interest or importance while otherwise accepting the recommendations of the committees. And in some instances a Senator may influence his colleagues by influencing their constituencies.

Some may regard this process of mutual accommodation as unethical. I do not regard it as unethical, because I do not place my own wishes and judgments on a plane above those of my colleagues. There are no areas of public policy

[6] "Comments on the Dominican Republic," *Congressional Record*, October 22, 1965, p. 27465.

in which I am absolutely sure of the correctness of my opinions, but there are some in which I am reasonably confident of my judgment; it is in these areas that I try to make a contribution. There are other areas in which my knowledge is limited, and in these I prefer to let others take the lead. There are still other areas in which I am proscribed from leadership or initiative by the strong preferences of my constituency.

A politician has no right to ask that he be absolved from public judgment; he may hope, however, that he will be judged principally on the basis of his performance in the areas of his principal effort. He may hope that he will be judged not as a saint or paragon but as a human being entrusted by his constituents with great responsibilities but endowed by the Lord with the same problems of judgment and temptation that afflict the rest of the human race.

Hampered though he is by human limitations, the American politician of the 1960s has respon-

sibilities which no politician in any country in all history has had before. His is the world's most powerful nation at the moment in history when powerful nations have acquired the means of destroying the human race. All of the traditional attitudes of our ancestors, about war and peace, about the conflicts of nations and the brotherhood of man, have been called into question and are in need of re-examination. It is the responsibility of the politician to lead in that fateful re-examination; to do so surely is to act upon a higher patriotism. And, in so doing, in the words of Albert Camus, "if at times we seemed to prefer justice to our country, this is because we simply wanted to love our country in justice, as we wanted to love her in truth and in hope."[7]

[7]Albert Camus, "Letters to a German Friend," Second Letter, December 1943, in *Resistance, Rebellion, and Death* (New York: Random House, 1960), p. 10.

FOREIGN POLICY LEADERSHIP AND COORDINATION
President John F. Kennedy's letter to all U.S. Ambassadors, May 29, 1961
Department of State Foreign Affairs Manual Circular Number 385, March 4, 1966

Given the proliferation of agencies and programs through which the United States has attempted to pursue its foreign policy purposes in the last twenty-five years, one problem that has been discussed almost *ad nauseam* is the need for policy leadership and program coordination for these varied activities. There has been a great deal of debate over who should perform the leadership and coordination roles, and how.

In its overseas dimensions, the answer that was reached fairly early in the game was that the United States ambassador was the obvious choice to provide overall guidance and control of official American activities in his country. President Kennedy's letter of May 29, 1961 represents the culmination, to this point in time, of a gradual process of increasing the power of American ambassadors abroad.

The two paragraphs that deal with military forces overseas and the relationship between their military commander and the ambassador were only sent to those countries where U.S. military field forces were in fact stationed. They indicate the one remaining gap in the authority of the ambassador, a gap that at least some observers feel should be filled by a further general grant of authority to the ambassador. (See the comments by Ausland in the selection in Chapter Two.)

Also worth noting are the ambassador's power to ask any member of the U.S. mission to leave the country and the stipulation that, when there are disagreements with other agency representatives, his decisions are governing until contrary instructions are received from Washington.

The organizational machinery set forth in Foreign Affairs Manual Circular (FAMC) 385 (see below) represents one set of devices for dealing with the much more difficult problem of foreign policy leadership and coordination in Washington. The President has nominal and ultimate responsibility in this field, but it is obvious that he cannot handle all the detailed actions personally. It then becomes a question of whether to develop a very large staff to do this job at the Presidential level or to rely primarily on one of the line departments, which usually means the Department of State, the traditional and still the most important foreign affairs agency of the government. The latter is the solution that recent Presidents have espoused, at least in principle.

The State Department must, then, work with and provide leadership to the other agencies with foreign affairs responsibilities and programs. A standard device for doing so has been some system of interdepartmental committees. FAMC 385 represents one such arrangement; those who developed it in the last years of the Johnson Administration emphasized that it stated much more clearly and emphatically than any previous document the dominant leadership position of the Secretary of State and his department in foreign affairs. However, early in the Nixon administration the plan of organization described in FAMC 385 was abolished. The point to be kept in mind is that whatever the mechanisms and nomenclature developed by the Nixon administration and others that may follow, the problem that they will be trying to cope with is a most difficult one, particularly in Washington where the great departments and agencies of the U.S. government inevitably vie for larger budgets, greater powers and responsibilities, and more autonomy for their own activities.

PRESIDENT JOHN F. KENNEDY'S LETTER TO ALL U.S. AMBASSADORS, MAY 29, 1961

DEAR MR. AMBASSADOR:

Please accept my best wishes for the successful accomplishment of your mission. As the personal representative of the President of the United States in ——, you are part of a memorable tradition which began with Benjamin Franklin and Thomas Jefferson, and which has included many of our most distinguished citizens.

We are living in a critical moment in history. Powerful destructive forces are challenging the universal values which, for centuries, have inspired men of good will in all parts of the world.

If we are to make progress toward a prosperous community of nations in a world of peace, the United States must exercise the most affirmative and responsible leadership. Beyond our shores, this leadership, in large measure, must be provided by our ambassadors and their staffs.

I have asked you to represent our Government in —— because I am confident that you have the ability, dedication, and experience. The purpose of this letter is to define guidelines which I hope may be helpful to you.

The practice of modern diplomacy requires a close understanding not only of governments but also of people, their cultures and institutions. Therefore, I hope that you will plan your work so that you may have the time to travel extensively outside the nation's capital. Only in this way can you develop the close, personal associations that go beyond official diplomatic

circles and maintain a sympathetic and accurate understanding of all segments of the country.

Moreover, the improved understanding which is so essential to a more peaceful and rational world is a two-way street. It is our task not only to understand what motivates others, but to give them a better understanding of what motivates us.

Many persons in —— who have never visited the United States, receive their principal impressions of our nation through their contact with Americans who come to their country either as private citizens or as government employees.

Therefore, the manner in which you and your staff personally conduct yourselves is of the utmost importance. This applies to the way in which you carry out your official duties and to the attitudes you and they bring to day-to-day contacts and associations.

It is an essential part of your task to create a climate of dignified, dedicated understanding, cooperation, and service in and around the Embassy.

In regard to your personal authority and responsibility, I shall count on you to oversee and coordinate all the activities of the United States Government in ——.

You are in charge of the entire United States Diplomatic Mission, and I shall expect you to supervise all of its operations. The Mission includes not only the personnel of the Department of State and the Foreign Service, but also the representatives of all other United States agencies which have programs or activities in ——. I shall give you full support and backing in carrying out your assignment.

Needless to say, the representatives of other agencies are expected to communicate directly with their offices here in Washington, and in the event of a decision by you in which they do not concur, they may ask to have the decision reviewed by a higher authority in Washington.

However, it is their responsibility to keep you fully informed of their views and activities and to abide by your decisions unless in some particular instance you and they are notified to the contrary.

From *The Ambassador and the Problem of Coordination,* a study by the Historical Studies Division of the Department of State for the Subcommittee on National Security Staffing and Operations, Committee on Government Operations, U.S. Senate, 88 Cong. 1 sess. (1963), pp. 155–56.

If in your judgment individual members of the Mission are not functioning effectively, you should take whatever action you feel may be required, reporting the circumstances, of course, to the Department of State.

In case the departure from —— of any individual member of the Mission is indicated in your judgment, I shall expect you to make the decision and see that it is carried into effect. Such instances I am confident will be rare.

Now one word about your relations to the military. As you know, the United States Diplomatic Mission includes Service Attachés, Military Assistance Advisory Groups, and other Military components attached to the Mission. It does not, however, include United States military forces operating in the field where such forces are under the command of a United States area military commander. The line of authority to these forces runs from me, to the Secretary of Defense, to the Joint Chiefs of Staff in Washington and to the area commander in the field.

Although this means that the chief of the American Diplomatic Mission is not in the line of military command, nevertheless, as Chief of Mission, you should work closely with the appropriate area military commander to assure the full exchange of information. If it is your opinion that activities by the United States military forces may adversely affect our over-all relations with the people or government of ——, you should promptly discuss the matter with the military commander and, if necessary, request a decision by higher authority.

I have informed all heads of departments and agencies of the Government of the responsibilities of the chiefs of American Diplomatic Missions for our combined operations abroad, and I have asked them to instruct their representatives in the field accordingly.

As you know, your own lines of communication as Chief of Mission run through the Department of State.

Let me close with an expression of confidence in you personally and the earnest hope that your efforts may help strengthen our relations with both the Government and the people of ——. I am sure that you will make a major contribution to the cause of world peace and understanding.

Good luck and my warmest regards,

Sincerely,
[Signed] John F. Kennedy

Subject: Direction, coordination and supervision of interdepartmental activities overseas

1. Authority and responsibility of the Secretary of State

To assist the President in carrying out his responsibilities for the conduct of foreign affairs, he has assigned to the Secretary of State authority and responsibility to the full extent permitted by law for the overall direction, coordination and supervision of interdepartmental activities of the United States Government overseas.

2. Activities not included

Such activities do not include those of United States military forces operating in the field where such forces are under the command of a United States area military commander and such other military activities as the President elects to conduct through military channels.

3. Definition of "interdepartmental" activities

Activities which are internal to the execution and administration of the approved programs of a single department or agency and which are not of such a nature as to affect significantly the overall U.S. overseas program in a country or region are not considered to be interdepartmental matters. If disagreement arises at any echelon over whether a matter is interdepartmental or not in the meaning of this circular the dissenting department or agency may appeal to the next higher authority as provided for in the following paragraph.

4. The concept of executive chairmen

The Secretary of State will discharge his authority and responsibility primarily through the Under Secretary of State and the regional Assistant Secretaries of State, who will be assisted by interdepartmental groups of which they will be executive chairmen, i.e., with full powers of decision on all matters within their purview, unless a member who does not concur requests the referral of a matter to the decision of the next higher authority.

From *The Secretary of State and the Problem of Coordination*, New Duties and Procedures of March 4, 1966, Subcommittee on National Security and International Operations, Committee on Government Operations, U.S. Senate, 89 Cong. 2 Sess. (1966), pp. 4–6.

5. The Senior Interdepartmental Group (SIG)

To assist the Secretary of State in discharging his authority and responsibility for interdepartmental matters which cannot be dealt with adequately at lower levels or by present established procedures, including those of the Intelligence Community, the Senior Interdepartmental Group (SIG) is established. The SIG shall consist of the Under Secretary of State, Executive Chairman, the Deputy Secretary of Defense, the Administrator of the Agency for International Development, the Director of the Central Intelligence Agency, the Chairman of the Joint Chiefs of Staff, the Director of the United States Information Agency, and the Special Assistant to the President for National Security Affairs. Representatives of other departments and agencies with responsibility for specific matters to be considered will attend on invitation by the Chairman. Such other departments and agencies may raise matters for consideration of the SIG.

The Chairman of the Senior Interdepartmental Group (SIG) may designate the Under Secretary for Economic Affairs or the Deputy Under Secretary for Political Affairs to chair the SIG in the Chairman's absence.

The SIG will assist the Secretary of State by:

   a. ensuring that important foreign policy problems requiring interdepartmental attention receive full, prompt and systematic consideration;

   b. dealing promptly with interdepartmental matters referred by the Assistant Secretaries of State or raised by any of its members, or, if such matters require higher level consideration, reporting them promptly to the Secretary of State for appropriate handling;

   c. assuring a proper selectivity of the areas and issues to which the United States Government applies its resources;

   d. carrying out other duties and responsibilities of the Special Group (counterinsurgency), which has been abolished;

   e. conducting periodic surveys and checks to verify the adequacy and effectiveness of interdepartmental overseas programs and activities.

The SIG will encourage interdepartmental action and decision-making at the Assistant Secretary level to the greatest extent possible.

The SIG will meet in the Department of State regularly and specially at the call of the Chairman.

The Chairman will be supported by a full-time staff headed by a Staff Director who will also serve as the Special Deputy Executive Secretary of the Department. Staff personnel will be furnished on the Chairman's request by the departments and agencies represented on the SIG. The Chairman may request departments and agencies to designate a point of contact for the Staff Director on matters affecting their interests.

The Staff Directors of the Interdepartmental Regional Groups will assist the Staff Director of the SIG as he requires by providing staff support on regional matters of interest to the SIG.

6. The Interdepartmental Regional Group (IRG)

To assist the Assistant Secretaries, an Interdepartmental Regional Group (IRG) is established for each geographic region corresponding to the jurisdiction of the geographic bureaus in the Department of State. Each IRG shall be composed of the regional Assistant Secretary of State, Executive Chairman, and a designated representative from Defense, AID, CIA, the Organization of the Joint Chiefs of Staff, USIA and the White House or NSC staff. Representatives of other departments and agencies with responsibility for specific matters to be considered will attend on invitation by the Chairman.

The regional Assistant Secretaries, in their capacities as Executive Chairmen of the IRGs, will ensure the adequacy of United States policy for the countries in their region and of the plans, programs, resources and performance for implementing that policy. They will be particularly watchful for indications of developing crises and when such matters require higher level consideration, will recommend appropriate measures to higher authority for dealing with emergent critical situations in their regions.

A regional Assistant Secretary may designate a Deputy Assistant Secretary to chair the IRG in the Chairman's absence. IRG meeting and staff procedures will be patterned on the SIG.

7. Interdepartmental leadership and coordination of country matters

A new position of Country Director will be established in the regional bureaus to serve as the single focus of responsibility for leadership and coordination of departmental and interdepartmental activities concerning his country or countries of assignment. In particular he will:

a. provide continuing departmental and interdepartmental leadership in planning, coordination, and implementation of decisions;

b. raise specific matters for consideration by the IRG, and bring detailed knowledge to IRG discussions when so requested;

c. serve as the base for crisis task force operations as necessary.

The Country Director will be responsible for seeing that the Ambassador's needs are served both within the Department and government-wide. He will ensure that the mission is fully supported in the full range of its requirements: policy, operations and administration.

Each Country Director will organize and develop such contacts, channels and mechanisms as are appropriate to and necessary for full interdepartmental leadership on country matters, and for full support to the Assistant Secretary.

To assist in providing guidance and direction to the Country Director, the Assistant Secretary will have one or more Deputy Assistant Secretaries whose areas of responsibility will be defined by the Assistant Secretary.

Positions of Office Director and officer-in-charge will be abolished as the transition is made to the establishment of Country Director positions.

PLANNING-PROGRAMMING-BUDGETING
Staff Memorandum, Senate Subcommittee on National Security and International Operations

PPBS AND FOREIGN AFFAIRS
Thomas C. Schelling

While there is considerable controversy about the net worth of the performance of Robert McNamara as Secretary of Defense, most observers seem to agree that he made a major contribution to rationalizing the decision-making processes in the military establishment and that while various particulars will no doubt be modified, the essential elements — program budgeting, systems analysis, and cost-effectiveness studies — seem almost certain to remain. (For a balanced discussion and evaluation of these, see the selection by Posvar in Chapter Two.)

Indeed, McNamara's efforts in the Pentagon seemed so strikingly successful that it was finally decided to apply the general approach on a governmentwide basis. The result was PPBS, instituted in 1965. The two selections that follow are an attempt to assess the possibilities and the limitations of such an approach. The staff memorandum prepared for the Senate subcommittee takes a broad look at national security implications while Professor Schelling's comments for the subcommittee are specifically focused on foreign affairs.

Both are somewhat skeptical, the Senate subcommittee bluntly so. For a more positive statement of what was hoped for by the Johnson Administration, the testimony of various administration officials before the subcommittee should be examined. (See *Planning-Programming-Budgeting*, Hearings before the Subcommittee on National Security and International Op-

erations of the Senate Government Operations Committee, 90 Cong. 1 sess. (1967), Parts 1, 2, and 3.)

It might be noted in passing that this subcommittee, chaired by Senator Henry M. Jackson (D., Wash.), is the latest embodiment of a group that has been examining critical national security issues, substantive and organizational, under a variety of names since 1959. From 1959 to 1961, it was the Subcommittee on National Policy Machinery; from 1962 to 1964, the Subcommittee on National Security Staffing and Operations. The present subcommittee was instituted in 1965. The work of all these subcommittees has been extremely helpful, in my view, to students and practitioners alike in the foreign policy and national security fields.

STAFF MEMORANDUM, SENATE SUBCOMMITTEE ON NATIONAL SECURITY AND INTERNATIONAL RELATIONS
Introduction

In August 1965, President Johnson directed that a Planning-Programming-Budgeting System (PPBS) be installed throughout the Executive Branch, to be supervised by the Bureau of the Budget. The Subcommittee on National Security and International Operations is reviewing the application of this system in the national securi-

From *Planning-Programming-Budgeting*, Subcommittee on National Security and International Operations of the Senate Government Operations Committee, 90 Cong. 1 sess. (1967).

ty area. The purpose of this staff memorandum is to provide a guide to questions on which the subcommittee may wish to take testimony during the 90th Congress.

PPBS: What is it?

Sitting at the apex of the Federal Government, a President is keenly aware of the shortage of resources for pursuing desirable goals of public policy, and of the difficult choices this hard fact of life imposes. Some goals must be eliminated, some postponed, others reduced in order to tailor the desirable to the feasible. A President needs the best help he can get in establishing an intelligent scale of priorities, choosing policies that would achieve desired results at the least cost, and marshalling, through Congress, the required resources.

In matters of defense and foreign policy, a President seeks aid from many quarters—State and Defense, his own staff, the National Security Council, task forces, other departments and agencies involved with national security matters, members of Congress, and private citizens. In addition, the budgetary process helps to bring things into focus—to weigh domestic versus foreign needs and to set priorities, to compare costs and benefits of competing programs, and once the budget has been fixed, to exercise Presidential direction and control of the operations of the Executive Branch.

The Planning-Programming-Budgeting System is one more step in a continuing endeavor to make the budgetary process a more versatile and helpful instrument of the President and his principal advisers. As its name suggests, it is an effort to tie forward planning to budgeting via programming. Key elements in the approach are program budgeting and systems analysis.

The traditional budget has been prepared and presented in terms of objects of expenditure, or "inputs," in the new jargon. In this form the budget has not shown the link between agency spending and agency purposes—between the resources an agency uses and its missions or tasks, now, of course, called "outputs." By linking resources to purposes, inputs to outputs, in a program, and by planning ahead for several years, the program budget is expected to contribute to better appraisal by decision-makers of what a budget cut or increase would mean in terms of an agency's program—the goals to be pursued and the goals to be sacrificed or deferred.

Systems analysis is intended to present decision-makers with a systematic and comprehensive comparison of the costs and benefits of alternative approaches to a policy goal, taking advantage of techniques variously described as operations research or cost-effectiveness studies. There is an emphasis on quantitative analysis. Computers have made it possible to handle large quantities of data and applied mathematics has provided ingenious statistical techniques for dealing with some kinds of uncertainty.

Some of the less historically-minded proponents of PPBS strongly imply that it is something brand new, providing decision-makers for the first time with a rational basis for choosing between alternative policies. Actually, cost-benefit analysis seems to have begun in the Garden of Eden (see *Genesis*, 3), and the problem from the outset has been to avoid an underestimation of costs and an overestimation of benefits. Costs and gains have been compared throughout our government's history whenever a decision to spend or not to spend had to be made, and Congress explicitly called for cost-benefit studies as far back as the Rivers and Harbors Act of 1902. Operations research demonstrated its usefulness in World War II. Statistical control, pushed by Robert Lovett as Assistant Secretary of War for Air in World War II, was the forerunner of many functions of the Comptroller of the Defense Department and a predecessor of systems analysis. The idea of performance or program budgeting can be traced back at least to President Taft's Commission on Economy and Efficiency, which published its path-breaking report, "The Need for a National Budget," in 1912. And program budgets for periods extending well into the future have long been the rule in progressive banks and business firms.

PPB may for the first time identify these techniques as a "system," give them a special name, and advertise them, but the approach itself is as old as the problem of the buyer who would like to make two purchases and has money only for one.

Some of the more enthusiastic advocates of PPBS seem to suggest that it can work miracles in all corners of government. But it is no magic wand. It is a set of sharp tools which in experienced hands and guided by sound judgment can be a helpful aid in some of the business of government.

In his original statement of August 25, 1965,

directing the extension of PPBS throughout the Federal Government, President Johnson said that, once the new system is in operation—

   . . . it will enable us to:

(1) Identify our national goals with precision and on a continuing basis

(2) Choose among those goals the ones that are most urgent

(3) Search for alternative means of reaching those goals most effectively at the least cost

(4) Inform ourselves not merely on next year's costs, but on the second, and third, and subsequent year's costs of our programs

(5) Measure the performance of our programs to insure a dollar's worth of service for each dollar spent.

These are high hopes. It remains to be seen to what extent PPBS will fulfill them.

The experience in Defense

The major experiment to date with PPB began in the Department of Defense in 1961, and the system has been applied to six defense budgets—Fiscal Years 1963 through 1968.

Very strong claims are made for the contribution of PPB to Defense. Charles Hitch, who as Comptroller of the Defense Department had the primary responsibility for fashioning and directing the system, summarized his view of it in these words:

. . . we have provided for the Secretary of Defense and his principal military and civilian advisors a system which brings together at one place and at one time all of the relevant information that they need to make sound decisions on the forward program and to control the execution of that program. And we have provided the necessary flexibility in the form of a program change control system. Now, for the first time, the largest business in the world has a comprehensive Defense Department-wide plan that extends more than one year into the future. And it is a realistic and responsible one—programming not only the forces, but also the men, equipment, supplies, installations, and budget dollars required to support them. Budgets are in balance with programs, programs with force requirements, force requirements with military missions, and military missions with national security objectives. And the total budget dollars required by the plan for future years do not ex-

ceed the Secretary's responsible opinion of what is necessary and feasible.

With this management tool at his command, the Secretary of Defense is now in a position to carry out the responsibilities assigned to him by the National Security Act, namely, to exercise "direction, authority, and control over the Department of Defense"—and without another major reorganization of the defense establishment.

This Defense PPB system has, of course, been applied only during a period of rising national defense budgets (from $54.3 billion in FY 1963 to about $75 billion in FY 1967). It is not clear that the system would ease the problems of managing a contraction of the military services and of deciding, in a period of declining appropriations, what combination of forces would best promote the national interest.

Even in Defense the benefits of the PPB system have been overplayed by its proponents. It is not a statistical litmus paper, scientifically sorting good projects from bad. It may be used as easily to rationalize a decision as to make a rational choice. It is no substitute for experience and judgment, though men of experience and judgment may find it helpful.

The PPB approach was used to justify the purchase of a $277 million oil-fueled aircraft carrier that was obsolete before it was launched. Also, a perversion of cost-effectiveness was used, after the fact, in the largest single military aircraft contract in history, to rationalize the choice of an airplane whose costs are soaring, if not its performance. The latter case demonstrates that cost-effectiveness study, like any other management tool, can be misused—to becloud rather than illuminate judgment in the Executive Branch and Congress.

A major goal of PPB, according to Charles Hitch, was to enable the Secretary of Defense to run his Department on a unified basis, and PPB has meant a greater centralization of decision-making and control. A consequence, whether intended or not, is that it may be more difficult for voices of doubt and dissent at lower levels to make themselves heard at high levels. It means, among other things, less bargaining between OSD and the service departments and the services. This in turn makes it easier for OSD to ignore or simply not to hear things it would rather not hear—other beliefs about technological change, different estimates of costs and gains, conflicting views of the contingencies and the uncertainties. Defense programs may therefore be more nearly tailored to one estimate of the future and to one cost-benefit calculus than in a period when decision-making was less centralized.

All this underlines the fact that "unifying" is not without its dangers, particularly for the innovation of new weapons systems. Professor Roland McKean points out: ". . . rivalry under a rather decentralized system more than good analysis was probably responsible for the early development of Polaris and the subsequent Air Force interest in reducing vulnerability." The evidence is not all in on how increased centralization has affected major force-level decisions, aircraft production rates, and initiatives on new major weapons systems, including the ABM. But there are obvious risks to which the President and Congress should be alert and which may suggest the need for reforms in Defense, at the Presidential level, and in Congress.

PPB aims at a systematic analysis of significant costs and benefits of alternative policies. But as a politician knows, sometimes the costs of an action, or failure to act, are heaviest not in dollars, but in a loss of confidence or a failure of will or a collapse of morale. Benefits also may show up in an improvement in these intangible factors of will and psychology rather than on the cash register. Priceless is not a synonym for worthless. An analysis which emphasizes cost-effectiveness and gives special attention to quantification runs the risk of short-changing or ignoring non-quantifiable costs and benefits. Skybolt presumably did not meet the Defense tests of cost-effectiveness, but one wonders whether, in estimating the costs of its cancellation, allowance was made for the impact on the British Government and perhaps on French policies in Atlantic and West European affairs.

These questions might be asked:

1. The programming system as it evolved under Charles Hitch is being modified in a number of respects by Robert Anthony who became Comptroller in September 1965. To what shortcomings in the system are the reforms directed?

2. A generally acknowledged difficulty has been the excessive detail, complexity and burdensome requirements of the defense programming and procurement process. Can it be simplified? Would a simpler approach help to identify major issues early and to raise them

promptly at the Presidential level, so that they will not be submerged in the clutter of smaller problems to be settled at the OSD or, hopefully, a lower level?

3. How has PPB been relevant or useful in Vietnam?

4. What lessons can be learned from the Skybolt decision, the level-of-U.S.-forces-in-Europe case, and from other decisions of importance to our allies?

5. Within the Defense Department program budgeting has appeared to be helpful in some programs and less useful in others — for example, General Purpose Forces and Research and Development. How might this experience bear on the application of PPB in non-Defense areas?

6. How has the introduction of PPB in Defense affected Congressional consideration of the defense budget?

Relevance to the State Department and related agencies

The State Department, like a number of other agencies, may find PPBS of little use. The differences between decision-making in defense and in foreign affairs, of course, make it impossible just to transfer budgetary procedures from Defense to State, AID, USIA and other national security programs.

In the nature of things, Defense must plan and program far ahead because of the time required to turn ideas into weapons. Foreign policy is more sensitive to day-to-day actions of other governments.

Furthermore, the difficulties of quantifying objectives, costs and benefits in Defense are minor compared with the difficulties in foreign affairs. Defense deals in large part with end products that one can see, touch, measure, test-fire and ride in. State itself has virtually none of that; it deals mainly with the battle of ideas and interests called diplomacy. Also, the budgetary process as a whole does not serve effectively to bring foreign policy choices into focus.

Even apart from these factors, there has been no preparatory work in the foreign policy field remotely comparable to the decade of intensive work by RAND and others which preceded the large-scale application of programming and systems analysis in Defense, and the number of people trained and skilled in both the conduct of foreign affairs and the techniques of modern management is very limited. Charles Hitch himself has sounded a cautionary note:

. . . there are risks and dangers as well as opportunities in trying to move too far too fast in the application of new management techniques like these, including the risk of discrediting the techniques.

The foreign affairs agencies are still grappling with PPBS to learn what it means for them.

A special problem: the Office of the Secretary of State has not yet found means to take the proffered role of Presidential agent for the "overall direction" of interdepartmental activities overseas, and to play it vigorously. The difficulties are great, and it is unlikely that PPBS provides an answer to the problem. An effort has been made to assist State by establishing a Senior Interdepartmental Group (SIG) with the Under Secretary of State as its Executive Chairman, and Interdepartmental Regional Groups (IRG), chaired by the regional Assistant Secretaries of State. This experiment, however, seems to be languishing.

These questions follow:

1. What problems have been encountered in implementing the President's directive on PPBS with respect to State and related agencies?

2. To what extent are the difficult foreign policy decisions that must be faced by the President, the Secretary of State, and the heads of related agencies ones on which budgetary considerations are of great or determining influence?

3. At this stage of the development of systems analysis, can it play a constructive role in foreign policy decision-making?

4. Are some aspects of the operations of State, AID, and other foreign affairs agencies adapted to programming and cost-benefit analysis?

5. Would PPBS be helpful in any way in the work of the Senior Interdepartmental Group (SIG) and the Interdepartmental Regional Groups (IRG)?

6. An attempt is being made to develop an "inter-agency foreign affairs programming system." Does this contemplate a more prominent role in policy-making for the Bureau of the Budget in relation to State and other departments? What arguments are advanced by proponents and opponents of the system?

Implications for the President and Congress

Does PPBS provide a wholly rational basis for decision-making? Have we arrived at that technocratic utopia where judgment is a machine-product?

Not even the zealots of PPBS would answer these questions affirmatively, although some of them talk as though we should be moving in this direction. Professor Frederick Mosher, for example, has noted the frequency of authoritarian language:

In all the literature I have read about PPBS . . . only a very few authors have even mentioned the executive and legislative processes of review and decision. The President and Congress seem to be regarded as enemies of rationality . . . . Much of the literature of PPBS resembles that of the technocrats of the thirties; its aim seems to be to eliminate *politics* from decisionmaking.

It would be as easy of course to take H_2O out of water as to take politics out of decisions. Our political system is a system for making decisions on matters of public interest. We do not propose to delegate this task to a dictator, no matter how benevolent, or to an expert, no matter how objective, or to a computer, no matter who programs it. Indeed, we do not propose to leave it to any one person, but have built what we call "checks and balances" into our decision-making system. At the heart of our democratic form of government are the principles of executive accountability and Congressional review of Executive action.

The temperate proponents of PPBS claim only that their approach will help to sharpen the intuition and improve the judgment of decision-makers by providing them with more, better, and more timely information. They do not aspire to replace our decision-makers although they might want to arrange the contents of their in-boxes.

It is easy to agree that good analysis is preferable to poor analysis. If the President and his principal assistants believe that PPBS studies and analyses are helpful and an improvement over what they had before they will surely want to see the techniques developed and extended.

It is not clear however that PPBS will win or should win a President's unqualified support. A President needs and wants, for example, freedom to shift his plans and respond flexibly to new situations. Professor Aaron Wildavsky points out:

It is well and good to talk about long-range planning; it is another thing to tie a President's hands by committing him in advance for five years of expenditures. Looking ahead is fine but not if it means that a President cannot negate the most extensive planning efforts on grounds that seem sufficient to him. He may wish to trade some program budgeting for some political support.

To some extent, the planner and the politician are and ought to be at odds. The planner tries to foresee, in order to plan intelligently. A plan rests on today's best estimates of future needs. A politician knows how dimly we can foresee at best, how inadequate the information on the basis of which he must decide and act, how full of surprises history is, how desirable, therefore, to postpone decisions that can be postponed, and how much one depends, in the final analysis, on intuition and judgment based on experience.

A President will look at a program budget skeptically—or should—for he will sense that some costs may have been overlooked and some benefits overestimated—and he may also sense the temptation of assistants to write plans and programs that rationalize their hunches. He will take seriously the lesson of the struggle to get nuclear propulsion for the Navy—a lesson described in these words by Admiral Rickover:

Nuclear power has served to demonstrate the fallibility of expert cost accountants. In so doing, this issue has served a useful purpose. This has resulted in delay in achieving a stronger Navy, but in the long run it may have been worthwhile.

Out of this issue has again been demonstrated the fact that politics is more difficult than physics or cost accounting, and that it is politicians who saw the truth before the cost accountants. The primacy of politics should not again be subordinated to the doctrinaire and unproved claims of specialists—particularly when these specialists are in a position of overall authority and do not encourage or permit contrary views to be voiced or to be asserted.

Congress, too, may not welcome all the implications of PPBS. The experience to date does not suggest that the Department of Defense is likely to place before Congressional committees the analyses of costs and benefits of competing policies and programs on which the Department

based its own choices. Without such comparisons, however, Congress will be in the dark about the reasons for selecting this policy over that. It may be that Congress will wish to improve its own capability for systematic analysis of public problems in order to compete on more even terms with the Executive Branch. Furthermore, the more centralized decision-making becomes in the Executive Branch, the more important some competition of this sort from Congress might be.

Congress may also be concerned with the impact of PPBS on the distribution of power within the Executive Branch. The centralizing bias of PPBS may be more important than the anticipated technical improvements of the budgetary process, because of a lessening of competitive forces within the Executive Branch. Congress will also be interested, of course, in how the changes in the Executive Branch will affect the role of Congress in the formulation of national security policy and the establishment of national security budgets.

If PPBS develops into a contest between experts and politicians, it will not be hard to pick the winners. They will be the politicians in the Congress and the White House. It has been said, and correctly, that as interesting as observing what happens to government when confronted with PPB will be watching what happens to PPB when confronted with government.

PPBS AND FOREIGN AFFAIRS

Thomas C. Schelling

I respond with diffidence, as anyone must, to your invitation to comment on PPBS in relation to foreign affairs. Foreign affairs is a complicated and disorderly business, full of surprises, demanding hard choices that must often be based on judgment rather than analysis, involving relations with more than a hundred countries diverse in their traditions and political institutions—all taking place in a world that changes so rapidly that memory and experience are quickly out of date. Coordination, integration, and rational management are surely desirable; but whether it is humanly possible to meet anything more than the barest minimum standards is a question

From *Planning-Programming-Budgeting*, Subcommittee on National Security and International Operations of the Senate Government Operations Committee, 90 Cong. 1 sess. (1967).

to which an optimistic answer can be based only on faith.

PPBS as a tool of evaluation

Furthermore, PPBS is a method or procedure whose worth depends on the skill and wisdom of the people who use it. Identifying coherent objectives, relating activities to objectives, identifying costs with activities, comparing alternatives, and weighing achievements against costs, are bound to be unimpeachable activities if properly done. But human ingenuity is so great that hidden assumptions can be introduced into any analysis, benefit of the doubt can be prejudicially awarded, quantitative data can be subtly made prominent to the detriment of important qualitative considerations, and even the objectives themselves can be gathered into the wrong packages. The success of PPBS in the Department of Defense over the past half-dozen years — and I think there can be no doubt that the system has been a great success — may be due as much to the quality of the people engaged, and their confidence in each other, as to the logic of the system.

I should like to emphasize something that is implicit in the testimony you heard from both Charles Schultze, Director of the Budget, and Alain Enthoven, Assistant Secretary of Defense (Systems Analysis), but that they perhaps made too little explicit. PPBS, backed up by a competent analytical staff, can hardly fail to be helpful to a decision-maker who insists on making his own decisions and on understanding how he makes them; it can be a seductive comfort, and in the end an embarrassment, to a lazy executive who wants his decisions to come out of a process in which his own intellect does not participate. PPBS can be a splendid tool to help top management make decisions; but there has to be a top management that wants to make decisions.

Let me use an analogy, if I may. A court-room adversary proceeding has been evolved as a comparatively good way to provide the judge in the dispute with the arguments and evidence on which to base a decision; but the crucial element in the proceedings is the judge himself. Systems analysis and other modern techniques of evaluation require a consumer, some responsible person or body that wants an orderly technique for bringing judgment to bear on a decision. PPBS works best for an aggressive master; and where there is no master, or where the master wants the machinery to produce his

decisions without his own participation, the value of PPBS is likely to be modest and, depending on the people, may even be negative.

A third point I would emphasize is that PPBS works best, and historically has been mainly applied, in decisions that are largely budgetary. Budgetary choices are typically choices among *good* things, some of which are better than others, when there are limits on what things or how much of them one can have. The questions are not, "What is good?" but, "Which is better?," not whether more is better than less, but whether it is enough better to be acquired at the expense of something else. A budgetary proposal never arises in the first place unless someone thinks it has merit. A bad budgetary judgment is usually — not always, but usually — bad in proportion to the money that is wasted; there are probably few things that the military services have proposed for purchase that would not have been worth having if they were free of charge.

Outside the budget, big mistakes are cheaper.

It is noteworthy that your committee, in questioning Secretary Enthoven about the sufficiency of bombs for bombing missions in Vietnam, did not ask what PPBS would say about a bombing truce, or the bombing of targets in Cambodia. These are not decisions for which money or economic resources are the main considerations. Having more bombs than necessary is bad only because they cost money; using bombs, or failing to use them, can be bad irrespective of what the bombs cost.

In foreign affairs, more of the hard decisions are of this nonbudgetary sort. That is, bad decisions are not merely wasteful of money, and good decisions do not merely promote efficiency. Even in defense there are plenty of decisions that are not mainly budgetary; the defense budget, though, is so big that the scope for good budgetary practice is ample, and no one can deny the significance of PPBS if it "merely" helps to spend 50 to 75 billion dollars per year more sensibly.

In foreign affairs, quite broadly defined, annual expenditure is about a tenth of that. The Director of the Budget cited a figure of 5.6 billion dollars to your committee, exclusive of expenditures on military forces and intelligence. No one will claim, I am sure, that decisions made in the field of foreign affairs are only one-tenth as important as those made in the field of military affairs; and indeed a good many of the non-procurement decisions in the field of military affairs can be construed as a specialized part of foreign affairs.

I shall not question the worth of being more efficient in the use of 5 billion dollars, even though the amount seems small compared with the defense budget. Furthermore, those of us who think that foreign affairs sometimes receives stingy treatment in Congressional appropriations, compared with defense procurement, must be especially concerned that scarce resources not be wasted. Nevertheless, few among us—and I suspect I can include most of your subcommittee here—when we think about the management of foreign affairs, have an overriding concern with how the 5.6 billion dollars gets spent. Money is not the primary consideration in nuclear proliferation, recognition of the Greek military regime, or new commitments to Thailand. Your committee's interest in the Skybolt affair indicates, furthermore, your concern that PPBS, being focused on costs and other "tangibles," may even divert attention from those elements of a decision, sometimes dominant elements, that cannot be translated straightforwardly into budgetary terms.

There is consequently genuine concern that PPBS and other techniques of management that are essentially budgetary or quantitative may be not only of less positive value when applied to foreign affairs but even, through their tendency to distort criteria and to elevate particular kinds of analytical competence, to be of positive harm. A rather striking manifestation of this concern is the extreme reluctance with which any among us, including perhaps your committee and the Director of the Budget, approach the question of whether the Central Intelligence Agency is part of "foreign affairs" and ought to be subject not only to similar program planning but to the same process of planning, programming, and budgeting.

I believe the spirit of PPBS, even some of its most familiar techniques, is as much needed in handling non-quantitative and nonbudgetary "costs" as in the more traditional budgeting; the "costs" of, say, meeting certain objectives in Jordan or India may be the sacrifice of certain objectives in Egypt, Algeria, Israel or Pakistan, and the disciplined judgment that PPBS demands may prove an advantage. The estimates will have a higher component of judgment in them, a lesser component of organized data; at the same time, the temptation to hope, or to pretend, that the "system" gives answers, instead of merely providing the framework for disciplined judgment and confrontation, will be correspondingly smaller.

PPBS as a means of control

My fourth general observation is that any discussion of PPBS is unrealistic unless it is acknowledged that budgetary processes are a means of control, as well as a means of evaluation. Secretary McNamara surely did not use PPBS and other techniques of financial management merely to cut waste and to improve efficiency or to save money. He took advantage of his central role in the defense-budgeting process to exercise what he believed to be his authority over military policy. Some people have more instinct than others, or better training than others, for using the purse strings as a technique of management and a source of authority; but almost anyone concerned with administration sooner or later discovers that control of budgetary requests and disbursements is a powerful source of more general control. (This is true of universities as well as government agencies.) Anything that makes budgeting more effective will add to the authority of those involved in the budgeting. Budgetary procedures provide invaluable opportunities for holding hearings, demanding justifications, spot-checking the quality of planning, identifying objectives, and even enhancing competition among lethargic subgroups. Furthermore, the budgetary process being geared to an annual cycle, it provides a regular and systematic way of repeatedly examining into these subjects.

My own experience was quite vivid. In 1951 Congress passed the Mutual Security Act. All aid funds were appropriated to the President, who could delegate authority to the Director for Mutual Security. Appropriations for all aid programs were first authorized and then appropriated in a single Act, the titles of which were differentiated by region, not by agency or program. Both in going up to the Hill, through the Budget Bureau and the President, and in getting apportionments of appropriated funds, the several operating agencies were subject to coordination by the Director for Mutual Security. An extraordinary degree of centralized coordination occurred. It was accomplished by a small staff working closely with the Bureau of the Budget. The extent of coordination was undoubtedly more satisfying to the coordinators than to the coordinated; but there can be no question that coordination occurred, and that it occurred precisely because the Director for Mutual Security was put directly at the center of the budgetary process.

This is important. It means that in talking about enhancing the budgetary effectiveness of the Secretary of State or his Office, we are talking about enhancing much more than that. A real test of whether an aid program, an information service, an agricultural program, an intelligence activity or a peace corps is subordinated to the executive authority of the Secretary of State is whether, and how aggressively, he exercises authority over their budgets. (His authority over their personnel ceilings would be a second such test.) I have no doubt that the coordinating role of the State Department in respect of foreign aid would have been greatly enhanced, perhaps permanently so, had the Mutual Security Act of 1951 given budgetary authority to the Secretary rather than to a Director for Mutual Security. (And I have little doubt that the Congress knew exactly what it was doing.)

The question of a foreign affairs budget

My fifth and final observation about PPBS and foreign affairs — and the one most directly related to whether the experience in Defense could be translated into the State Department — is that the budget does not yet exist to which PPBS might be applied in the field of foreign affairs. When Secretary McNamara assumed office, he was at least fifteen years ahead of where the Secretary of State is now in having a recognized budget. There is a "Defense Budget"; there is not a "Foreign Affairs Budget." Both legally and traditionally the defense budget is fairly clearly defined; around the edges there are the Atomic Energy Commission, some space activities, perhaps the Maritime Commission, that one may sometimes wish to lump into a comprehensive "defense total," and over which the Secretary of Defense does not exercise direct budgetary authority. But he has always had his 50 billion dollars or more that were unmistakably his responsibility; and money spent by the uniformed military services evidently came under his authority. The Secretary of Defense makes an annual comprehensive presentation of his budget, typically in the context of a broad evaluation of the military threat to the United States; it is a "State of the Union" insofar as national security is concerned. The committees in Congress that deal with the defense budget

have no doubt that they are dealing with national defense and no doubt about what budget it is that they are considering.

Not so the Secretary of State, whose own budget of about a third of a billion dollars a year corresponds, to take a very crude analogy, to the budget that the Secretary of Defense might present for the operation of the Pentagon building and the people who work in it. The 5.6 billion dollars cited by the Director of the Budget is neither a "State Department Budget" nor a "Foreign Affairs Budget." It is a composite figure that makes a lot of sense to the Director of the Budget but has no official status and corresponds to no appropriations procedure. I have no doubt that his composite is a reasonable one; but if I were to present you my own figure I'm sure that it would be different, because there is no official definition that keeps me from adding, on the basis of judgment, a few things that his figure leaves out or deleting, on the basis of judgment, a few things that he and his staff think it expedient to include. Even he acknowledges that his figure leaves out intelligence as well as all expenditures on U.S. military forces; and while I may agree that it makes practical sense at the present time to put intelligence in a wholly separate category, it is not for "official" reasons. We know that the CIA is outside the defense budget because we know what the defense budget is; we do not know whether the CIA would be outside a "Foreign Affairs Budget," because we do not even know whether there ever will be a foreign affairs budget.

Let us imagine that Mr. Charles Hitch had been, instead of Assistant Secretary of Defense (Comptroller), Assistant Secretary of State (Foreign Affairs Comptroller). If he were to perform a task in the field of foreign affairs comparable to what he and Secretary Enthoven and others did for Secretary McNamara, he would have had to invent a budget, not merely to rationalize one. There would not have been a history of "Foreign Affairs Reorganization Acts" defining his budgetary jurisdiction. Nor could he have simply folded into one comprehensive foreign-affairs budget the budgets of several subordinate agencies; not all the agencies would have been subordinate, and some programs over which he might have wanted some coordinating authority would have been lodged in agencies, like the Department of Agriculture, whose primary responsibilities were not in the field of foreign affairs. By a heroic exercise of both intellect and authority, and with the full cooperation of the Budget Bureau, he might have achieved a welcome consolidation of budgetary plans on their way through the White House to Capitol Hill, but there the whole package would have had to be disintegrated to correspond to the Congressional appropriations structure. This would have been a different task, and in many ways a harder one, than the budgetary task that he actually took on—and that one itself was a task that an ordinary mortal would have shrunk from.

A dilemma of state department organization

I called my fifth generalization "final," but I'd like to make one organizational comment about the Department of State. It has been widely remarked, especially in the early years of the McNamara regime, that there were frictions between civilians and the military in the Pentagon, that "civilian control" was occasionally resented, that there was not always mutual trust and respect as between civilians and the military, and that the civilians lacked direct experience in military command and the conduct of ground, air or naval operations. Just suppose the reverse had been true, and the Chief of Staff of the Army were *ex officio* Secretary of Defense, all his Assistant Secretaries chosen from the Army, all of their "whiz kids" being bright, promising young Army officers. I think the situation would have been impossible. The entire OSD, being strictly Army, would have had no experience in naval command or the conduct of modern strategic air operations; professional bias and service loyalty would have made it beyond the credulity of the Air Force and Navy that they were receiving fair, sympathetic and impartial treatment. Secretary McNamara had the disadvantage that he and his staff were a class apart—civilians —but he had the great advantage that he was unambiguously a civilian, not identified with a particular service, with no special bonds of personal sympathy or loyalty to any one service, and not obliged to devote part of his time to running one service while being the rest of his time the President's executive manager of them all.

The Secretary of State presides over, or can aspire to preside over, a number of civilian services and operations. But he is also traditionally identified with one particular service, the Foreign Service. The Department of Defense is essentially OSD, "the Office of the Secretary of Defense"; the Department of State is both OSS—"the Office of the Secretary of State"—and the Foreign Service. (It is also quite ambiguously related to ambassadors abroad, who are nominally the President's representatives, but who are more and more expected to be professional graduates of the Foreign Service.) The Congress has never quite recognized the OSS function of the Department of State; putting the Marshall Plan under an independent agency, the Economic Cooperation Administration, was a Congressional vote of "no confidence" in the executive talents of the State Department. Resentment and distrust of "State" by people in foreign aid programming, through a long sequence of agency reorganizations, has been not wholly dissimilar to the distrust that the military allegedly have for civilians in OSD.

Furthermore, by putting some of the specialized professional responsibilities in quasi-independent agencies like AID, USIA, Peace Corps, and so forth, the Executive Branch and the Congress have precluded the State Department's acquiring the professional talents, the internal organization, and the executive experience to lord it over these other agencies. No uniform distinguishes the AID official from a country director, or Deputy Assistant Secretary of State; but he may feel a little the way an Air Force officer would feel if the Congress had created the Defense Department by elevating one service into executive status while preserving the operating role of that service.

I have to discuss this because, as I mentioned earlier, techniques and procedures that are intended to enhance the budgetary role of a particular office tend, when successful, to enhance the executive authority of that office. The matter is not simply one of providing better analytical staff work to a senior official of the government; more than that, the issue is how to generate more coherent planning and better coordinated operation in the field of foreign affairs. The first thing to decide is whether we want more coherence, more coordination, and an identified responsibility for executive direction. If we do not, then PPBS probably becomes an analytical specialty that is not really worth the attention of your committee. If we do, then I believe we have to recognize that the Department of State presently combines both what might be called the "Office of the Secretary of State," and the Foreign Service, and that this constitutes an encumbrance that the Department of Defense did not have to suffer.

Now let me turn—"finally," if I may use that word again—to the first rudimentary step in the establishment of PPBS. It has nothing at all to do with computers, little to do with systems analysis, and in the first instance little to do with analysis of any kind. It harks back to the first elementary thing that Secretary Hitch did in the Department of Defense and that Secretary Enthoven may have emphasized too little, partly because of the progress he has made and partly because of the general interest in the mystique of systems analysis.

The most crucial thing that Secretary Hitch ever did was to identify his basic "program packages"—what are sometimes called the "outputs" of the defense budget. It is important, in thinking about a "foreign-affairs budget," not to pass on too readily to the examination of "program elements," and all the techniques of analysis that can thereafter be applied. Eventually most of PPBS is likely to be concerned with the evaluation of "program elements" and comparisons among them, with cost estimates and so forth. But this is already way beyond what first needs to be done in foreign affairs; that all comes after the basic program packages have been identified.

What is it that corresponds, in the field of foreign-affairs planning, to the original program packages that were developed under Charles Hitch? I believe the Director of the Bureau of the Budget gave you his answer when he said, "First,"—and I am glad he put it first—"*individual countries constitute useful categories* under which to analyze an agency's foreign affairs activities as a means of achieving U.S. objectives." Let me say it differently: Individual countries are the basic "program packages" for foreign affairs budgeting. (I do not at this point want to argue with people who think that regions rather than countries are the basic packages; I think they are wrong, but they are not the ones I want to argue with.) The basic package is not the program—Peace Corps, intelligence, AID, agricultural surpluses, technical assistance, Ex-Im bank credits—but the country. Secretary Hitch identified originally, I believe, about seven basic packages. I wish in foreign affairs we could get along with as few; as Charles Schultze indicated, the number of countries we now recognize in the world has grown to 119. I'm afraid this is an irreducible

minimum number of packages, except as we can exercise selectivity in treating some as far more important than others.

Mr. Schultze understated it; individual countries are more than "useful categories," they are *the basic packages* for not only budgetary decisions but most other policy decisions. Countries cannot, of course, be treated in isolation—India separately from Pakistan, Jordan separately from Syria and Israel, Thailand separately from Vietnam and Cambodia. But neither can the Defense Department's strategic defenses be considered wholly in isolation from strategic offenses, or "general purpose forces" from sealift and air-lift. The point is that the basic program package is not Peace Corps, financial aid, military aid, agricultural surpluses, propaganda, or diplomatic representation; the basic package is the country.

Maybe somebody can think of a better package. But what we are presently struggling for in our budgetary procedures is an identification of the objectives or "outputs" toward which our programs are supposed to be oriented. Just getting recognition that the country, rather than the agency or program, is the basic unit of analysis would be a heroic step. After that the people with specialized analytic talents, with schemes for the orderly collection of data, and with professional training in PPBS can go to work. The first step toward PPBS is officially identifying program packages; and that step has not yet been taken.

Who coordinates foreign policy?

To say that the basic program package in foreign affairs is the individual country can provoke either of two objections—that it is wrong, or that to say so is trivial. Those who object that it is wrong do not worry me; I share their discontent with the country as the basic package, but do not believe they can identify a better package, and in the end we shall, equally discontent, settle on the individual country as the least unsatisfactory basic package for foreign affairs budgeting.

Anyone who says that the individual country is so obviously the basic package that in saying so I have said nothing, is plain wrong. What I have said is trivial as far as analytical budgeting is concerned; but bureaucratically it is revolutionary. Charles Schultze is a sensible and responsible man; that does not mean he is not revolutionary, only that he makes his revolution slowly, carefully, and responsibly. The revolution is in considering all programs for a country together, rather than all countries for a program together. It is examining what the United States does with respect to Greece, Thailand, Brazil, India, or Nigeria, rather than what the United States does with aid, Peace Corps, agricultural surpluses, military assistance, and propaganda.

This is revolutionary not just because somebody would be looking at the totality of U.S. programs with respect to a particular country all together, relating them to the same set of objectives, comparing them with respect to their effectiveness, demanding that the same set of objectives be acknowledged in the consideration of each program, eliminating inconsistency and reducing duplication. Nor is it that, once the basic country packages are identified, countries would be compared with each other as claimants for U.S. resources and U.S. attention.

No, what would be revolutionary is that somebody or some agency has to do this, and it has to be decided who or which agency would do it. (It also has to be decided whether the Congress wants this done; and that may depend on who does it.)

Who should do it? An easy answer is that the Budget Bureau should do it; the Budget Bureau is the centralized agency that brings consistency and compatibility to the claims of diverse governmental programs, foreign and domestic. But what I said earlier about the relation of budgeting to control commits me to the belief that we are talking about the question, "Who coordinates foreign policy?" I do not believe the answer should be the Bureau of the Budget.

Maybe the answer is "nobody." Maybe, as a practical matter, the answer is that the coordination will be fragmented, and the Budget Bureau will exercise a good part of the coordination. But if both the President and the Congress want this responsibility fixed unambiguously, in the absence of a drastic reorganization of the Executive Branch it would be hard to identify any formal locus of responsibility except the Office of the Secretary of State.

But to put this responsibility on the Secretary of State is to give him both a means and an obligation to assume the kind of executive authority that has never, in spite of executive orders and the logic of ideal government, either been wholly acceptable to the Department of State or freely offered to it. This is to put the purse strings directly into the hands of the Secretary of State with encouragement to use them in the executive management of foreign policy.

I think it makes sense, but I am not sure that this is what the Congress wants nor sure that this is what Secretaries of State and their senior staffs want. But this is where we are led by the philosophy of PPBS; and we are led there not by fancy analytical techniques but by the simple logic of "program packages" and the need to develop policies, as well as budgets, in a coherent process that recognizes the country as the primary unit of budgeting and policy-making.

I am not trying to lead your subcommittee, through any line of reasoning or casuistry, to a particular conclusion. If we were concerned exclusively with architecture, we would end up with a good case for demanding of the Secretary of State that his Office do this kind of budgeting and do it with the impartiality that would estrange the Foreign Service from the Office of the Secretary of State. But these issues cannot be settled by reference to the aesthetics of organization charts. These are pragmatic questions. Do we want coordination at the price of centralization? Can we split the Department of State into an executive foreign-affairs office and the Foreign Service? Does coordinated, centralized programming undermine the decentralized initiative and responsibility of programs like the Peace Corps, AID, or cultural exchanges? Does the Congress itself lose bargaining power when the Executive Branch gets better organized for foreign affairs, and is the Congress willing to encourage this?

I should like to see the Office of the Secretary of State accept the philosophy according to which it is the executive arm of the President for foreign affairs, and emancipated from the Foreign Service. I should like to see it use the budget process to clinch its authority and to rationalize its decision processes. I should like to see all overseas programs and activities brought under the purview of an "Office of the Secretary of State," streamlined to provide executive direction. And I should like to see the Department of State enjoy the benefits of modern analytical techniques of the kind that Secretary Enthoven has brought to the Department of Defense, as well as other kinds. But I cannot—I wish I could, but I cannot—declare with any confidence that this can be done. I come back to the remarks with which I began this memorandum. Foreign affairs is complicated and disorderly; its conduct depends mainly on the quality of the people who have responsibility; decisions have to be based on judgments, often too suddenly to permit orderly analytical processes to determine those decisions. The best—the very best—performance that is humanly possible is likely to look pretty unsatisfactory to the Congress, to Washington correspondents, to the electorate, even to the President who presides over the arrangement. The system can be improved, but not to anybody's complete satisfaction. In this improvement, PPBS will eventually have a significant role.

THE FLOW OF POLICY MAKING IN THE DEPARTMENT OF STATE
Charlton Ogburn, Jr.

Mr. Ogburn's essay was originally prepared as part of a Brookings Institution study of United States foreign policy formulation. It has since been anthologized many times, and for good reason. It captures better than any other single piece of writing in print the sense and flavor of foreign policy decision-making activities as they are typically carried on in the Department of State.

Time has left its mark on Mr. Ogburn's essay as on all else. Consulate General Brazzaville is now American Embassy Brazzaville; the fifth-floor location of the Secretary of State and his top aides in New State has become the seventh floor in new New State; Dependent Area Affairs are no longer dealt with by a separate office in the Bureau of International Organization Affairs; but Africa does have a separate office to analyze its problems in the Bureau of Intelligence and Research.[1]

But these are minor changes. Ogburn still reflects brilliantly the variety of pressures and problems with which the American foreign policy machinery must contend and some of the typical work-patterns through which it attempts to cope with them.

The Department of State is an organism that is constantly responding to a vast assortment of stimuli. A new Soviet threat to Berlin, a forthcoming conference of Foreign Ministers of the Organization of American States, a request from Poland for credit, a solicitation for support of a candidacy for the Presidency of the United Nations General Assembly, a plea from an ambassador that the head of the government to which he is accredited be invited to visit the United States officially, a refusal by another government to permit the duty-free importation of some official supplies for a U.S. consulate, a request from the White House for comment on the foreign affairs section of a major presidential address, an earthquake in the Aegean creating hardships which it appears the U.S. Navy might be able to alleviate, a request for a speaker from a foreign policy association in California, a transmittal slip from a Member of Congress asking for information with which to reply to a letter from a constituent protesting discriminatory actions against his business by a foreign government, letters from citizens both supporting and deploring the pólicy of nonrecognition of Communist China, a continuing inquiry by a press correspondent who has got wind of a top secret telegram from Embassy Bonn on the subject of German rearmament and is determined to find out what is in it, a demand by a Protestant church group that the Department take steps to prevent harassment of their coreligionists in a foreign country, a request by a delegation of a federation of women's clubs for a briefing on southeast Asia and suggestions as to how its members might be useful in their planned tour of the area, a request from Consulate General Brazzaville for a revision of cost-of-living allowances, a visit by a commission of inquiry into the operations of U.S. foreign aid programs, a notification from the staff of the National Security Council that a revision of the National Security Council paper on dependent areas is due, a telegram from a U.S. embassy in the Near East declaring that last night's flareups make a visit by the Assistant Secretary for Near Eastern and South Asian Affairs, now in mid-Atlantic, inopportune at the moment, a warning by a European Foreign Minister of the consequences should the United States fail to support his nation's position in the Security Council, and a counter-warning by an African representative at the United Nations of the consequences should the United States do so—this is a sample of the requirements made of the Department of State in

From Charlton Ogburn, Jr., "The Flow of Policy Making in the Department of State," in H. Field Haviland, Jr. and Associates, The Formulation and Administration of United States Foreign Policy, a Report for the Committee on Foreign Relations of the United States Senate (Washington, D C.: The Brookings Institution, 1960), pp. 172-177.
[1]Burton M. Sapin, The Making of United States Foreign Policy (Washington, D.C.: The Brookings Institution, 1966), p. 383.

a typical day. Of course it does not include the oceans of informational reports that come into the Department by telegram and air pouch or the countless periodicals from all parts of the world that arrive by sea.

What is required to begin with is that the flow be routed into the right channels. This does not apply to press correspondents and foreign embassy officials; they usually know where to go without being directed. For the rest, almost every piece of business—every requirement or opportunity for action—comes within the Department's ken first as a piece of paper. These pieces of paper—telegrams, dispatches (or "despatches," as the Department prefers to call them), letters—must be gotten as speedily as possible into the hands of the officers who will have to do something about them or whose jobs require that they know about them.

The telegram and mail branches of the Division of Communication Services, a part of the Bureau of Administration, receive the incoming material and, after decoding and reproducing the telegrams, indicate on each communication the distribution it should receive among the bureaus or equivalent components of the Department. If, in the case of a letter or a dispatch, there are not enough copies to go around, the recipients are listed one after another and receive it consecutively, the original going first to the bureau responsible for taking whatever action the document requires. With telegrams, the deliveries are simultaneous. Several score copies of a telegram may be run off. A yellow copy, called the action copy, like the original of a dispatch or letter, goes to the bureau responsible for taking any necessary action; white copies go to all others interested.

A telegram (No. 1029, let us say) from a major U.S. embassy in Western Europe reports the warning of the Foreign Minister of X country that a grave strain would be imposed on relations between X and the United States should the latter fail to vote with X on a sensitive colonial issue in the United Nations General Assembly. Such a telegram would have a wide distribution. The action copy would go to the Bureau of European Affairs. The action copy of a telegram to the same purpose from the U.S. delegation to the United Nations in New York, quoting the X delegation, would go to the Bureau of International Organization Affairs. This is a matter of convention.

Information copies of a telegram of such importance would go to all officers in the higher echelons—the Secretary of State (via the executive secretariat), the Under Secretaries, the Deputy Under Secretaries, the counselor. They would also go to the Policy Planning Staff, to the Bureau of African Affairs because of the involvement of certain territories within its jurisdiction, to the Bureau of Far Eastern Affairs and the Bureau of Near Eastern and South Asian Affairs because the telegram concerns the incendiary question of European peoples' ruling non-European peoples, and of course to the Bureau of Intelligence and Research. Other copies would go to the Department of Defense and the Central Intelligence Agency. The executive secretariat would doubtless make certain that the Secretary would see the telegram. In addition, its staff would include a condensation in the secret daily summary, a slim compendium distributed in the Department on a need-to-know basis. If classified top secret, it would be included in the top secret daily staff summary, or black book, which goes only to Assistant Secretary-level officials and higher.

In the bureaus, incoming material is received by the message centers. There a further and more refined distribution would be made of telegram 1029. Copies would go to the Office of the Assistant Secretary (the so-called front office), to the United Nations adviser, to the public affairs adviser (since the United States is going to be in for trouble with public opinion in either one part of the world or the other), and to whatever geographic office or offices may seem to have the major interest. In the Bureau of International Organization Affairs, this would be the Office of United Nations Political and Security Affairs. Another copy, however, might go to the Office of Dependent Area Affairs.

In the Bureau of European Affairs, the yellow action copy of the telegram goes to the Office of Western European Affairs and thence to the X country desk, where it is the first thing to greet the desk officer's eye in the morning. As it happens, the desk officer was out the evening before at an official function where he discussed at length with the first secretary of the X embassy the desirability of avoiding any extremes of action in the United Nations over the territory in question. In the front office of the Bureau, the staff assistant has entered in his records the salient details of the problem the Bureau is charged with and has passed the telegram on to the Assistant Secretary.

The following scenes are now enacted:

The X country desk officer crosses the hall to the office of his superior, the officer-in-charge, and the two together repair to the office of the Director of the Office of Western European Affairs. The three officers put in a call to the Assistant Secretary for European Affairs and tell his secretary that they would like as early an appointment as possible.

The Director of the Office of United Nations Political and Security Affairs (UNP) telephones the Director of the Office of Western European Affairs (WE). He says he assumes WE will be drafting an instruction to the U.S. embassy in X to try to dissuade the Foreign Office from its course, and that UNP would like to be in on it. He adds that they had thought of getting the U.S. delegation to the United Nations (US Del) to present this view to the X mission in New York but that there seemed to be no point in doing so since the latter would already be advising its government to take account of world opinion.

After the Secretary's morning staff conference, where the matter is discussed briefly, a conference is held in the Office of the Assistant Secretary for European Affairs to decide on a line to take with the X government. The X desk officer is designated to prepare the first draft of a telegram embodying it. The draft is reviewed and modified by his officer-in-charge and the Office Director for Western European Affairs.

The telegram instructs the U.S. embassy in X to make clear to the X government our fear that its projected course of action "will only play into hands of extremists and dishearten and undermine position elements friendly to West" and suggests that the X government emphasize its policy to take account of the legitimate aspirations of the indigenous population of the territory in order to improve the atmosphere for consideration of the problem by the General Assembly. The Assistant Secretary, after scrutinizing and approving the telegram, finds it necessary only to add the Bureau of Near Eastern and South Asian Affairs to the clearances. Those already listed for clearance are the Deputy Under Secretary for Political Affairs, the Bureau of International Organization Affairs, and the Bureau of African Affairs. He says it can be left to the Deputy Under Secretary for Political Affairs to sign the telegram; he does not see that the telegram need go higher.

It remains for the drafting officer to circulate the telegram for approval by those marked for clearance. In the Bureau of African Affairs the telegram is termed extremely gentle to the X government but is initialed as it stands. The Officer of United Nations Political and Security Affairs (UNP) wishes to remind X that the United States, setting an example of its adherence to the principle of affording the widest latitude to the General Assembly, had even accepted on occasion the inscription of an item on the agenda accusing the United States of aggression. The X desk officer states, however, that WE would not favor such an addition, which might only further antagonize the X government. Thereupon, UNP, yielding on this point, requests deletion of a phrase in the telegram seeming to place the United States behind the X contention that the question is not appropriate for discussion in the United Nations. The drafter of the telegram telephones the Director of the Office of Western European Affairs who authorizes the deletion, having decided that he can do so on his own without referring the question to his superior, the Assistant Secretary.

With that, the Director of the Office of United Nations Political and Security Affairs initials the telegram for his Bureau, and the X desk officer "hand carries" the telegram (in the departmental phrase), with telegram 1029 attached, to the Office of the Deputy Under Secretary for Political Affairs and leaves it with his secretary. At 6 o'clock he is informed by telephone that the Deputy Under Secretary has signed the telegram (that is, signed the Secretary's name with his own initials beneath) without comment. The desk officer goes to the fifth floor, retrieves it, and takes it to the correspondence review staff of the executive secretariat, where the telegram is examined for intelligibility, completion of clearances, conformity with departmental practices, etc., before being sped to the Telegram Branch for enciphering and transmission.

The next morning, all officers of the Department participating in the framing of the telegram receive copies of it hectographed on pink outgoing telegram forms. The telegram, bearing the transmission time of 8:16 p.m., has entered history as the Department's No. 736 to the embassy in X. The X desk officer writes "telegram sent," with the date, in the space indicated by a rubber stamp on the yellow copy of the original telegram 1029, and the staff assistant in the front office makes an equivalent notation in his records. The yellow copy is then sent on to the central files, whence in time it will probably be consigned to the National Archives. Only the white copies may be kept in the Bureau's files.

In this case, however, no one is under any illusion that the matter has been disposed of. Scarcely 24 hours later comes a new telegram 1035 from the embassy in X reporting that, while the X government may possibly make some concessions, it will certainly wage an all-out fight against inscription of the item and will expect the United States to exert itself to marshal all the negative votes possible. The question is, what position will the United States in fact take and how much effort will it make to win adherents for its position? No one supposes for a moment that this explosive question can be decided on the bureau level. Only the Secretary can do so—as the Secretary himself unhappily realizes.

At the end of a staff meeting on Berlin, the Secretary turns to the Assistant Secretary for Policy Planning and asks him to give some thought within the next few days to the alternatives open on the question. The official addressed sets the wheels in motion at once. A meeting is called for the next morning. Attending are: the Assistant Secretary for Policy Planning himself and several members of his staff (including the European and African specialists), the Director of the Office of United Nations Political and Security Affairs, the Western European officer-in-charge, the X desk officer, a member of the policy guidance and coordination staff of the Bureau of Public Affairs, and two intelligence specialists, namely, the Director of the Office of Research and Analysis for Western Europe and the Director of the Office of Research and Analysis for the Near East, South Asia, and Africa.

The discussion explores all ramifications of the issues involved and is generally detached and dispassionate. The object of the meeting is to help clarify the issues so that the Policy Planning Staff may be sure all relevant considerations are taken into account in the staff paper it will prepare for the Secretary.

The Secretary is in a difficult position. The President's views on what course of action to take are somewhat different from his. The Congress is also of divided view, with some Members impressed by the irresistible force of nationalism among dependent peoples, others by the essential role of X in NATO and European defense. The ambassadors of some countries

pull him one way, others another. One of the Nation's leading newspapers editorially counsels "restraint, understanding and vision." At the staff meeting he calls to arrive at a decision, the Secretary perceives that his subordinates are as deeply divided as he feared. He takes counsel with each—the Assistant Secretaries for Policy Planning, European Affairs, African Affairs, and Near Eastern and South Asian Affairs. At the end he sums up and announces his decision. Thereupon the following things happen:

The Assistant Secretaries take the news back to their bureaus.

An urgent telegram is sent to the U.S. Embassy in X reporting the decision.

Telegrams are sent to embassies in important capitals around the world instructing the ambassador to go to the Foreign Office and present the U.S. case in persuasive terms.

A similar telegram is sent to the U.S. delegation in New York for its use in talks with the delegations of other United Nations members.

Conferences attended by representatives of the geographic bureaus concerned, of the Bureau of Public Affairs, and of the U.S. Information Agency, are held. Afterward, the representatives of the U.S. Information Agency return to their headquarters to draft guidances to the U.S. Information Service establishments all over the world. Such guidances tell how news of the U.S. decision is to be played when it breaks.

The more important the problem, the more the upper levels of the Department become involved. In a crisis—one brought about, say, by the overthrow of A, a Western-oriented government in the Middle East—the Secretary himself will take over. However, the bulk of the Department's business is carried on, of necessity, by the lower ranking officers. Even when a crisis receives the Secretary's personal, day-to-day direction, the desk officer and the officer-in-charge are always at hand to provide the detailed information only specialists possess, while in the intelligence bureau, country analysts and branch chiefs will be putting in 10-hour days and 6- or 7-day weeks. Generally, moreover, the crisis will have been preceded by a good deal of work on the part of lower level officials.

In the case suggested, it was apparent for some time that all was not well in A. The U.S. Embassy in A was aware of growing discontent with the regime through its indirect contacts with opposition political elements, from information from Cairo, from evidences of tension, from clandestine publications. Additional straws in the wind were supplied by the public affairs officer in A both to the embassy and to the U.S. Information Agency because of his special contacts among professional groups. On the strength of these reports and of dispatches from American foreign correspondents in the area, and equipped with analyses from the Bureau of Intelligence and Research, all pointing in the same direction, the desk officer at a staff meeting of the Office of Near Eastern Affairs imparts his disquiet. He is directed to prepare a memorandum which, if convincing in its presentation, the Office Director undertakes to put before the Assistant Secretary.

What the desk officer has in mind will require national action, so what he drafts takes the form of a memorandum to the Secretary. It embodies a statement of the problem, the actions recommended, a review of the facts bearing upon the problem, and a conclusion. At the end are listed the symbols of the offices of the Department from which concurrences must be sought. Backing up the memorandum will be supporting documents, especially telegrams from the embassy, each identified by a tab. The mass fills a third of an in-box.

The problem is defined as that of strengthening the present pro-Western regime of A. By way of recommendation, the desk officer is especially sensitive to the problems and needs of the country for which he is responsible. He calls for more detachment of the United States from A's rival, B, expediting U.S. arms deliveries to A and the supply of certain recoilless rifles and jet fighter planes the A government has been requesting, support for A's membership in various United Nations agencies, a Presidential invitation to the Prime Minister of A to visit the United States. Much of what the memorandum recommends has to be fought out in the Bureau and even in the Office since it conflicts with the claims of countries (and the desk officers responsible for them) in the same jurisdiction. While neither the Office Director nor the Assistant Secretary doubts that support of B is a handicap in the region, they consider that a proposal for a radical departure would simply doom the memorandum by preventing anyone from taking it seriously.

As it finally leaves the Bureau with the Assistant Secretary's signature, the memorandum is considerably revised, and further change awaits

it. The Department of Defense cannot provide the desired recoilless rifles and jet fighters. The Bureau of International Organization Affairs cannot offer any undertakings at this stage with respect to the question of membership in United Nations agencies. The Deputy Under Secretary for Political Affairs rules out a request of the President to invite the A Prime Minister for an official visit because the number of those invited is already too large.

Among recommendations in memorandums to the Secretary, as among salmon battling their way upstream to the spawning grounds, mortality is heavy. Almost everywhere in the world, things are far from satisfactory, but the United States cannot be doing everything everywhere at the same time. And A, far from seeming to cry out for attention, looks like the one Middle Eastern Country about which it is not necessary to worry.

Then the uprising occurs in A. Early in the morning, the officer-in-charge of A and one other country is awakened by the ringing of the telephone. In a flash, before his feet have touched the floor, he has visualized every conceivable disaster that could have befallen his area and has picked the overthrow of the monarchy in C as the most likely. Or did the security people find a top secret document under his desk?

On the telephone, the watch officer at the Department tells him that a "Niact" (a night action telegram, which means "Get this one read immediately even if you have to rout someone out of bed") is coming off the machine and it looks serious—he had better come down. En route, the officer-in-charge turns on his car radio and picks up a news broadcast, but nothing is said about A. Uncle Sam has beaten the press agencies.

At the Department, he finds the telegram wholly decoded and reads the hectograph master. There is revolution in A. The top leadership has been either murdered or banished. The officer-in-charge could legitimately awaken the Assistant Secretary, but for the moment it seems there is nothing that can be done, so he decides to hold off until 6 a.m. and then call the Office Director and put it up to him. He does, however, call the A desk officer and tell him to get on his way. To share his vigil beside the watch officer's window there is a representative of the executive secretariat, who will have the telegram ready for the Secretary to read immediately on his arrival. In the Bureau of Intelligence and

Research—it being now after 4 o'clock—the morning briefers have arrived to go over the night's take and write up items of importance, with analyses, for the Director's use in briefing the Secretary's morning staff conference. The briefer for the Office of Research and Analysis for the Near East, South Asia and Africa—a GS-11 specialist on India—takes one look at the Niact on A and gets on the telephone to the A analyst.

By the time the Secretary has stepped from his black limousine and headed for the private elevator a good deal has happened. In the Bureau of Near Eastern and South Asian Affairs, everyone concerned with A from the Assistant Secretary down, and including the officer-in-charge of Baghdad Pact and Southeast Asia Treaty Organization affairs and the special assistant who serves as a policy and planning adviser, has been in conference for an hour laying out the tasks requiring immediate attention. Two more Niacts have come in from A, one reporting that so far no Americans are known to have been injured but offering little assurance with respect to the future. The Assistant Secretary has already put in a call to the Director of Intelligence Research to ask that all possible information on the new leader of A and his connections be marshaled and that the Central Intelligence Agency be informed of the need. For the rest, the following represent the Assistant Secretary's conception of what should be done first:

1. The Department of Defense must be apprised of the Department of State's anxiety and be requested to have transport planes in readiness at nearby fields for the evacuation of Americans if necessary in accordance with prearranged plans. There must be consultation on what instruments are available if American lives have to be protected by force.

2. The U.S. embassy in C, a friendly neighbor of A's to which the Niacts have been repeated, will be heard from at any moment, and the Special Assistant for Mutual Security Coordination in the Office of the Under Secretary for Economic Affairs and, also, the Office of International Security Affairs in the Department of Defense will have to be alerted to the possibility of emergency military assistance for C.

3. Anything in the pipeline for A should be held up. The Special Assistant for Mutual Security Coordination must be advised of this.

4. The possibility of a demonstration by the U.S. 6th Fleet in support of C's independence and integrity will have to be discussed with the Department of Defense.

5. A crash national intelligence estimate will be requested of the Central Intelligence Agency, provided the Agency does not consider the situation too fluid for a formal estimate to be useful.

6. The public affairs adviser will get in touch with the Bureau of Public Affairs, the departmental spokesman and the U.S. Information Agency to agree on the kind of face the United States will put on the affair.

7. The B Ambassador will probably have to be called in and apprised of the critical need for his government's acquiescence in overflights of B for the purpose of getting supplies to C. The B and C desk officers had better get busy immediately on a draft telegram to embassy B (repeat to C) setting forth the case the ambassador should make urgently to the B Foreign Office.

At 9:12, anticipating that he will be called to accompany the Secretary to the White House, the Assistant Secretary instructs his secretary to cancel all his appointments for the day, including one with the dentist but excepting his appointment with the C ambassador. ("Mr. Ambassador, you may assure His Majesty that my Government remains fully determined to support the sovereignty and territorial integrity of his nation.")

At 9:14, 1 minute before the scheduled commencement of the staff meeting, the Assistant Secretary joins his colleagues in the Secretary's anteroom, prepared to hear the estimate of the Director of Intelligence and Research and to give his own appraisal and submit his plan of action.

INTELLIGENCE AND FOREIGN POLICY: DILEMMAS OF A DEMOCRACY

William J. Barnds

As Mr. Barnds suggests in his essay, nothing aside from the war in Vietnam has generated as much controversy for the United States government in recent years as its intelligence operations. Its covert activities have been particularly vulnerable. There have been some widely publicized failures overseas, like the Bay of Pigs operation in 1961, and more recently the upsetting (to many) revelation that certain American student organization activities had been subsidized by the CIA.

In a relatively brief essay, Mr. Barnds covers most of the critical issues in this field, both from the point of view of substantive foreign policy problems and requirements and the peculiar dilemmas involved in carrying on such activities in a democratic society like our own. In my view, his analysis is balanced and judicious and helps put a controversial and emotionally charged subject into clearer perspective.

With the obvious exception of Viet Nam, nothing the U.S. Government has done in recent years in the field of foreign policy has created so much controversy as its intelligence operations, especially the secret subsidizing of private American institutions. The attack on the *Liberty* with the loss of 34 American lives during the 1967 Arab-Israeli war and the capture of the *Pueblo* by North Korea in 1968 brought home to the American public the dangers involved in one type of intelligence collection and embarrassed an already beleaguered Administration. Of all the U.S. intelligence organizations, the Central Intelligence Agency has been the most vociferously attacked. It has been accused of perpetrating the 1967 Greek coup, arranging the death of Ché Guevara and even fanning the flames of the recent student riots in Mexico as a means of influencing the Mexican Government to adopt an anti-Castro stance in hemispheric affairs.

Some critics of CIA view it as omnipotent and evil; others attack it as bumbling and incompetent. Although only a minority accepts either of these extreme characterizations, many Americans and foreigners are concerned about CIA's activities, and they are far from reassured by repeated official statements that it is an efficient and fully controlled instrument of the U.S. Government. The CIA has undoubtedly contributed more than other agencies to the alienation from the U.S. Government of an important segment of the academic-intellectual community and of young people; the arrival of its recruiters on a college campus is more likely to start a student riot than those of any other institution—with the possible exception of talent scouts from the Dow Chemical Company.

Present attitudes toward CIA represent a sharp departure from the situation a decade ago. Yet in the immediate postwar years there was considerable uneasiness about establishing such an organization. To do so seemed undemocratic and out of keeping with American traditions. Many Americans regarded spying as a dirty business, and looked on interfering in the internal affairs of other nations as inconsistent with our professed principles of nonintervention. Yet agreement slowly emerged that if the United States was to protect its interests and fulfill its international responsibilities in a harsh environment it had little choice but to engage in such activities.

This consensus, like so many others, has now vanished. Therefore it is appropriate to consider why CIA was created, how an intelligence agency operates, the relationship of intelligence activities to foreign policy, and the difficulties and dilemmas (as well as the capabilities) such an institution creates for a democracy which is also a major power.

II

The collapse of Soviet-American coöperation late in World War II gradually convinced most Americans that Soviet communism posed a critical challenge to U.S. security. The development of the cold war and the withdrawal of the European colonial powers from Asia made it clear that this country could not escape a much deeper involvement in world politics than had formerly been the case in peacetime. Complex and difficult decisions had to be made on a bewildering variety of issues in a rapidly changing international environment. The United States was becoming involved in areas of the world about which it knew next to nothing. It was uncertain about the capabilities and intentions of both friendly and unfriendly nations—and sometimes not sure which was which. The implications of the scientific revolution for world politics and military affairs were difficult to discern with any clarity, and the relationships between American interests in different parts of the world were obscure.

It soon became apparent that the United States lacked not only a foreign policy adequate to cope with this new situation but even the institutions within the U.S. Government necessary to develop and carry out an effective policy. Institutions and procedures had to be established which would enable the President to bring together the key U.S. officials who dealt with the various aspects of foreign policy to consider the relevant facts, weigh the alternative courses of action, make the necessary policy decisions and see that they were carried out. The result was the National Security Act of 1947, which created the National Security Council to help the President formulate foreign policy and established the Department of Defense as a step toward unification of the armed forces. This Act also created the Central Intelligence Agency; it was the nation's first separate peacetime intelligence organization.

Those responsible for U.S. foreign policy in this period felt keenly the need for more and better information on many unfamiliar areas and problems, and they decided that the task of providing much of this information should rest with men who had no direct policy responsibilities and thus no position to support, no interest to defend. American leaders also concluded that the United States needed an organization able to perform certain tasks in the execution of policy that fell between the traditional instruments of foreign policy and the open use of armed force. Thus CIA was given three general functions: (1) to gather information by covert as well as overt means; (2) to combine the information it collects with that of other agencies, to evaluate it and to present it in useful form to the policy-makers; and (3) to be prepared to intervene covertly in the affairs of other nations when so directed.[1]

The communist seizure of power in China and Peking's involvement in the Korean War greatly intensified the cold war. This led to a major expansion of U.S. military forces and of CIA and other U.S. intelligence organizations. A less tangible but perhaps more important effect of the communist gains in East Asia, coming so quickly after the imposition of communist rule

on Eastern Europe, was to create in American minds the image of a worldwide movement of incredible unity and dynamism pressing hard on a disunited and weak non-communist world. America was the only serious obstacle to even more dramatic communist gains, and American leaders were determined that this country would not fail in its responsibilities as it had after the First World War.

When uneasy stalemates developed in Europe and East Asia, the struggle between the communist bloc and the West shifted to Asia and Africa. In view of the inherent weaknesses and immense problems of most Afro-Asian countries, few people were confident that communism could be successfully combatted in all these lands. CIA was assigned an important part of the task of turning back the communist offensive—partly because in the atmosphere of those years Congress would not have openly provided funds for those liberal or leftist groups which were often the most effective in opposing the communists. U.S. covert operations during the late 1940s and the early 1950s were successful in a variety of situations. CIA was generally regarded as something new, exciting and effective, and it stood rather high in public esteem.

Simultaneously, the advent of hydrogen weapons and intercontinental ballistic missiles made it of crucial importance that the U.S. Government have reasonably accurate knowledge about enemy capabilities. Fortunately, the technological revolution which led to the development of such weapons also made it possible to develop means of penetrating the Soviet veil of secrecy. The U-2, reconnaissance satellites and electronic intercept stations around the edges of the communist world enabled the United States steadily to increase its knowledge of the Soviet military establishment.

These technological advances first came to public attention in connection with the Soviet downing of the U-2 on the eve of the 1960 Summit meeting. The U-2 affair, followed by

[1]CIA was thus the central element of the intelligence community, and the Director of Central Intelligence was made responsible for coördinating the intelligence activities of the U.S. Government. The intelligence community is now composed of CIA, the Department of State's Bureau of Intelligence Research, the Pentagon's Defense Intelligence Agency, the National Security Agency (which is responsible for communications intelligence), the intelligence components of the Army, Navy and Air Force, and—on certain matters—the intelligence units of the Atomic Energy Commission and the Federal Bureau of Investigation.

the spectacular failure of the Bay of Pigs operation in 1961, ended the relative immunity of such operations from public criticism. Those members of Congress who had long been convinced that the legislators should exercise a more formal and extensive control over CIA renewed their push for creation of a Joint Committee on Intelligence. The press began to take a more critical view of American intelligence operations, and gradually became eager to disclose information about them. From then on there were periodic revelations of past U.S. intelligence operations, and after each disclosure there was a new outcry for more control over CIA and less reliance on it. (It was only among the novelists and television producers that the intelligence agent remained the hero par excellence.)

The more critical public attitude was also stimulated by changes in this country and abroad and by the impact these developments had on American views of the world. The Sino-Soviet split, the declining intensity of the U.S.-Soviet conflict (especially after the Cuban missile confrontation), the growing awareness that the intense nationalism of the Asian and African nations limited communist prospects in these countries, and the upheavals in China gradually convinced many Americans that the external dangers were declining. By the time Viet Nam had reached crisis proportions, the case for according higher priority to domestic affairs was winning growing support, especially among young people. To them Stalin was but a name from the past, and the Cuban missile crisis was either a blurred memory or was looked upon as an aberration in Soviet policy. In this atmosphere the revelation in 1967 that CIA had been supporting the National Student Association and other private institutions led to such bitter and sustained attacks on the U.S. Government and on CIA as to force a basic reëxamination of American intelligence activities.

Perhaps the most important lesson of these events was to make it clear that even supposedly secret intelligence organizations do not and cannot operate outside and apart from the American milieu or mood. Clearly, American attitudes toward intelligence activities are closely related to the public view of the external dangers facing the United States and the foreign policy the nation should pursue. Yet today the task of reaching even general agreement on these matters is most difficult. As the danger is

seen less clearly, confusion concerning U.S. goals has correspondingly increased. The United States is coöperating with the U.S.S.R. on some issues and competing with it in others. The decline in many Americans' fear of communism and the lack of agreement on foreign policy has led many to argue that covert operations should be drastically curtailed if not eliminated. This raises the question whether the intelligence community can continue to perform effectively without some degree of consensus as to the threat we face.

III

Although CIA's covert operations have received most public attention and criticism because of their dramatic nature, far greater resources are devoted to the less spectacular effort of collecting, analyzing and reporting intelligence. These activities permeate the entire foreign-policy process; important policy decisions and the allocation of billions of dollars often depend on the judgments and conclusions reached by U.S. intelligence organizations. In such circumstances, intelligence judgments inevitably become involved in domestic political controversies.

It is simple to state the formal responsibilities and to describe the work, varied and voluminous though it is, of the U.S. intelligence community in the area of intelligence production as distinct from operations. It is to give the policy-makers judgments as to what the situation actually is in the world at any given time, what it will be in the future, and (to a degree) what the implications of such judgments are. A task simple to state, but awesome to contemplate. Historians dispute the meaning of past events, students of contemporary affairs are seldom wholly persuasive when they describe current events and their implications, and the difficulties of forecasting even general trends are obvious to all who have tried it and remember their record.

To carry out its responsibilities the U.S. intelligence community has become one of the largest consumers and producers of information in the world today—and thus in history. It gathers masses of facts, rumors and opinions by reading everything from *Pravda* to the cables of U.S. missions abroad and the reports of secret agents, and from the photographs taken by satellites to the information gleaned from National Security Agency reports. Even though much of this information goes no farther than the intelligence analysts themselves, the intelligence organizations regularly produce a variety of reports (National Intelligence Estimates, daily and weekly intelligence journals, special memoranda and various studies in depth) and send them forth to compete for the attention of the overburdened and harassed policy-makers.

In theory, the intelligence officer does not recommend policy, but his decisions as to which facts are relevant and the way in which they are presented can make a current policy look or sound silly. He does not fulfill his role unless he brings unpleasant as well as welcome facts and analysis to the attention of the policy-makers. Yet the latter, who must also consider U.S. domestic needs, may have quite different ideas about which facts are relevant. And if the senior policy-makers are to fulfill their responsibilities to inform the public, they must present some of the facts upon which U.S. foreign policy is based; the danger is that their use of intelligence data and judgments will be selected in a manner designed primarily to justify their policies. Thus the relationship between intelligence officers and policy-makers is as complex and varied as the personalities involved.

Yet despite the inherent tensions and frictions in this relationship, U.S. leaders have an indispensable asset in the U.S. intelligence community. It is worth the policy-makers' time and trouble to keep the appropriate parts of the intelligence community informed of all significant policy matters coming up for decision, and to learn where and how to tap into the intelligence apparatus in order to ask the right questions of the right people. It is also important for U.S. leaders to let the intelligence community know their opinion of the quality of its output. For the great danger is that the intelligence officer, often involved in tedious and painstaking work, will come to feel completely cut off from the policy-making process. When this happens, he either becomes a time-server or else studies his subject only for its own sake rather than in the light of its importance to the United States.

But, one may fairly ask, has the quality of American intelligence research and analysis been such as to warrant this effort, or even to warrant the cost of the intelligence apparatus? Even the informed part of the public probably has only a vague impression of a few spectacular intelligence failures and of some of the outstanding successes, but no real feel for the general quality of the effort. CIA's researchers and analysts have produced a broad range of studies of a quality that often matches the best turned out by universities and private research organizations. Other parts of the intelligence community have done very good work in more specialized fields. On the whole, the performance of the intelligence community has been effective, especially when one remembers America's lack of experience and the complexity of the problems involved. None the less, there have been more failures and, less excusably, more mediocrity than the United States should be willing to accept.

In any case, there is no room for complacency. The volume of information to be processed will continue to increase and, while computers will in time be of growing value, sound human judgment will remain the crucial element. Moreover, the tasks of the future are likely to be more difficult than those of the past, for international affairs probably will become more fluid and complex. If greater complexity and more rapid change characterize the world of the future, the importance of appraising the attitudes, capabilities and intentions of other nations will increase rather than decline. Yet prediction is especially difficult regarding nations striving to modernize, for in such countries traditional and modern attitudes are intricately interwoven. In such circumstances, the intelligence analyst's perennial problem of deciding when a political leader or a nation will act "out of character" and then of convincing his colleagues and his readers to be ready for a discontinuity of behavior becomes acutely difficult. These problems will remain even if American involvement abroad becomes more selective than it has been in the past.

The size of U.S. intelligence organizations gives them a great capability for research in depth, but their size also imposes limitations, for subtlety of thought is not the most noteworthy trait of any large organization. Special efforts will constantly be necessary to see that thoughtful, unorthodox views and individual insights are encouraged rather than stifled by the system.

IV

The tasks of the CIA clandestine service are at least as varied as those of the intelligence analysts and reporters, and much of what has been written about its activities has condemned or supported its efforts rather than analyzed its functions. Essentially, a clandestine service performs four different types of activities: (1) it collects information secretly—traditional espionage or spying activities; (2) it has a counterintelligence role—protecting the United States against penetration by other intelligence services; (3) it works with the intelligence services of allies and, at times, other nations—exchanging information with them and sometimes helping them to protect their own societies against penetration or upheaval; (4) it conducts covert political operations, which include advising foreign politicians, conducting covert propaganda, supporting labor unions or political parties, and occasionally attempting to overthrow a foreign government.[2] These diverse activities can be separated in theory more easily than in fact, since a CIA station abroad is at times involved in several activities simultaneously, and they thus tend to interact and overlap.

The most widely accepted of these activities is the counterintelligence function, for it is difficult to criticize a government for striving to protect itself against penetration by foreign agents. The counterintelligence function is not the exclusive responsibility of CIA, however, for the military services and the Federal Bureau of Investigation are also deeply involved in this area. The difficulty of this task in a world of shifting and uncertain loyalties is attested to by the varied list of men—Richard Sorge, Klaus Fuchs, Kim Philby and Oleg Penkovsky, to name but a few—who long served governments other than their own.

Most of the critics of CIA also accept the necessity of clandestine intelligence collection, but there is considerable public confusion as to its purpose, value and limitations. All governments try to keep certain of their actions and plans secret, and every government of consequence tries to secure as much of this information as it deems necessary to protect itself against the actions of other nations and to formulate its own policies on a sound basis. Properly conceived and operated, a clandestine collection system is essentially an extension of a government's overt information system, and represents an attempt to gain key pieces of information that cannot be obtained from open sources or through other channels.

The intelligence supplied by a Richard Sorge or an Oleg Penkovsky can be of momentous importance. As Hugh Trevor-Roper said in his penetrating article on Kim Philby: "To have a reliable, intelligent, highly-placed agent in the center of a potentially hostile power, with access to 'hard' evidence, is the dream of every intelligence service. . . . A well-placed agent of known fidelity and intelligence who can advise his masters, answer specific questions, comment on the disjointed texts which any Secret Service picks up, correct the illusions to which it is prone, has a value which transcends the occasional questionable scoop."[3]

But there are few Sorges, Penkovskys or Philbys, and the real question concerns the value of the information supplied by the typical agent. Everyone with any experience in collecting or reading clandestine reports recognizes that they range from the uniquely important to the routine, which at best confirm information obtained through other channels and at worst mislead. Wherever the norm truly lies, it is natural that officers of the clandestine service tend to place a higher value on the intelligence they acquire than do many foreign service officers or even intelligence analysts.

Covert political action—and particularly the use of private American institutions, sometimes with the knowledge of few if any of their officials—is the principal cause of the controversy surrounding CIA in recent years. A more recent criticism by an increasing number of Americans opposed to the basic thrust of U.S. foreign policy is that CIA's coöperation with foreign intelligence organizations in the area of counterintelligence demonstrates that it is a prime instrument of a government intent on upholding repressive régimes against revolutionary movements dedicated to social justice. These activities have led to a broad and sustained barrage of criticism, ranging from the thoughtful and serious to the wild and irresponsible, and have even led some to suggest that CIA is an invisible government which really runs the foreign policy of this country. Whatever CIA is, it is neither invisible nor a government.

Is there adequate control of CIA within the executive branch—by the White House, the Department of State, and (when appropriate) the Department of Defense? (In this connection, it is important to distinguish control from *influence*, for many of the charges that CIA is

[2]Technically, covert political action is not an *intelligence* activity, but since it is carried on by intelligence organizations it must be considered in any discussion of intelligence activities.
[3]Hugh Trevor-Roper, "The Philby Affair: Espionage, Treason, and Secret Services," *Encounter*, April 1968.

not adequately controlled reflect the conviction that the Agency has too much influence.) CIA has always secured approval from the senior policy-makers before initiating covert political action. Although for some years the procedures for approval of new programs were informal and established programs often were not subjected to critical scrutiny, these weaknesses have steadily diminished. Today covert political activities are approved and reviewed by a top-level committee composed of senior members of the White House staff, the State Department and the Defense Department. Moreover, projects are now initially discussed at lower levels with the relevant assistant secretaries in the Department of State or Defense. Ambassadors in the countries involved are also almost always brought into this decision-making process. Control procedures have thus improved steadily over the years, and they enable the appropriate policy-makers to exercise effective and flexible control over the initiation and continuation of covert operations. However, these procedures will remain effective only so long as the officials involved remain determined to make them work rather than let them become a formal ritual.

If control is not the problem, what have been the reasons for the troubles CIA has experienced? And how damaging have these troubles been in comparison to the substantial contribution made to American security by covert operations, many of which remain secret to this day? I make no pretense of having the background necessary to answer the second question. Probably only a handful of men have, and none of them is likely to reveal the evidence which would support his conclusions. However, it is obvious that covert operations have caused considerable trouble and that continual efforts to improve them are indispensable.

CIA's covert operations have suffered from several specific weaknesses. Briefly, the clandestine service has not been able to maintain adequate standards of secrecy and has overestimated its ability to operate secretly, especially for prolonged periods. The U.S. Government's policy of virtually automatic denial when accused of conducting a covert operation compounded the problem once an operation was compromised. Finally, Washington has often overestimated its ability to influence and manipulate the internal affairs of other nations, and has sometimes exaggerated the importance of doing so. This latter criticism applies to its overt as well as to its covert activities. The Government's successes with both types of activities during the height of the cold war led many officials to fail to recognize that America's capacity to influence situations abroad would decline when conditions changed. In time they also discovered that some projects which were successful in the short run had no lasting effect. All of these shortcomings tend to reinforce one another.

The United States intervenes in the affairs of foreign countries in a variety of ways which clearly pose political and ethical questions, but intervention is not prima facie immoral simply because it is covert. People will differ as to whether the ends justify the means in particular circumstances; policy-makers can perhaps agree as to whether a proposed intervention is necessary, judicious and well conceived. What is required is a sense of proportion and a determination not to be unduly influenced by short-term considerations, and these are qualities difficult to gain and hold. Guidelines can be set forth for some aspects of covert activities, but not for all of them, and it is important to understand the differences involved.[4]

These political and moral problems, as well as those of secrecy, are most acute with regard to covert support of private American institutions. Whatever the arguments once advanced for this practice (and some were compelling), they are no longer persuasive. On the basis of the Katzenbach (Gardner and Helms) recommendations, following the 1967 disclosures, the U.S. Government has announced that it has abandoned secret subsidies to private voluntary American institutions. The Katzenbach report did state, however, that in cases involving overriding national security interests individual exceptions should be made, provided extremely stringent procedures were followed. This is a sound basic policy, but should be supplemented by a major effort by the Administration to secure Congressional approval for one or more publicly financed agencies to extend support to private institutions when it is in the national

---

[4]If the CIA's sharpest critics—the radicals who favor support of revolutionary movements—were to gain power in the United States, they would almost certainly have to rely on covert operations to achieve their aims. Reactionary and oppressive régimes are not easily dislodged, as Rhodesia and South Africa demonstrate, and will not fade away because of moral disapproval or even economic boycott. An activist policy short of direct military intervention would lead such critics to adopt the very instruments and methods they had formerly denounced.

interest to do so. If some new institutional arrangement is not made, the Government may in a time of danger feel compelled to resort to covert subsidies again, and if this became known the domestic and foreign political impact could be extremely severe.

V

A second area where a basic policy change would be helpful concerns government-press relations. The disclosure of intelligence activities in the press in recent years is a clear national liability. These disclosures have created a public awareness that the U.S. Government has, at least at times, resorted to covert operations in inappropriate situations, failed to maintain secrecy and failed to review ongoing operations adequately. The public revelation of these weaknesses, even though they are now partially corrected, hampers CIA (and the U.S. Government) by limiting those willing to coöperate with it and increasing those opposed to it and its activities. As long as such disclosures remain in the public mind, any official effort to improve CIA's image is as likely to backfire as to succeed.

Moreover, in the present atmosphere the press will seek and publish any information about intelligence activities it can acquire, probably arguing that, if it can learn about such activities, other governments already know of them. Even if some parts of the press were disposed toward discretion the problem would remain formidable. Voluntary press restraints would have to be accepted by virtually the entire newspaper, magazine, radio and television industries or they would quickly break down. Legislation, whether regarded as desirable or not (and even ignoring the Constitutional problems) is impossible to achieve in the present climate, and it would be unwise to count on improved prospects in the future.

There is one change that could be made to diminish these difficulties. The U.S. Government in the past almost automatically and immediately denied any charge that a particular event had resulted from a U.S. covert operation. Sometimes this ended the matter, but too often enough evidence came to light to strip the denial of its credibility or even to force the United States to admit the truth, thus getting itself into the worst possible position. Gradually the Government has shifted from a policy of virtually automatic and instant denial toward one of re-

fusing to comment on such charges. Refusing to comment should become a firm policy — whether the charges are true or false — and the Government should make clear from the outset that this is now the basic information policy. A policy of refusing to comment would not be easy to initiate and maintain, especially if an accusation was causing a furor in a foreign country, but it would in time substantially improve the public position of the U.S. Government regarding covert operations.

Many critics and some supporters of CIA have suggested two other changes involving American intelligence activities which they think would substantially improve the situation. One is to divide CIA, separating the clandestine service from the intelligence research and analysis function. The other involves the creation of a Joint Congressional Committee on Intelligence to oversee the activities of CIA and perhaps the intelligence components of other government departments as well.

The arguments for and against a division of CIA are intricate and complicated. The arguments in favor are: (1) the organization that produces finished and evaluated intelligence conclusions which influence policy should not be the same organization which often executes the policy decided upon — even though these functions are organizationally separated — lest the possible bias of the operators affect the judgments of the analysts; (2) given the present reputation of CIA as a vast manipulator of events, its reorganization probably would ease public concern at home and abroad; (3) a separation of functions would lessen the alienation between much of the academic-intellectual community and youth on the one hand and the intelligence agencies on the other, and would ease recruiting problems; (4) a reorganization along these lines probably would make it easier to improve the cover of clandestine officers and increase their capability to act secretly.

Equally weighty arguments can be advanced against dividing CIA. These are: (1) CIA's ability to secure money from Congress has been due in part to the variety of tasks it performs, which has give it a broad Congressional constituency. It is questionable whether the part of CIA responsible for research and analysis could secure its present level of funding if it were separate from the clandestine services, while the latter might suffer a similar fate after an operational failure had become known; (2) the

Director of Central Intelligence cannot be a strong independent force as the President's principal intelligence adviser and continue to be responsible for coördinating the intelligence activities of the U.S. Government unless he heads a broadly based organization; (3) it would be difficult to devise a different organizational cover for the clandestine service which would be any more secure; (4) CIA's capability in the scientific field is an important asset, and any division of the Agency probably would divide this group and weaken its capabilities; (5) operators and analysts each benefit from the other's substantive knowledge and experience.

On balance, the benefits of maintaining CIA as it is now organized presently outweigh the advantages of splitting it, but it would hardly rank as a disaster if it were divided.

The case for creating a Joint Congressional Committee on Intelligence rests largely on the view that such a committee would ease Congressional and public concern about CIA activities. Advocates argue that the present subcommittees of the military and appropriations committees in the House and Senate do not really influence and supervise those activities in the way Congress should and would if there were a Joint Committee solely involved in this task. On the other hand, such a committee should logically be responsible for all intelligence organizations and activities, and the Armed Services committees are unlikely (to put it mildly) to relinquish their jurisdiction over military intelligence. A formal Joint Committee would also create additional pressure on CIA to adopt a cautious and bureaucratic approach in a field where imagination and flexibility are important qualities. Finally, the creation of a formal Joint Committee probably would reduce the willingness of foreign intelligence services to pass intelligence to, and coöperate with, CIA, because of their fear that such relationships would become known and create domestic political problems. These disadvantages seem persuasive, and to date a majority of Congress has reached the same conclusion.

Moreover, it is misleading to suppose that organizational structures or executive-legislative relations are the basic problem involved in covert operations, for changes in these areas would not touch the central issue. This is the question of policy: under what circumstances should the United States resort to covert operations? It would be immensely useful if a set of rules or even guidelines could be developed, but this is probably impossible unless one is willing to decree an absolute prohibition of specific kinds of operations, and few Americans want their Government to be this rigid. Even Senator J. William Fulbright, in an article which attacks many of CIA's activities and points out the corrosive effect they can have on American values, says that in times of supreme emergency such a rigid rule cannot be applied. "We are compelled, therefore, to lay down a qualified rule, a rule to the effect that the end almost never justifies the means, that our policy must almost always be open and honest and made in accordance with constitutional procedure."[5]

Thus we cannot escape reliance on human judgment, and our judgment will depend on how we view our place and responsibilities in the world. This will involve us in painful dilemmas, for the United States is trying to do two quite different things simultaneously. It is trying to adhere to certain principles and values which often seem in conflict with the means employed to protect its security and advance its interests. The decisions we make in the field of intelligence will ultimately reflect the interaction between our estimate of the danger we face and the values we hold. American leaders will need a sense of proportion, a combination of boldness and caution, a thorough knowledge of men and nations, and the uncommon quality of common sense. Finally, they should have the vision and strength of character to think in terms of years and even decades rather than weeks and months. These are difficult qualities to come by, but unless they are possessed in large measure by American leaders the United States will be unable to conduct a successful foreign policy in any area.

[5]Senator J. William Fulbright, "We Must Not Fight Fire with Fire," *The New York Times Magazine*, April 23, 1967.

CHAPTER 5

MAJOR POLICY PROBLEMS

FOREIGN POLICY ANALYSIS

For all the thousands of articles and books that have been devoted to the discussion of public policy issues, the level of rigorous analysis that has been developed is disappointingly low. The broad field of economics would be one notable exception to this characterization. The literature dealing with foreign policy, unfortunately, illustrates the point all too well.

This is not to imply that the state of relevant academic knowledge puts us at the threshold of a "science of foreign policy," with hypotheses systematically generated and investigated, significant dimensions of problems translated into quantitative terms, and then manipulated with the aid of contemporary computer technology. Movement in this direction certainly must be explored on a continuing basis. However, much of the writing on foreign policy does not even satisfy simpler rules of logical analysis and problem solving. At times, it seems that the same criticism could fairly be directed to foreign policy decision making within the government.

What follows is a rather simpleminded effort to suggest a framework for the analysis of foreign policy—questions and concepts that the outside observer can bring to bear on the foreign policy statements and other materials made available to him. The inevitable caveats are also

included because these are difficult analytical problems to deal with under the best of circumstances, and the conditions and pressures under which they must often be dealt with inside the government fall far short of the ideal.

Intelligence: Defining external situations

Foreign policy can be defined as the result of the interaction of national interests and values with an international setting or environment having certain characteristics. Thus, one critical factor in the foreign policy-making process is defining the nature of relevant external situations. This usually involves not only statements about the past and the present but predictions about the future.

We are, necessarily, interested in what is likely to be happening in a great many places around the globe. Furthermore, our interest is selective; it is limited to those situations or events that could affect American interests and policies. Thus, the external intelligence side of the policy equation is doubly difficult: it involves identifying situations that are or could be relevant to American interests, and then making predictions (usually stated in terms of probabilities and possibilities) about how they are likely to develop over time.

It must be conceded that making the predictions is usually far more difficult than identifying situations that require attention. For example, assessing the capabilities and intentions of the Soviet Union and Communist China represents an absolutely fundamental requirement for American foreign policy and, therefore, an urgent, continuing problem for the American intelligence community.

One has the impression that American knowledge about Soviet and Chinese military strength and advanced weapons is rather good. Anticipating what those two governments are likely to do in the short run is a much more hazardous enterprise, although even here the enigmatic quality may be exaggerated. The most difficult kind of intelligence analysis, though, is the longer-range assessment of underlying political, social, and economic trends in eastern Europe and the Soviet Union and what they may mean for the foreign policies of those nations and their relations with the West. By their very potential for dangerous as well as promising consequences, they nevertheless require attention.

The United States, of course, is not merely concerned to understand the actions of other nations; it is often trying to influence them. Another aspect of intelligence analysis therefore involves assessing the probable or possible consequences of planned U.S. actions on the behavior of others. (This kind of analysis is not the exclusive preserve of the intelligence expert; interested policy analysts and policy makers will have their own views and predictions.)

Whoever may do it, it is tricky business. Have the Russians avoided attacking western Europe because they were deterred by American nuclear power, or would they have been too cautious to do so even without the American deterrent? What effect did the United States bombing of North Vietnam, begun in 1965, have on the policy makers of that country? Did it help bring them to the negotiating table in Paris in 1968? Would they have continued their effort in South Vietnam without negotiations if there had not been, first, a limited and, then, a complete halt in the bombing? These are most difficult questions to answer, even after the fact.

Scholars working peacefully in the academy often cannot even agree on the meaning of the past. Most, however, would agree that prediction in the social sciences is at a very early stage of development. Clearly, governmental intelligence estimaters have a thankless and frustrating task. (The United States has an elaborate organizational machinery and set of procedures designed to produce estimates on matters of considerable importance; the products are known as National Intelligence Estimates or NIEs.)

From an academic viewpoint, this process might be improved if predictions about the future, particularly where U.S. actions are involved, were more often phrased as hypotheses; if the nature of relevant evidence tending to confirm or disconfirm these hypotheses was specified in advance; and if the empirical data and assumptions underlying characterizations of present situations, and predictions regarding their future development, were made explicit and as precise as possible, quantitative where feasible.

Motivation: national interests and objectives

The motive thrust for foreign policy is provided by national interests and purposes, translated in turn into objectives, policies, and specific actions and programs. The sources of policy motivation can be traced back as far as the patience and imagination of the researcher will take him, perhaps all the way to original sin. History provides general and sweeping explanation; a specific event, like the Monroe Doctrine, may become established as a tradition and guidepost and exercise a continuing influence in the present. In the development of American foreign policy, the protection of the oceans and the presence of weak neighbors north and south have long been commented on as geographical factors of importance. The American character and the American creed or value system, if their nature can be agreed upon, must be considered. For example, the American foreign aid program probably cannot be adequately understood or assessed without attention to phenomena that fall under these headings.

Getting more specific, prior commitments, obligations, and even courses of action previously embarked upon provide their own momentum or, at times, inertial force. Some commitments seem firmer, more clearly defined, more vital to national interests than others. For example, the commitment to defend western Europe from attack, embodied in the North Atlantic Treaty, would seem to rank far higher on all these counts than the commitment to Southeast Asia reflected in the Southeast Asia Treaty Organization (SEATO).

For present purposes, the more fundamental sources of policy must be taken as given. National interests are usually stated in rather basic terms—national security, economic well-being, maintenance of valued American institutions. Some commentators have laid heavy emphasis on the concept of "*The* national interest," but it seems to me more useful to use the plural. *The* national interest concept assumes that in foreign policy situations, it will always or usually be clear to all rational and honest men what ought to be done to best advance the nation's interests.

My assumption, on the contrary, is that in the toughest, most critical situations, honest, rational, well-intentioned men will often differ, and sometimes radically so. Foreign policy making frequently involves choosing among shades of gray or, even worse, among less bad rather than positively good alternatives. At times, the latter may be thought of as choosing which horn of the dilemma to impale yourself upon.

The further assumption, then, is that the choices usually get more difficult as situations and objectives get more specific. The translation of basic national interests into a broad set of goals vis-à-vis the international system usually raises no hackles; few will quarrel with a vision of peaceful, prospering, increasingly democratic nation-states, willing to live and let live with their neighbors and to settle their differences without resort to force.

How one is going to bring about this millennium or, more modestly and realistically, keep the globe from going up in smoke raises much more difficult choices and, along with them, wider disagreements.

Making policy choices

An *objective* is usefully defined as a *desired state of affairs. Policies,* simply stated, represent *rules and/or actions.* A great deal of nonsense has been written and spoken about policy: e.g., does the United States have a foreign policy? At times in the past, the U.S. may not have had a very active, aggressive or well-conceived foreign policy, but it certainly had rules or norms that guided its actions. In effect, a nation is either engaging in actions which, hopefully, make clear what its preferences and concerns are or is stating that under given circumstances, it is prepared to take certain actions. In either case, it is trying to establish what its objectives are and what it is doing, or is prepared to do, in their pursuit.

Complications and difficulties arise in a variety of ways. First of all, desired states of affairs are sometimes not precisely or clearly set forth.

Sometimes, indeed, they have not been clearly or fully thought through by the policy makers. There are occasions, however, when the ambiguity of objectives is quite calculated. In other situations, the clarifying of objectives is not easy to do, given the many uncertainties involved. For example, a major complaint of critics of the Vietnam policy has been that the U.S. Government did not clearly set forth the state of affairs in South Vietnam that it insisted upon or would settle for. Perhaps the policy makers were not clear in their own minds on this point; more likely, the South Vietnamese situation was too fluid to allow for such precision in the specifying of objectives. To do so, furthermore, might have been to lock the United States into a policy position without bringing any compensating advantages in terms of diplomatic bargaining.

This last point suggests the next stage, analytically speaking, in this process. Assuming that desired states of affairs can be and have been specified, what American courses of action seem most likely to accomplish said objectives? Here, a number of previously noted caveats are relevant.

First, American leverage on foreign situations is limited, sometimes quite narrowly so. Furthermore, some of the objectives we are attempting to accomplish, for example in the less-developed countries, are so fundamental and far-reaching, are directed at such deep-seated social problems and processes, that it would be presumptuous to expect more than the most limited success. The problems of development or modernization in the less-developed countries illustrate another fundamental handicap for the American foreign policy or program official: he must make operational choices in situations which even the academic experts say are not well understood. It should not be surprising, then, that policies and programs do not always achieve stated objectives.

If policies and programs are often on such uncertain ground, it becomes most difficult to decide what resources to allocate to them, to evaluate results vis-à-vis costs, and to compare the effectiveness of one program with another or the same program as carried on in a number of countries. Some of the problems involved are suggested by the discussion of the federal government's Planning-Programming-Budgeting System (PPBS) in Chapter Four. All that can be noted at this point is that the translation of policies into detailed programs, and then into specific budgetary items, represents another painful and critical stage in foreign policy development and analysis.

Further difficulties of another sort are raised by objectives and policies that conflict. At times, the United States has had to choose between policies designed to support and strengthen its NATO allies in Europe and others aimed at gaining the confidence and friendship of the newly free, less-developed countries of Asia and Africa. Areas still under European colonial control (e.g., the Portuguese African colonies of Angola and Mozambique) have provided prime occasions for such exercises in policy priorities. In the Portuguese case, the situation is further complicated by the presence of important American military installations in the Portuguese Azores. In the interest of realism, it should be pointed out that policy makers will "waffle" or "fuzz" these policy differences when they can, rather than striving for the intellectual neatness of clear-cut policy priorities. Their rationale: why antagonize another nation unless absolutely necessary.

Policy differences are sometimes generated by the different time frames of various objectives. This is sometimes stated more simply as long-range vs. short-range objectives and policies. For example, it is argued that assistance to a right-wing, authoritarian regime or military junta may produce short-term gains of local support for the U.S. and a temporary political stability but at the price of repressing needed social change and encouraging eventual extremist solutions to political and socio-economic problems. This is, to many Americans, an attractive argument on the surface; however, it glides by an insistent present reality to a scenario of things that may, or may not, happen. The policymaker who must cope with the present reality probably deserves a sympathetic hearing before he and his policy are dismissed out of hand as reactionary, or worse.

Planning

This plea for sympathy for short-range policy considerations may be the appropriate point to comment on the nature and desirability of foreign policy planning. A good brief definition of planning is "thinking ahead with a view to present action." The intellectual or analytical activities involved are very much like those discussed in this essay. The essential difference is the time frame. Because the operational per-

sonnel in most organizations tend to be fully engaged in coping with current problems and situations, it has become increasingly common to establish separate planning units, to assure that someone in the organization is taking the longer-range view of its problems on a regular, continuing basis.

The American and other military establishments have been doing this for many years. American foreign policy agencies, including the State Department, have come to it on any scale only in the last 20 years.

There are many kinds of planning activities. Scholars and practitioners alike differ on the usefulness of foreign policy planning. For present purposes, the point to be emphasized is that it is not intrinsically different, as an intellectual activity, from the foreign policy analysis discussed above. Presumably, it is more difficult, challenging, and frustrating, perhaps worthless, yet possibly quite significant because of the more ambitious time frame in which it is set.[1]

Grand strategy

We have been attempting to pull apart the intellectual elements of foreign policy. Now, it may be useful to put them back together again and look at the overall picture, at what is sometimes referred to as "grand strategy." If a nation has a coherent, well-defined set of national objectives, a clear notion of the major forces at work in the international system, and a guiding concept of how the latter must be dealt with to accomplish the former, we can credit the nation in question with a grand strategy. The containment policy developed by the United States in the late 1940's to deal with the Soviet Union was such a strategy; it involved meeting Soviet expansionist probes with "situations of strength." It did not involve, as perhaps it might have and some indeed proposed, efforts to roll back the Iron Curtain.

In recent years, a growing number of critics of U.S. foreign policy, notable among them Senators J. W. Fulbright and Eugene McCarthy, have been arguing that the original containment policy degenerated over time into a rigid and unimaginative anti-Communist policy, in which the United States took it upon itself to oppose the spread of communism everywhere, even by internal if violent change within countries,

[1]For a more detailed discussion of planning, and of some of the other matters treated in this introduction, see Sapin, The Making of United States Foreign Policy, ch. 10.

without much weighing of the American interests and objectives involved and the possible costs and risks to the United States. Vietnam and the Dominican intervention of 1965 are cited as prime examples of the negative consequences of such a stance. Thus, we have been instructed about the limits of power, warned about the arrogance of power, and soberly counseled about the discipline of power.[2]

These criticisms seem to me oversimplified and unfair. However, what the critics have called for is quite appropriate (and in fact already under way), namely, a critical look at our guiding foreign policy concepts or grand strategy. It seems clear that the time is ripe for it. The result is not likely to be any radical change in the foreign policy stance of the United States but rather a more relaxed approach to some of the world's problems, a willingness to do less in certain situations and to let other nations do more and take on greater responsibilities (if they are willing), a recognition that not all external situations require our active attention and involvement. Perhaps some Presidential speechwriter will come up with an appealing label for this posture, if adopted.

Hopefully, this brief essay has illuminated some of the problems of the foreign policy maker as he engages in foreign policy analysis and decision making and, at the same time, provided the student with some critical apparatus that he can bring to bear in his own study of foreign policy issues.

It should be emphasized that the policy analyst and the policy maker will not always be confronting these problems in a cool, rational, insulated working milieu. Bureaucratic rivalries and suspicions, within as well as between agencies, may affect their product and what can be accomplished with it. The personalities of key officials may be important. The political power, broadly speaking, of those involved is sometimes a factor. No doubt these political pressures become more important, more urgent, as the policy choices involved become more critical. In any event, a framework for policy analysis, such as the one presented above, should not be mistaken for a description of how the foreign policy machinery operates.

It is not, furthermore, a guide for the making of difficult choices—for example, in the running of risks, in the discounting of uncertainties in intelligence, in the allocation of scarce resources, in the weighing of external as against domestic political pressures. Here, no doubt, we are more in the realm of art than science. The justification for the analytical approach suggested above is not the elimination of wisdom, seasoned judgment, and intuition. It is aimed, rather, at providing the maximum analytical and empirical base as point of departure for them, minimizing the area in which such delicate and at times unreliable mental tools must be employed.

[2]The following were among the more widely noted critiques: J. William Fulbright, *The Arrogance of Power* (New York: Vintage Books, 1966); Eugene J. McCarthy, *The Limits of Power* (New York: Holt, Rinehart and Winston, 1967); Edmund Stillman and William Pfaff, *Power and Impotence* (New York: Random House, 1966); and Ronald Steel, *Pax Americana* (New York: Viking Press, 1967). A more balanced and positive view was to be found in George W. Ball, *The Discipline of Power* (Boston: Little, Brown, 1968).

THE ABM, PROLIFERATION AND INTERNATIONAL STABILITY

Robert L. Rothstein

Among the critical national security issues that will face the United States in the 1970's are: what kind of defenses, if any, to build to protect the country against possible attack by Soviet or Chinese Communist intercontinental ballistic missiles; the likely spread of nuclear-weapon capabilities beyond the five nations that now possess them and what can be done about it; the possible intensification of the strategic arms race between the United States and the Soviet Union; and, finally, the effects that developments in these first three categories might have on U.S.-Soviet relations, including some possibly dangerous ones.

Clearly, American policies on all of these matters are closely related. Indeed, they illustrate very well the premise, set forth at length in Chapter Two of this book, that foreign policies and military policies are deeply and fundamentally linked. It is impossible to understand contemporary relations between the United States and the Soviet Union without a considerable grasp of modern weaponry, particulary in its nuclear and missile dimensions. Similarly, it would be naive, or worse, to plunge ahead with strategic weapons decisions without making some judgments or assumptions about their possible effects on Soviet behavior. Presumably the foreign policy expert is better equipped to analyze the latter than the weapons developer or even the military strategist.

The United States has already made some important decisions in this general area. In 1968 it was decided to proceed with the building of a "thin" antiballistic missile (ABM) defense system. In March 1969 President Nixon modified this decision in favor of an ABM system, now called "Safeguard," designed primarily to protect selected missile sites, rather than cities, against a possible Soviet "first strike." While Professor Rothstein's point of departure is the earlier decision, his analysis is still quite relevant to this problem area.

He illuminates some of the complex ways in which the deployment of ABM systems is related to nuclear proliferation as well as to the continued, intense competition between the United States and the Soviet Union in the field of strategic nuclear weapons; and, also, some ways in which these military developments interact with international political relationships in a number of parts of the globe.

Rothstein does not mention another major, and possibly destablilizing, development in military technology—missiles with multiple warheads, so-called MIRV's (multiple, independently targeted re-entry vehicles), being developed by the United States and the Soviet Union.

The contemporary strategic era, dominated by ballistic missiles, has appeared to possess a curious kind of stability. Despite its uncertainties and dangers, two factors were apparently beyond dispute. On the one hand, neither the Soviet Union nor the United States could eliminate the other's missile forces in a first strike or effectively defend against a retaliatory missile strike. The offense seemed to have made a quantum jump against the defense: the old pattern of oscillation between defensive and offensive superiority has apparently been superseded by a period in which, for the foreseeable future, defense would be definitely inferior and incapable of matching offensive gains. On the other hand, missiles were so expensive and required so much technical sophistication that very few countries could either afford them or build them. The vexing problem of nuclear proliferation thus appeared in a new light. Even if a state could develop a nuclear bomb, it was

assumed that it could not be a truly "effective" member of the nuclear club unless it also developed a missile to deliver it somewhere. The double task of building a bomb and a sophisticated delivery system inevitably seemed so difficult that the problem of preventing a thoroughly destablizing nuclear proliferation appeared relatively simple. At worst, the process could be "managed."

We may, however, be entering a strategic era in which neither factor holds true. Whether ballistic missile defense ever achieves the level of effectiveness (near perfect) some of its proponents foresee in the next decade, and whether the costs and difficulties of developing rocket vehicles are as sharply reduced as others contend (so that the ability to deliver the bomb in high style spreads rapidly) are obviously uncertain. But to the degree that these prophecies are accurate, or believed, the stability of the missile era may prove to have been very transitory.

At any rate, one point deserves emphasis. Deployment of an ABM system and the beginning of a process of nuclear diffusion (which may be directly related to the ABM decision), irrespective of whether they occur because of political or technological reasons, may thrust us into a new strategic environment in which even the tenuous stability of the present will evoke nostalgia. In the circumstances, policies which would have appeared dangerous or unnecessarily provocative yesterday may perhaps begin to appear more prudent and realistic today or tomorrow.

II

The recent announcement of the decision to begin installing a "thin" ABM system elicited a great deal of negative comment in the American and European press. This is hardly surprising for, on the basis of publicly available information, the arguments against the ABM seemed much more persuasive than those for it. In fact, anyone who troubled to read Mr. McNamara's statement on the budget in January 1967 would come away quite convinced that the arguments justifying early installation of an ABM system were at best premature and at worst spurious. Yet within the year Mr. McNamara had apparently changed his mind and committed the United States to early deployment of a partial ABM system. The San Francisco speech in which he announced the decision may, perhaps, be read as an ambiguous and even anguished justification for the ABM; but it still may have committed us decisively.

It is possible, of course, that there were objective military and political reasons for Mr. McNamara's about-face. A new technological breakthrough might have occurred or intelligence might have yielded firmer and more dangerous information about Soviet or Chinese capabilities or intentions. To a certain extent this indeed appears to have happened. Soviet development of a "fractional orbital bombardment system" (FOBS), reports of heavy Soviet investment in *both* offensive and defensive missile systems, new predictions about Chinese capabilities and significant advances in our own ballistic missile defense research (especially with X-ray warheads) all tended to point in the same direction: prompt deployment of a "thin" ABM system.

Now, it is a mistake to argue as if the installation of an ABM system would have only negative consequences and that a delay would have only positive consequences. Decisions such as these are a wager about the future and they are made — or ought to be made — "on balance," and with full realization that the possibility of unanticipated consequences or mistaken consequences is very high. In the circumstances, there is great temptation to buy insurance by developing everything that can be developed, and to do everything possible to reëstablish or maintain a situation which seems to be advantageous. The virtues which the Joint Chiefs of Staff have seen in immediate deployment of the ABM system may be regarded in this light. Their arguments, in isolation, seem persuasive: more effective deterrence, a reduction in the number of lives lost should deterrence fail, a reduction in the possibility of accidental or "catalytic" wars, a halt to nuclear proliferation and, above all, a stabilization of the *existing* strategic balance (*i.e.* one in which the United States possesses "dominance"). ABM deployment, according to the Chiefs, would "continue the Cuba power environment in the world. . . . At the time of Cuba, the strategic nuclear balance was such that the Soviets did not have an exploitable capability because of our vastly superior nuclear strength."

None of these arguments is as clear and uncontroversial as the Joint Chiefs of Staff appear to assume. Mr. McNamara himself apparently found them unconvincing as recently as a year ago. Under some circumstances, and in certain future contexts, an ABM system promised several limited advantages; on balance, however, they were apparently outweighed by the disadvantages. Under the best of circumstances, the ABM seemed prone to obsolescence (as new offensive missiles appeared), uncertainly effective,[1] enormously expensive and politically inexpedient. The obvious question is whether various technological developments in the past year, as well as new uncertainties about Soviet and Chinese behavior, justified a reshuffling of priorities and a definite decision to plunge into a new strategic environment. Even for those with access to all the available information it must have been an agonizing choice: the stakes are frighteningly high.

It ought to be said, however, that there are a number of very knowledgeable people in Washington who maintain that the foregoing considerations were irrelevant. They contend that the decision was almost completely a response to domestic political pressures.

While the argument is not very subtle, it is also not entirely implausible. With the political costs of the Vietnamese war accelerating, the Johnson Administration may well have felt that it could not risk providing the right wing (both Democratic and Republican) with another security issue in the forthcoming elections. It may be, as some have said, that the Administration overestimated the degree of Congressional pressure for an ABM system. However, it was quality not quantity which was probably decisive: the Congressmen who were most vociferous on this issue were also among those who could harm Mr. Johnson most in the next year. In addition, the Joint Chiefs, whose discontent is frequently noted, had to be pacified: their leverage on the President and the Secretary of Defense went up as their threats to resign became increasingly dangerous in political terms.

That the decision to begin deployment of a "thin" ABM system was not the result of a considered evaluation of all the military and political evidence may perhaps be inferred from the confused manner in which it was publicly justified. While it was said to be aimed solely at the emerging dangers of a Chinese nuclear

[1]As one Department of Defense expert has noted: "Any defensive system can really do no more than to raise the entrance price which an attacker must pay in order to destroy a target." Charles M. Herzfeld, "BMD and National Security," *Annals of the New York Academy of Sciences*, 1965, reprinted in *Survival*, March 1966, p. 74. The best analysis of the ABM problem which I have found is J. I. Coffey, "The ABM Debate," *Foreign Affairs*, April 1967.

strike against the United States, and not at the Soviet Union, against which it was patently ineffective, both Mr. McNamara and various military officers indicated that it would indeed have an indirect effect on the Soviet-American strategic balance. By providing point defense for our Minutemen it clearly would cut down the effectiveness of a Soviet strike against them. However, since the Administration was in the throes of a public and private effort to convince the Soviets that the ABM deployment was not aimed at them, and that discussions to curtail ABM deployment were necessary and possible, "clarification" was needed.

A public speech by Assistant Secretary of Defense Paul C. Warnke attempted to provide it. Mr. Warnke argued "that our Chinese-oriented ABM deployment should make it easier, and not harder, for countries in Asia to sign the NPT [nonproliferation treaty]." The ABM, he maintained, would make the American commitment to defend Asia credible, since henceforth Detroit or Los Angeles, etc., would be safe from Chinese retaliation. He also maintained that it would emphasize the "unique disparity" between the United States and China, and thus make it "even clearer" to the Asians that they could safely sign the nonproliferation treaty. He concluded by declaring that the Soviets "knew" that the system was not designed for use against them, and therefore need not respond to it —surely one of the more naïve imputations of faith in recent years, especially given the contradictory testimony from other officials of his own Department.

Mr. Warnke's analysis of the possible effects of the ABM is peculiar in that he apparently presumes that it can be deployed while everything else in the strategic and political environment remains static. The Russians will not respond, or will respond by agreeing to arms-control measures, because they believe in our good intentions. The Asians will agree to forego nuclear weapons because their faith in our good intentions will rise. The Chinese, who have no faith in our good intentions, will "finally" realize that we can destroy them and will behave more rationally. And our European allies will, of course, realize that, as we have from time to time maintained, our efforts to improve our own defense have nothing to do with our commitment to come to their aid; and it is merely a nasty impertinence to insinuate in Gaullist style that we are leaving them exposed and ignored.

Many of our strategic analysts have tended to view strategic problems from a systemic point of view, almost to the exclusion of other vantage points. As a result, particular events or developments have been assessed primarily from the global perspective of the superpowers. Since the strategic configuration which has existed over the last twenty years has, for the most part, reflected conditions of American dominance and relative stability, new developments have inevitably been foreseen as destabilizing unless they were controlled by, or symmetrically limited to, the superpowers.

The response to the problem of proliferation is a case in point. Granted it is potentially very destabilizing, how does one prevent it? The usual answer has been by persuading potential nuclear powers that their efforts will be extremely costly and that, anyway, they will be useless if not counter-productive against the United States or the Soviet Union. That is, the systemic perspective has been maintained: the behavior of small and middle powers has been evaluated almost wholly in terms of its possible impact on the whole system. Since we have favored the status quo, our efforts have been limited to trying to convince others not to rock the boat. The whole syndrome can be perceived in the arguments designed to convince France not to join the nuclear club; they were perfectly logical but also irrelevant. To Paris, and perhaps to many potential nuclear powers, the problem appeared in a wholly different perspective when evaluated in terms of national (i.e. sub-systemic) interests.

Mr. Warnke's speech may be read in this light. Again, it is assumed that other states will perceive the situation in the same way as we do and will be as concerned with international stability as we are. There is no attempt to examine the problem from other points of view. If we do attempt to interpret the impact of the ABM decision from local perspectives, the picture which emerges is not nearly as optimistic as the one drawn by Mr. Warnke.

III

We can begin by discussing China's possible reactions. It is doubtful that anyone seriously believes that the ABM, as currently described, is aimed at China. However, since public justifications have insisted that the essential aim of the ABM system is deterrence or defense against Chinese threats, the argument must be examined.

It should be clear that the political and psychological advantages of China's nuclear weapons are not directly related to American defensive capabilities. There is thus no sense in the simplistic argument that an ABM system will actually induce the Chinese to forego missile development. In addition, the assumption that the Chinese will react to an increase in our defensive capabilities by decreasing their offensive capabilities is not psychologically convincing: the opposite reaction may be more likely.

The usual contention, however, is not that the Chinese will give up their missile program but that a "thin" ABM system will substantially lessen the impact of a Chinese nuclear attack. What is the probability of such an attack? To some, the likelihood is high; the Chinese are more aggressive and less rational than the Soviets and will strike rather than accept humiliation. In effect, a Cuban missile crisis with the Chinese is destined to have a different scenario. To others, the behavior of the Chinese has been as cautious and nonprovocative as that of the Soviets and the probability that they would strike the United States seems very low. Acceptance of the latter point of view has to be tempered by several considerations. The first, obviously, is the current internal instability of China, which might lead to extreme or irrational behavior in a crisis. Another point is that China has not yet reached the stage where war—as the fashionable argument goes—becomes increasingly unpalatable and unlikely as energies are concentrated on the accomplishment of domestic tasks. Finally, the Chinese tradition is different from our own, we have miscalculated their response before, their standards of rationality may diverge as much from ours as Japan's did in 1941—and so on. In short, it is not altogether unreasonable to worry about aggressive and irrational behavior by the Chinese. The critical question concerns the relationship between that assumption and the installation of an ABM system.

Reports on Chinese missile capabilities suggest that they might have a small but operational ICBM force in the early 1970s. What damage that force could inflict upon the United States depends on a range of factors which defy simple summation. The "thin" ABM system promises area coverage of the whole land mass of this country against a light attack. Thus even if the Chinese were willing to trade payload for range (and reach cities considerably east of the Mississippi), it would do them little good since those cities would be as protected by the ABM as our west-coast cities. They could, in theory, saturate one or a few areas with all their missile strength, but the effectiveness of that tactic would depend on the capability of our ABM system and the actual number of ICBMs the Chinese could launch.

It is difficult to take these calculations very seriously. It is hard to imagine a set of circumstances in which the Chinese would actually strike first with their small ICBM force, and one is inevitably obliged to create scenarios of ever increasing degrees of improbability. They *could*, in some *Götterdämmerung* fashion, launch all of their force against San Francisco; or they could spread it out in the belief that our ballistic missile defense was a "paper wall"; or they could gamble on odd forms of delivery (the proverbial bomb in the cargo hold, or nuclear torpedos against coastal cities, or small planes launched from ships and carrying small bombs, etc.). But the probability of their doing so is surely very low. And since we cannot prepare for *all* potential dangers, regardless of plausibility, and since even reasonably prudential calculations suggest that a Chinese ICBM attack on the United States is highly improbable, an ABM system justified by reference to Chinese threats to ourselves does not make much sense. This is the more true because lead times are such that we could still meet the threat if it became less improbable at a later date.

The case seems even stronger if we try to foresee the response Peking might make to our ABM system. It is very unclear at the moment, especially to anyone not privy to whatever information we are collecting about the mainland, just what the Chinese are attempting to develop. They will probably produce some ICBMs, if only to prove that they can do so. However, they are most likely to concentrate on medium-range missiles in order to threaten neighboring states in Asia. This would allow them to delay investing heavily in an ICBM until they are capable of producing an improved second-generation weapon. The Chinese could, in a sense, hope to duplicate the efforts of the Soviets in the late 1940s and 1950s, when, being clearly inferior to the United States in strategic power, they deployed their ground forces and short-range missiles to threaten Western Europe. The message was clear. If we attacked Moscow, confident that *we* would not be hurt badly, we were warned that Europe would be devastated in the process. An asymmetric balance seemed to exist, and the weaker side appeared to deter the stronger by threatening an area which the stronger valued but could not easily protect.

Though the analogy is obviously imprecise, the odds definitely favor a Chinese strategy designed to threaten us only indirectly, at least until that day, probably in the later 1970s and 1980s, when the Chinese are able to produce a force capable of achieving nuclear parity or stalemate with ours (and the Soviets'). In the meantime, the ABM system we are committed to install will rapidly become obsolescent. In sum, against the Chinese, our ABM system promises advantages only if the Chinese are foolish enough to launch an attack on us with their first generation ICBMs.

Presumably, then, the ABM system must serve other purposes. The one most frequently cited is the possibility that it will enhance the credibility of any commitment we offer to a non-nuclear country (*e.g.* India or Japan) threatened by a nuclear power. The idea has a certain plausibility in that, in a world in which all calculations were rational, the possibility of limiting destruction to ourselves ought to convince our friends that we are more likely to live up to our commitments to them. If true, they will not need to develop their own nuclear weapons and can then sign the nonproliferation treaty, for they will be assured that we will counter mortal threats to their existence.

It is difficult to speculate on this point, for the evidence is both slight and ambiguous. The Suez episode of 1956 provides one illustration of a nuclear threat against a non-nuclear state (France), but it is probably not a reliable analogy. At any rate, it did nothing to convince the French that they were better off without nuclear weapons of their own. India's reaction to the Chinese bomb is also ambiguous: at the least, India has begun to consider seriously the possibility of becoming a nuclear power.

Unfortunately, one is left with the impression that the contention that our ABM system will facilitate nonproliferation reflects profound hopes and desires, but not a very realistic judgment about how other states will view their own interests. Improvement in our defenses is likely to be of only marginal significance in affecting Asian calculations. Given the inherently low credibility of our nuclear guarantees outside Western Europe (and it has not been spectacularly high there either), the critical question is not *our* "damage limiting" capability, but that of the Asians. Japan or India, threatened by a Chinese nuclear attack, will undoubtedly prefer an American guarantee to nothing at all. But it is possible (even probable?) that they will view it as only a temporary umbrella while launching a crash program to develop their own nuclear weapons.

The only way to short-circuit this process may be to provide threatened states with an effective ABM defense of their own. If we really want them to forego developing nuclear weapons, we must provide a direct defense of their territories. This could be accomplished in several ways, but some combination of an explicit American guarantee, the provision of a reasonably effective area ABM system (preferably at least initially under our control), and perhaps even the promise of a small, offensive nuclear force if a threat of a specified nature arises—all these may be necessary to make our guarantee credible and thus inhibit the process of proliferation.[2] It is an extreme policy, and can be justified only in terms of the kind of environment it may be forced to contend with. The costs would be very high, not least in the sense that promising or providing a nation with an ABM system may be the first step toward its acquiring offensive nuclear weapons—on the uncertain but not implausible presumption that an ABM system without a complementary offensive capability is as unsatisfactory as entering a battle with a shield but without a sword. Moreover, the problem of defending against an MRBM is almost insuperable, given their limited flight time, and especially if they are delivered in number. Hence, the pressure for offensive weapons as a deterrent will be heavy.

This suggests that the possibility of signing an effective nonproliferation treaty is bound to decline rather sharply in the near future; that many states will be seeking their own nuclear

[2]The worst danger of a guarantee policy is that it might commit us to involvements we would prefer to avoid; the decisive question, which cannot be discussed here, is the extent to which we really have a viable option of noninvolvement open to us. The idea of a seaborne ABM force under our control may be worth investigating and might even be reasonably effective against a relatively small and unsophisticated Chinese missile force.

defenses; and that we shall have to consider new nuclear arrangements if we want to do more than wring our hands piously as the environment becomes more and more dangerous.

IV

What effect may our ABM system have on our relations with the Soviet Union and our European allies? The argument that an ABM system would "continue the Cuba power environment in the world," and thus reinforce our ability to deter the Soviet Union, is superficially plausible until it is placed in context. The assumption that the installation of an ABM system will enhance our ability to deter the Soviets depends on what kind of system we build and how the Soviets respond to it. Some systems and the responses they evoked would decrease our ability and increase the chance of an even more destructive war.

All the denials notwithstanding, our ABM system is primarily designed to counter an apparently growing Soviet threat. In the past, we have tended to assume that the way in which we developed or deployed our weapons systems signaled something to our enemies about our military intentions. It has never been very clear that the Soviets actually read these signals in the desired fashion. They may simply have been following their own technological genie wherever it led them: that is, they may have developed and deployed weapons not in response to what we did but simply as a response to their own technological capabilities.

At any rate, it is difficult to resist some such reasoning in the light of the Soviet decision to begin installing their own ABM system. After all, if they were "reading" us accurately, they should have known that we would respond by building our own ABM system and by increasing our offensive missile capability to penetrate their defenses. They would then be in an even more inferior strategic position and would have expended scarce rubles for very little return in security. Our rearmament in 1950-53 and our reaction to the "missile gap" are only the most obvious illustration of our unwillingness to remain behind.

Yet the Soviets have apparently rebuffed all efforts to reach an agreement prohibiting ABM deployment—almost as if our response left them indifferent. The normal explanation offered by Western analysts is the extreme defense-mindedness of the Soviet Government and people.

Marxist theory, a history of invasions and fears of encirclement apparently justify what seems to be an excessive concentration on defense—a phenomenon the Anglo-Saxon powers have always found, for obvious reasons, difficult to comprehend. Nevertheless, defense-mindedness alone does not seem a sufficient explanation for Soviet behavior.

Another rationale is that, as a relatively weaker power, the Soviets may feel considerably more threatened by the proliferation of small nuclear forces than we do. The French and Chinese nuclear forces, and the possibility of a West German force, not only have the potential of inflicting considerable damage on the Soviet Union but also—given Soviet history and predilections—might appear more likely to be actually used than we presume. To a weaker state, weaker nuclear forces appear more dangerous: the attacking smaller state could no doubt be destroyed in retaliation, but in the meanwhile it might have hurt the Soviets grievously and exposed them to American retaliation. If one presumes that they have reordered their hierarchy of threats and have upgraded the dangers of living in a "world of nuclear powers," the installation of a primitive ABM system does not look quite so "irrational." That it simultaneously worsens relations with the United States could be accepted as a reasonable price to pay.

Still, this argument could be completely wrong. The Soviets may still see us as the prime threat, and the ABM system may be designed to deter us and to limit damage in the event of a major war. The geographical placement of their ABM sites would seem to confirm this. In that case, the rationale for the Soviet decision remains very unclear, and the disagreements on this issue among Soviet leadership groups very understandable. To many Western observers, however, the Soviet decision seems to be a manifestation of a kind of intellectual lag in strategic thinking which has persisted for two decades. The Soviets have seemed to be several years behind us not only in weaponry but also in drawing the political, psychological and military implications of various technological developments. Current ABM systems thus seem more effective when compared with the capabilities of an earlier generation of missiles. The Soviets may in fact have much greater faith in the technological capacities of their ABM than we tend to credit them with—a circumstance which could be dangerous.

What effect will the mutual emplacement of ABM systems have on the strategic balance between the United States and the Soviet Union? There is no clear and unambiguous answer. It will obviously depend on the kind and extent of the systems installed, and, perhaps even more, on each side's subjective estimates of the likelihood of war or probable behavior of its antagonist in major crises.

It can be said, though, that ABM defense — at least a less than perfect defense — is of more relative utility to the aggressor than to the defender, whose retaliatory force must strike back in a weakened condition against a fully alerted defensive force. And since there is no situation in which striking first is not of *some* relative advantage, defensive forces can have a very destabilizing impact on any strategic balance to the degree that they make it appear as if striking first is becoming a more and more "attractive" possibility to either or both sides. This is especially true if one side is aware that it holds the weaker cards in any strategic exchange and is less than firmly convinced of the peaceful intentions of its adversary. Its propensity to gamble on striking first in a crisis may then be fairly high. This is a familiar syndrome and it suggests why many analysts argue that installation of an ABM system will force a return to the dangerous and unstable years in which we were troubled by the "consequences of expecting surprise attack."

The way in which each side deploys its ABM system is thus of great significance. But as long as the Soviets remain the weaker side, their decisions are somewhat less important than ours. That is, we possess a larger margin of error and therefore can be more flexible. If our system is designed only or primarily to protect our retaliatory missiles, the decision may not be too destabilizing; the Soviets will still retain the capability to destroy our cities in retaliation, just as we would theirs. However, the area system we are on the point of installing is, for the moment anyway, designed to protect cities from weak missile attacks. It is not intended to protect our Minutemen. It *looks* as if it is designed to handle a Chinese attack or some sort of accidental firing by virtually anyone. But it may not be read that way by Soviet leaders.

Unfortunately, many hints and suggestions are already appearing that the system ought to be expanded. We cannot have it both ways: if it is to deter the Chinese, extension of the system is unnecessary, for they do not have a techno-

logical capability to endanger our missile sites. If it is against the Soviet Union, official spokesmen are not only lying about our true intentions but also have begun installation from the wrong direction: obviously protection of missile sites is the first task.

These circumstances suggest that it is a fair presumption that our "thin" system will shortly begin to put on weight. Whether it is in reaction to Soviet offensive or defensive moves, or whether it is done in response to other considerations (*e.g.* domestic political pressures), is not especially important. In either case we will have begun a major new phase of arms competition with the Soviet Union. Whatever else one can say about the resulting situation, it is unlikely that it will be very stable or that it will actually reduce damages in a war. In effect, an ABM system guarantees decreased casualties *only* if both sides refrain from simultaneously increasing their offensive capabilities, or if the system achieves virtual perfection. Both are unlikely. Moreover, by another familiar dynamic — the "self-fulfilling prophecy" — we may actually increase the likelihood of war by acting as if it is more and more possible. Our ability to deter the Soviets may decline as we begin to threaten them in a more dangerous fashion, and our ability to defend more successfully (to lower casualties) may also decline as offensive force levels increase.

The decision to expand the "thin" ABM system may not be inevitable. The burden of the foregoing argument is that it ought to be resisted as long as this remains feasible. The point is not that installation of a larger ABM system is wrong in all circumstances; rather, that, on balance, it seems wrong in the set of circumstances determining strategic calculations at the moment and for the next few years. Compared to us, the Soviet Union is clearly the weaker power. The choices before it on the ABM issue are not only fewer but also starker. They have to respond to our actions, whatever the cost, unless they willingly accept an acknowledged state of conspicuous inferiority. We are not so narrowly constrained (except domestically): as the stronger power we need not meet every Soviet increase in strength with a symmetrical increase in our own force structure.

The underlying rationale for restraint on our part is twofold. On the one hand, given our current superiority and given our lead-time advantages, we do have some time in which we can safely delay expansion of the ABM system — at least until we believe that the Soviet ABM system represents a significant threat to our retaliatory force. On the other hand, restraint now represents what may be our last significant opportunity to delay the emergence of an environment in which stability is increasingly tenuous. In so far as possible, we should not only refrain from expanding our ABM system but should also limit the expansion of our offensive forces to whatever minimum seems safe. A too extensive expansion of our offensive force, so that it appeared capable of a credible first-strike attack, could be as destabilizing as the installation of the wrong kind of defensive system.[3]

It is still much easier to increase the striking power of offensive forces than the damage-limiting capabilities of defensive forces. It is possible, therefore, to limit our response to increasing our offensive capability to penetrate the Soviet ABM system; our cities would still be hostage to a Soviet strike and the Russians would not necessarily have to increase their own retaliatory force substantially. We could still penetrate their defenses and they could still penetrate ours, defense expenditures would not be extravagant, and some element of stability—albeit the uncertain stability of a nuclear balance—might still persist.

V

Something ought to be said about the presumed impact of our ABM system on our European allies. Official spokesmen have been very quiet on this aspect of the decision. When pressed, they have contented themselves with platitudes about common interests and the like: anything we do to improve our defenses must, by definition, improve Europe's defensive situation also.

The Europeans do not see it this way. Many of them, and not only Gaullists, see the ABM as increasing their vulnerability. They stand wholly exposed between our missiles and Soviet missiles. Moreover, the British and French nuclear forces are inevitably downgraded as deterrents, for the ABM systems have a much higher probability of success against small strikes. Some of our commentators have seen this as a virtue, since it presumably would inhibit potential nuclear powers from joining the club and perhaps even induce the French to bring their force under our umbrella.[4] Unfortunately, this is likely to be true only if the French and other potential nuclear states have developed or will

develop their nuclear forces to garner *military* advantages vis-à-vis the superpowers. That is not the case: their nuclear forces have been, and will be, designed to extract political and psychological advantages from the superpowers and to serve a military purpose only on the local level.

Great Britain and France are not going to dispense with their nuclear forces, or turn them over to our control, solely because of developments in ABM technology. On the contrary, our defensive efforts will probably succeed only in exacerbating present disagreements. Our minimal effort to consult our allies before making decisions is not conducive to good relations. Worse yet, they may respond by seeking their own ABM systems. This would probably signal the end of the nonproliferation treaty, for signing it would preclude independent development of the necessary technology. While the Europeans may not rate the probability of Soviet military action very high, they will not be able wholly to ignore the military significance of a new arms race between Washington and Moscow. Moreover, the task may be so difficult (since the direct threat against Europe consists of a large number of medium and short-range missiles against which the defensive problem is fantastically difficult and expensive) that they will prefer to decrease their ties with the United States. It may appear that this is the only way in which they can reduce their chances of being an exposed pawn in a resurgent cold war.

This article has suggested that the deployment of ABM systems may have a number of

[3]After this article was written, Secretary McNamara, in his farewell report, announced that the Soviets are apparently not installing a full-scale ABM system (though they have substantially increased the size of their ICBM force). He said that the Galosh system around Moscow had not been expanded or extended to other cities and that the Tallinn system across the Soviets' northwestern approaches is no longer believed to have "any significant ABM capability." It is difficult to take a charitable view of why a different impression had been given earlier, for serious doubts about the reliability of the evidence concerning Soviet ABM installations have been justified from the beginning. At any rate the arguments in this article are reinforced by the Secretary's admission; there is even stronger reason to slow down (if not halt) our own installation of an ABM system; thus far no move has been made to do so.

[4]Thus one writer argues that "possession of ABM systems by the great powers could deter non-nuclear countries from obtaining nuclear weapons while at the same time increasing the deterrent value of the great powers' nuclear forces." (Lewis A. Frank, "ABM and Nonproliferation: Related Issues," *Orbis,* Spring 1967.) This piece seems to me a classic example of the tendency to overemphasize the degree to which decisions by the United States and the Soviet Union about their forces will affect the decisions of non-nuclear states.

unfortunate consequences, none of which have been sufficiently stressed—and, perhaps, understood—by official spokesmen. There are undoubtedly ways in which these developments can be avoided or at least mitigated. If they do come about, it will not be because we are prisoners of some inexorable technological process or because the demands of security can be met only by policies which are ultimately self-defeating, but because of very human errors of will and foresight.

Finally, if this writer has not been misguided, two propositions must be emphasized: first, in our own security interests we should under-respond to Soviet ABM deployments, at least in the immediate future; and second, our friends and allies have every right, not to say obligation, to place what we (and they) can do for *their* security—not what we can do to limit damage to ourselves—in the center of their calculations.

THE ECONOMIC DEVELOPMENT SYNDROME
Jacob J. Kaplan

From its very beginnings in Truman Doctrine aid to Greece and Turkey and Marshall Plan aid to western Europe, foreign aid has been a much-debated and politically vulnerable program. (For some of the reasons why, see the selection by Professor O'Leary in Chapter Three.) At least in part because of its political vulnerability, the executive branch has had a tendency to oversell it, either by exaggerating its likely accomplishments or the foreign threats to which it was a response. There have been recurring promises that the aid programs had terminal dates in view. There have also been periodic efforts to "repackage" the programs or reorganize them to increase their salability.

In the selection that follows, Mr. Kaplan takes a critical look at one of the more recent guiding concepts in the economic aid field—economic development. It should be kept in mind that Kaplan himself is a former government official with long experience in the foreign aid program and is a strong supporter of foreign aid programs, and indeed of economic development as one possible goal of foreign aid. This kind of critical rethinking of premises and purposes is probably essential if the trend toward sharply reduced foreign aid expenditures is to have any chance of being reversed, assuming the latter is regarded as desirable.

The search for a new rationale led back to the concept of development. Enunciated in the late 1940's as the objective of Point Four, development remained a persistent if intermittent theme in the foreign aid program. The degree of emphasis varied, as did the conception of both the development goal and the means of achieving it. Though the purpose was frequently described

as economic and social development, the economic emphasis was predominant. Economic development could be defined in such measurable terms as capital projects completed or growth of the national income. Social development, a vaguer and less quantifiable idea, has received much less attention, both in evolving concepts and in actual aid operations.

The use of aid as a device for promoting economic development was the fruit of two separable strains of thought. The World Bank had first conceived of its development mandate in rather narrow administrative terms, confining itself to the partial financing of isolated capital projects. Toward the end of the 1950's, it was receiving the flattery of imitation from the expanded operations of the Export-Import Bank, the Development Loan Fund, and a number of bilateral and regional project lending institutions. However, by this time the Bank was itself increasingly dissatisfied with its own early doctrine. The Bank's criteria had satisfied neither the needs of the developing countries nor its own preoccupation with selecting good credit risks. It was beginning to recognize that the project approach neither assured the ability of clients to service loans nor necessarily accelerated their over-all economic growth. A need for more flexible instruments was implicitly recognized with the decision to establish a "soft-loan" window. The Bank's operations were progressively freed from the narrow con-

From *The Challenge of Foreign Aid*: Policies, Problems and Possibilities, by Jacob J. Kaplan; Frederick A. Praeger, Inc. Publishers, New York, 1967. Reprinted with permission.

fines of the profitable project approach, a process that still continues.

The Bank was further impelled to enlarge its perspective on economic development by the views of the economics profession. A great renewal of interest in long-term economic growth had swept the profession, producing a flood of research, writing, and teaching. By the late 1950's, this outburst had yielded a substantial consensus, relating insights into the process of economic growth to the ways in which development could be accelerated through foreign aid. Implicitly or explicitly, economists became committed to the view that foreign aid should be used primarily for economic development, except perhaps in limited and exceptional circumstances. They clamored for a policy that was preoccupied with economic growth in developing nations—to a degree that may have been sought but was never achieved for older views about internal U.S. policy.

The economists' consensus found an uncritical response in the aid-giving community, thanks to an existing policy vacuum. Those responsible for U.S. national policy toward developing areas felt both the necessity for more foreign aid and the absence of an intelligible explanation about how it could and should be used. For lack of an alternative, the new rationale took over.

This consensus first emerged in some studies commissioned by the Senate Committee on Foreign Relations in 1957. By 1961, it was fully developed. The first foreign aid program presented by the Kennedy Administration to the Congress was essentially an economic development program.

CHARACTERISTICS OF THE SYNDROME

The ten principles

The consensus may be described in the following ten propositions. Though they oversimplify professional views of both the nature of the growth process and the role of foreign aid, they embody the essential rationale as presented and understood by nonprofessionals—the public, the Congress, many aid executives, and the developing nations themselves. The propositions, as they are stated here, created an intellectual foundation for policy and action that was widely accepted and pursued. As usual, the "ifs" and "provided thats" of professional literature fell by the wayside.

1. An increase in the total volume of invest-

ment is the essential requirement for initiating economic growth. Herbert Feis has characterized this proposition as "a faith in the procreative power of invested capital."[1]

2. If some prospect for democratic institutions is to be preserved in developing nations, economic development cannot be based on forced savings. Foreign assistance must finance much of the initial increase in investment, since voluntary domestic savings are unlikely to provide an adequate initial thrust.

3. An ever-increasing proportion of the additional output resulting from increased investment should be available for savings and reinvestment. Thus, once adequately launched, the process of growth tends to be self-generating. The compound-interest principle learned by every schoolboy will translate a properly sustained increase in investment into accelerating economic growth.

4. At some point, this self-generating process will produce enough domestic savings to support adequate further growth. Foreign aid can then be suspended. Still later, foreign aid supplied in the initial stages can be repaid with interest out of the ever-increasing volume of savings based on ever-rising levels of production.

5. If the developing nation does not mount a substantial "self-help effort," the amount of foreign aid required will be unreasonably large. Even if such larger sums were available, the process will probably fail to work itself through. At the least, foreign aid should not replace domestic savings, permitting them to be diverted into consumption. At the most, it should assure the highest rate of savings acceptable to the populace through incentives provided by fiscal and monetary policies. High on the list of crucial self-help policies are honesty in government, noninflationary financing of development programs, appropriate exchange rates to encourage exports and discourage unnecessary imports, and the encouragement of private enterprise, including foreign private investment.

6. A development plan is the first essential self-help requirement. Its purpose is to assure the most efficient use of resources, including foreign aid. It should thus minimize the need for aid and maximize the rate of growth possible at any given level of aid. The plan should include the expected availability of resources and

[1] Herbert Feis, *Foreign Aid and Foreign Policy* (New York: St. Martin's Press, 1964), p. 20.

the expected rate of growth in parts of the economy. A proper plan requires not only orderly programming of resources but also procedures, policies, and administrative machinery for their effective implementation.

7. Foreign assistance should therefore seek to maximize incentives for preparing better development programs and policies and for establishing the administrative machinery necessary to their execution. Accordingly, countries that seem ready to execute such a development program should receive generous foreign assistance. Since development plans must be prepared on a multi-year basis, good plans should be rewarded with unqualified promises to furnish the necessary foreign aid over the entire life of the plan. Those governments that engage their energies primarily on other objectives, or are unwilling to make the requisite sacrifices to help themselves, should receive minimal foreign assistance. Those that are determined to develop and willing to sacrifice, but lack the capacity to prepare and organize a program, should be helped to acquire that capability through education and other technical-assistance programs.

8. Military-assistance programs should be reduced to the barest minimum essential to meet obvious and immediate threats. The more military matériel delivered under aid programs, the more manpower, managerial skills, and budgetary funds must be diverted to deploy and maintain the new weapons.

9. Whether resources are provided in the form of investment projects, raw materials, semifinished goods, or technical assistance is a matter of indifference to contributors of foreign assistance, provided that a country has a well-conceived development program. Nor need the donors be concerned with how local currencies generated by the sale of imported aid supplies are used. Therefore, the negotiating leverage of foreign assistance donors can and should be concentrated on obtaining improvements in development programming, minimizing the diversion of resources from development objectives and maximizing the self-help contributions of the receiving country.

10. The administrators of U.S. aid should not be diverted from such concentration by the siren of political advantage, and particularly not by short-term political gains. Funds should be provided without political or military strings; they should be allocated solely on the basis of the prospective productivity of the investment.

Early appeal and renewed torpor

Webster's Dictionary defines a syndrome as "a group of signs and symptoms that occur together, and characterize a particular abnormality." In their preclusive preoccupation with economic development, the foregoing principles as a whole do characterize an abnormality. The unexceptionable character of the individual propositions conceals the irrationality of acting as if economic development completely dominates the motivation and behavior of governments, whether those that provide aid or those that receive it. However, as in the case of individual behavior, an aberrational national policy may nevertheless seem very attractive, particularly before its consequences become evident.

The initial appeal of these principles is easy to understand. They offered an internally consistent and purposeful set of propositions on which to base a program that had previously seemed negative, defensive, and rudderless. The goals were positive, idealistic, and constructive. Moreover, they were relatively simple and provided an observable test of success — the annual rate of growth of the GNP.

Offering a distinct prospect, however distant, of an eventual termination of aid, they pandered to a popular yearning that dated to the very origins of foreign assistance. This happy prospect was joined by another: foreign aid could be regarded as a retrievable investment. Recouping funds might be far off and uncertain, but nonetheless possible, if only the investment were managed on the stated sound principles. Such an aid philosophy was manifestly more in consonance with the American ethic than maintaining an unending stream of gifts to governments that were friendly and responsive as political allies but incompetent, if not downright corrupt, in managing the internal affairs of their nations.

The plausibility of the structure of principles and the clear-cut prescriptions for aid policy that followed seemed to satisfy the need for a foreign aid rationale. They were seized upon by the new administration that took office in 1961. The doctrine dominated the presentation of a "new program" to the Congress, and continues to permeate succeeding presentations. However, once the initial burst of enthusiasm had passed, it failed to enlist either a national commitment to the problems of the developing nations or support for foreign aid appropriations.

Such rapid withering of appeal was unthinking insofar as the public is concerned, but an intuitive recoil is not hard to explain. The economic development rationale rested on debatable assumptions. Time and events have tended to confirm the muted voices that questioned their validity at the time. Moreover, it proved easier to formulate the new doctrine than to install corresponding changes in the use of Congressional appropriations. Facts and motives that the principles would not readily tolerate proved to have a stubbornly unyielding reality. The allocation of funds proved to be not very different from that under the preceding collection of illogical and poorly related justifications. When Congressional converts to the economic development rationale responded by offering legislative amendments in order to give it a more mandatory character, the executive branch offered firm resistance. Increasingly, it has become clear that the doctrine is adequately related neither to the facts of international life nor to the priority interests of the United States as a donor of aid to developing nations.

. . . [T]he official rationale for foreign aid continued to be focused on economic development. The connection between development and the national interest has rested on administration assurance that the relationship is positive and important. The response has been fitful and insecure.

A democratic political structure requires heed to widespread public skepticism about national policy, however intuitive it may be. An abiding democratic faith suggests that the public mood may prove to be well founded in reason. It is to such reason that we now turn.

DEVIATION FROM REALITY: DUBIOUS ASSUMPTIONS AND INCONVENIENT FACTS

Economic growth as the priority U.S. interest

The first dubious assumption of the economic development doctrine is that economic growth is the priority U.S. interest in the poorer nations of the world. Perhaps a more tenable variant is that economic development should have an overriding priority because it alone can pave the road to other objectives that may ultimately be more important.

The mid-1961 presentation devoted virtually all of its 189 pages to explaining *how* countries would be helped to expand their economies. *Why* the United States should care was answered largely by a quotation from the President's Inaugural Address: "because it is right." A rhetorical reference can be found to the de-

cade of decision between a decade of development and a decade of crisis. A cryptic reference was made to a choice between freedom and totalitarianism. One can read very carefully without finding the phrases "national interest," "national security," "anti-Communism," or even "friendly country"—phrases that had been the touchstones of support for foreign aid from the time the Greek-Turkish program was enacted in 1947. The President's message accompanying the presentation sought to redress this deficiency, largely by strong assertion that the economic growth of the developing nations would strengthen their resistance to Communist blandishments and thus strengthen American security.

In his sympathetic and sophisticated study of the dismantlement of the colonial system, Rupert Emerson had gently challenged the assumption that economic growth must serve U.S. interests.

The West, and particularly the United States, pays larger attention to the political consequences which are presumed to accompany development. The three major ones are the laying of stable foundations for presently unstable societies, curbing the appeal of Communism and making friends for the West, and eliminating dangerous threats to peace. Regrettably, an irrefutable case can be made for none of these.[2]

Events provided both refutation of the presumption and confirmation of the "larger attention" paid to political events.

Economic development enthusiasts argued that if economic growth could be sustained, the social institutions, political behavior, and economic environment would be transformed in the direction of democratic political institutions, protection of private property rights, and respect for the Western nations that had set the good example at home and contributed to its realization abroad. The analogy with the Marshall Plan on this score is dangerous, for the value system of the United States was derived from the very countries whose economic growth it sought to revive by means of Marshall Plan aid. The values of the developing nations, with the possible exception of Latin America, can only be described as having independent traditions and different histories and priorities from

[2]*From Empire to Nation* (Boston: Beacon Press, 1960), p. 413.

those prevalent in the West. In Europe, economic revival might reasonably be expected to strengthen, modernize, and reinvigorate traditional values. In the developing world, an accelerated rate of economic growth is more likely to shake traditional value patterns to their core. New institutions and value systems will have to evolve to replace the old, and their character is at best highly unpredictable. Deviation from Western norms, not conformity to them, is more likely to result from imposing advanced technology and modern systems of production on the traditions of the less developed world. Moreover, a high rate of economic progress, achieved at considerable cost to the political and social stability of nations, may encourage and facilitate international adventures and jeopardize the peace. It is just as reasonable to assume that a slow rate of economic progress will permit a more gradual adaptation of new techniques to old values, and hence a greater probability that the new institutions will conform to those that have been successful in the industrialized societies of the West.

A more defensible position would admit that the relationship is uncertain, and yet would advocate a U.S. association with, and major contributions in support of, economic development. Such advocacy could be justified either as an act of faith despite uncertainty, or as an alternative that is more promising than the refusal to help.

This more reasonable position, however, destroys the operational simplicity of the economic development rationale. It suggests that the American interest in development is of different intensity in different lands. It requires analysis of whether American interests are better served by an accelerated rate of development in some lands and a slower pace in others. It leaves unanswered queries about whether the purposes of the aid donor are more effectively furthered by increasing the incomes of particular groups, either because they are sympathetic or because they are restive. Or perhaps it is desirable to increase the consumption of certain services—education, health, defense—because they are urgently wanted, even if such use of resources fails to maximize the rate of growth in national income. In brief, this position accepts economic development as one purpose of foreign aid or as one means of furthering U.S. interests. It requires that economic growth compete with other goals for aid funds on the open market of specific interest to the United States.

Reluctance to offer a pledge to the Pakistan Consortium meeting scheduled for mid-1965 demonstrated how poorly the development rationale fitted the principal preoccupations of the United States. It demonstrated that economic development is neither the sole nor the overriding U.S. priority. Pakistan's economic performance in the preceding year had earned high commendation; on economic development grounds, it was entitled to a substantial pledge. On the other hand, Pakistan found itself at the time in increasing conflict with the United States about its closer relations with Red China and its threatened use of force in Kashmir. United States support of Pakistan's "good development program" might also have appeared as acquiescence to cooperation with a major U.S. antagonist and as indifference to threats to peace. United States behavior demonstrated that its interest in economic development was indeed subordinate to other considerations.

Development as the priority interest of the developing nations

A second questionable assumption is that economic development is so high on the effective priority lists of governments in developing countries that they will be prepared to subordinate all other interests—that if only they have a realistic choice and a prospect of economic success, they will pursue it single-mindedly. Adequate foreign aid can certainly provide both the possibility of choice and a better prospect of success.

Evidence in support of this assumption is elusive, to say the least. Evidence to the contrary is almost universal. To be sure, there is no dearth of protestations in developing countries about the primary importance of economic development; few political leaders can refrain from proclaiming dedication to the economic progress of their people. However, a more meaningful test is the actual choice among alternative courses of action when developing countries are faced with decisions. In practice, even governments of poor nations prove to have sundry and conflicting goals and to subordinate readily their attachment to economic progress. Even those countries that have already achieved a high rate of growth are prepared to divert very large resources from accelerating the growth process—witness Israel, Greece, and Taiwan. When one turns to countries whose economies are less successful, decisions contrary to the strict requirements of economic growth are even more striking. Brazil, Argentina, Pakistan, India, Indonesia, and Egypt come quickly to mind, but it is certainly unfair to single out any country in this regard.

The economic growth "buff" readily criticizes "noneconomic" policy behavior in developing nations. However, before he seeks a higher priority for economic growth in their decision-making, he might heed the mote in his own eye. The priority accorded comparable economic objectives in U.S. internal policy is high, but scarcely pre-eminent. Are the noneconomic priorities of developing nations then really irrational or censurable? Or are they deeply embedded in the nature of man and hence reflected in the behavior of groups of human beings, whether they be associated in rich or poor communities?

The government of the United States loudly proclaimed its dedication to the goal of full employment and economic progress throughout the 1930's while behaving too cautiously to reduce unemployment very much. In the 1950's, other values again impeded the adoption of policies and programs to reduce unemployment to minimal levels. Among them were national security and foreign policy interests, internal income distribution, social security, the social importance of the family farm, the balance of power between local and federal government, reluctance to enforce the proscription of racial discrimination in all employment situations, and unwillingness to enlarge the role of the government in spending the national income. Where the federal government desired to subordinate other national goals, it had to explain and await a greater degree of public concurrence. Both the effective priorities and caution in pursuing them are requisites of a democratic political process.

The developing countries are also societies with plural values. They do seek economic development. They also have other national interests and objectives that frequently override economic growth when put to the test. Sometimes the apparent priority given to non-growth objectives is the result of venality, sometimes of a lack of confidence in the efficacy of the advice of their economists, and sometimes of a lack of ingenuity on the part of economists in suggesting less objectionable paths to growth. More often, it represents the effective expression of true priorities as reflected by the existing politi-

cal power structure. Because that structure seeks to retain power, its choices do correspond, however imperfectly, to the nation's operative priorities. It hardly suffices to say that these countries are too poor to indulge themselves in noneconomic values. Noneconomic goals are not the prerogatives of the rich. American society respects such goals within its aid programs to less fortunate segments of its own population.

The political leadership of developing nations, like our own, is ordinarily impelled to consolidate its hold on political office. However idealistic, it must try to enlarge the consensus of political support upon which its tenure is based as a prerequisite to its larger aspirations. The weaker the political base on which that tenure is founded, the more it must be guided in day-to-day decision-making by short-term internal political considerations. Governmental leadership consists in being a short step ahead of the country, but not so far ahead that the ability of the government to execute decisions is itself threatened. Thus when the government of a developing nation is confronted by a difficult economic policy choice, the decision appropriate to its economic development objective may seem rather clear cut. But before proceeding, it must weigh the effects on such groups as the military and the clergy, landowners and manufacturers, local business interests and investors, students and peasants, one region of the country or another, various racial or tribal groupings, schoolteachers and bankers.

If one recalls the broad range of relevant decisions, one will appreciate that their political incidence is very great. They include such questions as: the size of additional taxes and upon whom they will be levied; the allocation of government tax revenues among such competing claimants as the military, the police, the school system, highways and railroads, different regional governments; the allocation of government-controlled investments between social overhead (schools, medical facilities, public recreation, public administrative facilities) and facilities more directly related to the production of marketable goods and services, such as agriculture, power, transportation, and industry; whether the banking system will restrict or expand the extension of credit to the government on one hand or to the private sector on the other; how scarce materials or scarce foreign exchange will be allocated between government and private uses and among various governmental and private claimants. The very decision as to whether the allocation of credit, supplies, and foreign exchange will be accomplished through a market or an administrative mechanism will itself have different effects on various components of the body politic.

Even if it is assumed that the government is strong enough to insist that the sacrifices required in the name of economic growth should be imposed and borne, it must further be assumed that the overriding interests of the society as a whole lie in economic development. Yet few would urge countries that feel insecure about the integrity of their national boundaries or about highly organized internal conspiracies to neglect their military defense or their police force in order to divert resources to investment purposes.

Sacrifices by individuals or groups in the name of the future welfare of the country presuppose a sense of identification with the broad community encompassed within the national boundaries. For many governments the more pressing problems may be the creation of just such a sense of national identification. A willingness to subordinate tribal or local loyalties to the country; a willingness to compromise religious, racial, and language differences; the transfer of power and responsibility from expatriates, who inevitably symbolize vestiges of colonialism; the creation of a tangible and beneficent presence of the national government—all these considerations may legitimately deserve priority over the more measurable requirements of economic development.

Indeed, "the search for nationhood" may be a precondition for the inauguration of a meaningful economic development program with realistic prospects for effective implementation. The nationhood requirement frequently explains some of the pet peeves of economic developers about "waste" of resources by developing countries—the building of sports stadiums and imposing government buildings, the elaborate celebration of official holidays, the establishment of uneconomic national airlines, radio and television facilities, and large department stores.

In the long run, constructive progress in dealing with any of the problems of a developing nation—be it the sense of nationhood, or security, or redistribution of income, or political reforms—will contribute to economic growth and may be a precondition for sustained economic progress. Any use of aid toward the solution of a national problem, economic or not, thus becomes a contribution to economic growth, given an appropriate span of time. A higher rate of consumption of resources and a lower rate of investment may even be conceived as the best path to a successful economy. Such use of resources may involve a low rate of growth in national income in the immediate future while promising faster expansion at a later date. At this point, the economic development principles once again lose their clear prescriptive value for either justifying or managing foreign aid programs.

Knowledge about how to maximize the rate of economic growth

Third, the economic development doctrine presupposes a rather high degree of certain knowledge about the kinds of economic policy decisions that do maximize economic growth in developing countries.

The problem of inadequate and unreliable data is evident, but the development expert argues that it is better to base decisions on whatever quantitative material is available than on judgments that defy objective evaluation. Aid recipients are particularly skeptical about this argument and are resistant to advice based on statistics they distrust. It is not uncommon for differences between aid-receiving and aid-giving agencies to be rooted in a choice between the judgment of individuals who know their country and its ways and the judgment of foreign experts who are inevitably dependent on the application of tests of logical internal consistency to partial and even misleading data. Both groups suffer from an inadequate basis for making the decisions that nonetheless must be made.

Even where reasonably adequate statistics are available, the analytical tools may be much too dull to suggest unequivocal policy conclusions. Noneconomic goals such as security, political stability, and national loyalty may affect such vital imperatives of economic development as the willingness to undertake investments with long gestation periods, to save and pay taxes, to render disinterested service in public office. The relationship, however, is scarcely quantifiable. Moreover, the available techniques for objective calculation cannot prescribe the allocation of funds between such needs as defense, police, and public buildings, and such conventional investments as highways, power production and distribution facilities, and factories. Even if productivity were the dominant criterion, many major decisions concerning the use of resources must be largely subjective.

Much the same is true of such social overhead as education, health, and housing. Again a positive relationship may be presumed to exist between such expenditures and the economic growth of the country, though they may be, and usually are, justified in terms of their noneconomic contributions. This relationship is easier to define and measure than that between "nation-building" expenditures and economic growth. Indeed, some investigators have concluded that the contribution of social overhead expenditures to a rising national income is much greater per dollar than that of conventional investments.[3] As their contribution to economic growth is better understood, the wisdom of giving them more emphasis in planning for economic development may be confirmed. In the meantime, they remain as politically important claims on the resources of all societies, since people want education and medical services whether or not it makes them more productive. Any government that neglects such desires because other expenditures promise more future income may find its political power lost and its good development programs discarded.

Even within the areas of investment, where more precise quantitative evaluations of the contributions of alternative expenditures are attempted, definitive policy prescriptions must be regarded with a wary eye. Cost-benefit ratios are numerical results, but the spurious nature of their precision is apparent to anyone who understands the pyramid of hazardous forecasts on which they are based—prices, costs, demand, and the time period required to complete construction and to reach the predetermined degree of operational proficiency.

Perhaps the crucial gap is in knowledge of the importance of rates of savings and investment. Economic development theory treats the investment rate as the critical determinant of the rate of increase in production; the rate of savings is supposed to be the principal test of an effective self-help effort. Other things being equal, the theory is unquestionably sound, but the "other things" appear to be grossly unequal in poor societies. At any rate, the lack of a positive relationship between savings and investment rates

and growth in GNP in various developing nations is very disturbing to the usefulness of the theory for policy purposes.

In 1964, an AID research project assembled such data for twenty-five countries, covering the years 1957 through 1963 for all, and going back to 1950 for many.[4] The data showed that thirteen countries had maintained an increase in savings and investment adequate to support a 2.5 per cent per capita growth in GNP. The others had not. Seven of the thirteen countries with adequate rates of investment nevertheless failed to sustain a 2.5 per cent growth in output; four out of the dozen countries with inadequate investment rates did achieve such an increase. The deviations from an adequate rate of investment, on the one hand, and from a 2.5 per cent per capita growth of GNP, on the other, appear to be unrelated. Moreover, some countries with low rates of savings managed to achieve high rates of growth anyway, achieving large increases in production per dollar of investment. Others with high rates of savings and investment have failed to attain a high rate of economic growth. The procreative power of invested capital appears to vary considerably from one country to another. . . .

It would be malicious and mischievous to conclude from the foregoing that economic development is an uncharted sea that must be sailed without foreknowledge or rational calculation. The more appropriate lesson to draw is that we are far from ready to turn the helm over to programmed computers or even to the consensus of professional opinion. The proper course to be followed is so uncertain that intuitions based on firsthand experience may be correct, while a mass of calculations based on incomplete and incorrect data may steer the ship onto the reefs. Such data and analytical competence as we possess can contribute and do need to be brought to bear more often and more effectively. But political judgment, based on experience in leading the particular society in question and directed toward amelioration of noneconomic tensions, may best steer a country on a progressive course, carrying economic progress along in its wake. It certainly should not be overridden by calculations, whatever the

[3]F. Harbison and C. A. Myers, *Education, Manpower and Economic Growth* (New York: McGraw-Hill, 1964), chap. i.
[4]Mimeographed statistical tables reproduced by AID under the title *Economic Growth, Investment, Savings and Foreign Trade, Selected Less Developed Countries, 1950–1963.*

validity of their underlying data, nor by a preference for logically consistent analysis, however debatable its assumptions.

The early prospects for self-sustaining growth

Finally, skeptics have never been convinced by the promise of self-sustaining growth. The record to date is largely on their side. The picture of needy countries receiving first soft loans, then borrowing normally in the capital market, and finally relying on their own savings is too enticing to be either rejected or believed. The problems are perhaps less those of false assumptions than of false time perspectives. Ample evidence exists to suggest that such an evolutionary process is no mere wishful thinking. The examples of the United States and Japan do exist. However, no basis exists for assuming that self-sustaining growth will soon be upon us in many of the aid-receiving countries.

The professional literature is replete with caution about the "preconditions" for a rapid movement toward self-sustaining growth, but few of the developing nations today possess these "preconditions," except in the eyes of the most optimistic observers or in the words of those who would solicit or justify foreign aid by the development rationale. In his deservedly renowned book *The Stages of Economic Growth*, Rostow described the preconditions stage with great sophistication and professed to see evidence that a wide variety of countries either were emerging or already had emerged from that difficult condition. He believed that Turkey and India, for example, had reached the next stage of "take-off" in the 1950's. Today a reader can easily assume that his discussion of the "preconditions for take-off" well describes both countries in the 1960's, though Turkey's continuing problems appear much more tractable. Perhaps the disappointingly slow rate of economic growth in both countries is the best evidence of his excessive optimism about the pace of the process he pictured so well.

It is sometimes forgotten that Rostow found that the "take-off" stage continued for twenty to twenty-five years after the country first entered that stage; presumably it is during these years that large amounts of economic aid are most needed. It is only in subsequent years that self-sustaining growth is attained, with its capacity to borrow and pay normal rates of interest on debt.

It is unrealistic to expect self-sustaining growth in Africa or Asia within the next quarter-century, nor is it possible today to foresee the moment when many of the nations of these continents can dispense with foreign aid. The Alliance for Progress was originally envisaged as requiring a full ten years of sustained aid to Latin America on a substantial scale, after which it was expected that the need for aid would decline and an increasing number of countries would be able to progress satisfactorily without further aid. By mid-1965, the Alliance for Progress experts, themselves under pressure to justify aid as a contribution to imminent self-support, began to warn that the task would require more than a decade. By mid-1966, the United States Government formally acknowledged that its aid commitment would need to be of longer duration. Yet few would question that more of the preconditions for rapid economic progress exist in Latin America than can be expected in Asia for some years to come, and in Africa for many more years to come.

To be sure, the discovery of oil or diamonds, a tourist boom, or some other windfall may reduce the need of some countries for aid. Others may be able to do without it for a while because their populations passively accept low levels of consumption or because favorable market conditions produce a spurt in their exports. However, economic progress for most lands will require the continued receipt of more resources than they can pay for with their own foreign exchange earnings. Indeed, as the growth process accelerates, as the preconditions are put into place, the need for resources is likely to expand. The more that countries with basically weak economies borrow now, the larger the volume of aid they will need for some years to come in order to pay interest and dividends and amortization. Certainly this has been the experience of all but a handful of developing nations with the loans contracted in the years since World War II.

Yet ephemeral prospects of self-sustaining growth and the end of aid are held out to the Congress and the public. A "numbers game" is played, listing countries that have passed from the aid rolls as evidence that self-sustaining growth is possible. The bulk of the list consists of developed countries; they received aid for reconstruction, not development. Almost without exception the rest fall into special categories. Some have benefited from windfall additions to their foreign exchange position, from petroleum production or from offering a safe haven for the funds of the petroleum rich (Lebanon). A few have renounced small aid programs for political reasons (Cambodia). Others continue to receive aid from sources other than AID appropriations—food programs, military equipment donations, or contributors other than the United States. A few have benefited from large amounts of aid in the past on a grant basis and have been pushed off all "assistance" rolls to borrow substantial sums from private lenders, the Export-Import Bank, and international institutions. Whether these borrowing countries will be able to service such rapidly accumulating debt remains to be seen. Surely it is only this latter handful of countries that may properly be cited as having demonstrated the capacity of developing nations to achieve self-supporting growth within a brief time span.

The promise of a not-too-distant cessation of aid carries in its train the seeds of another wave of disillusionment with foreign aid, and perhaps even of new tensions with less developed lands. Because India has failed to make the predicted progress, it is belabored for failing to make an adequate self-help effort. Self-help efforts can and should always be improved, India's perhaps more than most. However, the fault probably lies as much with unrealistic donor expectations as with inadequate self-help. India is perhaps already the victim of the intellectual fantasies of half a decade ago. . . .

DEVIATION FROM REALITY: PRACTICE INCONSISTENT WITH PRINCIPLE

The foregoing reservations and qualifications are prevalent in the professional literature and are taken into account by the practitioners of foreign aid. An examination of the actual uses to which funds have been put shows considerable deviation from the development rationale. To conclude that U.S. aid, after the full-fledged adoption of the development rationale in 1961, has been guided much more than previously by its tenets requires a determined resolve to be enslaved by the language of legislative appropriations categories. . . .

Whether the substance of the program has in fact been as radically transformed as the form of the legislation depends on the answers to other questions. Were countries with strong indigenous development efforts rewarded with more assistance and laggards penalized by reducing their aid? Were the priorities in discussions with aid-receiving countries radically revised to reduce the use of aid as leverage for U.S. security and foreign policy purposes? Has discussion and negotiation of better domestic economic programs and policies assumed a much greater importance in U.S. relations with other countries than in the past? Has there been a significant increase in the quantity and quality of economic development planning?

The record to date is, at best, ambiguous. If changes have occurred, they appear more as minor shifts of emphasis, as variations on the periphery of the aid program rather than dramatic changes in its character and direction. Were it otherwise, notable variations should have taken place in the amounts of money received by individual countries before and after the 1961 legislation. Good development plans would have been rewarded; slothful and corrupt governments would have been penalized. Allies would be relatively less well endowed, since presumably some of them were rewarded previously for their friendship rather than their economic merit.

A comparison of the program for fiscal year 1963 with fiscal year 1960 shows little change in the allocation of funds among countries. The changes that did take place are more readily explained by factors other than a strict application of the development rationale. In both years, economic aid commitments under the Foreign Assistance Act were about the same amount for countries outside the Western Hemisphere. Hence a comparison of the sums provided to individual countries in the two years should give evidence of a radical change in purpose.

Aid commitments to Latin American countries under this act were sharply increased, from less than $100 million to some $550 million, fulfilling the promise made at Punta del Este in the summer of 1961, when the Alliance for Progress was formally adopted. The Bay of Pigs disaster had markedly strengthened the influence of Castro throughout Latin America, to the point where the United States felt threatened by increasing hostility in its own hemisphere. The potential dangers were readily apparent long before they were dramatized by the appearance of Soviet missiles in Cuba. While the long-term aid commitment was formally conditioned on the preparation of development programs and the adoption of a wide range of "self-help" policies, a billion dollars a year of U.S.

Government-financed aid of all sorts was promised and was provided without waiting upon Latin American peformance.[5] More than four years after Punta del Este, not a single Latin American country had an operational multi-year development plan; several were submitted but failed to receive international endorsement. Nevertheless, all Alliance members except Haiti were allotted larger amounts of U.S. aid in fiscal year 1963 than in 1960. Haiti offers a solitary example of withdrawing aid from a government that had been abusing past largesse. Brazil was promised a larger program in return for a major financial stabilization effort. When the effort failed to materialize, the additional aid was withheld but the aid level nonetheless remained much larger than in 1960.

Alliance aid has undoubtedly improved United States relations with its hemisphere neighbors, reducing both the attractions of Castroism and the proliferation of Communist adherents and apologists in key positions. The increased assistance essentially took the form of project aid, supplementing a further increase of similar assistance from the World Bank, the Inter-American Bank, and the Export-Import Bank. Because projects take time to carry out, actual expenditures by the United States Government on behalf of Latin America increased much less rapidly. Some economic and social progress will inevitably flow from these projects; the focus of the governments of Latin America on improving economic policies has undoubtedly been sharpened as a direct result of the Alliance. However, the notion that significantly increased aid would only be provided as reward for substantially improved economic performance has had hard sledding in the face of hemisphere political realities.

The record is even less clear cut in the rest of the developing world. In 1960, twenty-eight countries received assistance under the defense support and special assistance programs, with a dozen defense support countries receiving most of the money. Presumably, development was not the primary purpose of the programs for any of the twenty-eight. Despite the disappearance of the military alliance criterion from the new legislation and a drastic reduction in funds for the "supporting assistance" category, twenty-five of them were still receiving assistance under the act in 1963. Spain, Yugoslavia, and West Berlin were removed from the list. The rest were allotted about as much U.S. assistance in

1963 as in 1960, a reduction in Foreign Assistance Act funds being matched by an increase in other programs, primarily the Food for Peace legislation. Reduced allocations of Foreign Assistance Act funds were not primarily visited on those countries whose self-help policies were inadequate or whose development programs left much to be desired. Aid was reduced where the need for assistance was diminishing, whether as a result of greater production and increased foreign exchange earnings set in motion by a mixture of aid and better economic policies in the 1950's (Spain, Taiwan, and Greece) or as a result of finding oil (Libya). Moroccan aid was reduced because U.S. bases there were no longer needed and because the French resumed their assistance.

By fiscal year 1965, the original list of twelve defense support countries had been reduced to seven still receiving funds out of Foreign Assistance Act appropriations. However, eleven of the twelve still obtained substantial new commitments of economic funds of one sort or another. Cambodia was the exception, having itself renounced further American aid in a fit of political pique. The remaining eleven countries received commitments of $1.34 billion. Excluding Vietnam, total United States economic aid to the defense support countries was about the same in 1965 as in 1960.

Two-thirds of the Foreign Assistance Act savings on such countries in 1963 were used to increase aid to India. The rest made possible increased assistance to the Congo, Nigeria, East Africa, Israel, Egypt, and a number of other newly independent countries. Nigeria may offer a reasonable example of rewarding economic merit, though its role as a potential bulwark of Western influence in a disorganized and unstable continent undoubtedly influenced the decision to provide substantial aid. Israel was making a serious and successful enterprise of its economic development, but its need for increased aid was political and military, not economic. Aid to the Congo represented a response to a serious internal crisis with strong overtones of Communist intervention. The other African countries received increased project aid after achieving independence.

As for India, increased assistance was loudly advertised as the first application of the new

[5]Food, Export-Import loans, and contributions to the Inter-American Bank, as well as AID assistance.

principles. In fact, a major commitment was made to India even before the act of 1961 had completed its course through the Congress, nominally in recognition of the excellence of its development record. The soundness of its new Five-Year Plan had been endorsed by the World Bank and a group of international experts. Actually, India's economic performance has been less than exemplary.[6] Its growth rate has been modest under both second and third plans. While internal investment has been high, the resulting production increases have been unexpectedly small and export performance has been poor. Prior to 1965, aid was hardly used as an important lever for persuading India to improve its economic policies. The increased commitment in 1961 and thereafter more truly represented a revision of the previous policy of penalizing India for her neutrality. The political eclipse of Krishna Menon, the attack by Communist China, the moderation of an anti-Western tendency in India's neutrality, the elevation to leadership of a more moderate and pragmatic faction after the death of Nehru—these were the immediate events that produced increases in U.S. aid to India. Always in the background has been an awareness that only an increasingly prosperous India could thwart the expansion of Communist Chinese influence and power in Eastern Asia. To justify the program as a developmental one because India's intentions are serious, though her actions are ineffectual, may be no more than realistic. However, it does turn the development rationale into a justification for concentrated aid to many more countries than in fact receive it. . . .

SOME PROPOSED LOGICAL EXTENSIONS OF THE RATIONALE

As the Congress became sensitive to this disparity between professed rationale and the purposes for which funds had actually been allocated, a new wave of attack set in. It was joined this time not by the old enemies of any U.S. foreign aid, but rather by the more dogmatic converts to the economic development rationale. The first reaction was to reduce appropriations. The amounts approved for fiscal years 1963 and 1964 were slashed drastically below the President's request, and the same fate was avoided for fiscal years 1965 and 1966 only by the device of having the President anticipate the cut and make it himself. The roster of Congressional critics who have been asking for yet another

"new look" at the program continues to grow.

Attacks for failure to adhere more rigidly to the economic development criteria have been a natural consequence of the oft-reiterated rationale for the program. Most recent Congressional proposals for amendments to the legislation or changes in the program flow as a logical consequence from the development creed.

Thus the country programs that involve financing a handful of small projects in a given country—the so-called presence programs—have been challenged for their inconsistency with the rationale. Aid should have been concentrated in those countries with the best economic growth prospects. The small programs can be defended either by reverting to the earlier World Bank concept of development by project financing or by reference to the political advantages of maintaining some constructive contribution to the economy of the recipient, however minor its impact on the economy as a whole and however poorly the country may be using its own resources in general. The elimination of all programs where U.S. aid makes only a minor contribution to the economy would reduce the number of recipient countries from seventy to perhaps twenty at most. Some $275 million was divided by the AID among fifty countries in 1963. Even allowing for the small size and population of many of them, it seems unlikely that the size of their national incomes ten years hence would be noticeably affected by the continuation or absence of aid at this level. If one wishes to defend these programs, one must look elsewhere for a rationale.

Nevertheless, U.S. interests would certainly suffer if most developing nations were removed from its aid clientele because they have not fulfilled the preconditions or because they lack appropriate development programs. The notion that aid should be focused on a few prospects for early self-sustaining growth while the rest are left to mark time is hardly consistent with U.S. national interests in the external world. In 1960, prior to the Kennedy Administration reforms, the notion that aid might fruitfully be concentrated on the best development prospects was suggested to the Congress. A proposal to focus U.S. aid on "islands of development" produced protests from a vast number of excluded

[6]See Edward S. Mason, *Foreign Aid and Foreign Policy* (New York: Harper & Row, 1964), p. 43; and Wilfred Malenbaum, "Growth Theory and Indian Development," *The Indian Journal of Economics*, April, 1963.

countries and from the U.S. officials responsible for dealing with them. Someone dramatized the problem by asking in private whether the United States intended to leave the rest of the Third World in a "Slough of Despond." The effort that is under way to concentrate U.S. aid further and to reduce the number of recipients may appear inadequate to the proponents of economic development; it may also be damaging to more important U.S. concerns.

Other critics have attacked the "softness" of AID loan terms. Its interest rates have been increased somewhat since 1962, and a number of senators suggest each year that it be raised further. The case for "harder" terms is another logical extension of the investment philosophy of the development rationale, with its explicit preference for loans rather than grants and its promise of self-sustaining growth. If the investments will in fact yield high rates of return to the borrowing government in the form of rapidly rising national incomes, it might reasonably be asked to repay not only the principal but also a market interest rate, or at least the cost to the taxpayer of borrowing by the United States Government.

Finally, it is suggested that development loan money be turned over to an international institution such as the International Bank, for allocation among developing countries as well as for administration. The Chairman of the Senate Foreign Relations Committee, Senator Fulbright, long a thoughtful and perceptive student of the uses of foreign aid, has given unqualified support to this proposal.[7] Essentially the argument is that such an international institution would make money available only in response to economic development criteria, while decisions of the U.S. Government are inevitably influenced by noneconomic considerations. Once again the proposal is a logical extension of the development rationale.

These proposals have all been opposed by the Agency for International Development, by the Department of State, of which it is a part, and by the White House. The opposition must be based on a tacit admission that development is not the be-all and end-all of the United States program. Money appropriated by the Congress, even under development appropriations categories, has not been used in rigid conformity with development criteria, perhaps not even in loose conformity. The development purpose has been subordinate to other, higher-priority U.S. objectives, before the 1961 rationale and after. The United States cannot afford to eliminate or reduce aid significantly to the vast majority of countries that subordinate economic development to other considerations—as long as their policies are not in conflict with basic U.S. priorities. If funds had been used only when the development criteria were rigidly met, higher-priority U.S. purposes would certainly have been sacrificed in the process. Yet the failure to articulate these other goals clearly and effectively and to provide the Congress and the public with a better-balanced perspective on the relationship between economic development and foreign aid has been costly. It has deprived the executive branch of an effective explanation of what it is, in fact, doing with foreign aid money and why that use is, in fact, consistent with the best interests of the American people.

INADEQUACY OF THE ECONOMIC DEVELOPMENT RATIONALE

. . . This lengthy critique suggests the need for modifying the economic development rationale, not for discarding it. To argue that it is not the overriding concern of both the United States and the developing nations is not to suggest that it is unimportant or irrelevant. A realistic rationale must, however, allow for the priority U.S. interest in more basic objectives, which may be furthered by economic growth but need not be. It must alert aid recipients to the true order of U.S. priorities. It must signal that their aid will be jeopardized if conflict with basic U.S. interests becomes acute—irrespective of their economic performance. Room should be provided in the rationale for relating aid more directly to such strategic interests, rather than resting the relationship solely on the uncertain by-products of economic growth. The rationale should further allow for the legitimacy of noneconomic aspirations in developing nations. It should acknowledge the inadequacy of knowledge—both ours and theirs—concerning how foreign aid can best contribute to the various objectives of both sides, economic development among them. Finally, it should be chary of optimistic predictions about the early end of aid.

The economic development syndrome characterizes an abnormal interest in developing the economy, while a good government seeks to

[7]The New York Times Magazine, March 21, 1965.

develop the society. To the extent that the United States has an interest in the growth of a foreign country, it is again the society, not merely the economy, that should command its attention. If the society is to develop successfully, economic growth will surely be required, but a high rate of growth in the economy to the neglect of both social and national security problems is unlikely to serve the purpose of either the indigenous government or the United States. It may well even fail to sustain itself.

THE ATLANTIC MIRAGE
Ronald Steel

Few quarrel with the assumption that the political and economic state of Europe, particularly western Europe, will continue to be a vital concern of the United States in the '70's, and even farther. Where the disagreements become strenuous and, often, fundamental is in addressing the question of what specific American policies and objectives will best protect these vital interests.

Here, one is required to make judgments about such matters as the nature of the Soviet military threat to western Europe, likely trends in the relations between the Soviet Union and the other East European Communist states, and in the internal "liberalization" of the various Communist states. In this connection, should the United States continue to seek a more or less unified or integrated western Europe eventually becoming linked with North America in a broader Atlantic Community, or is the notion of a gradual drawing together, over decades, of western and eastern Europe a more desirable and realistic image of the future, particularly in view of the dilemma of a divided Germany?

These are most difficult questions. While Mr. Steel's style is journalistic and his approach somewhat polemical, his answers to them are challenging.

There is an eternal dispute between those who imagine the world to suit their policy, and those who correct their policy to suit the realities of the world. —Albert Sorel

NATO was the first of our entangling alliances, and it is still the most important. Around NATO we built our postwar diplomacy of containment and intervention. By pledging our lives, our honor, and our wealth to the war-weakened nations of Western Europe, we rejected the isolationism that two world wars had rendered impossible, and sought a new community with our friends across the Atlantic. Based upon the foundation of a common civilization and a common danger, NATO set the precedent for a series of global alliances. Although some of its offspring are often forgotten or ignored, NATO still remains close to our hearts. To many Americans it symbolizes our acceptance of world responsibility as the protector and defender of Europe.

Yet now, nearly twenty years after its founding, that dream has begun to go sour. The allies who once beseeched our help are now chafing under what they term our "hegemony." They claim that America dominates the alliance to such a degree that Europe is in danger of losing its identity. Some fear, or profess to fear, that the American nuclear guarantee is less credible now that the United States herself is vulnerable to retaliation. Others complain that Washington's attention is straying from Europe to the new nations of the Third World. This change in focus, some believe, might lead the United States to involve its allies in a war over an issue in which they have no interest. And among the cynical there is a suspicion that Russia and America might try to keep the Continent divided by rival military pacts in order to retain their own dominance.

Everywhere there are complaints, suspicions, and, in France, an outright rejection of NATO itself. America's postwar role as protector of Europe is in danger now that Europeans no longer feel so threatened. The Kennedy administration's dream of a Grand Design embracing America and a united Western Europe in "equal partnership" is beginning to seem unduly optimistic and even outdated. It is not even certain that NATO itself can much longer survive in anything like its present form. The North Atlantic Treaty Organization, which found its inspiration in a moment of common peril, is giving way to the détente.

Today, nearly twenty years after its creation

NATO seems to have fulfilled its purpose. But in the unsettled conditions of the late 1940s it was a vital demonstration of America's intention to resist Russian expansion. It was not, as some of its more obstreperous European critics seem to imagine, an American plot foisted upon helpless allies. Nor was it an instrument of aggression designed to force the Soviets out of Eastern Europe. Rather, it was a defensive response to the chaotic conditions of postwar Europe; part of the Continent lay under Russian domination and the other part was so weak that it threatened to fall to communist-inspired coups from within.

Postwar America would have been quite happy to withdraw from Europe once the Nazi armies were defeated. But we could not leave the Continent to the mercy of the Russians, who had installed communist dictatorships in Eastern Europe to replace the mainly right-wing, and occasionally fascist, ones of the prewar era, and who menaced the war-weakened nations of Western Europe with various forms of blackmail and subversion. With the electorally powerful communist parties of France and Italy threatening to come to power via the ballot box, with communist rebels fighting the royalist government of Greece, with the Russians making threatening moves in Iran and around Berlin, and with Czechoslovakia dragged behind the Iron Curtain by a *coup d'état*, it became obvious that the United States could not insulate herself from the dangers that faced postwar Europe. The victory over Hitler was not meant to be succeeded by the creation of a communist empire ruled from Moscow.

With the Truman Doctrine of March 1947 the United States intervened directly against communism in Europe with military support for the Greek government. Two years later this intervention in the defense of non-communist Europe was consecrated by the signing of the North Atlantic Treaty Organization pact. The logical corollary of the Truman Doctrine, NATO was designed "to restore and maintain the security of the North Atlantic area" by making American military protection available to those nations which were too weak to defend themselves. It was a wise, and indeed an essential, measure to re-establish a military balance in Europe against the powerful Soviet forces in the East. The West Europeans needed American protection, and they welcomed NATO as the codification of our assistance.

Considering the inspirational sentiments the alliance evokes today, its original intentions seem exceedingly modest. It was not intended to be the foundation for a political union between America and Western Europe—nor for any other kind of union, for that matter. Rather, it was conceived as a simple guarantee of American protection, meant to tide the Europeans over until they were able to provide for their own defense. The purpose of NATO, according to the report of the Senate Foreign Relations Committee, which approved the treaty, was to "facilitate long-term economic recovery through replacing the sense of insecurity by one of confidence in the future." NATO, in other words, was to be the military component of a formula in which the Marshall Plan was the basic ingredient: a temporary wall behind which the Europeans would use American economic aid to patch up their wartime wounds and rebuild their defenses. This effort, it was hoped, would be accomplished within twenty years. For this reason, the member nations were given the option to drop out after 1969, a provision particularly important to the United States Congress, which had no intention of committing the nation's fortunes to Western Europe indefinitely.

If the original aims of the alliance were modest, they did not remain so for long. The treaty was scarcely a year old when the communist North Korean army moved across the 38th parallel. With the decision to intervene with American troops in the defense of South Korea, the Truman Doctrine was extended from a war-weary Europe to a revolution-torn Asia. The impact of the Korean war was immediately felt in Europe, where the United States, fearful that a Soviet assault was in the offing, demanded a massive military build-up to achieve parity with the Russians on the western front. This, however, could be done only by enlisting the support of the Germans, who at that point were still under Allied military occupation. Consequently, in September 1950, three months after the outbreak of the Korean war, Secretary of State Dean Acheson called for the rearmament of the three western zones of Germany and the incorporation of twelve German divisions into NATO. The creation of a new German army was to be made tolerable by the establishment of an "integrated" NATO command to which the German units would be pledged. NATO, it was argued, would serve as the safety latch on German military independence.

Whatever limitations NATO offered, most Europeans were deeply disturbed by the prospect of a new German army. The scars were too deep and the memories too fresh to welcome the reappearance of German soldiers, even if they were now dedicated to the defense of the West and formally "integrated" into a multination NATO command. Nor were the Germans themselves eager to rearm after the debacle of their last effort. Chancellor Konrad Adenauer, despite his desire to please the Americans, continually dragged his feet, with the result that the *Bundeswehr*, which Dean Acheson declared to be so urgently needed in 1950, did not achieve its full twelve-division strength until a decade and a half later, by which time the threatening situation it was designed to meet had diminished considerably.

In addition to their understandable apprehension about the rearmament of Germany, the allies were unconvinced that any crash military program was really necessary. While they formally approved at NATO Council meetings the various strategic goals urged by the United States—including in 1952 a demand for a ninety-division NATO army—they never assumed that Western Europe was to be defended on the ground with foot soldiers. For the Europeans the real deterrent to Russian aggression was not the land armies they grudgingly assembled under American prodding, nor the GIs guarding the frontier between the two Germanys, but the awesome nuclear arsenal the United States threatened to unleash in case the Russians crossed the Elbe. All the rest was window-dressing. The Europeans, as Henry Kissinger has explained,

saw in the military contribution a form of fee paid for United States nuclear protection. The Europeans agreed to our requests. But they tried to see to it that their actual contributions would be large enough to induce us to keep a substantial military establishment in Europe, yet not so high as to provide a real alternative to nuclear retaliation.[1]

Nor, from their point of view, did the Europeans have to provide an alternative to nuclear retaliation. So long as American soldiers remained on the Continent, the United States would be obliged to come to Europe's defense. These GIs insure, in a way that no promise or treaty commitment ever could, that America will be involved in any European war from the first shot. They are the human trip-wire which, if broken by a Russian attack, would trigger the American nuclear deterrent. Thus the presence of these soldiers on the Continent has seemed essential to the Europeans, for they make the American nuclear guarantee fully credible. The troops are, in this sense, hostages.

By making modest efforts to fulfill their own NATO goals, the Europeans have been able to retain the American hostages. But they have not been able to prevent a technological revolution in weaponry which has changed the whole nature of the nuclear guarantee. When the United States pledged itself to Europe's defense in the late 1940s, it was virtually invulnerable to Russian retaliation. Because of the intercontinental missile, however, the United States now faces the same danger of instant obliteration that the Europeans have faced from the start. Without doubting America's good faith, some of the allies have begun to wonder whether the President of the United States would now unleash nuclear missiles on Russia in retaliation for an attack on Europe, since he knows that this would almost certainly mean the destruction of the United States itself. Some profess to see the Pentagon's new strategy of "flexible response"—with its call for larger European armies to prevent a war from immediately "escalating" to the nuclear level, and for American control of all NATO nuclear weapons—as a partial retraction of the old nuclear guarantee. They fear that the United States and Russia, in order to spare themselves atomic devastation, may prefer to conduct a "limited" war on European soil. But what would be "limited" for the super-powers would most likely be total for their allies. For this reason the British maintain their mini-deterrent, the French develop their *force de frappe*, and the Germans suffer from a nuclear inferiority complex. Among the larger allies there is a feeling, expressed by Canadian Prime Minister Lester Pearson, that:

An alliance for defense only is an anachronism in the world of 1966, especially when nuclear power is not shared, by possession or by control, among its members. . . . A guarantee of nuclear support against aggression simply does not now have the credibility that would make it a fully effective deterrent and therefore a guarantee of security.[2]

[1] Henry Kissinger, "Coalition Diplomacy," *Foreign Affairs*, July 1964, p. 534.
[2] Lester Pearson, address at Springfield, Illinois, June 11, 1966. *The Congressional Record*, June 14, 1966, p. 12501.

Such criticisms as these reflect a deep anxiety among the allies that the interests of Europe and America, however similar they may be, are not identical where questions of national survival are concerned. Thus the allies prefer the old strategy of "massive retaliation," which threatens the Russians with instant obliteration should they move across the Elbe. Faced with such a threat, Europeans believe, the Russians would never dare risk even a conventional probe. As a result, the allies have refrained from building the thirty-division army the Pentagon has urged upon them. Indeed, even the United States does not appear to take its own strategy seriously, since it has pulled troops out of Europe to send to Vietnam and would like to cut the 225,000-man American army in Germany if it could assuage German anxieties. With the withdrawal of French forces from NATO and the cutback in both the British and the American armies in West Germany, any Russian attack would almost certainly have to be met with atomic weapons. "Flexible response" still remains the official policy, but "massive retaliation" more realistically describes the situation.

Because of these rather dizzying changes in strategy, NATO has come to mean something different from, and perhaps a good deal less than, what it did in the past. It is no longer, if indeed it ever was, a united body in which the defense of one is the defense of all. Militarily, the Europeans were never able to offer the United States much more than advance bases from which to strike at Soviet power. Now intercontinental missiles and Polaris-firing atomic submarines, long-range F-111 fighter-bombers and giant military transport planes, have drastically reduced the need for such strategic bases. Today whole divisions can be flown across the Atlantic in hours. Ten of these transport planes could have handled the Berlin airlift; 42 of them could complete in half a day the transfer of 15,000 troops to Europe that required 234 airplanes in 1963 and took nearly 3 days. Advanced technology has rendered the NATO bases, with their elaborate military pipelines and their brass-heavy bureaucracies, far less necessary to the defense of Europe. Thus there have been persistent calls—supported by General Eisenhower, Senator Mansfield, and the Senate Democratic Policy Committee—for sharp reductions in American troop strength in Europe. Technological innovation, the demands of the Vietnamese war, and the steady drain on United States gold

reserves have served to intensify these appeals.

The declining need for overseas bases has stimulated not only a strategic revolution, but perhaps a political one as well. Once the United States and the Soviet Union developed the means to obliterate each other with weapons fired from their own territories, the importance of their European allies inevitably diminished on the strategic scale of priorities. For both sides the most vital concern has switched from the defense of ideological allies to the prevention of nuclear war. Fearful of being dragged into an atomic conflict against their will, America and Russia have developed a common interest in keeping their allies out of the nuclear business. The Russians have not the slightest intention of giving atomic weapons to their East European comrades, and the United States has discouraged France's efforts at nuclear independence. President Johnson has wisely put into the deep freeze his predecessor's plan for a multilateral nuclear force (MLF) under mixed NATO ownership and control, and has firmly told the Germans that their desire for nuclear sharing must take a back seat to the Russo-American détente and the wider interests of European peace.

Today, as in the past, the Europeans have no real control over American strategy, nor over United States diplomacy outside the Atlantic area. The American deterrent, which comprises about 95 per cent of NATO's nuclear power, rests entirely in United States hands. The allies cannot insure that it be used for a cause they may consider vital, nor prevent it from being used for a cause they may disapprove of. The Cuban missile crisis and Vietnam clearly revealed the limits of collective decision-making within the alliance. From an American point of view, these limits are eminently reasonable and desirable. As the nation which bears the major responsibility, and the major cost, of defending the Atlantic area, we clearly cannot tolerate having vital decisions over our security made anywhere but in Washington.

However reasonable this may seem to most Americans, it is an attitude not shared by some of our European allies—and particularly not by General de Gaulle. Shortly after returning to power in 1958 he tried to establish a three-power directorate with America and Britain to coordinate NATO policy on a global level. When this met with a cold reception in Washington, he sought to increase Europe's leverage within the alliance by striking a special entente with Bonn. This effort, however, collapsed with the departure of Adenauer from office. De Gaulle then fell back on the assertion of French autonomy within the Atlantic alliance, an autonomy backed up by the *force de frappe* and by a diplomatic line open to Moscow. Having announced in February 1965 that France would soon end "the subordination known as 'integration' which is provided for by NATO and which hands our fate over to foreign authority," he carried out his threat scarcely a year later by withdrawing from the military structure of the alliance.

De Gaulle, of course, could not have done this had he believed that it involved any real danger for France. But behind his action is the assumption that the alliance will continue without the system of military integration under NATO, and that such integration is, in any case, no longer essential to the defense of Europe. Deterrence, he believes, rests in the American atomic arsenal, not in the NATO command structure. And the deterrent, he is convinced, will continue to cover France just as it covers the other members of the alliance, and even such neutrals as Switzerland and Sweden. This has nothing to do with the structure of NATO, but with vital considerations of national interest. The United States cannot allow Europe to fall into Russian hands. This would be true whether NATO existed or not. And this is why, for purposes of nuclear deterrence, NATO is largely irrelevant.

Seizing upon a widespread discontent with the subordinate role to which Europe is still confined, de Gaulle has tried to establish France as the leading challenger to American "hegemony" in Western Europe. By detaching France from NATO and throwing out her diplomatic lines to the emerging countries of the Third World, he has gained for France a freedom of maneuver that is denied the other members of the alliance. In so doing he has tried to show that Europe must be something more than a pawn in the struggle between the super-powers. More important, he has expressed, and even helped to create, a sense of European resistance to the United States that is complex in its origins but quite widespread in its effects. It is compounded of pride in what Europe has accomplished during the past two decades, embarrassment at being totally dependent upon the United States for protection, apprehension at the growing role that American industry plays in the European economy, and fear of becoming involved in America's revolution-squelching interventions in the southern hemisphere. As Washington has become increasingly preoccupied with "wars of national liberation," the Europeans have given vent to a detachment that is not yet neutralism but determinedly resists any involvement.

In challenging America's domination of the alliance, de Gaulle has brought to the surface tensions and disagreements that have long been concealed by the patina of NATO unity. He has revealed and even intensified these tensions, but he did not create them. The disputes within the alliance over politics and strategy began long before de Gaulle returned to power, and are likely to continue long after he leaves the scene, for they rest upon the realities of power, not upon the provocations of an irritating personality. "You can eliminate de Gaulle completely from the picture," the former supreme commander of NATO, General Lauris Norstad has said,

and you would not eliminate the problem. You could eliminate France from the picture but you would not eliminate the problem. The problem has been fundamental all the way through. It is always convenient to have a whipping boy. It excuses us from our action or inaction.[3]

The reality de Gaulle has revealed is that the conditions that originally inspired the alliance — a menacing Russia, an invulnerable America, a helpless Europe — have been overtaken by events. The Russians have become outspoken practitioners of "peaceful coexistence" and have been more interested in holding their own shaky political bloc together than in threatening Western Europe. The United States is still the world's greatest military power, but her defense policy for Europe is based upon a threat to commit national suicide. The Europeans have recovered from their wartime wounds to such a degree that they can now ponder the possibility of a reunited Continent from which both Russian and American troops will have disappeared. The sense of common danger and common weakness that inspired the Atlantic pact has given way to a new sense of security that is

[3]General Lauris Norstad, statement to the Senate Subcommittee on National Security and International Operations, May 6, 1966.

the undoer of alliances. Having achieved so much of what it initially set out to do, NATO is in danger of foundering now that its virtues no longer seem so necessary. In this sense it has become the victim of its own success.

This decline of NATO could be considered a source of satisfaction, for it means we may be approaching the point where the Europeans can take over the major burden of their own defense, and where it will no longer be necessary for us to assume such extraordinary dangers and costs on behalf of once-indigent allies. But our satisfaction with the stability and security of today's Europe has been muted by our disappointment over the failure of NATO to stimulate the united European community we desired. For most Americans, NATO was always more than merely a defense alliance: it was to be the means by which the old European enmities would be healed, by which Germany could make her peace with her neighbors, by which corrosive European nationalism would be buried, and by which the states of Eastern Europe could eventually be pried loose from the Soviet Union. Having twice been drawn into Europe's civil wars, we believed that Europe had to be made into something better than it had been. Applying the virtues of our own federal system to the chronic troubles of the Continent, we believed that the Europeans could end their endemic rivalries by forming a more perfect union: a United States of Europe.

This ambition was not selfish, for it was shared by many Europeans, and particularly by those who saw it as a means of ending the self-destructive rivalries of modern European history. Inspired by visions of a post-nationalist Europe, statesmen on both sides of the Atlantic drew up blueprints for a united Continent with a single army, a single parliament, and a single diplomacy. The communist capture of Eastern Europe limited the scope of this vision, but it also offered the opportunity of achieving the experiment on a smaller and more manageable scale in the countries west of the Iron Curtain. In this "little Europe" some of the great experiments in postwar cooperation were introduced: the Marshall Plan, NATO, the Coal and Steel Community, Euratom, the West European Union, and, perhaps most important of all, the Common Market.

From a fragmented, fratricidal Europe there would arise a great new power in the world, one which would be an "equal partner" to America

in the Atlantic alliance, and which would exert such a powerful attraction on the communist states of Eastern Europe that the Russians would be forced to relinquish their empire peacefully. This was what came in time to be known as the Grand Design, a blueprint for a transatlantic partnership between the United States and the western half of Europe. Within the restricted scope of the Atlantic pact it promised the hope of One World that had been frustrated by Soviet ambitions and the collapse of great-power unity. To the former isolationists whom the cold war had transformed into fervent interventionists, the Grand Design affirmed the wisdom of American institutions by transposing them to a corrupted Europe. To the liberals committed to a benevolent imperialism, it affirmed America's readiness to assume the burdens of world leadership. Through the fusion of their economies and the federation of their governments, the nations of Western Europe would help the United States combat the communist menace, aid the underdeveloped states, lower tariff barriers, and even, in the words of President Kennedy in his "declaration of interdependence" at Philadelphia on July 4, 1962, offer the means by which "we can help to achieve a world of law and free choice, banishing the world of war and coercion."

It was an inspiring vision, noble in sentiment, honorable in aspiration, and deeply felt in its idealism. It was also a bit specious, more impressive in the effusion of its rhetoric than in the depth of its analysis. In positing a permanent "equal partnership" between America and a united Western Europe, it held out the hope of a world that might have been, rather than of one that was in process of becoming—as Kennedy himself grew to suspect before his death. From the start it should have been clear that the allies did not have the same conception of the partnership as did Washington. At best it could only be a substitute for the kind of Europe that the Iron Curtain and the cold war had made impossible. This was particularly true when it became obvious to Europeans that the United States did not intend to participate in the equal partnership on an equal basis: that it had no intention of tearing down its tariff walls, sharing its deterrent, or subordinating the United States Congress to a European parliament. Nor did Washington ever seem to realize that a Europe that would be an equal partner would also want to be equal in the implements of power—that it would expect to have its own economic policy, its own diplomacy, and perhaps even its own Bomb. Equality, if it is to be anything more than rhetoric, means the ability to follow independent policies. Even those Europeans most desirous of some form of Atlantic partnership see a united Europe as something more than America's alter ego and spear-carrier. "Partnership," in the words of Walter Hallstein, president of the Common Market Commission and thus Europe's highest-ranking bureaucrat,

means the opposite of a monolithic Atlantic community in which the European states would play the part of a bridgehead towards the East, as were the Hellenic settlements in Asia Minor. . . . Free Europe must develop its own personality in order to become a partner for America and to serve as a magnet for the countries of Eastern Europe.[4]

American diplomacy has run parallel to European interests because it has been based upon the military containment of Russia. But now that the fear of Soviet attack has subsided in Western Europe and American attention has focused on the unstable states of the Third World, there is no longer the same clear convergence of interests between the United States and her NATO allies. Washington's attempts to solidify the détente with Moscow have raised apprehension among some of the allies, particularly the Germans, who fear that Russia and America may choose to keep Germany partitioned in the interests of European stability. Outside the Atlantic area, the United States has found that the Europeans have maintained a distance from our diplomacy that borders on open detachment. Only France has so far openly criticized American interventionism in such places as Vietnam and Santo Domingo, but none of the NATO allies seems to share our concern about the expansion of communism in Southeast Asia, or our estimate of the aggressive intentions of China. In fact, they rather admire China for her accomplishments, see her as a potential market for European manufactured products, and recognize the usefulness of Peking as a counterbalance to Russia in the East.

Even in such mundane affairs as economics, European and American interests are not identical and sometimes not even complementary. The long and painful negotiations during the "Kennedy Round" for mutual tariff reductions have dramatized just how determined the Europeans are to protect their economic interests, and how much leverage they have gained by joining together in the Common Market. Tariff reductions have been achieved where they were to the advantage of both parties, but the hyperbole of Atlantic partnership has not secured American products a privileged entry into the Common Market, nor induced the Europeans to take on a greater share of foreign aid for the underdeveloped countries.

As they try to build large-scale industries for their expanding consumer markets, the Europeans have become alarmed by the level of American private investment on the Continent, and particularly by its concentration in such vital fields as computers, automobiles, chemicals, and photographic equipment. The avalanche of American corporations jumping the Common Market tariff wall by setting up European subsidiaries has stimulated charges of "economic colonialism" that are no monopoly of the Gaullists. Many fear that the enormous American lead in growth industries such as electronics, plus the vastly greater amounts of funds available in the United States for basic research, will ultimately reduce Europe to the role of an economic satellite fated to produce American-designed products in American-owned factories on American licenses. "Europe," declared the French Socialist leader Gaston Deferre, "will be colonized by the United States unless we decide to pool our resources in order to create industrial concerns comparable in size to the American ones and able to compete with them on an equal footing."

These fears are not as imaginary as they may seem to skeptical Americans. Within recent years there has been a mounting invasion of Europe by American dollars, today in excess of $5 billion in the United Kingdom, and $6 billion on the Continent—or six times what it was in 1954. More than $2 billion is invested in West Germany alone, with another $1.5 billion in France and nearly $1 billion in Italy. The Common Market has become not only America's single most important customer and supplier, but also a magnet for United States capital in search of investment opportunities. In many respects this infusion of American funds has helped stimulate and expand European

[4]Walter Hallstein, quoted in David P. Calleo, *Europe's Future: The Grand Alternatives.* New York: Horizon Press, 1965, p. 78.

industry, providing the technical know-how and the competitive spirit that have been lacking in many areas of the European economy. But by its concentration in certain key industries, it has given rise to apprehension over foreign control. The computer industry, which holds the key to technological innovation, is controlled almost entirely by two American corporations. A similar situation applies in agricultural equipment, synthetic rubber, and chemicals. American ownership means that key areas of the European economy lie outside the effective control of European governments. "However much we welcome new American investment here as in other parts of Europe," Prime Minister Harold Wilson declared in words that sound suspiciously Gaullist, "there is no one on either side of the Channel who wants to see capital investment in Europe involve domination or, in the last resort, subjugation."[5]

The European problem is not how to keep American firms away, for Europe needs American capital and technological skill, but how to make sure that the control of the European economy remains in European hands. This is not easy at a time when the French and Italian computer industries have been swallowed by IBM and General Electric, when the British government-owned airlines are buying American-built jets while Britain's own aircraft industries hover on the verge of bankruptcy, and when fledgling European nuclear-power programs are being threatened by the American electrical giants. How can the Europeans compete so long as they do not have the continental-scale markets and the enormous federal research funds enjoyed by American corporations? How can they hope to challenge the United States in the basic growth industries when a single American firm such as General Motors has annual sales greater than the gross national product of the Netherlands or than that of a hundred other countries? The answer is that Europe cannot compete unless there is a domestic market comparable to that in the United States, unless European industries are able to merge into cartels as large as American corporations, unless there are massive infusions of government funds into basic research, and unless American companies can be prevented from controlling key areas of the European economy through subsidiaries. These goals cannot be achieved through an Atlantic community, since this would only institutionalize Europe's tech-

nological weakness. They can be realized only through unification—through expansion of the Common Market across the Channel and eventually across the Elbe. Whether this will happen remains to be seen. But unless there is some kind of wider economic integration, Europe cannot hope to compete with America as an equal.

European apprehension about American competition has not been confined to industry, but spreads to agriculture as well. For the past twenty years the United States has found an eager market in Western Europe for its farm products. European purchases helped cover the deficit in our balance of payments caused by overseas military expenses and foreign aid. But the same mechanization that modernized Europe's factories has also modernized her farms to the degree that the Common Market now has a farm-surplus problem of its own. Whatever their friendship toward the United States, the members of the Common Market have a primary obligation to their own family. There is nothing anti-American in the desire of European farmers to sell the crops with which a beneficent nature has provided them, but it does mean that the United States cannot much longer expect to meet its payments deficits out of money earned from selling surplus grains to Europe.

These economic disagreements have revealed just how much undue optimism there has been in Washington's vision of a free-trade area within the Atlantic community. Although an admirable design for trade liberalization on the classical model, it is full of pitfalls the Europeans are determined to avoid. Because they did not want to have their industries crushed by mass-production American imports, they have retained an external tariff. And because they wanted something more than a simple free-trade zone—more than a European supermarket—they rejected Britain's plans for diluting the integrationist ambitions of the Common Market. The Common Market nations are, in a sense, protectionist. But in that game nobody enters the arena with clean hands, not even the United States.

From these economic disagreements—which are only shadows of more important political differences—it is apparent that there has been a good deal of unjustified optimism, and even of

[5]Harold Wilson, quoted in *The New York Times*, December 1, 1966.

cant, in Washington's dream of a unified Western Europe joined to America in an Atlantic community. A united Europe of 180 million people in the richest and most industrially advanced nations of the earth would be a great power in its own right, capable of defending itself and pursuing its own foreign policy. While it might be a partner to America in areas where their interests overlapped—such as the containment of Russia—it would have interests of its own to pursue, and the strength to make those interests felt. It could not be expected to remain permanently dependent on our protection, since it would have the capacity to build a Bomb of its own. Nor would it be content to play deputy sheriff to Washington in the unruly states of the Third World. A unified Europe would want a dominant voice in working out an eventual political settlement with Moscow, and in time it might even find a tamed Russia a useful ally in balancing the overwhelming weight of American economic power. As is already apparent, it would hardly share Washington's phobia about China. The Grand Design was honorable in inspiration, but too much has happened since that Fourth of July when President Kennedy outlined his sweeping vision of an Atlantic partnership. The communist empire is breaking up, the little Europe of the NATO pact has grown too small to Europeans looking beyond the Iron Curtain, and America's new role as revolution-extinguisher has instigated a growing European desire to be counted out.

The United States has been deeply involved in European affairs for half a century. Because of Europe's vital importance to our national interest, we must remain deeply concerned by what happens on the Continent. Europe will probably always remain our first line of defense, as it has long been the anchor of our deepest cultural ties. But this does not make us a European power, any more than playing a saxophone turns a man into a musical instrument. Europe is important, but it is only one of the areas of concern vital to the United States. The Atlantic demands our attention, but so do the Pacific and the Caribbean. A community is one form of political organization, but it is not one which is natural to nations separated by 3000 miles of ocean and with great discrepancies of size, wealth, power, interests, and ambitions. Our alliance with Western Europe represents our stake in Western civilization, but the lands beyond the Iron Curtain, and even Russia herself,

are also part of that civilization. Europe faces west toward the Atlantic, but it also faces east toward the Urals. A Europe which is becoming absorbed in the quest for reunification will not remain forever tied to a military alliance premised upon the indefinite division of the Continent. An Atlantic community may be desirable, but it can never be built at the expense of a European community that would bring the communist nations in the east back into the European family. Nor can we allow the parochial interests of some of our NATO allies to impede the détente with Russia.

America and Europe will probably always be joined by bonds of friendship and interest, and even by some form of alliance so long as Russia remains a threat. But although they are complementary civilizations, America and Europe are not identical, and the common mold has long since been broken by two centuries of an evolving American experience. The American impact on postwar Europe has been enormous in everything from the packaging of soap to the packaging of culture. But the so-called Americanization of Europe, reflected in supermarkets and motels, is really little more than Europe's postwar adaptation to mass consumption and mass production. Prosperity has modernized the face of Europe, rebuilding its cities and jamming its narrow streets with cars. But modernization is not the same thing as Americanization, any more than hair-tinting is psychoanalysis. Despite surface similarities shared by most industrial societies, the differences between America and Europe run deep—in culture, in society, in personal relations.

This does not mean that America and Europe must, or will, become hostile, but rather that the relentless pace of industrialization may be stimulating differences even as it creates similarities. In the long run it may make it even more desirable for the peoples of the New World as well as of the Old to guard their cultural differences as a means of preserving their identities. Joined by a common heritage, sharing common cultural values and common riches in a world of poverty, America and Europe are not necessarily political partners. These two great societies are on parallel rather than identical tracks, as Americans consolidate their own unique civilization, and as Europeans strive to maintain the cherished values of their shared history and to seek a new future in some form of unification.

We had a dream of what Europe should be: a politically unified West European federation linked to the United States. It was a dream inspired by the cold war and given flesh by the existence of the NATO alliance. But in embellishing this vision we lost sight of the reason which brought us back to Europe two decades ago: to defend our friends from the Russians until they were capable of defending themselves and of achieving a political balance with the countries of Eastern Europe. Now that our allies are beginning to turn their attention to this long-neglected problem, we treat this change as though it were somehow a defeat. We have forgotten what we wanted to accomplish in Europe, and in so doing are in danger of causing a new instability on the Continent.

The time has come to stop mourning over formulas that served so well in the past, over blueprints for the future that have been made obsolete by changing events. What was reasonable in 1949 is often unreasonable today; what was visionary in the mid-1950s is reactionary in the late 1960s. What is essential in contemplating the future of NATO is that we not allow ourselves to become prisoners of our own rhetoric: that we not pursue roads that are no longer open, proclaim goals that are no longer possible, substitute a certain conception of Atlantic unity for a reconciliation of Europe, impose an abstract solution upon an intractable problem, become so mesmerized by projects that we lose sight of ends. The true issue facing us today is not one of holding desperately to an organization that was conceived in the late 1940s, or of trying to force the Europeans into certain rigid forms of political union, but of encouraging the creation of a political climate that will allow the two Europes to reconcile their differences and achieve a wider community stretching across the Elbe.

This rebuilding of the European community is the ultimate objective which we originally envisaged when we returned to Europe twenty years ago. It would be foolish and self-defeating to allow our preoccupation with certain organizational forms of Atlantic cooperation to impede this process. It would alienate our European friends and negate much of what we have tried to accomplish during these past two decades. It could even leave Europe in a more dangerous condition than the one in which we found it. This need not happen, and it would be tragic if it did. Yet it could well result if we continue

trying to impose our own conception of unity upon a reluctant Europe.

NATO as a military alliance has served us well in the past and it is a construction in which we and our allies may take a good deal of pride. But it was a specific response to a specific situation, and the situation has changed so radically that the response is no longer the proper one. A revitalized Europe, a chastened Russia, a vulnerable America—these are not the conditions to which NATO is appropriate. The NATO Organization, which was appended to the North Atlantic Treaty as a military afterthought, has now largely served its purpose. It is breaking down—with the withdrawal of France, the reluctance to meet military goals, and the arguments over money—because the members themselves no longer agree upon its necessity. It is, in Walter Lippmann's striking phrase, "no longer a genuine military investment but an expensive and deteriorating ruin . . . like a mansion, once the pride of the neighborhood, from which the tenants have moved away, for which no new tenants can be found."[6]

Although NATO now seems doomed to extinction as a military organization, some form of military cooperation is likely to continue between America and Western Europe so long as our allies feel themselves threatened by the Russians. The alliance does not depend upon the organization, and the demise of the organization does not preclude the need for mutual defense arrangements. Even General de Gaulle has underlined the need for an Atlantic alliance that would assure Europe of American nuclear protection. But just as the alliance is not the same as the organization we call NATO, so the alliance is not necessarily the prelude to an Atlantic "community." An expression of the cultural, economic, and social bonds between America and Western Europe, the Atlantic community will always exist as a manner of speech and a frame of reference. What we must not do, however, is to confuse this community of values shared by the diverse peoples who border the Atlantic with a particular form of political organization between America and Western Europe. The former is a living reality based upon three hundred years of shared history; the latter is a by-product of the cold war. A politically

[6]Walter Lippmann, New York *World Journal Tribune*, December 15, 1966.

unified Atlantic community was a noble dream: but it is no longer so desirable as it once was to a Europe now in search of reconciliation, and to an America which may be tempted to achieve a private accord of its own with Russia. Perhaps one day it may be resurrected in another form, but in the new climate of détente, the emphasis in Europe is on reconciliation with the East —and in Washington, on collaboration with the Soviet Union.

Having for so long been bemused by our role as Europe's protector, and having been in search of an Atlantic mirage, we have allowed ourselves to become oblivious to the realities of a Europe that may be nobody's partner in tomorrow's world.

CONTAINMENT IN ASIA RECONSIDERED
David P. Mozingo*

Any serious American strategy and set of policies for Asia must rest on some basic assumptions. They must take into account the military, economic, and politico-diplomatic capabilities of Communist China and attempt a realistic assessment of the latter's intentions. They must also evaluate the capabilities, and the vulnerabilities, of the other countries of Asia, particularly those that are not under Communist control and may be presumed to be facing some sort of Communist threat. Finally, with a view of the Asian environment in hand, the policymakers (and their critics) must attempt to define as clearly as possible the interests and objectives of the United States in that part of the world.

As has been suggested at a number of points in this volume, this is not an easy task under the best of circumstances. It has proved particularly painful and difficult for the United States in recent years with regard to the Far East. While Dr. Mozingo's essay does not provide all the answers, his particular view of the Asian environment is a serious and challenging one that must somehow be taken into account in any effort to rethink American policies for that part of the world.

Since the Korean War, United States policies in Asia have gradually developed along the lines of the "containment" doctrine so successfully applied in Europe after 1947. Washington has increasingly seen the problem of Chinese power in Asia in much the same light as that posed by Soviet power in Europe and has behaved as if both threats could be contained by basically the same kinds of responses. In both Asia and Europe, containment measures have reflected a perceived need for complementary interaction between military policies and aid programs in order to prevent aggression by Communist powers and to foster the internal stability of nations in the area. Although difficulties have arisen in seeking the best balance of these components of the containment policy in Europe, most of the essential American objectives in the West have been attained.

For some time, however, it has been apparent, particularly in Southeast Asia, that the application of containment measures in the Far East has not yielded results comparable to those achieved in Europe. While it is widely recognized that this disparity in results reflects special Asian problems not encountered in Europe, there has been a general reluctance to question whether the containment philosophy really addresses the basic sources of the instability in Asia that alarms the United States. It is time to analyze the relative failure of the containment doctrine in Asia by considering both the obvious special difficulties confronting the United States there and the inherent differences between the situation in Asia and that in Europe.

Had the sense of historical perspective exerted a more prominent influence on Asian policy formulation, it is likely that containment's central objective of establishing a hard political and military line between a U.S. and a Chinese sphere of influence would have seemed infeasible from the beginning. In Western Europe, the basis for effective U.S. containment measures was soundly conceived because these measures were applied in defense of communities long-established within the framework of a nation-state system. Moreover, special ties bound the United States to Great Britain and France. By applying the containment doctrine in the West, the United States, for the third time in this century, reaffirmed the strategic principle that had

From *World Politics*, by permission of the Rand Corporation, copyright April, 1967.
*The views expressed in this paper are those of the author. They should not be interpreted as reflecting the views of The RAND Corporation or the official opinion or policy of any of its governmental or private research sponsors.

formerly governed Britain's policy toward Europe: No single continental power was to be permitted to conquer or dominate the European nation-state system. Further, the U.S. measures to contain Russia in Europe were strengthened by the historic determination of the Western democracies to preserve their established order and values.

In Asia, the containment doctrine has been applied to an area where a nation-state system is only just beginning to emerge amid unpredictable upheavals of a kind that characterized Europe three centuries earlier. It is only since 1949 that the restoration of a strong, unified China, the withdrawal of the Western colonial powers, and the formation of new independent countries have created the beginnings of a modern nation-state system in Asia.

The question in Asia is not how a traditionally functioning system can be rehabilitated but how a very new system will evolve and mature. The kinds of American technical and economic power that helped to restore the historic vitality of the European system would seem to have, at best, only partial relevance to the Asian situation. It may be doubted whether the kinds of tools and power available to the United States can induce stability in an environment in which most countries are experiencing a profound and rapid transformation of their societies, values, and attitudes. Much of the American experience and structure of values has already shown itself to be not only inapplicable but also not even wanted. The results of the competition between the United States, Russia, and China in Asia thus far seem to indicate that attempts by external powers to shape the emerging Asian system are unlikely to succeed. None of these powers has been able, whether by appeals to ideology or common national interests or by large-scale economic and military aid, to exert enough influence to draw the more important Asian powers into close alignment. In the absence of firm ties and mutual interests of the kind that have bound the United States to Western Europe (and these did not emerge overnight), a policy of containment in Asia must rest on unstable foundations.

THE EFFECT OF NATIONAL RIVALRIES ON A CONTAINMENT STRATEGY IN ASIA

The Soviet threat to Europe has been regarded primarily as a military one. Even when the Western part of that continent was most weakened, immediately after World War II, Communist parties were unable to take power in any country by popular consent. Western Europe's economic recovery was rapid. National conflicts were not so severe as to prevent the formation of an alliance. Until very recent times there was broad agreement among the Western powers about the nature of the Soviet threat and how to meet it. Consequently, it was possible to lay a firm political foundation for the NATO structure.

The political conditions that were indispensable to the creation of security arrangements in Europe are absent in Asia, where very few powers see their security interests in the same way. Except for Taiwan, all of the Asian powers have an enemy or enemies whom their leaders apparently regard as more threatening than China. Japan, for example, still regards Russia as at least as great a threat to her security as China. Moreover, the common threat to South Korea and Japan that developed as a result of the Korean War has yet to result in a real rapprochement between these two countries; but without such an understanding, no "little NATO" in Northeast Asia can be built. For these and other historical, economic, and psychological reasons it is doubtful that any anti-China security arrangement can win Japan's enthusiastic participation. In fact, only the United States and South Korea have indicated interest in an alignment with Taiwan against Peking.

In Southeast Asia, the menace to Thailand, Laos, and South Vietnam comes in the first instance not from China but from a very independent and highly nationalistic regime in Hanoi. North Vietnamese expansion into Southeast Asia also alarms Cambodia, but not as much as her fear of Thai and South Vietnamese aspirations to recover lost territories at Phnom Penh's expense. Prince Sihanouk believes these two historic enemies have aligned themselves with the United States, not so much to contain China or North Vietnam as to secure the arms and tacit backing of the United States for the pursuit of their irredentist claims on Cambodia—hence, his close ties with Peking and deference to Hanoi. Similar fears influence Pakistan, whose government (understandably) believes India is gearing her defenses less to protect the subcontinent from Chinese invasion than to dominate Pakistan. In Rawalpindi's view, New Delhi is using the boundary dispute with Peking to secure U.S. and Soviet aid that will more likely be used against Pakistan. Indonesia, the Philippines, and Malaysia are geographically beyond the reach of Chinese power. They have predominantly the same racial composition. In spite of these favorable conditions, in recent times the relations between the three countries have been strained by harmful rivalries they themselves have generated, not Peking.

Such strife among Asia's non-Communist powers, for which their own governments are responsible, has been far more beneficial to China's aspirations and interests as a great power in the Far East than have any actions she has initiated herself. It is therefore difficult to see how a containment policy directed primarily against China can be truly effective as long as the Far East seethes with conflict between jealously independent rival nationalist regimes whose policies are essentially their own. To a certain extent it would seem that previous U.S. attempts to back one or another potentially anti-Communist state and to promote the growth of its petty military power have not so much deterred or contained the dubious military threat from China as they have sharpened the very national conflicts, internal and external, that undermine local stability and hence frustrate the development of a broader basis for conciliation among the nations in this region. American objectives would perhaps have been better served by policies that emphasized the American role as a "conciliator" in Asia (for example, in the India-Pakistan, Indonesia-Malaysia, or Cambodia-Thailand-Vietnam disputes) than by so much emphasis on building anti-Communist "positions of strength" through military alliances aimed at China. Actually, the United States has the strongest kind of interest in promoting conciliation between all the states of Asia in this century of intense nationalism. This interest includes even such issues as the Sino-Indian boundary dispute. However, it is clear that the incessant conflict and rivalry among Asia's non-Communist states go further to destabilize Asian politics than do the actions taken thus far by the Peking regime.

The existence of intense rivalries among Asia's non-Communist powers, rivalries that result from their own conceptions of national interests and objectives, has produced a response in Asia to the fact of Chinese Communist power that is altogether different from Europe's reaction to the Soviet threat. At no time has there emerged anything like an Asian consensus about how to regard Chinese military or political intentions. It would be difficult to show that any Asian countries capable of independent action

have accepted the United States' assessment of China. This judgment is supported by the fact that the United States has been unable to construct, even informally, an alliance structure in the Far East, directed against Peking, which includes the major Asian powers. It is well known that even some allies of the United States, given the balance of power that so heavily favors Russia and the United States, do not regard Peking as a serious military menace to themselves. At the same time, there can be scarcely a government in the Far East today that is not aware of how useful it is, in dealing with the United States, to invent or exaggerate fears of a Chinese bogeyman.

The United States, far removed from Asia and from direct threat by China, stands almost alone in emphasizing the urgent menace of Peking, while most of the countries in the region, who ought to be highly sensitive to any Chinese threat, have taken a more conservative view of their Chinese neighbor's intentions. Even India's bitter hostility to Peking has not produced anything like the devil-theory of China that has grown up in the United States. To sum up, the states of Asia have not agreed on the existence of a common external threat; but such an agreement seems to be an indispensable condition for the success of policies modeled on European-type containment.

APPRAISING CHINA'S INTENTIONS

It is not only the inherent differences between the political structure of non-Communist Asia and Western Europe that cast doubt on the validity of applying European-type containment doctrines to the Far East. The aims and direction of Chinese Communist policy—indeed, the nature of the Communist challenge in Asia itself —must be evaluated in terms that are largely irrelevant to European experience. Menacing Soviet actions in Europe presented such a clear and present danger to all concerned that they provoked the creation of the NATO alliance. Since the Russian forward pressure came after the Western powers had already acquiesced in considerable territorial and political concessions in Eastern Europe to meet alleged Soviet security interests, there was general agreement in Western Europe that Moscow's intentions were not defensive in nature. The American effort to equate China's intervention in the Korean conflict and her use of force in the Taiwan dispute, in Tibet, and on the Indian boundary with Soviet behavior in Eastern Europe has obviously failed to convince most Asian governments that China has aggressive intentions toward them. This failure suggests why the United States has been unable to crystallize opinion in these countries behind any genuine Asian regional security arrangements to curb a supposed threat of Chinese expansion.

In explaining Chinese action, Pakistan, Burma, Cambodia, Nepal, even Indonesia and our ally Japan, have tended to give more weight to traditional, nationalistic, and defensive motives than to purely "aggressive" Communist revolutionary impulses. This is not to say that these non-Communist Asian countries have been unconcerned about China's actions, her power, or her Communist system. But it is clear that most of these countries rely on their own perception of their Chinese neighbor, and their perception is such that the United States is unlikely to succeed in arousing a high level of Asian fear about China unless Peking behaves in a manner far more threatening to them, collectively and individually, than she has done to date. It is recognized in a number of Asian capitals that China's belligerence is largely a function of her special rivalry with the United States over Taiwan and other issues. Hence these countries have chosen to avoid alignments that would conflict with their own interest in stabilizing relations with Peking. Their aim has been, quite obviously, to avoid inflaming relations with China, and they do not wish to be drawn into the Sino-American quarrel. Asian reactions to the issues raised in Korea, Taiwan, Tibet, India, and Vietnam have been extremely varied and at no time has any of these conflicts produced an Asian front against China similar to that which the Soviet Union brought on herself by her actions in Europe. The disparity of views among the non-Communist Asian powers, and between them and the United States, about China's intentions robs the policy of containment of the basic consensus that was essential to its success in Europe.

China's foreign policy has also helped to undermine the appeal of the Containment doctrine in Asia. The basic direction of her foreign policy in Asia since 1954 has been toward seeking an adjustment of contentious issues between herself and such of her neighbors as were not allied with or seemingly under the control of the United States. Thus, for more than a decade, China has worked to normalize relations with Afghanistan, Burma, Pakistan, Cambodia, Ceylon, Nepal, and Indonesia. Peking is outspokenly hostile to all members of the American anti-China bloc. She seeks in various ways, including the threat to support revolutionary elements, to convince their leaders that making common cause with the United States carries certain risks; that it is not possible for any of them to support the United States in opposing China and have friendly relations with Peking at the same time. Even in relation to countries in this category, however, China's actions—as distinguished from her verbal condemnations—have been cautious and restrained. To those Asian governments that decline alignment with the United States, Peking offers such explicit rewards as border settlements, aid, and China's nonsupport of insurrectionary tactics by local revolutionaries. This Chinese stance reflects not only the limitations on Peking's military capabilities for large-scale aggressive actions, but, vastly more important, her recognition that naked and unprovoked aggression against her neighbors would threaten the collapse of her entire diplomacy in Asia. Since the Bandung Conference, China has attempted to compose her relations with any genuinely nonaligned neighbors in order to identify and isolate the United States as the aggressive power and to find common ground with Asian nationalism for the purpose of organizing opposition to the policies of the United States.

Since the mid-1950's, China's diplomatic efforts to prevent her neighbors from being drawn into the American anti-China alignment have consistently enjoyed priority over Peking's commitment to support Communist revolutions. The Chinese position on revolution, which is central to an accurate understanding of her policies in Asia, should not be misunderstood or distorted. China encourages armed "revolutionary" action on the part of Communists or other dissidents in countries where special conditions exist—that is, where the so-called "imperialist" powers have interposed themselves, as in Taiwan, South Korea, Japan, Laos, South Vietnam, and most recently, Thailand (after U.S. military forces arrived in that country). Ostensibly nonaligned governments, as in India, have also to reckon with Peking's anger when they adopt "anti-China" policies. One listens in vain, however, for the strident Chinese call to "revolution" in any Asian country that is clearly independent of American tutelage and pursues a policy of accommodation with Peking.

Where supporting revolution conflicts with China's hope to wean non-Communist Asian governments away from the United States, revolution is pushed into the background. China has advised in her ideological pronouncements on revolution that local Communist parties, though they should learn from Chairman Mao, must in the final analysis find their own formulas for taking power. In those Asian countries that remain independent of the United States and friendly to China, Peking shuns calling upon the local parties to attempt "adventurist" revolutionary actions that conflict with her own diplomacy. Toward governments in this category, China's basic policy for more than a decade has been to concentrate wherever possible on currying favor with nationalist leaders (some of whom, from the Communist viewpoint, can scarcely be described as "progressive") and to encourage the local party to develop the art of skilled united-front tactics. Local Communists are expected to exploit the various "contradictions" in their own country so as to place themselves in a position to take power when the old incompetent order collapses. Peking encourages local parties to take power by the parliamentary or peaceful path if they can, but she points out that there is no instance in which the bourgeois classes have permitted a Communist party to win power "democratically." Hence, the Chinese argue, it is indispensable that a real Marxist-Leninist party organize for and be prepared to use armed revolutionary struggle. Otherwise the chances are very slim that a Communist party could come to power, much less be strong enough to carry out a dictatorship of the proletariat.

Peking's actual behavior and her ideological theses on revolution reveal that she is prepared to refrain from direct interference in the competition (whether peaceful or violent) between Communist parties and the "bourgeois" classes in Asian countries, so long as the United States also does not directly intervene in these countries' politics.[1] This is the essence of the Chinese version of peaceful coexistence in Asia, formulated more than ten years ago at the Bandung Conference.[2] China has not violated her own ground rules in relation to any independent Asian country, regardless of its social system, except where the United States has come to play a direct role in support of "bourgeois"

regimes' competition with local Communist parties. The dispute with Moscow on the meaning of peaceful coexistence has arisen over the issue of what the policy of the Communist powers should be in situations where the United States rushes in to prop up a non-Communist regime that is in danger of losing the competition with its local Communist opponent. China argues that the Communist bloc should try to deter, or by various means oppose, attempts by the United States to use her own power unilaterally to determine the outcome of the competition between the bourgeois elites and the Communist forces. The Chinese leaders' view of their own national interests requires this position, for they regard the United States as bent on organizing all Asia into a belt of client-states opposing Peking. These fears are less disturbing to the Soviet leaders, who have long betrayed noticeable ambivalence about the desirability of fully opposing the United States in Asia if to do so would benefit the interests of the Chinese state.

As her power increases, of course, it is possible that China may abandon her present compromise with independent Asian nationalist regimes and, under the protection of her own nuclear deterrent, energetically attempt to impose Communist regimes on her neighbors. That possibility cannot be dismissed lightly, but it is a course of action fraught with grave risks for Peking. While it is conceivable that China might attempt to invade small neighboring countries or to foment and support revolution in them, it is far less likely that she will feel confident enough to undertake such measures against large Asian powers such as India, Pakistan, Indonesia, and Japan. Some of these nations will be able to move in the nuclear direction at some future time; should Peking, without provocation, take an aggressive attitude toward these countries, she would run the risk of hastening the development of an anti-China nuclear club. Nothing would seem so well calculated to drive non-Communist Asia closer to the United States (or Russia) as an attempt by Peking

[1]The definitive statement of the Chinese position on "peaceful coexistence" with other non-Communist states was set forth in the Sixth Comment on the Open Letter of the Central Committee of the CPSU, "Peaceful Coexistence—Two Diametrically Opposed Policies," published December 12, 1963. The full text is in *The Polemic on the General Line of the International Communist Movement* (Peking 1965), 259-301.

[2]For complete texts of Chou En-lai's three speeches at the Bandung Conference on relations with Asian countries, see *China and the Asian-African Conference (Documents)* (Peking 1955).

to coerce her neighbors into unconditional surrender to Chinese demands.

Seen dispassionately, China's policies in Asia are more characteristic of a traditional great power than of a revolutionary renegade. The commitment to revolution plays a special part in Chinese policies, but in aspiring to great-power status, Peking emphasizes such traditional and conventional instruments as diplomacy, economic power, and the presence or threat of force. The demands of the Chinese regime for certain irredentas, spheres of influence, and concessions to its security interests are opposed by the United States and the Soviet Union, each of them much more powerful than China. Peking cannot hope to force concessions from either of these powers by provoking a direct test of strength. But it is quite evident that Communist China does not intend to accept passively a position and influence in the world, particularly in Asia, that she regards as being dictated either by the Soviet Union or by the United States. It is doubtful that any Chinese leadership born in this century would react differently. But the Chinese leaders are not the only ones in Asia and in other areas with aspirations that go beyond the position Russia or America would assign to them. China's call to "revolution" is directed primarily to existing and potential elites in Asia and elsewhere whom she regards as likely to share with her an interest in altering any status quo imposed by U.S. or Soviet policies.

The model she has offered to these potential Communist and nationalist allies, in the hope that their revolutionary efforts will shake U.S. and Soviet domination, is one derived from Chinese Communist revolutionary experience. The Chinese leaders believe that under favorable conditions, well-trained and indoctrinated Communist parties can integrate this model with their own concrete situations and can ultimately take power. The Chinese do not say that revolution can or should be launched everywhere; they actively support unrest only in certain carefully defined revolutionary situations: where "imperialism" (i.e., the United States) is present, and where the prescribed local conditions of success exist. Peking is the master, not the servant, of its revolutionary ideology.

The entire Chinese line on revolution has been fashioned to support the great-power policies Peking pursues in her contest with the United States and the Soviet Union. Where China's leaders have believed their interests in this fundamental struggle could be best served by supporting foreign Communist revolutionary movements, they have done so. But wherever they have believed they could advance in the contest with Moscow and Washington by supporting an odd assortment of friendly nationalist, militarist, or monarchial regimes, they have not hesitated to leave local Communist parties to their own fate. Had Peking's actions conformed to the devil-theory of China that has grown up in the United States, the appeal of the containment policy in Asia would no doubt be much greater than it is today.

OBSTACLES TO CHINESE PREEMINENCE IN ASIA

It is not surprising that a state with China's present power and long history should aspire to regional preeminence. But the task of transforming such ambitions in Asia into reality promises to be very difficult. Various forces in Asia, independent of American power, seem likely to curb Peking's influence.

The position of the Chinese state in Asia is not comparable to that of the United States in the Western hemisphere or to Russia's position in Eastern Europe. In addition to the United States, Peking confronts, in Russia, Japan, India-Pakistan, and Indonesia, large powers which, irrespective of their political order, have reason to oppose mainland China's hegemony in Asia. Russia's and Japan's interests are very different from China's, and the power complex developing in both these countries would act as a major curb on Chinese expansion in the most decisive theater, Northeast Asia, even in the unlikely event of a total withdrawal of American power. The departure of the United States from Asia would no doubt gratify Peking, but it would not clear the path for Chinese hegemony. Rather, it would set the stage for a different kind of power struggle in the area.

Since the nineteenth century, both Japan and Russia have tried to be expansionist powers at China's expense. No Chinese government is likely to rid itself of the old fear that these two powers might again take the path of aggression against China or combine against her interests in Asia. If a disengagement were ever to occur between the United States and China, it seems very probable that China's attention would turn to the older problem of opposing Russian and Japanese penetration of the Asian mainland. In the twentieth century this old three-power rivalry might take a different form than it did in the past, but the steady rise of Russian and Japanese power would continue to be a basic obstacle to Chinese hegemony. The longer and much deeper history of China's fear of Russia and Japan may one day exert a powerful influence on future Chinese leaders' attitudes toward the United States, if a major conflict between the two powers does not come to pass.

The natural direction for Chinese expansion, it is usually thought, is into Southeast Asia, where China has historically exerted influence. China's nearness and the absence of strong indigenous military powers have led to the assumption that she is destined to dominate Southeast Asia unless resolutely deterred by the United States. This fits in neatly with theories about power vacuums. But the major Southeast Asian countries themselves have strongly resisted the idea of being drawn into China's orbit (or anyone else's). All of the countries in this area, including Vietnam, share an antipathy toward Chinese pretensions to superiority and dominance, whether on the part of local Chinese populations or of the Peking government. Nearly all the countries of Southeast Asia possess impressive geographic barriers against a major Chinese invasion. Moreover, they all are well aware that Soviet and American power interests are also opposed to Chinese predominance, although not all agree with the United States about how to deal with China. Contrary to the experience of past centuries, when her spreading culture was a powerful vehicle for claims to regional predominance, China's influence as a whole has been declining in Southeast Asia. Recently excluded from the area by the Western imperial powers, China now faces the intense nationalism that has captured the successor states since World War II.

The existence of fraternal Communist parties, the most successful of which have been every bit as nationalistic as the Chinese party, has not constituted an unmixed blessing as far as Peking's search for preeminence in the area is concerned. These parties have been useful and necessary allies, as in Vietnam and Laos, in opposing the American effort to turn the 1954 Geneva agreement on Indochina into an anti-Communist and anti-China front. On the other hand, some of these highly nationalistic and ambitious Communist parties, like the Indonesian one, often complicate China's diplomatic dealings with nationalist governments. The stronger Asian Communist movements have all shown an independent temper, and this has increased their freedom to take actions contrary to China's interests.

The Chinese leaders believe that the removal of Western influence from Asia, coupled with prolonged internal instability, will eventually aid local Communist movements in coming to power. But China's leaders, no less than Russia's, are already discovering in their relations with North Vietnam and North Korea that ideological affinity and territorial proximity between Communist states do not result in the subordination of the smaller partners. Already it is evident that North Korea and North Vietnam will develop their own distinctive national personalities and forms: neither is now or is likely to become simply a small replica of "the thought of Mao Tse-tung." In the past, both regimes have shown a willingness to depart from the Chinese line on key issues. Should other Communist regimes emerge in Southeast Asia—in Vietnam, say, or possibly in Indonesia—Peking cannot assume on the basis of past experience that they will follow her lead. Actually, China must remain worried that such regimes may seek more freedom of action by currying favor with the Soviet Union—or, for that matter, with the West. Consequently, it is by no means clear at this point that China's leaders would prefer the development of stable, independent, diverse, and highly nationalistic Communist regimes in Southeast Asia in preference to the prolonged continuation of weak non-Communist regimes led by men willing to defer to China's interests in return for Peking's respect of the essential sovereignty of their countries.

None of the elites of the principal Asian nations—Japan, India, Pakistan, Indonesia—on whose political and military stance a great deal of China's ultimate position and influence in Asia depends, have shown themselves to be anybody's pawns—Russia's, China's, or America's. The United States and Russia have failed on the whole in their attempts to manipulate Asian nationalism so as to support their own state strategies in the cold war. By now it ought to be apparent that there is not going to be either an American or a Soviet solution to Asia's postcolonial problems. By its nature that goal was never really attainable, but it seemed to be a serious aspiration at one time because both Russia and America have been attracted, to a different degree and in very different ways, to the notion that they have special world ideological missions. Peking may believe China can succeed where two vastly richer and stronger superpowers failed, but the post-World War II history of Asian nationalism indicates very clearly that none of the great powers will be likely to succeed in this endeavor.

It should not be forgotten that between 1948 and 1951, during the heyday of Sino-Soviet cooperation, the Communist parties of Asia tried very hard to use armed insurrection as a means of discrediting and destroying such leaders as Nehru, Sukarno, U Nu, and others. In every instance where the non-Communist leadership could lay genuine claim to representing the force of nationalism, the Communist rebellions were crushed. So complete was the failure of these parties' assaults on nationalism that the Communist movement was forced to come to terms and to shift to policies of peaceful coexistence—a new line first championed by the Communist parties of China, India, and Indonesia, and only later by the Soviet Union. It should also be added that except for the special case of Malaya, the most politically significant defeats inflicted on Communist movements have come at the hands of non-aligned nationalist governments, and, as the recent suppression of the Indonesian Communist party again demonstrates, these defeats were brought about without the assistance of the United States.

The fear, expressed in the argument that neutralism or nonalignment is simply a temporary way station on the road to communism, that Peking and other Communists can push over popular nationalist regimes like "dominoes" once a Communist revolution succeeds somewhere else, is overwhelmingly contradicted by the proven vitality of Asian nationalism in the last twenty years. The Chinese Communists were the first to recognize, more than a decade ago, that genuine non-Communist nationalism was nobody's pushover and that efforts by local Communist parties to prove the contrary would bear bitter fruit. In Asia, it is only where an existing leadership has not earned, and therefore cannot claim, the mandate of nationalism that Communist parties have been able to make a serious challenge for power—a challenge based on their own attempt to seize power from those who either lost that mandate or never had it.

THE REAL AMERICAN PROBLEM IN ASIA

Much discussion about the threat of Chinese Communist expansion exaggerates what Peking is capable of doing both now and later and underplays the role of indigenous forces at work in neighboring countries affected by Chinese policies but clearly free from Chinese domination. This is a critical distinction to make, for the fact is that China is assigned far more responsibility than she deserves for the disturbances that lie at the roots of American anxiety about Asia. It is simply not true that Peking or any other Communist power can successfully "turn on" a Communist revolution wherever it chooses. Neither Peking's actions nor her ideological pronouncements have created the essential conditions that have energized the growth of the Communist movement in Asian countries. Local Communist parties have scored impressive gains, invariably, in those countries where native non-Communist elites have, by their own actions, failed to gain or retain their people's recognition as popular, effective nationalists. Local non-Communist elites themselves, not Peking, created the basic sources of internal discord in Laos, Vietnam, and Indonesia, where the most successful Communist movements to date have developed. Communist strength in these countries would be far less today had the non-Communist political elements subordinated their private rivalries to the larger task of national consolidation. Where the competition among the non-Communist elites has not reached the point of destroying the national fabric—for example, in Japan, Thailand, Pakistan, Burma, Cambodia, Ceylon, India, Malaysia, and the Philippines—the Communists have been unable to make a serious bid for power.

The plain fact is that Asian communism's greatest asset is not, and never has been, Communist China's potential military threat or her support of revolution. It has been, and continues to be, primarily the existence of incompetence and corruption and the lack of a genuine, socially progressive, nation-building ethic within the non-Communist elite in every country where communism has made serious advances. Conversely, the most effective deterrent to Communist gains has proved to be the existence of a non-Communist elite dedicated to solving its country's problems and therefore capable of holding the loyalty of its own people. American military power and aid, in themselves, have not proved adequate to find, to build, or to replace a dedicated, hard-working, non-Communist elite.

In the absence of indigenously inspired civil strife, gross incompetence among the non-Communists, or a foreign colonial enemy, no Communist movement in any Asian country has come even close to taking power, through either revolutionary or conventional political strategies. The political, economic, and social upheaval indispensable for a successful "people's war" cannot be manufactured abroad, and it does not burst on the scene overnight. Fundamentally, the prospects for successful Communist movements in Asia depend far less on contriving armed insurrection than on the character and ability of the non-Communist elites. Asia's non-Communists, the Chinese believe, will do the basic job of disintegrating their own societies and reputations to the point at which Communist parties can effectively exploit the situation. If the Chinese are right, and the evidence suggests that in some countries they are, the Communist threat to Asia would not disappear if Communist China's presence vanished from the scene tomorrow.

There most certainly are both immediate and long-range prospects that the kind of future the United States would like to see develop in Asia will not come about. And the nature of the threat to idealized U.S. hopes is primarily the potential rise of authoritarian or totalitarian regimes in response to a broad pattern of grievances long felt and long uncorrected. But this danger comes not from the Left alone, in the shape of communism, but also from the Right, in the form of authoritarian, oligarchic regimes representing the military, the privileged social classes, and the commercial element. There are numerous examples—Laos, Indonesia, Vietnam, Kerala—to show that when the Communist parties are likely to take power, whether through elections or revolution, the rightist classes are likely to agree on a coercive political solution of their own invention, rather than to accept one formulated in Moscow and Peking.

For a long time, United States assumptions about political developments in Asia have contained the unwarranted expectation that somehow national communities based on some form of democratic consensus ought to, or are likely to, flourish in the area, provided an assumed Communist threat to their institutions is checked and economic development is encouraged. It is quite natural that the United States, in view of her values and traditions, should act to promote economically viable and politically responsible regimes wherever there is a *clear* indication of local purpose and desire. But successful policies for the long run—not based merely on the year-to-year fluctuation in Com-

munist fortunes—must take account of the limitations on what the United States, great though her power is, can realistically expect to achieve in a vast and varied part of the world that has very different traditions from her own. History thus far would appear to show that overt Communist military aggression can be defeated and that artificially contrived "people's wars" do not succeed in countries whose leaders command the consent and loyalty of their own people. There is, however, serious reason to doubt that any foreign power, including the United States, can redeem the image of harsh and unpopular governments or can persuade or force unwilling governments to take those measures of reform that alone can win the support of their own populations or build a nationalist following where one does not exist.

Unfortunately, the painful truth is that Asia's strongest political tradition is the very authoritarianism that stands in the way of such reforms. The variations in this authoritarian tradition have been either despotic or benevolent but have remained authoritarian. The sharing of state power under the rule of law is an alien conception in many parts of Asia. Moreover, the desirability of political Westernization is not at once obvious to most Asians, as it is to Americans. Except where Western institutions have been imposed forcibly by Western powers, there has been little lasting, indigenously sustained commitment to socially progressive or politically democratic ideas in any Asian country. There is no "free Asia" counterpart to the Western democratic traditions on which to build except in our own imagination. The United States can have hope for and can act to sustain Japan's, India's, or any other country's adoption of consensus-type political communities, but there should be no illusions. The foundations of transplanted Western political and social ideas in Asia are weak. Institutions based on them have already been overturned in Burma, Korea, Pakistan, Laos, and Indonesia; they have hardly existed in other countries of the Far East. One may even fairly doubt that Western political forms would survive in India or Japan in the event of a serious crisis.

In Asia, however, the absence of quasi-democratic, pluralistic institutions has not proved to be an insuperable obstacle to maintaining stable political communities based on the tacit or expressed consent of the governed. Indeed, some Asian societies are likely to find what they regard as the appropriate balance between the conflicting demands of progress, justice, and order best achieved within a traditional-authoritarian political system that is in harmony with their historical development. What has proved to be the indispensable condition for maintaining a stable non-Communist political order is that the government and its leaders win and retain the confidence of their people as genuine exponents of nationalism. Where this common bond of nationalism links leaders and citizens, no Communist movement in Asia has been able to sever it at the polls or on the battlefield.

All this is true even in an era when U.S. military power has been overwhelming and when vast sums have been made available for aid to any regimes that would hoist the anti-Communist banner. The United States has been at no disadvantage compared to the Communists in her resources for waging the contest in Asia. Quite the opposite is true. The real difficulties that beset the United States arise primarily from the nature of the task she has set out to achieve. That task has become, evidently, nothing less than to act as a vehicle shaping basic forces of change in a vast part of the world that not only is entering the nation-building stage of development, but is also undergoing at the same time the profound experience of total cultural transformation. But the United States has virtually no ties linking it to the traditions that are bound to govern the evolution of most Asian countries. In the context of the profound upheaval now occurring in Asia independently of great-power action, it would be well to ponder whether even the United States can reasonably expect to exert a decisive molding influence on the form or spirit of new national communities that must ultimately reflect their own diversity, peculiari-

ties, needs, traditions, and aspirations. It is leaning on a weak reed, in truth, to base long-range policies on assumptions that the United States, or any combination of Western technological expertise and aid, will somehow be able to channel and mold the vast revolution in human attitudes and behavior that is painfully under way not only in Asia but in three-quarters of the world. But if the United States is determined to substitute American power for the absence of indigenous, non-Communist nationalism and to attempt a basic transformation of the elites and the societies of the far-off countries of Asia, let *that* true purpose be defined for what it really is, not displaced onto the myth of a Chinese Communist bogeyman.

It is primarily the evolution of nationalism, not the foreign policies or ideology of the Peking government, which frustrates the United States in Asia. The power fundamentally to change the basic indigenous forces shaping the development and character of nationalism in Asian countries lies in neither Peking nor Washington. No internal or external Communist power has yet been able to force the submission of an independent Asian country, however poor and whatever its political system, whose non-Communist leaders can justifiably claim the mandate of nationalism. It is incredible to suppose that the United States can, by the exercise of her own power, claim that mandate for any non-Communist elite that has not earned it from its own people. And until the United States comprehends the full meaning of nationalism in Asia, Communist and non-Communist alike, the gap between America's expectations and the real world around her will remain frustratingly large.

PERSPECTIVES

The Study of Foreign Policy

The study of foreign policy has been more noteworthy for the quantity than the quality of its intellectual products. Three recent, developing trends in this field give some hope that tomorrow will be better. They should provide analytical tools and improved empirical research that will be helpful to the practitioner as well as the student of foreign policy.

In brief, scholars in this field are beginning to approach the subject matter with a more *theoretical* orientation, a *comparative* approach, and a concern to strengthen the study of policy *substance* along with policy *structure and process*. None of these orientations are really surprising because they reflect broader trends in the effort at a more scientific approach to political phenomena. Indeed, given the laggard state of teaching and research in foreign policy, they represent something of an effort to catch up.

There has been considerable interest in the development of conceptual frameworks, testable propositions, and more ambitious models and theoretical statements in the study of international politics. However, these have for the most part been directed to the study of relations among nations (e.g., alliances, conflict and conflict resolution, voting and other political behavior in the United Nations) and to interstate relationships viewed as *systems* of activity. The one notable exception was a conceptual framework oriented to state decision-making, but it was not developed into a full-fledged set of hypotheses and relatively little empirical research was done in *its* precise terms.[1]

Thus, what one might refer to as state behavior, as distinct from interstate relations or international systems, has received relatively little theoretical attention. Those not committed to the more scientific study of political phenomena (and, hopefully, even some who are) might well answer—so what? The answer is that in the absence of a concern with theory, some fundamental, and tough, questions have not been asked or, to be more precise, have not been systematically investigated.

There has been a great deal of research focusing on one or another of the components of the American governmental and political system —voting behavior, the press, pressure groups, the Congress, various executive units or agencies, career or noncareer personnel—and how *it* affects American foreign policy. Very rarely, however, has this factor in turn been placed in the context of the larger system and some effort made to *weigh* its impact and importance. The impression one tends to be left with is that a lot of internal factors affect U.S. foreign policy, but it is far from clear what their net effects are. For example, the limitations imposed on the American system by the separation of powers modified by the checks and balances may be so fundamental that changes in the organization of the Department of State are bound to be only marginally significant in terms of impact on the quality of foreign policy performance. The point is that we have tended not to ask this kind of question and that the pressure of having to develop a theory of national foreign policy behavior is probably the most effective scholarly means of getting it asked.

It may be argued that all the domestic factors are, together, of marginal importance when placed beside the compelling character of external events and situations. Even if they do not completely determine foreign policy choices, their impact, it could be said, will far outweigh domestic considerations and limitations.

This is a moot point. For present purposes, it suffices to point out that we have not even systematically explored the connections or "linkages" between external events and situations and foreign policy perceptions and responses in a variety of political systems. Scholars in the field are simply not in a position to state with confidence how different political systems respond to identical or equivalent classes of external situations.

This kind of theoretical orientation leads very quickly to another observation and set of questions. It is clear that the study of international politics in the United States has been much too parochial. In our international politics courses, considerable attention is often given to the United States role in world affairs, and the examples used to illustrate more general points are often, understandably, drawn from American experience. The felony is compounded, if felony it be, by the follow-on courses offered at most American colleges and universities on *American* foreign policy and policy-making.

The inevitable emphasis on the study of American political institutions and behavior —American government—has been balanced in the past 15 or 20 years by the very rich growth of courses in comparative government and politics and, in more recent years, by the burgeoning of first-rate research and theory development in the comparative government field. Both have been given added interest and support as a result of greatly expanded attention to the politics of the less-developed countries.

The comparative approach has finally begun to extend to the foreign policy field, although the number of comparative foreign policy courses being offered and the number of comparative foreign policy or national defense studies being prepared or produced is still quite small. There may be some bandwagon or faddist elements involved in this development, but there are also legitimate and worthwhile intellectual purposes to be served.

To state them briefly, the comparative study of foreign policy should help put American pat-

[1] See Richard C. Snyder, H. W. Bruck and Burton Sapin (eds.), *Foreign Policy Decision-Making* (Glencoe, Ill.: The Free Press of Glencoe, 1962).

terns and problems in clearer perspective and, at the same time, sensitize the American interested in the foreign policies of other nations to the factors likely to have most influence on them. Further, the systematic, comparative study of foreign policy formation and implementation in many countries should provide a firmer empirical base for the development of theories of foreign policy behavior which have some general applicability rather than being glorified propositions about *American* foreign policy performance.

Some illustrations may be helpful. Typically, American students of foreign policy have viewed the role of the Congress in foreign policy-making critically, negatively, sometimes with resignation, often with despair. In my view, Professor Waltz, in his *Foreign Policy and Democratic Politics* (see Chapter Four), has helped put the Congressional role in better perspective by comparing it to the role of Parliament in the British *political* system.

Waltz assumes that national foreign policy performance will be more effective in a political system where major policy issues tend to be directly confronted and grappled with, and in the process given a full public airing; where, consequently, the public has some notion of the nature and dimensions of major policy problems (and, therefore, a general base of support is usually available for the major directions of policy, if not all of its tactical details); and where elected executive officials and their subordinates in the great governmental bureaucracies are kept more alert and self-conscious by the ever present possibility and the recurring reality of detailed legislative scrutiny of their activities. Waltz concludes that the American separation of powers, the built-in legislative-executive rivalry and suspicion, and the considerable political power that still resides in Congress and its committees contribute significantly to such consequences.

It is not necessary to argue that the motives involved are all pure, that the traditional structure and institutions of the Congress are ideally suited to the needs of the late twentieth century, or that the results would warrant the highest rating from some philosopher-king. These are patently absurd propositions. What Waltz is saying, and with much to support him, is that if one looks past the messiness of the process and the unappetizing character of some of the individuals involved to the net foreign policy consequences, these are on the whole positive and de-sirable. And the point becomes much more effective when the functioning of the American political system is compared to that of its British precursor, usually assumed to be its superior in political performance and outputs.

Waltz's effort to compare at the level of a total *political system* is daring and somewhat risky in terms of the state of our knowledge. Nevertheless, there would seem to be some real pay-offs, in both increased understanding and stimulation of new research, in approaching foreign policy-making at this level. To do such comparative analyses with increased rigor would require specification of those characteristics and abilities that make for effective foreign policy performance by any nation; and, further, some hypotheses regarding those characteristics of a political-governmental system likely to contribute to such effectiveness.

All of this is bound to be somewhat speculative at the start, but it is speculation aimed in the right direction. The examination in these terms of Western democratic systems, of various authoritarian systems, of varieties of less-developed countries, should prove most enlightening. Theories of foreign policy will have a broader empirical basis while our understanding of the patterns and problems of individual countries, including the United States, should be much improved.

Finally, I should emphasize that the approach at the level of the overall system represents just one among a number of useful paths of inquiry. It does have the virtue of forcing the observer to weigh net consequences of individual elements and assess overall foreign policy performance. However, there is still room for useful comparative studies of foreign service personnel, of foreign policy-military policy coordination, of foreign aid programs, of public opinion and foreign policy, and of intelligence and planning activities, to name just a few. The more general comparative study of public administration that is developing should produce relevant results for the student of foreign policy administration, as should the very substantial work in comparative political systems, if more of its attention is focused on the externally oriented activities of these systems.[2]

The third of the recent trends that give hope

[2]For more detailed comments on some of these points, see James N. Rosenau, "Pre-theories and Theories of Foreign Policy," in R. Barry Farrell (ed.), *Approaches to Comparative and International Politics* (Evanston, Ill.: Northwestern University Press, 1966), pp. 27-92.

for improved research and teaching in foreign policy relates to the *substance* of policy, as distinct from the various structures and processes that help influence and shape it. One preliminary comment is in order. The expanded attention that is now beginning to be devoted to the more systematic and, hopefully, scientific analysis of policy substance is broadly directed to the *public* policy area; it is neither exclusively nor even substantially focused on *foreign* policy issues. Thus, it is somewhat optimistic and even misleading to label it a trend in the study of foreign policy.

Having put foreign policy in its place, we can now proceed to examine some of the newer concerns and the glaring weaknesses they may help to remedy. In the introduction to Chapter Five of this book, a rather simple set of concepts and related questions was presented as a first step in the direction of improved foreign policy analysis. There is much more that can and should be done.

While recognizing that much that is relevant to policy and program choices will either be unknown or uncertain and that wise judgment and choice will always be necessary elements in any political system, there is still considerable room for improvement in the analytical underpinnings of policy. Underlying assumptions about interests, objectives, and salient characteristics of the external environment (including the behavior of other states and how it can be influenced) should be made explicit, spelled out in detail, and examined critically. Where appropriate, assumptions about the possible consequences of one's actions should be stated as hypotheses and some effort devoted to specifying in advance what will be regarded as confirming and disconfirming evidence.

Most foreign policy practitioners will dismiss such suggestions as the typically naive proposals of the ivory-tower academician. Without bothering to offer "real world" credentials, it can at the outset be conceded that such efforts, even if carried on more assiduously in the bureaucracy, will often seem fruitless. Furthermore, they cannot guarantee the avoidance of major mistakes. What is essential is a critical posture and approach to policy problems and the habit of taking nothing for granted, of questioning what seems unquestionable.

In the field of national defense policy, many of the relevant factors can be translated into quantitative terms, thus facilitating the application of more sophisticated techniques of analysis. As indicated in several selections in Chapter Two, the ability to do this kind of analysis has improved dramatically in the last decade and in fact become an integral part of military establishment decision-making. Used critically and responsibly, and with an awareness that the results obtained will depend on the assumptions made (not all assumptions being equally well-founded empirically), the economics and systems analysis approaches to defense policy can contribute to the increased rationality of choices in that field.

The significant parameters of foreign policy choice do not lend themselves so easily to quantification. However, where it is possible to make such a translation (for example, in foreign economic or military assistance programs), it should be done — not to produce some illusory sense of scientific precision but rather as another effort at self-consciousness and rigor in dealing with problems that can so easily be dealt with intuitively or impressionistically.

Where programs are being funded in pursuit of specified objectives in particular foreign countries, there is no reason why the resources devoted to various objectives in a single country, or similar objectives in a number of countries, should not be quantitatively measured, compared, and critically evaluated. Such analyses will not make it any easier to deal with foreign governments and their problems, but it may provide a more reliable basis for the evaluation of vulnerable programs and the allocation of limited resources. Here, as was indicated in Chapter Four, there have been notable governmental developments.

The State Department began to introduce its own Comprehensive Country Programming System in the early 1960s; more recently, a Planning-Programming-Budgeting System (PPBS) has been introduced on a government-wide basis. These innovations will probably not make basic policy choices any easier, but they should improve the ability to measure and compare programmatic activities and choose among them where necessary.

Public policy and program issues often involve "experimentation" in the sense that there is considerable uncertainty about the nature of the relevant factors and that proposed or actual courses of action are, in effect, exploratory or tentative efforts to see "what will work." Public officials are rarely willing to acknowledge such a state of affairs and, as was suggested above, there is insufficient concern with premises, hypotheses, the nature of meaningful evidence, and so forth.

Since he usually has less familiarity with or leverage on the external environment than the domestic policy-maker does vis-à-vis the internal environment, the foreign policy practitioner is less willing to approach his problems in an experimental frame of mind. Here, help is now at hand in the form of developments in the field of gaming and simulation. The foreign policy official can now attempt an experimental creation or re-creation of a real world problem — be it another Berlin blockade, Dominican crisis or some other — and let policy officials, professors, college students, and the like attempt to cope with it. It can be played in a variety of versions or replayed with the same scenario but a different group of simulated decision-makers.

If he is more ambitious intellectually, the policy maker can even use the computer to simulate international systems of considerable complexity. By varying assumptions about national relationships and the amounts and importance of such factors as military capabilities or economic resources, a great variety of international situations and systems of relationships can be simulated, examined and compared as they unfold over time. The critical problems come at the stage of making assumptions about the dynamics of international relationships because what one is doing, in effect, is devising a theory of international politics that can then be translated (programmed) into the language of the computer.

This kind of analysis is at its beginning stages, but if it proves a successful innovation, it should provide the policy official, as well as the academic theorist, with a tool for exploring many possible assumptions and hypotheses about the international arena.[3]

There are other interesting avenues opening up in the study of public policy. Some political scientists with value or normative concerns are interested in clarifying the problems of priori-

ties among values and, even more fundamental, the question of precisely how value choices are manifested in specific empirical situations or problem areas. No doubt the pragmatic public policy official spends little of his time agonizing over such intellectual dilemmas, but it is clear that he is in a business which involves almost constantly making choices regarding highly complex situations in which a number of values, sometimes conflicting, sometimes not clearly seen, are enmeshed. Once again, advances in the sophistication with which such analyses can be carried on should provide practical as well as philosophical benefits.[4]

In short, it looks as if the poverty of imagination and rigor with which public policy, and particularly foreign policy, problems have been studied is beginning to be remedied. Regarding this trend and the others briefly discussed in this essay, some perspective is in order. The study of international politics, comparative politics, foreign policy, and military policy in the United States has expanded in breathtaking, unbelievable fashion since the end of World War II. Nevertheless, it does not greatly strain modesty and honest self-doubt to suggest that all of these fields are at a relatively early stage of development in terms of viable theory and reliable data. Hopefully, in a decade or two we will be able to look back at this period and recognize it as a rich and necessary period of experimentation and exploration. For the moment, a certain modesty on the part of student and practitioner alike is probably an appropriate posture with which to approach contemporary problems of foreign policy and national defense.

[3]For a broad survey of the possible applications of the computer to foreign affairs, written by an experienced Foreign Service Officer, see Fisher Howe, *The Computer and Foreign Affairs* Some First Thoughts (Washington, D.C.: U.S. Government Printing Office, Department of State Publication 8156, November 1966.)

[4]Some of these matters are discussed in Charles E. Lindblom, *The Policy-Making Process* (Englewood Cliffs, N.J.: Prentice-Hall, Inc., 1968), particularly Part One.